MAERSK

TO RULE THE WAVES

HOW CONTROL OF THE WORLD'S OCEANS SHAPES THE FATE OF THE SUPERPOWERS

BRUCE D. JONES

SCRIBNER

New York London Toronto Sydney New Delhi

Scribner
An Imprint of Simon & Schuster, Inc.
1230 Avenue of the Americas
New York, NY 10020

First Scribner hardcover edition September 2021

SCRIBNER and design are registered trademarks of The Gale Group, Inc., used under license by Simon & Schuster, Inc., the publisher of this work.

For information about special discounts for bulk purchases, please contact Simon & Schuster Special Sales at 1-866-506-1949 or business@simonandschuster.com.

The Simon & Schuster Speakers Bureau can bring authors to your live event. For more information or to book an event, contact the Simon & Schuster Speakers Bureau at 1-866-248-3049 or visit our website at www.simonspeakers.com.

Manufactured in the United States of America

1 3 5 7 9 10 8 6 4 2

Library of Congress Cataloging-in-Publication Data

Names: Jones, Bruce D., author.
Title: To rule the waves : how control of the world's oceans shapes the fate of the superpowers / Bruce D. Jones.
Description: Hardcover edition. | New York : Scribner, 2021. | Includes bibliographical references and index.
Identifiers: LCCN 2021023017 (print) | LCCN 2021023018 (ebook) | ISBN 9781982127251 (hardcover) | ISBN 9781982127275 (ebook)
Subjects: LCSH: Shipping—History. | Sea-power—History. | World politics. | Power (Social sciences)
Classification: LCC HE571.B68 2021 (print) | LCC HE571 (ebook) | DDC 387.5—dc23
LC record available at https://lccn.loc.gov/2021023017
LC ebook record available at https://lccn.loc.gov/2021023018

ISBN 978-1-9821-2725-1
ISBN 978-1-9821-2727-5 (ebook)

Photo Credits
Title page: Chris Peters, Brookings Institution; pages 8–9: Chris Peters, Brookings Institution; pages 88–89: courtesy of the author; pages 158–59: Aja Jackson; pages 238–39: courtesy of the author.

To the memory of
Stanford and Beulah Jones

Contents

Part IV:
The Power of the Seas

Prologue – A Box in the Jungle

The heart of the Amazon is more than a thousand miles from the ocean. To get there, one must fly to Manaus, Brazil, in the very center of the rainforest. First established as a fort by Portuguese explorers in 1669, the outpost was of little account for its first century and a half until the industrial revolution created a demand for a plant brought back from the Amazon—rubber. Bendable, shapable, useful for thousands of purposes, rubber became an essential component in industrialization, and at the time could not be sourced anywhere but from the Amazon. In the race for profit that followed, German, Portuguese, and American businessmen vied for access to the Amazonian rubber tree, and Manaus become a hub of imperial commerce. The fossils of that period adorn the city to this day—from a seven-story mansion in the style of a Bavarian *Schloss*, a market building built as a replica of Paris's Les Halles, and the Teatro Amazonas, to a pink and white opera house topped by a dome covered with thirty-three thousand ceramic tiles painted the yellow, green, and blue of the Brazilian flag—one of the more surprising marvels of the late imperial age. It's a gritty town of wilderness and industry and eccentricity surrounded in every direction by over 1,500 miles of rainforest.

The vastness of the rainforest is broken only by the Amazon River, which courses along the banks of Manaus, three miles wide and seven hundred feet deep—neither the widest nor the deepest stretch of the Amazon, but still moving an astonishing volume of water.* Manaus also borders another river, the Rio Negro, or Black River, which runs

*Across its epic span, the Amazon River carries more water than all of the rivers of Europe combined.

1,400 miles southwest from the highlands of Colombia, emptying into the Amazon. Its name comes from the color of the water, a kind of translucent chocolate black, like someone had poured the world's supply of Coca-Cola into a riverbed. Where the two rivers meet and start to flow together at Manaus, a strange natural phenomenon occurs. For the space of three and a half miles, the two rivers flow through the same wide channel, but their waters do not mingle: they flow alongside each other, one chalky and the color of sand, the other thin and dark—two parallel streams of water surging, touching, occasional eddies swirling together, but not merging. This is caused by the radically different densities of the two bodies of water, the one full of vegetable residue accumulated as it runs through the upper stretches of the rainforest, the other scraped clean of anything other than minerals by its long descent down the mountains. In Manaus it is known as the "Meeting of the Waters," though that hardly captures the wondrous oddity of the sight.

One may take a riverboat out to see the Meeting of the Waters, and the aquatic life it attracts. Of particular appeal is a subspecies of pink dolphins unique to the Amazon. They concentrate at the confluence of the two rivers, where the separate streams mingle and churn up an abundance of fish on which to feed. The giant Amazonian pirarucú, or arapaima, is a staple of the dolphins' diet, and of the cuisine found in the restaurants of Manaus.

There, amid the whimsy of the remote city and splendor of the rainforest, I saw a familiar but wholly unexpected sight: a stack of sky-blue metal containers, neatly piled on a small container ship steaming its way upriver against the strong current. The boxes were instantly recognizable by their color and logo—a seven-pointed star painted white against the sky-blue backdrop—the symbol of Maersk, a shipping giant headquartered in Copenhagen, Denmark, a distance from Manaus of six thousand miles as the crow flies.

That Maersk had a wide global reach did not surprise me, but to find some of its containers on the deck of a transport ship 1,500 miles up the Amazon was eye-opening. If there was ever a visible symbol of the total worldwide penetration of modern globalization, this was surely it. And the sight established for me something I had understood intellectually but not viscerally: that it is sea-based trade that is the primary driver of modern globalization. There in the heart of the rainforest was the evidence.

* * *

Shipping containers are now a ubiquitous feature of the modern world. Once you start looking for them, you can't stop seeing them. Drive down the highways and byways of the United States or Europe and you notice these containers everywhere. The 18-wheeler is a storied part of the American history of continental trucking; but it's been displaced by the "prime mover"—a flatbed truck onto which is latched one of these shipping containers. Containers have also remade rail: watch a train transport at a road crossing and you are bound to see the Maersk logo on container boxes stacked two high on these freight trains, alongside containers from Taiwan, Korea, South Africa, Germany, and many points beyond. There's a secondary market for containers for housing and industrial design. You can even buy used containers on Amazon. But at the core, they are an instrument of global trade—the most visible, but as it turns out far from the only, manifestation of the way bulk shipping has transformed the world economy—and is starting to transform world politics.

The penetration of Western trade into central Brazil was just one part of a wider phenomenon that has been unfolding over the past three decades. Brazil was one of several important, populous countries—China and India being two essential others—that decided at the end of the Cold War to open up their economies and join the maelstrom of globalization. The entry of more than 2.5 billion people into the global economy has had dramatic effects. Many of those changes have been for the good. China, India, and Brazil between them pulled more than a half a billion people out of poverty and created a global middle class. Internationally, more than sixty countries were pulled out of poverty by the ever-further expansion of the world economy, and by China's huge appetite for natural resources and exports of cheap manufactured goods—a dynamic made possible by changes in global shipping. Having grown into an economic giant, China helped the United States navigate the global financial crisis, and Chinese growth helped the rest of the world recover from that shock. The Singaporean diplomat-turned-writer Kishore Mahbubani, one of the foremost chroniclers of the rise of Asia, made popular in his book *The Great*

Convergence the application of an old aphorism to the phenomenon of modern globalization: "A rising tide lifts all boats."

The tides were also critical to a second part of the changing story of the global economy: energy. Here, too, Brazil played a key role, though not in the Amazon. For it was in the long gentle slopes of the continental shelf off of Brazil's eastern shore that deep-sea energy exploration first took hold outside of the United States. Pulling other countries into globalization meant huge economic growth, and that in turn put major pressure on the world's supplies of oil and gas. The plumbing of the ocean depths for new sources of those fuels has been a critical part of the changing patterns of trade and geopolitics in the past decade, from Brazil to the East China Sea to the Arctic Ocean.

But it was also in the tides that early signs appeared suggesting that all was not well with the rise—or more accurately, the return—of these giant nations. In 2009, China made a sweeping claim to a huge stretch of the South China Sea, asserting a historical right to waters claimed by several other nations and dominated by the US Navy since the end of World War II. It was a move that presaged a mounting competition between the United States and the rising power of China—a competition playing out first and foremost in Asia's contested waters.

Between the mounting tensions in the South China Sea and the scale of global sea-based trade and energy discovery, I began to realize quite how central were transactions on and across the world's oceans to the texture of the changing times. Here, in the middle of the Amazonian rainforest, was a signifier of these global pressures, a stack of humble shipping containers, hidden in plain sight.

* * *

This book looks at the struggle for political and economic power from the vantage point of the world's oceans.

Four simple facts organize inquiry into this topic. First, the world's oceans are rapidly becoming the most important zone of confrontation between the world's great military actors—the United States and China above all, but also Russia, Japan, India, and others. How these powers manage their naval rivalry will shape the next half century. Second, when we hear the word "globalization" we think of airplanes and high-tech information flows, but the reality is that more than 85 percent of all global commerce is a function of sea-based trade. That trade flows across the Atlantic and Pacific Oceans bound in bulk carriers and mega container ships. Third, the oceans are vital to modern communications; we rarely think about the oceans in connection to the internet or finance or our smartphones, but the reality is that more than 90 percent of global data flows along undersea cables. Fourth, oceans play a surprisingly central role in the realities of energy, and in the global fight over climate change. Today's energy exploration is a story of tapping the vast resources of the seabeds from the Gulf of Mexico to the high Arctic, even as the oceans play a critical role in the changes to our weather that increasingly shape how we live.

I decided to see for myself how these dynamics were unfolding. My job required me to travel extensively, and starting in early 2017, I added a series of side trips to better understand and to visualize this new age of oceans. I sailed a fast boat out of the mouth of the Pearl River into the hills of Hong Kong and its great natural harbor, to put myself in the minds of the merchantmen and sailors of the English East India Company when they wrestled that island away from China nearly two centuries ago, in an act that reshaped the global politics and economics of the time. The commandant of the Port of New York toured me through the Coast Guard facilities there and around that vital harbor. I inspected the world's most important counter-piracy coalition, operating out of Changi Naval Base in Singapore—also the gateway to the most important choke point in modern trade. A Chinese friend arranged for me to tour the vast container port on Donghai Island, south of Shanghai, the world's largest. In Hawaii, I inspected the most advanced Aegis-class destroyer in the Pacific Fleet—once again the first line of defense against an ambitious Asian power. In the northern Arctic I saw how all these dynamics—warming seas and cooling relations—are reshaping the modern world.

And for ten days in the summer of 2019, I sailed on what was then the world's largest trading ship—the *Madrid Maersk*—across the world's most contested waters, in the Western Pacific: the Singapore Strait, the South China Sea, the Philippine Sea, and the East China Sea. The notes from that voyage frame each part of this book.

As I traveled, I read everything from the epic histories of imperial battles at sea to the labor economics of ports to marine insurance statistics to the engineering reports of deep-sea energy discovery and the complex science of ocean chemistry. Everywhere I turned I discovered entire worlds of history and science and politics.

Along the way I noted nuggets of history or modern life that seemed to illuminate patterns or politics not often discussed. Like the fact that the longest-running overseas military engagement in American history is neither the long war in Afghanistan nor even our seven-decade-long deployment to the demilitarized zone on the Korean Peninsula, but rather the near-century-long deployment of the US Navy in China, along the Yangtze River. Or the fact that to deploy troops to Afghanistan, the US armed services required the support of a Norwegian fleet of huge ferries, commercially owned and operated, that carry heavy equipment. That the use of nuclear weapons undersea is still an active part of the weapons planning of the world's major navies. Or that the testing of nuclear weapons at sea triggered some of the most important scientific study that would eventually result in careful documentation of what we now call climate change.

As I read and as I traveled, I experienced a phenomenon that surprised me. While the studies of globalization, energy, and even naval warfare gave me much that explained the technical or tactical dimensions of contemporary struggles, they cast little light on the *nature* of the rivalry. Instead, the older histories of imperial contest, of piracy, of the early days of ocean science, seemed to illuminate much more. Patterns set in the Age of Steam but that waned in the twentieth century seemed to be reemerging from the backdrop of modern history. Dynamics of trade and travel that would have been familiar to scholars and explorers in the late 1800s seemed to hew closely to the newest patterns of post–Cold War globalization.

Like other books that examine the role of sea power in the lives of nations, this one reaches back to the intellectual tradition of President Theodore Roosevelt's friend and confidant Alfred Thayer Mahan, who first sketched the naval foundations for what would become America's global role. Mahan would have been disoriented by the Cold War, an era dominated by continental superpowers and nuclear rivalry. But he would recognize the world coming into being now, where the urge to protect maritime commerce is stoking a global naval arms race. Unlike books that rest solely on the tradition of Mahan, though, this one also tackles issues he could not have foreseen—like the vast role the oceans play in our changing climate.

This book, I should add, is not *about* the oceans as much as it is a book *set on* the oceans. They are the screen against which the dynamics of our time plays out, a backdrop against which the shadows of history reveal themselves. They are a lens through which to watch a core struggle—what we might describe as the geopolitics of globalization.

The oceans are a metaphor, too, for the way in which the patterns of world affairs ebb and wash across our lives. History is often told as a series of events, sequenced in time and space. At moments, though, history moves like the ocean themselves, with currents that span continental shelves and patterns of waves that unfold over time, reaching far beyond their originating shores. Sometimes it behaves like a tsunami, where an earthquake in one area sends a shock wave through an adjacent ocean, barely noticed as it ripples across the waters, ultimately to be felt at a distant shore first by a receding of the tide, just before a huge tidal surge crashes onto land, wreaking destruction.

As we witness the epic scale of modern global trade, the mounting tensions of naval power, and the drama of climate change playing out in warming oceans, it's hard to resist the sensation that we are now at that moment just before such a tsunami, standing ashore when the tide has quietly flowed outward, far farther than normal—that eerie, quiet moment before the sea surges back in, destroying much of what we have come to know.

PART I

News from the Future

Awaiting the *Madrid*, Tanjung Pelepas, Malaysia

Algeciras, Spain, at the mouth of the Mediterranean. Lisbon, Portugal, Europe's westernmost vantage point, from where Portuguese conquistadors set sail on their voyages of discovery and violence, from Brazil to India. Muscat, Oman, where the Arabian Sea narrows toward the Persian Gulf. Kolkata, once Calcutta, that great historic trading entrepôt on the northern tip of the Indian Ocean, in the Bay of Bengal. Canton, now Guangzhou, where China first opened itself to foreign trade. And Shanghai, at the mouth of the Yangtze River, lifeline of China's economy, once dynamic, then closed, now risen again. These great ports, which have so shaped our history, would have been familiar to any trader or sea captain from Europe to the Middle East to East Asia as early as at the turn of the seventeenth century. Today, together with the great modern American ports, they form the spine of the route plan of the world's cargo fleet—a fleet that sails not in dhows or schooners or clippers, but vast floating factories of steel and oil that sew together the world.

Many of these ships, though, will dock at a port that did not exist in the world of those earlier legions of traders. That port is in Tanjung Pelepas, at the tip of the Malay Peninsula. It is the southernmost city in mainland Asia; only the islands of the Indonesian archipelago lie farther south. It has a long history as a fishing village, dating back to the thirteenth century, when this stretch of the Malay Peninsula formed the outer edges of the Siam empire. Now it's the industrial centerpiece of modern Malaysia, one of those rare places where in a single gaze you can take in relics of the long past, the arc of recent development, and the shadows of the probable future.

All this is best seen on the last remaining section of the city not given over to new-built apartment complexes or industrial warehouses. Guests and officials visiting the nearby port (or, occasionally, waiting to board a container ship like the giant *Madrid Maersk*) are often taken to a small stretch of coast off the old Jalan Sembilang road, where can be found a few remaining traditional restaurants and residences. Some of these are built on piers that reach forty feet out into the brackish waters where the Pulai River empties into the Johore Strait, at the northwestern tip of the long, shallow Java Sea. Even at low tide these waters lap up to the midpoint of the trunks of the mangrove trees and nearly cover the intertidal seagrass meadows that once lined far more of these shores. When the winds pick up and the tide is high, the waters rise to near the tips of the piers that have kept structures like these safe from the seas for several centuries. Standing on them, you can feel the visceral pull and power of the ocean as the tide pushes in and swells and briefly recedes and pushes in again, each movement of the water beneath your feet seeming to evoke long tides of history.

It is often in the shallows that we best perceive the power of the oceans. In Simon Winchester's lyrical history of the Atlantic Ocean, he imagines that moment when humankind first walked from the inland plains to the coast and encountered the "thrashing and thundering and roaring of an endless assault against the rocks that marked the margin of his habitat."[1] This sense that the oceans are most powerful at the shore is an illusion, of course; in the deep waters of the oceans, the currents are far more powerful still, pushing billions of gallons along the ocean floor and across continents. But when you are amid the endless gray expanse of the high seas, it's hard to place their span in human scale. It's only when they break their power against the coasts that we can situate our own scale in the context of their immensity.

On the coast of Tanjung Pelepas, these last remaining traditional structures carry with them the echo of the peninsula's long, contested history. Like much of the Malay coast, it was wrested away from Siam by the Malaccan empire, then claimed by the Portuguese, and then the Dutch East India Company. The Anglo-Dutch Treaty of 1824 divided the peninsula, and the area surrounding Tanjung Pelepas fell to the British. Directly south, the view on the horizon is dominated by a living relic of that period, the Horsburgh Lighthouse, which guides shipping through the Singapore Strait. It is named for a hydrographer of the East India Company, who first charted these waters for London. Nearby, though just out of sight, is the Sembawang Naval Base, where for more than a century the Royal Navy solidified its hold on Asia until Japan displaced the British during World War II, part of their bid to control the flow of oil and rubber in Southeast Asia.

After the turmoil of war, and as the "winds of change" blew through the farthest reaches of the British Empire, Malaysia and Singapore bid jointly for independence. They then parted ways in 1964. Singapore rapidly developed—aided by the comforting presence of the American navy, now docked in the Sembawang facility—and turned into a modern financial powerhouse. But Malaysia languished, one of the least developed parts of East Asia. In the early 1990s, then, Malaysia's government decided to open its economy to globalization—just as Brazil and India and dozens of others countries were doing the same. And as part of this bid to open their economy, they took the essential step for any country seeking to enter globalization. They built a modern port.

What is known locally simply as PTP—the Port of Tanjung Pelepas—occupies nearly two thousand acres of waterfront property along the dredged shores of the Pulai River, with a further 1,500 acres given over to an adjacent free trade zone. It boasts fifty-eight Super Post-Panamax cranes (technically, ship-to-shore gantry cranes)—the largest in the world. Each weighs approximately 900 tons, stands 177 feet tall, and has a reach of more than 229 feet. These load containers from its holding yard, which is 745.6 square miles in size, and is able to host more than 120,000 shipping containers at one time—the same size as the ones I saw in the Amazon. The port has an apartment complex for its day laborers, a health service, the authority to issue its own regulations, and its own police force.

PTP received its first ship in October 1999. The Malaysia authorities had anticipated a relatively steady early growth, but got lucky when the world's shipping giant, then named Maersk SeaLand, decided to move its operations from Singapore to Tanjung Pelepas. Two years later, another large shipping company, Taiwan Evergreen Marine, followed. Tanjung Pelepas rode the ensuing wave of globalization, and by 2015 had entered the top twenty ports in the world by value. The port anchors a far larger complex of industrial developments, housing complexes, byways, and land reclamation projects that have led Tanjung Pelepas to be labeled Malaysia's Shenzhen (China's first special economic zone).

The last remaining stretch of coast, though, did not fall to the port complex, but to a very different kind of development. Known as Forest City, it comprises a series of matched high-rise apartment buildings, twenty of them, an average of thirty-five stories tall. These are spread over four man-made islands, spanning 11.5 square miles of reclaimed land. The $100 billion complex of apartments is linked by a giant shopping mall, schools, and a medical facility. It even has its own beach, although the rising sea levels in the South China Sea threaten its long-term viability.

Throughout the project, the signage is in two languages: Malay and Mandarin. That reflects two facts: the anticipation of the owners that the majority of residents will be foreign, and most of them Chinese; and that the project itself is a Malaysia-China joint venture. The complex was built and financed in a partnership between the local Malay authorities and Country Garden Pacificview developers as part of China's Belt and Road Initiative. Their projection is that by 2050, when all phases of the project are complete, Forest City will host a whopping *seven hundred thousand* residents.

Now it is largely empty. Chinese nationals own most of the already-built apartments, but few live there; complex rules about residency and foreign ownership complicate the transactions. But that hasn't stopped Country Garden Group from continuing to build out the project, with strong government backing. Malaysia is torn between its deep economic ties to China and its suspicion of China's anti-Muslim policies; it's unclear where their eventual loyalties will lie. But if Malaysia moves increasingly in China's direction, Country Garden Pacific stands hugely to profit, and China would gain influence in Tanjung Pelepas and its growing port.

* * *

And so, standing on the shores of the Pulai River, in the gentle pull of the tides, we can see the echoes of Asia's long history, its violent encounter with Europe, the arc of its modern economic development, and the shadow of its likely future, where China's presence looms large. Just as we can see the competing realities of modern trade, embodied in the scale and dynamism of Port Tanjung Pelepas, and the continuing realities of Western naval power, encapsulated in the American presence in neighboring Sembawang. And if we look closely enough, we can see, too, in the rising tides and the erosion of the local shoreline, a whisper of the role the oceans are playing in our changing climatic future.

These glimpses of power dynamics past, and the rapidly changing future, are visible, too, in a very different locale on the other side of the globe; in the high north above the Arctic Circle.

1

Secrets of the High North

In the high north, above the 69th parallel, the deep of winter brings weeks of total darkness, day after day, when the sun never rises and only artificial light breaks the omnipresent black. By late January, though, the change in the Earth's axis relative to the sun is just enough to create a unique phenomenon known as blue night. While the sun never does crest above the horizon during this period, for a few hours each day just enough of the sun's light spills into the atmosphere to warm the darkness. A form of twilight emerges. Land, sea, hill, and sky all take on a silvery-blue hue, like the entire area has been dipped in liquid pewter. The daunting beauty of this frozen terrain shimmers in the ambient light.

In the blue night, it is hard to tell where land ends and the sea begins. All the more so because at this latitude, the Arctic Ocean spends part of the year under a thick blanket of sheet ice, impenetrable by all but the staunchest icebreakers. Even its littoral Barents Sea, off the coast of Russia's northern tundra, is frequently made impassible by ice floes.

The Norwegian Sea, southwest of the Barents, forms a kind of buffer between the cold, mineral-rich waters of the Arctic Ocean and those of the Atlantic, whose Gulf Stream currents start in the upwelling of the Southern Ocean, but are warmed on their way north by the heat of the Caribbean. The mixing of those waters plays a unique and consequential role in the flow of ocean currents worldwide, but they have a local effect as well, making the Norwegian Sea more navigable than its northern neighbors, ice-free year-round. It's still frigid, though, with an average temperature during the winter months around 37 degrees Fahrenheit, making it one of the coldest waters in the world that isn't trapped by ice. And during storms, high winds and thirty-foot swells pound against the mountainous coastline of the northern Finmark region, where the Scandinavian Peninsula arcs around its farther tip. The drama of the Norwegian Sea has given rise to legends, from the lore of the kraken sea monster to the epic tales of the maelstrom.*

The waters are not much warmer in the long, deep fjords that cut inland off the Norwegian Sea, but the fjords do at least provide protection from waves and wind. They shelter remote fishing communities, Arctic research stations, the occasional small city—and Cold War secrets.

The largest city in the area, Tromsø, lies at 69.64 degrees north, 18.95 degrees east, nearly 200 miles north of the Arctic Circle. It hosts a population of around 70,000 and serves as a hub for scientific research on the Arctic. And for tourism: several times a day small planes land at the airport in nearby Langnes, bringing European, Russian, and now frequently Chinese tourists to the high north. They spill out of planes clad in outdoor gear and carrying heavy boots and ice crampons and will soon head out into the snow on late-night dogsleds (or, for the less adventurous, dinner cruises) to catch a sighting of the glimmering fire of the northern lights.

Tromsø is located near the bottom of the largest fjord in this section of the coast, the Kaldfjord—literal translation, the "cold fjord." South of Tromsø, the smaller Balsfjorden runs for nearly sixty miles, broken at various intervals by still-smaller fjords that branch off from the main channel. These create highly protected deep-water inlets, secured from the winds by steep slopes on all four surrounding sides.

One such inlet lies fifteen miles south of Tromsø. The Ramfjorden forks east off of Balsfjord for three miles, and then curves sharply south to hit the mainland. Steep, high ridges protect it in every direction. Overhead to the south, the dramatic slope of the pyramid-shaped Piggtinden juts out from the surrounding Lyngen Alps, just visible in silvery relief.

*While the maelstrom depicted in Norse mythology and in Edgar Allan Poe's famous short story is legend, it's based on a real phenomenon—a series of powerful tidal eddies in the Norwegian Sea, including the Moskstraumen, one of the strongest whirlpools in the world. At maximum tide, it moves at sixteen knots and pushes more than ten million tons of water every hour through the narrow strait between the Lofoten Islands; it's one of the most dangerous pieces of water on the planet. (See Douglas Myles, *The Great Waves: Tsunami* (New York: McGraw-Hill, 1985).

If you cruise down the Ramfjorden, hugging close to shore, the blue night gives off just enough light to make out a small opening carved into the side of the mountain. Steer closer and you can see a tight tunnel, though the dark quickly swallows the little light that makes its way into this opening. A dark wall appears to indicate the end of the tunnel—even with limited visibility the smooth surface of the wall suggests something man-made rather than natural. But the swift current of the fjord makes anything more than a passing glance at this mysterious entrance hard to achieve.

A similar opening is carved into the same mountain two thousand yards to the northeast. This one can be accessed by road, though, assuming you have the right security clearances. And this one doesn't stop at an iron wall. It opens into a tunnel that penetrates the mountain for almost a mile. At eight feet wide and eight feet high at its peak, it's only big enough for a single car. Above the tunnel are hundreds of thousands of tons of solid gabbro, a dark, coarse-grained igneous rock. Driving into it, you are hard-pressed to avoid deep claustrophobia.

The road curves gently into the heart of the mountain, continuing for about a mile until it hits a T-junction. Turn left and you head deeper into the mountain for roughly one-fifth of a mile. Suddenly, the tunnel widens and the ceiling lifts and you find yourself in a large, well-lit chamber the size of a small airplane hangar. And the sense of enclosure gives way to one of astonishment as the dangerous secrets of the mountain reveal themselves. For there in front of you is not just another tunnel but a fully equipped submarine dock. This is no mere cavern: this is the Olavsvern naval base, a once-secret submarine facility carved into the very heart of the mountain.

Turning into the chamber is like stumbling into the heart of the Cold War, or onto the set of a James Bond movie come to life. The enigmatic approach, the physical scale, and the bewildering revelation of a naval base inside a mountain combine to confound expectations and senses alike.

The base is organized around two major components. The first is a long tunnel that comes in from a discrete eastern opening, and then curves into a straight lane just under one thousand feet long. Off this main channel are eight storage chambers, ranging from 160 to 220 square yards. These chambers are carved into the rock of the mountain, into which were then built a series of cement sheds, designed to store ammunition. Inside the largest of them, a series of red metal racks stacked on top of one another—like oversize milk crates—served to store torpedoes. An overhead crane, operated by a large remote hanging from thick wires in the ceiling, helped move the heavy weapons. Two of the storage sheds in the facility have small pools built into the floors: torpedoes operate on highly flammable fuels, and the water in the pools can absorb and extinguish any sparks from the clash of metals as the heavy weapons undergo inspections or repairs. The chambers themselves are enclosed by heavy steel doors, painted yellow. Remarkable pieces of military infrastructure in their own right, they were purpose-built for the compound, forged out of three feet of solid steel and built to a convex curve—so that an explosion in any other part of the base would ricochet off the doors and back out into the main channel, protecting the munitions within.

At the top of the channel is what is known innocuously as Hall 32—a large, empty chamber shaped like a dome cut in half. It's a vast blast chamber, curved and sweeping, designed to capture the shock waves from an explosion, turn them around, and send them shooting back out the tunnel toward the fjord. The blast would then hit the outer door by the eastern quay, a door made deliberately weak so that the pressure from the shock wave would be sufficient to blow it off its hinges, releasing the pressure out into the fjord, minimizing damage to the facility itself.

The second component is more impressive still. This is the submarine dock itself. It parallels the first channel and runs for one thousand feet inside the mountain. Unlike the first channel, though, this one is dug a farther twenty feet into the ground and flooded with seawater to just below dock level. A large metal door on a swivel operates like a canal door on the Erie or the Thames: sluices alongside the door can drain the water out of the rear portion of the dock, turning the chamber into a dry dock. On the ground under the water are a series of blocks of wood, like railroad ties, on which the base of a submarine can rest when the water is removed. Above, floodlights and cranes are set up to enable the ground crew to perform repairs or modifications to all parts of a waiting submarine. Powerful cabling enables electric-powered subs to recharge, while stores of fuel can reload their diesel counterparts. At the highest point in the channel, a cutout into the ceiling creates additional room for the base crew to effect repairs on a raised periscope.

Close by are a series of crucial support chambers: a secure communications room, a powerful engine room, and an area marked CBRN CLEANING—that is, a room designed to wash and scrub anyone exposed to chemical, biological, radiological, or nuclear materials.

For many years, this facility was NATO's northernmost vantage point. Originally commissioned just before the outbreak of World War II, the facility was dug out to exacting standards over the course of almost forty years. The eventual result: inside the mountain, almost three hundred thousand square feet of blast-proof space, carefully ventilated, wholly secure. Above, a thousand feet of solid rock protects the base from airstrikes or even a nuclear attack. The world's most powerful bunker busting bombs would come nowhere close to penetrating the outer shell of the mountain. At the water entrance, the facility is protected on four sides by the two fjords that create its enclosure. The steep slopes protect from more than just wind. Neither a fighter jet nor even a modern cruise missile can flatten out fast enough, having crested the peak of the surrounding slopes (which rise from the fjord at a near-vertical pitch), to penetrate the small opening. A series of additional security measures that cannot be revealed here protect the base from underwater attack.

The central purpose of the facility is the landing dock for submarines. Fully occupied, three full-size diesel submarines can be docked inside the chamber at one time. The wet dock is in fact large enough to berth even the largest nuclear-powered submarines in the NATO fleet, but for now the entrance to the cavern isn't wide enough to allow them in; there are plans to enlarge it. During the height of the Cold War, an additional, removable quay was floated just outside the entrance to the facility. Archived photographs from that era show the USS *Hampton*, the USS *Albany*, the USS *Toledo*, and unnamed Seawolf- and Los Angeles–class submarines docking at the external facility. It was at Olavsvern that the powerful US submarine fleet rested and refueled after shadowing Soviet submarines under the Arctic ice.

At the core of the facility is a command center. Abandoned when the base was given up at the end of the Cold War, the remnants of

Norwegian and NATO battle plans are still visible on faint outlines of a map etched into the main planning wall. Discarded Norwegian Defense Ministry nautical charts still lie atop the central table, and still fill the map drawers along the rear wall. Adjacent, a command office with a large domed window overlooks the map room, and is connected to a dedicated communications chamber that still shows evidence of the kind of security measures that would enable the facility to receive NATO's most secure communications.

It's no longer a secret that during the Cold War the purpose of the Olavsvern submarine facility was to help keep track of the Soviet fleet. Its location was perfect. For most of the 1,650 miles of the Norwegian land mass, Finland lies between Russia and Norway—and served as a neutral buffer between the Soviet forces and NATO. At its very tip, though, Norway borders Russia directly, creating one of only two land borders between NATO and the Soviet Union. But this is near-impassable terrain. The land trip to Tromsø from Murmansk, the largest town on Russia's northern-western edge, is an arduous fourteen-hour drive across the Finmark peninsula, a high mountain plateau whose roads are mere clefts in those high craggy peaks, blocked by ice and snow for most of the year; and so, easily defended. But Murmansk, and Russia's Northern Fleet, is only 590 nautical miles from Tromsø—just over a half-day sail for fast cruisers. If the Soviet Union was going to launch a sea-based invasion into NATO's north, it would have been in or around Tromsø that the attack would be most likely to start.*

When the Cold War ended, and in the relative calm in the region that followed, neither NATO nor Norway had any use for the base. It fell into disuse, and in 2008 it was decommissioned. Most of the steel doors were removed, and the command facility abandoned, stripped of its secure communication gear. Eventually, the Norwegian Ministry of Defense sold it into private hands. For several years, a private operator used it to rent storage for pleasure craft owners, to protect their boats

*During World War II, it was to Tromsø that the Norwegian government exiled itself when the country fell to the Nazi invasion; and from Tromsø that King Haakon—together with fifty tons of gold, several warships, and over a thousand merchant ships—was evacuated from Norway by the Royal Navy, acting on Winston Churchill's last orders given as Lord Admiral of the Navy, before he ascended to the role of prime minister.

during the deep-winter months. Some of its roadways and its storage channels held marine craft, yachts, Ski-Doos, sleds, Jeeps, and even classic cars—including a 1956 cherry-red X-Type Jaguar in mint condition. Its weapon bays were converted into storage chambers, practice bases for deepwater diving, and machine-tooling workstations. One was even converted into a facility for training show dogs. The juxtaposition between the show dogs' jumping gear and the base's original purpose stands now like some form of parodying monument to the leisurely excesses of the post–Cold War world.

And then, in 2018, the Norwegian armed forces reacquired the base. In September 2019, the Norwegian Defense Logistics Organization signed a contract with a marine engineering firm to operate the facility and restore it to defense standards. The contracting arm of one of the world's largest maritime logistics companies, the Wilhelmsen Group, began a swift program of rehabilitation to bring it back to military specifications. The objective was to have the base operational in 2020. By 2019, the United States was in negotiations with Norway to sign a "status of forces agreement" that would allow the US Navy to resume its access to Olavsvern, for submarine deployments to the high north.

The reasons why speak directly to the themes of this book.

* * *

Over the past quarter century, we've become increasingly accustomed to the material benefits of a globalized economy, a world where production moves and flows seamlessly across national boundaries, in seemingly limitless quantities and at ever-lower costs. Where the new middle classes of Asia and Latin America can afford modern housing and air-conditioning and cars and hugely improved health care and sanitation. A world in which American working parents can readily afford to feed and clothe their families, and to purchase goods that were once luxuries, like flat-screen TVs and laptops, by buying the inexpensive goods milled and manufactured by those same Asian and Latin American middle classes. A world in which Africa's cities have become hubs of innovation, and 400 million citizens of the continent carry cell phones. It's also a world where American city dwellers can drive German, Korean, Japanese, and Italian cars, buy raspberries and kumquats and pineapples in the middle of winter, and work and play on smartphones that are almost certainly the most globally integrated consumer good ever produced. Of course, it is also a world where American cotton plantations have been supplanted, for good and ill, by growers in Bangladesh and Laos; where steel factories in Ohio have been displaced by industrial production in Vietnam and China; where "American" airplanes use Russian steel and British engines and German software. By the same token, this is a world in which American and European service firms, engineering firms, technology companies, and banks have reaped huge profits from the ever-larger flow of trade. It's a world, as we shall see, born of trade by sea.

We've also become accustomed, over several decades, to relatively stable relations between the world's top military powers. Not free of tensions, to be sure, or of violence and war in the world's poorer regions; but a world in which the United States and its Western allies were free of existential threats; a world in which most countries, most of the time, could pursue their national ambitions and foreign policies free from the worry that one of the world's top military powers would seek to annex their territory, or that they would fall afoul of a militarized conflict between the world's nuclear powers. It was a world, as we will remember, characterized by the global reach of American military might—whose enabling feature was America's unrivaled blue-water navy.

And over a far longer period of time, we've become accustomed to the easy, inexpensive consumption of fossil fuels—the oil, the gas, and the coal that power the modern economy and every aspect of our lives—a practice made ever more possible, as we'll discover, by the sea-based flow of oil, and now also of natural gas.

As these economic and political dynamics of the last part of the twentieth century and the first phase of the twenty-first unfolded, they flowed together beside each other in relative harmony—relative comity between the world's most populous nations reflected in a deepening economic integration, and a sense of shared stakes and even a shared fate in the evolution of the natural world. But beneath the surface, older patterns of history—of rivalry, of distrust—were building strength. And over time, as these currents flowed beside each other, they began to intermingle—and to churn against one another.

* * *

All these patterns are on display in the high north.

In 1845, at the height of British imperial adventurism, the Royal Navy commissioned the HMS *Terror* to find a route through the Arctic—the fabled "northern route." It was a voyage that generated valuable scientific discovery—ever since, the ocean sciences have been a leading indicator of global power. But it failed to find a northern sea route, for the simple reason that there was none. For all of recorded history, the Arctic has been blocked year-round by a thick layer of sea ice. No longer. Just since 2000, the Arctic has warmed by an average of 2.7 degrees, which means that now for several months a year some of its waters are ice-free. The northern route so longed for by the British Crown has arrived.

This is a disturbing harbinger of the state of the natural world, but it is also in many ways an economic boon. No longer impeded by year-round ice, in 2018, a flotilla of Chinese container vessels sailed the route from Shanghai to Hamburg, Germany—almost six thousand miles shorter than the traditional route across the Indian Ocean, through the Suez to the Mediterranean, out through the Pillars of Hercules and up the western coast of the Atlantic. In time, this new route may prove as consequential to global trade—and to the geopolitical relations that underpin it—as the opening of the Suez Canal. What's more, the shallow continental shelf off the Norwegian and Barents Seas is increasingly accessible for energy exploration. In 2019, the largest oil and gas find in the world was in the Yamal Peninsula, off Russia's Barents coastline. And, somewhat ironically, the newly ice-free waters are generating an increasing yield in the already bountiful Arctic fishing grounds.

Yet for all the commercial prospects of the Arctic—indeed, partially because of those prospects—it's also emerged as a zone of military competition, as the world's naval powers vie for access and influence. Russia has moved important naval assets to its northern bases, from where it can threaten the Atlantic, while China has begun building a fleet of icebreakers to take advantage of the new northern route; and America is resuming its Cold War–era vigil underneath the residual sea ice. While much of the world's media attention has been in the warmer waters in the South China Sea, the cold waters of the north are yet another flash point in our rapidly changing world. It's but one part of a wider struggle this book charts—at the heart of which is a new global arms race, one that has navies playing the role that nuclear weapons played during the Cold War.

The Arctic is neither the sole nor even the most important exemplar of a changing climate; neither the sole nor the most tense flash point in the new global naval arms race; and not yet the most important new trade route on the high seas. But it is another of those rare places where we can witness how rapidly those patterns are changing, where we can see the relics of the past, the shape of the present, and the early signs of the future that awaits us. And once again the Olavsvern naval base will be the West's northernmost eye on that dangerous future.

* * *

The company contracted to rehabilitate the Olavsvern naval base is an interesting entity in its own right, and a brief consideration of its Norwegian parent company reveals the kind of linkages that exist between corporations and governments. That parent company is the publicly held Wilhelmsen Group, the largest maritime network operator in the world, with 2,200 locations around the globe, where it provides marine support services to companies and governments alike. Among its claims to fame, the Wilhelmsen Group is the world's largest operator of ro-ro boats.

But what on earth is a ro-ro boat?

"Ro-ro" is industry shorthand for "roll on, roll off." Ro-ro ships are basically giant ferries, square-sided, mammoth in scale. They are purpose-designed to transport rolling vehicles, primarily cars, to destinations around the world—in that, they're a perfect reflection of a changed world of global economic production. Buy a car in the United States, and chances are high that the vehicle spent part of its life on one of the fifteen decks of a large ro-ro ship, being transported from Japan or Korea or Germany to one of a dozen major port complexes on the eastern and western seaboards. But ro-ro ships have more uses than simply transporting cars. They are also used to transport heavy machinery and equipment—including for the US military.

The American military establishment likes to extol the virtues of its ability to put American power anywhere in the world, at short notice. Limited operations, like the deployment of Special Forces, can be handled by airplane or submarine. But any large-scale deployment involves getting huge amounts of military equipment—armored personnel carriers, tanks, light aircraft, helicopters—into position overseas. And for any purpose other than for a new invasion of Mexico or Canada, that involves large ships.

The US Navy operates a fleet of its own logistics ships and ro-ro carriers. But when a major mobilization is underway, even the US Navy has to contract out to the commercial market. That included when the US military mobilized at scale to mount the deployment to Afghanistan in the wake of 9/11.

That deployment of American power to central Asia—literally on the other side of the globe from New York's Twin Towers—may have marked the apogee of American power. Let's, for the moment, leave aside any policy questions about the endurance or conduct of the war. The launch of the war was, from a purely logistical perspective, an extraordinary thing. At no prior point in human history has a state power been able to launch first pinprick strikes, then heavy bombing raids, and then large-scale infantry deployments, fully half a world away from its home borders—and then to sustain them for years. At the very least it was the most logistically impressive feat of power projection since D-Day—whatever the results of the encounter. All the more remarkable, then, that the majority of the equipment deployed to Kabul and Kandahar and points beyond was sailed there by the ro-ro ships of the Wilhelmsen Group.*

There are several factors that go into the question of whether the military or other users of very heavy equipment can use a given ro-ro ship. One is simple size. The largest ro-ro ships, for example the Wilhelmsen Group's MV *Tønsberg*, the world's largest, can be up to 900 feet long, 100 feet wide, and have a total weight of 75,000 gross tons. Second is the weight of the hull. On the heaviest ships, the high decks on these ro-ros can withstand up to one ton of pressure per square foot, which means they're capable of carrying an armored tank. And a third factor is the dock. Ro-ro ships come with their own docks, self-propelled, mounted to the back of the ships, that enable them to port virtually anywhere in the world and off-load their weighty cargo. To drive a tank up the dock ramp requires a loading capacity of several

*The bulk of the equipment was loaded in Newport News, Virginia, and off-loaded in Pakistan, where it could move by road into Afghanistan.

hundred tons per square foot. A normal ro-ro ship ramp can handle 150 tons per square foot; the heaviest ro-ro carriers, like those used by the Wilhelmsen Group for the Afghanistan operation, can handle 500 tons per square foot.

It's another hidden feature of the modern realities of ocean traffic that even the world's most powerful military relies on bulk shipping in the private sector to be able to deploy overseas. This is yet another way in which America's fate and the dynamics of international security are bound up in command of the oceans.

* * *

That all of this matters to the US Navy, and to China and Russia, is evident. But to see how it links to the daily functioning of the economy, it helps to shift from the high drama of the north to the more quotidian realities of trade, and a location where the Wilhelmsen Group docks its ro-ro ships when not on special assignment to the US military. Like many of the features of contemporary changes to trade, it's plainly visible—in Newark, New Jersey.

2

The Outer Perimeter; or, Pushing the American Border Out

Every day, tens of thousands of New Yorkers climb into a taxi or an Uber to drive through the Lincoln Tunnel into Hoboken, New Jersey, on their way to Newark Airport. Along the way, many cross the Newark Bay Bridge on Interstate 78, one of the nation's most congested expressways. Most of them are watching TV shows on their iPads or texting and emailing from their phones—anything to avoid the bleak viewscape of chemical plants and storage facilities and rail yards that make up the industrial rim around New York City. Similar voyages make up the route to airports in Seattle, Boston, Houston, and other American locales—in each case, bypassing major seaports that no longer occupy central real estate in modern cities.

If these preoccupied passengers did look out the window and pay attention to their passing surroundings, along the route they would probably see at least one ro-ro ship docked in Port Newark, at the terminus of the Kill van Kull—the westernmost dock in New York's massive harbor, and easily the most important waterway that most people have never heard of. And chances are good that their car arrived in the United States on the decks of one of those ships, before being offloaded at Newark, New Jersey, and then moved by truck or rail to dealerships across the state, and as far away as Chicago.

New York's harbor has a long history. In 1524, Portuguese captain and explorer Giovanni da Verrazzano sailed aboard *La Dauphine* from a home port in Brittany under service to the French king, Francis I.

Nearly two months later, his ship neared an area now known as Cape Fear, off the Carolina coast. He then sailed northward, missing the Chesapeake Bay and the mouth of the Delaware River, and eventually encountering a large opening that he believed to be a lake. It was in fact the mouth of the Hudson River. Little did he know that the narrows he sailed past would end up bearing his name and be the sea-based gateway to the most important city of the twentieth century.

Today, few New Yorkers experience the old approach to the port and the harbor. They arrive by plane or train to the grim and grime of LaGuardia, Newark, or John F. Kennedy airports and to Amtrak's recently finished Moynihan Train Hall, which has replaced the dilapidated horror of Penn Station. But sailors aboard modern trade ships still enter by the old route. Having weathered the notorious storms and swells of the gray Atlantic, they approach New York City sailing west along Long Island's southern shore, and approach the Narrows from the east. Rounding the head, they sail under the huge suspension bridge named after Verrazzano—when it was built, at the height of American power, the largest suspension bridge in the world.

For the first few minutes after you enter the Narrows, the view is bounded by the headlands of Staten Island and Long Island. Then the field of vision opens to the wide expanse of the deep natural harbor where the East River and the Hudson River empty into the Atlantic. A small formation on the horizon soon reveals itself to be the Statue of Liberty. To the west lie the remnants of Fort Tompkins, named for Daniel D. Tompkins, governor of the state of New York during the War of 1812, when Britain's Royal Navy mounted a blockade of fledgling America off these waters.[1] To the northeast, the towers of lower Manhattan are outlined against the sky, their reflections shimmering in the surprisingly clear waters of the harbor.

In the days of sail and steam, and up through the 1960s, ships coming into New York Harbor from the Narrows would steer north up to the mouth of the East River and the piers at Manhattan's South Street port, or across the river on Brooklyn's shore. The Brooklyn Bridge—the world's first steel-wire suspension bridge—was built to provide a rail connection between Manhattan and the new Brooklyn shipping piers. From the early 1900s until the mid-1970s, New York was the largest and most important port in the world.

Not so for modern cargo ships. Indeed, the largest of those ships can't even enter New York Harbor, as it is too shallow at low tide to accommodate the draft of the ultra-large ships that make up the high end of the global trading system. These ships head farther south to the deepwater port of Charleston. But many other container ships—from the Maersk fleet, or from Orient Overseas Container Line, or Mediterranean Shipping Company, or Hapag-Lloyd—or ro-ro ships, oil tankers, grain steamers, or bulk carriers with shallower keels transit the Narrows, but instead of continuing north they turn southwest. There, they enter the Kill van Kull, a narrow channel that runs for three miles between Staten Island and the eastern shore of New Jersey. They have to navigate carefully—even modest-size cargo ships often have a draft of well over forty feet, and even after multiple dredging operations the Kill is only fifty feet deep at low tide. A slight wrong turn, a brief miscalculation, and a grounded ship would choke off dozens of billions of dollars of imports into the eastern United States.

Safely through, they dock at the piers at Elizabeth, New Jersey, just south of Newark.

The Inner Perimeter

If a cargo or container ship has made it this far into New York Harbor, it's already passed through several concentric rings of security—a vast system of interlocked intelligence gathering, cyber monitoring, Coast Guard operations, and overseas programs that put the United States at the heart of global trade security. The system is designed to protect the United States against terrorism, the import of weapons of mass destruction, and infectious disease, as well as the smuggling of drugs and counterfeit goods. And it effectively extends the American border outward seven thousand miles from each coast. We'll explore that in a moment. But having passed through that system and made it to the Kill van Kull, there are still two critical layers of protection to get past.

The first is a large but nondescript warehouse in the middle of the secured Customs and Border Protection zone in Elizabeth. This is the Centralized Examination Station, one of three, each encompassing 100,000 square feet of interior space, with sixty docking bays of container trucks. From inside the warehouse, agents of the Customs and Border patrol can inspect cargo inside the containers themselves, without having to unload the goods, unless they have specific intelligence or a reason to dig deeper.

The opened container doors reveal a bewildering array of packing methods, from the rigorous to the shambolic. In one container, an entire apartment's worth of furniture, clothes, carpets, and cleaning supplies are strewn across the container with no additional packaging or arrangement, like a college student in a rush has thrown their dorm room furniture into the back of their parents' truck—if that truck were one of twenty thousand containers on the world's largest cargo ship. In another, an old Mercedes is strung to the roof of the container using leather straps—as if being above a bunch of crates of toilet paper would somehow cause the customs agents not to notice. More commonly, every square inch of space inside the container is taken up with neatly stacked pallets or boxes, eight feet high by eight feet eight inches wide, and forty feet long. In one, dozens of cases of rum are boxed one on top of another—amazingly, not a single bottle broken during the twelve-day sea voyage across 7,500 nautical miles.

Not everything is inspected inside the container trucks, though. Acting on intelligence, a tip, or sheer gut instinct, the Customs and Border agents pull a selection of the goods onto the warehouse floor for more detailed examination. Their main job these days is counterterrorism—but the old-school agents still love the hunt for contraband. John V., a gruff old Irish customs agent, thirty-five years in the service, says with a grin, "We old-school guys do it old-school ways."

That involves stacking row after row of goods across the warehouse floor and doing a detailed inspection by hand. On a given day, the number and variety of goods arrayed across the Centralized Examination Station is staggering. There's a large row of neatly piled bags of turbinado sugar. A pallet of allspice. Dozens of bags of rice, next to sackcloth bags full of hibiscus leaves. Boxes of butane lighters next to old-fashioned boom boxes and pirated CDs. There are dozens of vacuum cleaners lying on their sides amid mops and brooms and pails and cleaning supplies. One row displays enough paper towels to wipe down a city block. There are hundreds of flat-screen TVs and stereos. A section of the warehouse is given over to furniture—dining room tables and chairs and living room sets, mattresses and pillows and blankets, all wrapped in translucent blue plastic. Crates of batteries. Boxes full of running shoes in every conceivable color combination, alongside T-shirts, jeans, and sweatshirts. There's an X-ray machine and a ventilator and a high-end laser printer. Stuffed animals and children's clothing and toys. A row of motorbikes, and several used cars—some of them in such appalling condition it's inconceivable that there's reason to import them. Car parts and canisters of fuel of every description. China dinner sets, toiletries, and an entire container full of sex toys. Reams of paper, paintings, wash powder, taxidermied animals, canola oil, laptops, headphones, winter coats, and pallets of dried flowers. Every possible facet of modern household consumption is arrayed here for inspection.

As are foodstuffs. Hundreds of sacks of potatoes and yams and rice. Coffee beans from Brazil, paneer from India, dried noodles from Pakistan and Thailand. And niche goods for specialty markets, like duck feet and chicken tongues and goose hearts. And every conceivable variety of pork product, mostly from China—pork tails, pork tongues, dried pork, smoked pork, pork hearts, pork livers, pork hocks.

Some of these goods are simply illegally imported and will be returned. Others are past their sell-by dates and will be destroyed. But there are also fresh goods and fruits designed for markets across the city and the entire eastern United States: crate after crate of persimmons and clementines and lemons. Pallets of tomatoes. Crates full of bananas. Pineapples, kumquats, avocados, lychees, and all of the other tropical produce that Americans have come to expect to be able to buy in their local markets. As well as fruit that is grown in the United States, but only seasonally, or that is cheaper to ship from Latin America than to fly from California—billions of dollars' worth of blueberries and strawberries and grapes and cranberries and mangoes and watermelons and apples.

There's a special inspection regime for live agricultural products. That doesn't mean sampling every piece of fruit—literally uncountable billions of pieces of fruit and vegetables enter this port every year. Instead, the agents work with the Plant Protection and Quarantine unit of the US Department of Agriculture to figure out scientific methods to test for disease. They conduct detailed experiments to measure the units per thousands of bugs, infestations, blights, and diseases that spread across specific types of plants, and sample against those ratios. Every single container that has agricultural goods is opened for inspection. The main concern is preventing the import of pests that could damage American crops, but it's also an important barrier against foodborne disease—foot-and-mouth disease and Asian swine flu being the two most pressing concerns. In the wake of COVID—and reports of potential new swine flu outbreaks in Asian markets—this function of the service feels particularly important.

A lot of what the CBP finds during these inspections are simply cheap knockoffs—counterfeit goods. You can almost monitor the popularity of various street brands by the quantity of knockoff imports inside the Centralized Examination Station. Yeezy shoes are the newest fad, and the newest catch. Timberland boots are a particularly common catch, with manufacturers using a series of tricks to try to get around counterfeit rules—like importing fake Timberlands that aren't adorned with the brand's distinctive under-sole label, which is produced domestically and glued onto the imported fakes if they make it past customs. There are fake Guccis, and Rolexes, and Nikes and Uggs and Beats headphones by the hundreds of dozens.*

And then there are the drugs. Lots of them, hidden in an ever more creative array of concealment techniques. So many that the customs agents dedicate a small portion of the warehouse floor to what they call their "concealment museum." Understandably, they don't display or talk about the latest methods. But even the methods that are now so routine that they aren't hesitant about displaying them are striking in their malign creativity. There's a bicycle whose tires had strips of marijuana hidden inside the inner tubes. A simple cardboard box: its contents passed inspection, but a clever agent noticed that the cardboard itself had a different consistency than normal, and tests determined that cocaine had been turned into a form of glue and painted into the ribs of the cardboard itself. A pallet of kitchen towels, seemingly innocuous, but actually with heroin baked into the fabric. A ceramic

*What's true on the way in is also true on the way out. The same agents can scan exported goods for sensitive American technologies, stolen vehicles, and illegal merchandise. But the vast majority of this enforcement function is now electronic.

toilet with meth hidden in its inner piping. Dates, still on the vine, imported from Algeria—and with cocaine soaked into the fruit. A stack of taxidermied lizards with LSD hidden in the stomach cavities—a clever idea but for the fact that the lizards themselves are a prohibited item. A 1992 BMW 750 whose gas tank was full of ecstasy pills. Every other variety of American appetite for vice is on display here as well.

They also find money. Once, $11 million stuffed into used truck parts. Another time, $150,000 hidden in bales of hay. And sometimes, simply a bundle of money left in the front of a container—a kind of standing bribe to look the other way at contraband.

The contents on display at the Centralized Examination Station give a glimpse both of the huge array of goods imported into the United States and of how much American consumption has come to rely on those imports. The scene is repeated in every major American port. And in port cities in every rich country in the world—highlighting the near-omnipresent nature of sea-based trade, no longer confined to specialty goods like spices and tea, but woven into the fabric of everyday household consumption and economic production.

Still, for all the diversity and scale of what's on display inside the Centralized Examination Station, only around 5 percent of the containers are pulled for inspection. The scale of what's imported now into the United States by ship is so large that if the customs agents pulled every container for inspection, it would drastically slow the entire American economy.

There's one critical exception, though: nuclear material.

The Last Line of Defense

In the wake of 9/11, with fears of a terrorist organization trying to smuggle a dirty bomb or radiological device or chemical weapon into the country, the Departments of Commerce and Homeland Security collaborated to put together new methods at Elizabeth to scan cargo coming into the country for radiological materials. That sounds very complicated, but after some trial and error and some technical innovations, this has been turned into a smooth operation. Containers coming into Elizabeth can be off-loaded from 6:00 a.m. to 8:00 p.m.,

Monday through Friday. As they do, they drive through a portal that checks for gamma radiation. It looks, quite simply, like an extremely large metal detector, the same kind you walk through when boarding an airplane. Only, this one is twenty feet high and twenty-six feet wide, painted yellow, covered in two-inch metal rivets, like the kind that hold airplane wings together. They stand two abreast, at the last exit from the port. Trucks pull up and drive slowly through the scanner one at a time, hundreds of them in any given hour. A few yards away, six officers sit crammed into a small shed, scanning the results.

The results are instantly displayed on a computer terminal, which shows the heat signature from the container on the back of the truck. The challenge for the CBP officers comes from the fact that many types of goods throw off some degree of radiation, including a variety of plastics, hospital equipment, even smoke alarms. Usefully, though, every type of radiation has a specific signature. For the most part, the officers inside the truck can tell the difference between the radiation thrown off from innocuous materials and those they should be worried about. The systems keep getting refined. When these "radiation portal monitors" were first installed at Port Elizabeth, up to two hundred containers a day would set off a flag that would require more detailed examination. With refinements in the technology and increased training for the agents, that's now down to twenty a day.

Sometimes still a red flag does go off. A container giving off the heat signature of cesium-137, for example, is indicative of nuclear or other radiological materials. That can still be legitimate, though: a hospital might be importing a complex piece of medical equipment that has a nuclear component, which is perfectly legal. The paperwork is inspected, and the container can move onward. If the signal is unclear, or the paperwork incomplete, the officers have to send the data source and the heat signature to one of the country's nuclear laboratories for further examination. A Washington, DC, lab monitors all this in real time and helps the officers to decide when to escalate for more complex screening. By now, that's down to one time a month, when a heat signature for cobalt-60 or another similar, prohibited substance gives off a large enough measure to worry about. Now 100 percent of containers leaving the port are scanned for radiological material.

Then the trucks carrying the off-loaded cargo head out into the complex of railway lines, highway terminals, and airports that surround Elizabeth—from there, feeding the entire eastern seaboard of the United States.

* * *

Elizabeth exists at the hub of a remarkable concentration of industrial and commercial logistics. Within a short radius of downtown Elizabeth can be found the nation's second-largest port, the main oil and gas pipeline into the American northeast, the world's most vital data cables, two of the nation's busiest airports, NY State Highway 89, the New Jersey Turnpike, several rail yards, and Wall Street.

For more than half a century, New York was the largest port in the world, and by most measures arguably the most important city of the twentieth century. Early in the twenty-first, New York's standing as the largest American container port was lost to Los Angeles/Long Beach—a reflection of the shift in economic weight away from Europe toward Asia, from the transatlantic trade to the transpacific. But New York still plays an outsize role in the global economy, in ways that are directly linked to sea-based flows. Taken as a whole, the port in New York and New Jersey is still one of most important economic pieces of real estate in the entire United States. The port area includes a system of waterways that make up some 650 miles of shoreline in New York City and northern New Jersey, as well as the region's airports. It's the second-largest port by tonnage and the busiest in the US, and it's vital to the most lucrative metropolitan region in the US. In 2018, the port alone imported more than $165 billion in value—more, if you count the oil that flows into nearby terminals. That's more than Turkey, South Africa, or Argentina.[2] The port system itself generates over four hundred thousand jobs, which is enough to employ the entire population of Tampa and more.[3]

It represents one of a handful of port complexes that anchor American trade. In 2018, the United States imported about $2.8 trillion in goods. And while those imports were spread over four hundred seaports, airports, and border crossings, the vast bulk of the imports—more than 60 percent of them—came into the country via one of ten major port complexes.[4] Those complexes—in Los Angeles/Long Beach, San Francisco/Oakland, Seattle-Tacoma, Miami–Fort Lauderdale, Laredo Texas, Anchorage, Houston-Sugarland-Baytown, Detroit-Warren-

Livonia, and Chicago-Joliet-Naperville—move more than $8 billion in goods *daily* in and out of the American economy. International trade accounts for nearly one-third of the country's entire GDP. And as we'll see at the end of Part II, that actually understates the importance of sea-based trade to the American economy, or to America's leadership role in the world.

Also: a little-understood role of modern shipping ports is that they are critical to major airports, too. Jets require very specific types of fuel, unsurprisingly collectively known as jet fuel. The supply of fuel for JFK, LaGuardia, and Newark airports, which combined represent the largest airport system in the United States, predominantly comes through Kill van Kull to oil terminals in New Jersey and New York.

All of this matters to New York, to the eastern seaboard of the United States, and to the entire American economy. But New York's port is vital in ways that extend far beyond its economic impact. It's a key hub in one of the most far-reaching and penetrating forms of American power—a system of trade intelligence and security that projects into the territories of dozens of countries worldwide with the goal of extending the American border outward; in the words of Customs and Border Protection, the objective is to "extend the zone of security outward so that American borders are the last line of defense, not the first."[5]

The Second Perimeter: Coast Guard Station New York

Jason Tama is in his midforties, with a wife and two young girls who occupy him when he's not surfing or skiing on the weekends, or cycling to and from his twelve-hour-a-day job in Staten Island, home to the main Coast Guard base for New York Harbor. Born in Maryland, near Annapolis, he's spent his entire adult life in the Coast Guard. His father worked as a civilian in the navy, and from both the surrounding geography and his father's influence, a life of service and a life at sea both came naturally. He was interested in both the navy and Coast Guard, but his father, despite his own path, convinced him to pursue the Coast Guard option—he thought his son would prefer the smaller service and the peacetime mission. A few weeks after graduating high school, at age seventeen, he reported to the US Coast Guard Academy in New London, Connecticut. Tama then served on ship and at shore, as well as in the DC headquarters, for twenty years. He took a master's degree in naval architecture from UC Berkeley and an MBA from the Sloan School of Management at MIT. He was then deployed as the Coast Guard's chief prevention officer in San Francisco.

In 2018, he was assigned as the captain of the Port of New York and New Jersey. From there, he was tasked to oversee every aspect of the Coast Guard's maritime safety, security, and environmental protection operations in the huge harbor, with approximately six hundred uniformed Coast Guard personnel under his command, as well as three hundred reservists and one hundred civilians. That included overseeing the blandly named Vessel Traffic Service—in reality, a war room that monitors the flow of commercial, naval, and recreational vessels in and out of New York Harbor: one vessel every eight minutes, 24/7; four thousand vessels every month, in addition to the hundreds of daily ferry transits crisscrossing the harbor.

Sit in Captain Tama's office for more than a few minutes and you're likely to witness him fulfilling his most important duty. His cell phone rings and he listens patiently to his deputy commander or watch chief at the other end of the line. He asks a clarifying question and listens to the answer. And then he says decisively, "I concur." He's just issued a "Captain of the Port Order." And in doing so, he's wielded a near-absolute authority, one that can't be overturned by the commandant of the Coast Guard, the secretary of Homeland Security, or even the president of the United States.

His Captain of the Port authorities go back to an incident in New York Harbor in July 1916, when a bomb was detonated in a stockpile of weapons on barges off Black Tom Island, just off the coast of Jersey City. The bomb destroyed a huge cache of weapons, over 2 million pounds of ammunitions, destined for a WWI resupply of the Allies. The explosion damaged the Statue of Liberty, buildings in Jersey City a mile away, and shook the Brooklyn Bridge. The shock wave was felt as far away as Philadelphia. It was the most important act of German espionage inside the United States during the war. The Black Tom incident led Congress to pass the Espionage Act of 1917, which for the first time established a domestic intelligence capacity for the United States. It also gave port captains sweeping powers to secure their ports.

For nearly a century, those authorities remained largely unchanged. Until 9/11. After that set of attacks, the fears of terrorists or rogue states using ships to smuggle weapons of mass destruction or related material into major cities caused Congress to pass an additional law, the federal Maritime Transportation Security Act of 2002. It took Captain Tama's substantial powers and expanded them. Indeed, it put him in the middle of a global web of intelligence collection and security operations.

In times past, the reach and authority of a Coast Guard captain was limited to the physical terrain of the port itself and the immediately surrounding waters. Given advanced warning of an illegal shipment or smuggling operation, the Coast Guard could interdict a ship just before it entered the port itself. More commonly, ships were inspected once they were already docked in harbor. Now the world's major ports are plugged into a twenty-four-hour-a-day web of information technology that connects hundreds of ports in dozens of countries into a single system of information designed to provide security to global trade.

If the radiation monitoring portal or the Centralized Examination Station in Elizabeth are the innermost layers of defense for American trade, then the most carefully guarded layer is the second—the entrance to New York Harbor. To protect it, the US Coast Guard, in close coordination with CBP, runs a worldwide program that requires ships to identify themselves and file vital information far offshore from the entrance to the harbor. From two hundred miles offshore, or ninety-six hours before docking, any ship wanting to enter an American port has to file with the Coast Guard what's known as an Advance Notice of Arrival (NOA). It lays out for the US authorities critical data they need to assess whether the ship poses a threat, or can be safely allowed into harbor. On its face, the document is innocuous enough: a simple list of ports of call, of crew members, and of the recorded contents of the cargo. In fact, it triggers a complex set of legal and operational authorities with global, national, and local law enforcement capacities.

One of the most important pieces of information on the NOA is the name of the last five ports in which the ship had docked. Those ports or the countries where they are located can ring an alarm bell if they are among the several dozen ports tracked by the US intelligence community—a list that is continuously updated and closely guarded. A combination of the NOA and intelligence flows come together in Captain Tama's office. Every single ship that enters the harbor has to pass by the scrutiny of his team.[6] If the port in question is on the watch list, or anything else about the NOA rings an alarm bell, Captain Tama issues a Captain of the Port Order and the Coast Guard swings into action. The ship is halted off the coast of New York, and a Coast Guard vessel motors out at high speed to intercept the ship prior to it passing through the Narrows.

The coordinated gathering and sharing of intelligence between the Coast Guard, CBP, and other law enforcement agencies has resulted in some huge seizures in ports across the country. For example: the largest cocaine bust in the history of US enforcement was three thousand pounds seized off the container ship MSC *Carlotta*, sailing up from Guyana. Based on local intelligence, the Coast Guard and local CBP agents boarded the ship as it was entering the Port of Philadelphia. They found forty thousand bags of cocaine hidden among hundreds of containers spread around the ship.

The Outer Layers

For a ship to leave an overseas port and head toward Captain Tama's port, it has already passed another layer of security. After 9/11, with enhanced fears about terrorist smuggling, the US adopted what's known as the Container Security Initiative (CSI), a system of port inspections, scanning methods, intelligence collection, and monitoring of port compliance that operates far beyond American borders. Fast-forward to 2019, and fully 80 percent of the goods imported into the United States by sea come to the US from a port that's participating in the CSI program. That includes all the major European ports, plus the main ports in Korea, Singapore, Japan, and even China. CSI, enabled by Congress's Fair Trade Act of 2007, requires any container or bulk cargo carrier seeking to sail toward an American port to disclose the manufacturer, seller, buyer, and destination; the location where the container was filled; the consolidator; the importer of record; the country of origin; tariff data; the vessel stow plan; and any and all updates on the status of the container. Seen in comparison to, say, the transport of people and goods by plane, this system seems mundane, obvious; but it brought a revolution in transparency to the opaque and under-regulated world of shipping.

And in real terms it means that US Coast Guard and Customs and Border Protection agents are stationed inside the port operations of the dozens of participating countries. They are constantly developing sources of information about potential smuggling operations—of humans, of drugs, of weapons—and can flag a specific cargo or a specific ship before it leaves a foreign port. If they don't give the ship a clean bill of health, it can't sail out of the port—at least not until it files a non-American destination. As Tama says, "Using big data and intelligence we can analyze threats much, much further up the supply chain."

The program is also designed to provide the US intelligence and Coast Guard communities with up-to-date information about the status of the security in ports worldwide and the question of whether a port captain can have confidence in the manifest of the ship that has emerged from suspect ports. The list of ports and countries subject to the watch list is closely guarded, but it would be no surprise if North Korea's Pyongyang were on the list, as well as Iran's Caspian Sea ports, and probably the Pakistani ports of Gwadar and Karachi.

If intelligence is received that gives the US authorities pause or concern, they can issue a "Do Not Load" order. This means that the container in question can't be loaded onto its intended ship. Of course, the United States can't physically block the loading of the cargo or the departure of the ship, but such a ship would never get anywhere near American shores—and the ship operator and cargo facilitator would find themselves subject to fines and extensive legal action in the US courts. And the shipowner would likely be barred from exporting to American ports. Denial of access to the vast American market is the kiss of death for any global manufacturer, so this is an imposing power.

These programs give the United States concrete tools to secure trade flows worldwide. They reflect a deep American security concept, one whose roots lie in the earliest days of the American Republic and the formation of the US Navy. It's the concept of "playing the away game"—that is, taking the fight to the enemies' shore so we don't have to fight on American soil. It's a concept of American foreign policy that has its roots at sea—as we'll see in chapter 3—and an astonishing conceptual extension of American might.

And these programs have this other effect: they put the American navy on patrol worldwide.

Sailing the Outer Perimeter

The largest hub of trade in the world is China. From ports outside Hong Kong, Shanghai, and Beijing, container vessels and tankers and cargo ships of every description sail east across the Pacific to Los Angeles and Seattle and Vancouver, or south to cross to the Indian Ocean en route to ports in Europe and the eastern United States. But a small number of ships do something very different. They turn off their locator beacons and head north for just over five hundred nautical miles, where they bunker off the boundary waters of North Korea. These are the sanctions busters: a form of modern-day smugglers, often private, sometimes state backed, who sell goods or weapons to a country that's been placed under sanctions. In this case, the target of the sanctions is the Democratic People's Republic of Korea: North Korea, the Hermit Kingdom, a country largely sealed off from the rest of the world by its own Orwellian government, and now also by multiple different sanctions imposed by the US and the United Nations. The sanctions were imposed both as punishment for its development of nuclear weapons, against rules set out in key international treaties, and to prevent North Korea from importing the materials or fuel to develop more.

The sanctions also prohibit the country from selling the shrimp, rice, minerals, and light manufactured goods that the country produces, and from importing manufactured goods, weapons components, and fuel. That is, all but a small supply of fuel, enough to heat its population, not enough to power its industry. That's where the smugglers come in. Ships sail out of the Yangtze River, or ports north closer to Beijing, and cross the Yellow Sea, usually under cover of dark. From reports from defectors, and by piecing together evidence from smugglers who have been caught, it seems that many of these ships sail to just over twelve miles off the North Korean coast, where they anchor in what are still technically international waters. Then they wait until local merchant ships steam out to meet them. The two ships then transfer their loads of coal or other fuels, which are then transported to land. It's estimated that by these means North Korea manages to smuggle roughly five times as much coal and other fuel as it is allowed under the sanctions.

Smuggling coal is one thing, smuggling weapons is another. In 2003, North Korea was caught doing just that. Early that year, the US intelligence community got wind of the fact that North Korea was smuggling rockets to ports in Yemen, in the Arabian Gulf, at that time an incipient stronghold of an ISIS affiliate. US agents managed to track down the *So San*, a North Korean–owned ship, as it was sailing through Spanish waters. The director for arms control at the State Department, none other than the feisty John Bolton, wanted to intercept the shipment. At the request of the US authorities, the Spanish naval frigate *Navarra* attempted to board the *So San*, which in turn tried to flee. The *Navarra* sent a shot across the bows and raked the stern of the *So San* with rifle fire, at which point the *So San* complied with the order to halt. The Spanish navy boarded the ship. And there, as warned, they found fifteen Scud missiles.

Bolton asked the State Department's lawyers to let him know which part of international law allowed him to seize these smuggled weapons. To his surprise the answer was "None." It wasn't illegal to smuggle the weapons on the lawless high seas, and Spanish and American lawyers determined that they had no legal basis to seize the weapons. Eventually, the missiles were allowed to proceed to Yemen.*

Bolton, furious, decided to remedy the situation. Building on the launch of the Container Security Initiative, the US called several allies together to join what became known as the Proliferation Security Initiative (PSI). Its signatories agreed not to use ships on the high seas to smuggle weapons. But more important, they agreed to allow the

* The US first got assurances from the Yemeni authorities that the missiles would be used for defensive purposes only. That held until 2015, when the missiles were used in attacks by Houthi rebels against Saudi Arabia.

United States, or another country with a claim, to board ships flying under their flags* if they were suspected of smuggling weapons of mass destruction or WMD-related material. PSI has been in operation ever since—used by American, German, Spanish, and other naval powers to intercept suspicious flows at sea.

These programs reflected the reality of the second decade after the end of the Cold War: that the United States was the undisputed leader of the international system, both architect and anchor of most international security arrangements, and in the leadership role to protect the flow of trade—above all, at sea. The Container Security Initiative reflected the long reach of the American market, and the ability of the United States to wield its market power to great effect. The Proliferation Security Initiative reflected a dual reality—that the United States alone operated a global blue-water navy, which sailed unchallenged; but that it used that navy, in part, at least, to enforce the rules and norms of open trade on the seas and to enforce decisions of the UN Security Council when other countries were abusing that open system. This notion of the navy as the guarantor of freedom of the seas was inherited from Britain's Royal Navy—one of the main legacies passed from that former imperial power to the United States in the wake of World War II.

A Sea of Data

All these programs rely on the constant and massive flow of data. But what happens if that data gets hacked? In 2019, Captain Tama was the

*"Flying under their flag": one of the oddities of international maritime law is that ships can fly the flag of any country that allows what's known as "registration of convenience." A ship can be owned by an American company, operated by a Dutch marine operator, sailed by an Indian crew, be sailing between Britain and South Africa, carrying Chinese, Japanese, and Thai goods; but for legal purposes can be registered in the Bahamas, or St. Kitts, or in any one of more than a dozen countries that allows the practice. This explains why the three countries in the world that lead with the number of ships registered to them are Panama, Liberia, and the Marshall Islands—countries with a combined population of circa 8 million. The business of assigning these "flags" is managed by the United States, specifically the straightforwardly named American Committee for Flags of Necessity.

first American port commander to board a ship on the basis of concerns about a cyber hack.

In February, a US-flagged container vessel filing its NOA en route to New York, verbally alerted the port that it believed that its data operations might have been penetrated by cyber espionage or interference. The NOA told Tama's team that the ship had docked in some high-risk ports in Asia and the Middle East and was transporting, among many other things, cargo for the Department of Defense. Now that they were reporting a potential hack, their route and cargo were points of serious concern. What was the intent? Was a state with adversarial intent seeking to gain control of the ship, or compromise its IT and navigation systems? Did terrorists want to ram the ship into the Verrazzano bridge and block the harbor, thereby disrupting a huge portion of the American economy?

Tama contacted the Coast Guard's nascent Cyber Protection Team, as well as the New York FBI's Cyber Task Force. Together—and with the ship's consent—they boarded it to investigate.

Tama was well trained for this operation. When serving in San Francisco, he frequently came into contact with executives from technology firms looking to develop projects in the harbor or off the coast of the Bay Area. When he returned to Washington, DC, he spent a stint developing recommendations to help the Coast Guard deepen their interactions with the West Coast tech firms, in large part to buttress cyber security.

In theory, many of the critical navigation systems of any ship entering New York Harbor are delinked from vulnerable networks to prevent hacking. But in practice, ships' crews, like all the rest of us, do not practice good cyber hygiene. When ships near ports, they need to communicate with the authorities, file records, and requisition supplies of fuel, food, water, and other goods. All this happens electronically. In the galley where the first officer of a ship works the bill of lading and oversees the onboarding and off-boarding of crew and containers, there may be dozens of thumb drives containing the relevant files from ports all over the world. These are routinely plugged into USB drives on the ship's operating system. The software that drives those gets automatic updates. And the notion that all of those updates are free from penetration is self-evidently false. On board the ship that reported the cyber hack, Tama and his team found an entire drawerful of thumb drives from ports all over the world, including from some on the Coast Guard's watch list.

In the end, software diagnostics proved that the ship had not been hacked by a malign nation, but simply infected by a piece of malware known as Emotet that had been attacking government institutions and corporations around the US. It seemed likely that the ship had not been deliberately targeted, but randomly infected. Still, it was a wake-up call for the marine industry, and for the Coast Guard.

A critical part of the data that ships use is what's known as the Automatic Identification System. The AIS is a post-9/11 innovation that requires ships to continuously transmit vital information like their position, their name, their size, their type of ship, their course, their speed, their cargo, their crew, and so on. Twenty or so pieces of basic information about every one of the ninety thousand ships that are sailing at any given time, all of it updated every minute, meaning that in a single day just over 2.5 billion pieces of data are flowing through the AIS, or more than 950 billion pieces of data per year. All of which can be penetrated by cyber hacks.

The biggest hack on shipping to date occurred on the afternoon of June 27, 2017.[7] Maersk employees in Copenhagen began to panic as one after another of their computer screens turned black. Earlier that year, hackers connected with the Russian military had hijacked the servers of a small, family-run software business in Ukraine, and in June, they used the back door they'd created to release a piece of malware called NotPetya. NotPetya spread like wildfire, attacking automatically and indiscriminately. It crippled companies across the globe—not just giants like Maersk, but also Merck, FedEx's European subsidiary TNT Express, and Rosneft. The hack hit more than sixty countries in Europe, the US, and beyond, and resulted in more than $10 billion in damages.[8]

The impact for Maersk reached across the world. In Port Elizabeth, where Jason Tama would arrive one year later, hundreds of truck drivers were stalled outside the port as the system that allowed them to come in and drop off their wares for shipping went black. Rail lines up and down the eastern seaboard were halted while they waited for cargo. No one could get in the gate. With no word from Maersk, the Port Authority announced that Maersk's terminal would close for the rest of the day. Shippers were stuck clamoring for either last-minute, expensive alternative shipping methods or temporary storage until the mess cleared. The same would happen at sixteen of Maersk's other loading terminals across the world.[9]

The computers on Maersk's ships weren't infected, but the computers monitoring and dictating the movement of those ships and all of their containers were. And key to that were the company's network's domain controllers, which among other functions set the rules that determine which users can access which systems. They only found one clean backup copy: in an office in Ghana, which happened to have been affected by a power blackout just before NotPetya struck and was thereby not vulnerable to the malware's attack. In a scene out of a spy thriller, Maersk raced to get the backup to London, where its IT department was based. With none of the Ghanaian staffers holding a British visa, the USB was handed off between two employees in an airport in Nigeria before being flown onward to London. It would be more than a week until Maersk terminals around the world began operating under any sense of normalcy. The attack alone cost Maersk between $250 and $300 million.[10]

All this to say that communications is key for the shipping industry. When trucks unload containers in ports for shipping, they are "checked in" similar to an airplane, given an identification number that not only details what is in the containers and where they are going but also feeds into an automated system that tells the truck where to unload the containers, then helps the cranes load them onto the ships, and so forth, until the container is returned to a new truck at the destination port. If something in that system breaks, the whole thing breaks—and the effects spread throughout the global economy.

From China's shores to America's, there's another critical way that sea-based traffic shapes the American economy: how data actually moves around the globe. It's commonplace when talking about the flow of data to talk about it "flying through the air"; and of course some data does move by radio waves. The vast bulk of data, though, moves by sea. That is to say, it flows through a system of cables that run along the ocean floor, connecting continents and linking economies. Fully 93 percent of all data traveling around the world ends up flowing through ocean cables. There's no part of our modern world of finance, internet communication, Zoom meetings, Amazon ordering, online commerce, Facebook, YouTube, and TikTok that isn't made possible by cables on the seafloor.*

In fact, a complex grid of more than four hundred seafloor cables link every major market in the world. Looking at their map is like playing a game of connect the dots between the world's major cities. Cables border the edges of every continent, hugging Europe from France to Portugal and then Africa from Morocco to South Africa. They cross in wide chunks from New York to nearly every part of Europe. They follow similar paths as do container ships, traveling the Mediterranean and passing through the Suez Canal before hugging India and traversing the Malacca Straits to Beijing and other coastal Chinese cities. There they group together to cross the Pacific, connecting to the West Coast of the United States—and everywhere in between. It's no accident that these cables concentrate in the world's key financial capitals, and it's no accident that those capitals are one and the same as the great harbors of the world.

That this global system of ocean floor cables requires continuous replacement and upgrade is not a revelation; what is perhaps surprising is that these cables were first laid in the 1850s, at the height of British maritime power. The famed HMS *Challenger* (whose voyage of discovery and scientific inquiry was celebrated by the first US shuttle launch) also undertook some of the first studies of the contours of the seabed and the conditions at seafloor depth that would affect the laying of various types of potential cable.[11] A scientist and engineer by the name of William Thomson made the key scientific breakthroughs about the design of cables that could sustain deep-sea conditions, and took to sea on the HMS *Agamemnon* in 1857 to begin laying cable. A series of failures and disasters did not deter Thomson or the shipowners, and in 1865 the first complete cable was laid. The onset of the transoceanic telegraph cable enabled quicker communications between Britain and its former colonial outpost, delivering news and data between journal-

*Which is why Microsoft and Facebook collaborated in 2017 to lay the fastest cable yet laid across the Atlantic, capable of transmitting data at a rate of 160 terabits per second.

ists, government officials, and trading and shipping companies, supplanting the sea "packets" that used to carry the mails between London and Newport, Rhode Island. In 1858, with the successful completion of the first transatlantic telegraph cable, the first message, on August 16, 1858, read, "Europe and America are united by telegraph. Glory to God in the highest." The next morning, one hundred guns saluted the connection in New York, with a grand parade and fireworks in September. William Thomson was knighted Lord Kelvin by Queen Victoria for his role in the effort.

Since then, cable speeds have kept getting faster—as a function of technology, military necessity, and the ravenous demands of capitalism. These cables link the great financial and trading hubs of the world, from New York to Hong Kong to London. "People don't understand how important the undersea cables are to our business," one financial trader told me. When the major firms are considering their trades, they're constantly calculating which undersea cable they should use to connect to specific markets; speed is a factor but redundancy and reliability are just as important.

All this profits the United States. Over the past three decades, the US share of world trade has gradually diminished to around 22 percent. Things look different if you examine the share of world profits taken by American financial firms. There, as of 2020, it was between two to three times that share.[12] Managing the flow of money that attaches itself to every single trade ship that enters the port of New York, to every trade transaction around the world that's brokered in US dollars, has become a huge part of what drives economic performance in the United States. In 2016, fully 50 percent of the profits recorded by American firms were in the financial industry. And all of this was made possible by seabed cables.

One of the tools that Captain Tama used to manage the security of the Port of New York and New Jersey is called an Area Maritime Security Committee. It brings together federal, state, and local authorities—and Wall Street. One of the country's largest financial firms sits on that committee, to help the Coast Guard perform its function. When Tama asked one of their executives why they paid attention to the Coast Guard's work, they answered: "You're a market mover. A disruption in the maritime supply chain would roil the financial markets."

* * *

So what's at stake is the American economy, American security, and America's role in the world as the banker to the global economy and the anchor of global trade security, a role that affects billions of people globally. It's a role that relies on American naval dominance, a position it inherited from the British Royal Navy—whose role in the eighteenth and nineteenth centuries was violent, sometimes immoral, but massively consequential to the shape of the twenty-first-century world.

3

Charting Today's World

How We Got Here

The Praia de Carcavelos stretches for more than a mile along Portugal's Atlantic coast, its deep, golden-colored sands serving as a weekend escape from Lisbon, eight miles away, around the headlands that separate the Tagus River from the swells of the Atlantic. Although well stocked with cafés and restaurants and bars, and well visited by Lisbon's burgeoning population, the Carcavelos beach receives few foreign tourists, who typically head farther south to the better-known beaches and resorts of the Algarve.

But Carcavelos has two important claims to attention. One is not easily visible; it's the hub of the first sea cable to connect mainland Europe to England, and thus to America, as well as Europe to Africa and then to India. On June 25, 1870, the *Illustrated London News* celebrated its conclusion:

> *The successful completion of the submarine telegraph line between Malta, Gibraltar, and Falmouth, in connection with the Anglo-Mediterranean and the British Indian submarine telegraphs, to form a direct submarine communication all the way from India to England, crossing only the land of Egypt, has been announced, to the public satisfaction.*

To this day, Carcavelos continues to serve as the hub of myriad undersea cables, with a particular concentration of cables connecting mainland Europe to Africa. The early company officials of the Falmouth, Malta, Gibraltar Telegraph Company (later, Cable & Wireless) who chose the Portuguese coast to anchor the Gibraltar section of the cable did so for a simple reason: it's the westernmost point of the European mainland.

That same geography matters for the beach's other important feature, the maritime defensive fortification of São Julião da Barra. The fort comprises an uneven pentagon that serves as its sea-level perimeter, defense posts overlooking the ocean, and a guard tower that anchors its central section. It is Portugal's largest maritime fortification, and from 2013 onward has been the official residence of the country's minister of defense. Although originally commissioned by King Manuel I, who ruled Portugal from 1495 to 1521, construction of the fort was delayed. It was completed between 1553 and 1558, one of a string of towers and forts that protected Lisbon from attack from the Atlantic.

It was from these shores, too, that Portugal's conquistadors set sail on their voyages of discovery, trade, conquest, and slavery that so profoundly shaped the modern world. The basement dungeons of São Julião da Barra, later famous for holding political prisoners during Portugal's fascist period, far earlier were also holding cells for slaves returned from West Africa. Several decades before the fort was constructed, Infante Dom Henrique of Portugal, Duke of Viseu, had established a trading post at Elmina, on the Ghanaian coast of the Gulf of Guinea, and brought African slaves back with him to Lisbon—the first African slaves to be brought to the European continent.* By the time of the completion of the Barra, Elmina was one of the major centers of the African slave trade, and many who were captured there spent time in the dank basements of the Barra.†

*I first visited these forts when I was seventeen, on a summer holiday with a school friend. While wandering through the dark halls of the fort's holding cells, I realized that I'd seen something similar before. As a schoolchild, I'd visited the other end of the traffic, the slaveholding forts of Elmina. It was an eerie realization, and one that shaped my earliest understanding of the role of empire in the forging of the world in which I lived.

†Three thousand miles away, Elmina fort still stands, well preserved, a three-hour drive west of Accra, Ghana. It overlooks the pounding surf and strong currents of the Gulf of Guinea. It's the oldest surviving European structure in sub-Saharan Africa, and a particularly redolent memorial to the brutality of that encounter. Just as in the Barra, its lowest levels were forged as holding cells for the slaves that passed through this fortification. Also on display at Elmina is the armor of some of the early Portuguese occupiers—surprisingly small in stature. At the height of the European slave trade (when Elmina had passed from Portuguese hands to the Dutch, before passing

No account of the role of European imperialism in forging the modern world should fail to emphasize the central, indispensable role of the transatlantic slave trade in its establishment, and of slavery in general in generating the wealth of Europe that allowed it to dominate world politics for the four and a half centuries that followed the construction of São Julião da Barra. Portugal's most consequential voyage, though, was not to its slaving colonies in the Americas or West Africa; it was Portugal's discovery of a solution to a riddle that had preoccupied Europe's imperialists and explorers and crusaders, and evaded rival Spain's Columbus—the sea route to the Indies. It's ironic that Europe's westernmost country would be the first to find the sea route to Asia, but it turned out that the key to doing so was to sail farther west across the Atlantic, there to catch winds that could fling a small ship into currents that pulled it south and east around the southern coast of Africa, up into the Indian Ocean—winds we know today as the trade winds.[1,*]

* * *

For the past five hundred years, the dynamics of world trade and military power have been shaped by oceans and the competition upon them. In that time, no state or empire has succeeded in sustaining a position as a leading world power without fielding a navy and merchant fleet capable of dominating the high seas. Alfred Thayer Mahan, the world's most renowned naval strategist, famously described the link between national power, economic power, and sea power: "Control of the sea, by maritime commerce and naval supremacy," he wrote, "means predominant influence in the world . . . [and] is the chief among the merely material elements in the power and prosperity of nations."[2]

In the modern period, the relationship between trade and naval power has been symbiotic in one way or another.[3] For some powers, trade followed where their navies plundered—in the parlance of the American navy, "trade followed the flag." Other nations inverted the

---

to the British), Elmina castle saw as many as thirty thousand slaves moved through its dungeons each year.

*Conventional wisdom to the contrary, the trade winds are not so named after the trade routes they came to support, but rather from the medieval phrase "blow trade," meaning in a steady course or direction. See Lincoln Paine, *The Sea and Civilization: A Maritime History of the World* (New York: Vintage, 2013).

relationship, letting trade serve as the leading edge of their power, which more forceful measures—and their navies—followed.

Prior to this period, for the Western nations who so profoundly shaped the modern world, oceans were the boundary of their experience, the frontier of societies, and the limit of knowledge. Not until the late eighth century did Norse Vikings sail and row across the North Sea to raid and then establish settlements in northern England—an impressive feat for the age, but in fact a voyage of only a few hundred nautical miles. More remarkably, around the turn of the eleventh century, Norseman Leif Erikson or his contemporaries (the historical record is imprecise) sailed across the Atlantic and established a settlement on what is now Canada's far-eastern shore.[4] But these were exceptions. For much of humanity the sea was a blank space on the rudimentary maps of the day. Instead of islands and waves, maps of oceans were marked by monsters and imaginary creatures—such was the limited understanding.

Only in the Islamic world was there greater movement and commerce across the oceans. The most recent history shows major trade across the Indian Ocean as early as the fourth century BCE.[5] It is no accident that it was an Islamic scholar, Ibn Battuta, who in 1328 or 1330 (his chronology is suspect) managed to sail from Jeddah in the Arabian Peninsula, southeast to Aden, against the prevailing winds in the Red Sea, and ultimately to Zanzibar, the fabled island off the eastern coast of Africa. At least a decade later, he also made it as far east as China.[6] Battuta's travelogue, the *Rihla*, only confirmed the extent of the cross-cultural and cross-continental trade in the Indian Ocean that reshaped the Islamic world in the fourteenth and fifteenth centuries.[7]

Europe was largely incidental to these developments. Only in the enclosed Mediterranean Sea did the European polities of the time compete in naval contest. The continent caught the echoes of wider developments in the trade of silk and slaves that connected it to the Islamic world, but only remotely. Most of that trade happened by camel and horse and foot, having only to cross a narrow section of the Mediterranean at its eastern edge to connect the Venetian empire to the wealth of the Islamic world.[8] What the European world understood of a rich market beyond its network of knowledge was shrouded in mystery and romanticism, like the legend of Prester John and his riches, which spurred many of the early, failed European efforts to find a sea route to Asia.

All that changed when pre-Renaissance Europe, rising from the devastation of the Dark Ages, developed new knowledge and techniques for long-range navigation. Tempted in large part by the lure of the spice trade, European adventurers began their excursions into Asia, Africa, and the Americas by means of ocean voyage.[9] The resulting encounters of commerce and violence forged our world.

Today we have a sense of the romance of the seas, but romance was not the point of Europe's ocean adventures—the point was prestige, and profit. As the most adventurous European powers of the day, Spanish and Portuguese explorers forayed into the "new" world, dismantling the Aztec and Mayan civilizations, and establishing for themselves far-flung empires of gold and silver and disease, spreading epidemics in their wake. And then Portugal went farther, charting a sea route to Asia, chasing the scent of profits as they tangled with the Mamluks of Egypt and the Ottomans of Constantinople over control of the spice trade.

Portugal's motives were religious as well—the Christian powers of Europe sought to weaken the influence of the Muslim world by pressuring them in their home territories. (It was the first but not the last time Western powers would decide that the right way to weaken the perceived threat from Muslims was to take the fight to the Arab world.) Such was the role of religion and perceptions of providence in early European exploration that the Portuguese king's orator once cast their ambitions in terms quoted from Psalm 72: "He shall have dominion also from sea to sea, and from the river unto the ends of the earth."[10] Combining religious zeal with advanced cannonry, Portugal's brutal explorers opened up trade routes that would become the precursors to contemporary globalization. Admiral James Stavridis, the first naval officer to become the head of NATO, wrote of this phase that "their great voyages of discovery inspired Europeans, exploited Africans (often with extreme brutality), and created the connections between the Atlantic and Indian oceans over the fifteenth and sixteenth centuries. Some have called this the dawn of the Oceanic Age."[11]

As the Portuguese and Spanish, and soon after the Dutch, vied for influence in the lands they encountered, dominance of the high seas became the most important measure and instrument of global power.[12] The age of empire, which so deeply shaped the modern world, was first and foremost an age of sail—of naval warfare and sea-based trade. It was a violent encounter. In his epic poem *The Lusíads*, the Portuguese poet Luís de Camões talked of

> *such storms and perils,*
> *That death, many times, seemed imminent;*
> *On the land, such battles and intrigue,*
> *Such dire, inevitable hardships!*[13]

This state-backed violence was a new phenomenon for the Indian Ocean they encountered. Roger Crowley, a historian of the imperial age, wrote about the Indian Ocean as the Portuguese encountered it in the 1400s. He described:

> *a complex interlocking of trading systems, maritime styles, cultures and religions, and a series of hubs: Malacca on the Malay Peninsula, larger than Venice, for goods from China and the farther spice islands; Calicut, on the west coast of India, for pepper; Ormuz, gateway to the Persian Gulf and Baghdad; Aden, at the entrance to the Red Sea and the routes to Cairo, the nerve center of the Islamic world. Scores of other small city states dotted its shores. It dispatched gold, black slaves and mangrove poles from Africa, incense and dates from Arabia, bullion from Europe, horses from Persia, opium from Egypt, porcelain from China, war elephants from Ceylon, rice from Bengal, sulfur from Sumatra, nutmeg from the Malaccas, diamonds from the Deccan Plateau, cotton cloth from Gujarat. No one had a monopoly in this terrain—it was too extensive and complex.*[14]

Portugal was not the only distant power of the era to flex its muscles in the Indian Ocean. So, too, did China, at the height of the Ming Dynasty. Earlier, Song Dynasty merchants had recorded large profits from seagoing ventures, but the depredations of two merchants during the waning days of Mongol rule confirmed traditional Confucian distrust of seagoing ventures, and bureaucrats put the lid on oceangoing trade.* China was visited by foreign explorers and traders, though, mostly from the Islamic world, whose arrival over land and by sea began to expose the Mings to the wealth to be found beyond the Middle Kingdom. At the dawn of the fifteenth century, the Yongle Emperor decided to break with that Confucian custom and set his sights on seaward exploration. He ordered his court to build a fleet of ships capable of sailing well beyond the coastal seas and into the far oceans.

What resulted has gone down in Chinese lore as one of the great exploits of the nation's long history. It has been described as "perhaps the most remarkable single phenomenon of the fifteenth century."[15] Under the command of one of the emperor's court loyalists, Zheng He, the Mings built a fleet of around sixty treasure ships, the largest of which had nine masts, and were likely at least twice the size of the single largest ship in the Spanish or Portuguese fleets (although their true size is disputed).[16] These ships were then loaded with goods and treasures from the Ming court, and accompanied by over two hundred troop, grain, battle, and supply ships. Historian Louise Levathes describes the voyage as it set sail: "In autumn of 1405, the fleet of 317 brightly painted junks with a total crew of more than 27,000 men was ready to depart from Nanjing. As the ships assembled in formation in the center of the Yangzi, the sculpted 'eyes' on the majestic bows looked anxiously downstream toward the open sea."[17] The so-called Treasure Fleet, voyaging together as an armada, set sail for ports west in 1405, past the Malay trading post of Malacca and out into the vastness of the Indian Ocean. For twenty-eight years these ships sailed to and from the major trading entrepôts of the day—from Malacca to Calicut to Malindi (near the island of Zanzibar) in an exercise of cultural diplomacy on a grand scale.[18] The voyage played an important

*According to a recent study of naval architecture, early Chinese ship designs actually informed some of the most important advances in industrial ship design, especially the strong internal bulkheads used by Chinese junks as early as the 300s. See Larrie D. Ferreiro, *Bridging the Seas: The Rise of Naval Architecture in the Industrial Age, 1800–2000* (Cambridge, MA: MIT Press, 2020). The superior design of these early junks was noted by none other than Benjamin Franklin in his "Marine Observations" of 1795.

role in quasi-stabilizing the Malacca Straits, until then an anarchic den of competing pirate clans.[19]

Few original writings of the voyage survive, but one is from Zheng He himself. He inscribed the following:

> *We have traversed over a hundred thousand li of vast ocean [and have] beheld great ocean waves, rising as high as the sky and swelling and swelling endlessly. Whether in dense fog and drizzling rain or in wind-driven waves rising like mountains, no matter what the sudden changes in sea conditions, we spread our cloudlike sails aloft and sailed by the stars day and night.*[20]

Zheng He is to China what Richard the Lionheart is to England—a figure of historical legend who embodies the early prowess of the nation, often invoked by Chinese patriots and nationalists aspiring to reclaim the lost glory of China's imperial past.[21] (And just as modern historiography has underscored the brutality of the Crusades, recent works of history have revealed that Zheng He's interactions across the Indian Ocean were far less peaceful than the official Chinese narrative would suggest.) But in 1433, after seven voyages of the Treasure Fleet, the Ming Dynasty under its new emperor, Xuande, pulled back the ships to preserve resources (the Mings were being attacked by the Mongols in the northwest), withdrawing back into its inland boundaries. "The timing of the Chinese maritime decline," writes the naval historian Bruce Swanson, "could not have been worse, for it coincided with European maritime expansion into Asia."[22]

And so the Portuguese (and soon their European competitors) encountered little resistance on the high seas of Asia. As Roger Crowley writes, "The great continental powers of Asia left the sea to the merchants. There was small-scale piracy but there were no protectionist war fleets, and little notion of territorial waters prevailed."[23] That was about to change. Had China stayed this maritime course, the first sustained encounter between the Middle Kingdom and the Christian empires might have played out very differently. But it was not to be. Portugal encountered an Indian Ocean free of Chinese sea power and was therefore able over time to gain an important advantage in the game of empires.*

For more than a century, Portugal's advantages on the high seas allowed it to develop the farthest-flung empire of the late fifteenth and sixteenth centuries, its exploits touching every peopled region of the world. From aforementioned Manaus in the central Amazon to the narrows that Verrazzano saw at the entrance to what is now the Port of New York to Goa on the west coast of India, Portuguese seafaring sketched the links in what would become a global chain of trade connections.[24] Wherever Portugal deployed its cannon, trade routes would follow: trade followed the flag. Since Portugal's rise in the 1500s, naval power and global trade have been inextricably linked—and remain so to this day.

By the late 1500s, England was challenging both Spain and Portugal on the seas. At a decisive battle in 1588 off the French coast at Gravelines, the English navy defeated the Spanish armada, demonstrating its growing mastery of the techniques of sail and naval battle. Its advances in shipbuilding would soon lead England to displace Portugal and then to build the largest and richest empire the world had ever known—until the US Navy helped forge the modern American equivalent.[25]

Globalization, that bugbear of modern politics, that much misused description of global economics, is often thought of as a contemporary phenomenon. Yet the history of the rise of Europe as early as the sixteenth century is a story of global trade. Not *free* trade, to be sure, but a global trade nonetheless. Indeed, to this day, global trade and power follows patterns and pathways set in the Age of Empire. The parameters of the contemporary world were set in large part by the way in which European colonial exploration intersected with the waning empires of the East in the late eighteenth and early nineteenth centuries.

Even smaller European empires like Sweden, puny actors by global scale, played important roles in this phase of imperial exploration

*The major competitors to the Portuguese in this period were the Ottomans. That the Ottomans were a sea power as well as a land power is often neglected in the recounting of the imperial age, but Portuguese-Ottoman competition shaped the development of the Red Sea, the eastern coast of Africa, and the Suez long before the arrival of the better-known Franco-British rivalries of the eighteenth and nineteenth centuries.

and trade.[26] Germany had a modest global footprint, as did Belgium, between them occupying and plundering in the most brutal manner imaginable the natural resources of Central and East Africa.[27] Of the major European powers, France joined the game late, moving in the 1700s to acquire possessions in the Americas, in West and North Africa, in the Middle East, and later a small foothold in Southeast Asia. Writing his magisterial account of the sea and civilization, Lincoln Paine comments of this oceanic activity: "They made possible the forging of new links between formerly unconnected regions of the globe, and laid the foundation of Europe's gradual ascendency on the world stage."[28]

But to fully understand that ascendency, and the shape of the modern world, it's chiefly Britain's economic, colonial, and eventually imperial role in Asia that matters. Britain reversed the Portuguese game—the flag followed the trade.

The Company

England's industrial revolution is often written about as a story of new technology and manufacturing prowess, and these were essential. What financed England's growth, though, was huge imports of cotton from India and other natural resources from its eastern colonies.[29] The flowering of European civilization in the eighteenth and particularly the nineteenth century was a product of the huge economic gains from a global trade—and, to be sure, of the system of suppression and indentured labor that undergirded it.[30]

Some of England's most important imperial interactions, though, came initially not through military occupation but commercial engagement. As early as 1553, a handful of British merchants formed what later became known as a joint-stock company, the aptly named Company of Merchant Adventurers to New Lands (also known as the Muscovy Company), formed to undertake trade with Russia.[31] Almost fifty years later, and more consequently, a similar mechanism was formed in 1600 to venture still farther east: the English East India Company. This move was quickly followed by the Dutch, Danish, Portuguese, French, and Swedish imperial courts, each of which would over the next decades establish their own similar "companies."[32] In today's parlance we would think of them as joint ventures, so entangled were they with the crown.* They became the tip of the spear of European exploration.[33]

Most consequential was the English East India Company, which by the mid-1700s was so large and so powerful it was simply known as The Company.[34] Over the course of two centuries, it wielded a combination of trade, commercial diplomacy, and private force—often backed up by official diplomacy and force from London. The story of The Company's gradual morphing from a commercial enterprise into a semi-sovereign force, both partner and competitor to the Crown, defies effective categorization between the private and the public sphere. William Dalrymple, the leading historian of the English in India, uses an evocative phrase to describe its tenure: he calls it, simply, "The Anarchy."[35] During its two centuries of operations, backed by the British Crown, it would progressively, purposely, and eventually brutally dismantle the Mughal Empire in northern India, along with the Burmese Kingdom, and absorb the remnants of the Deccan sultanates in southern India. And then, in a more gradual and subtle process, it would encounter and help to hasten the collapse of the Qing Dynasty in China.[36]

Though these empires were by most measures larger and more powerful than their European competitors, Europe's command of the high seas gave its adventurers a formidable advantage. Indeed, some recent scholarship suggests that it was the key advantage that the Europeans held over their powerful Asian rivals. In an important revision of some of the conventional assumptions of the time, J. C. Sharman's *Empires of the Weak* makes a compelling case that it was precisely their ability to control the high seas, not advantages of modernization or political systems or even weaponry, that enabled the European empires to gain mastery over the Asian empires. (It is also true that the heyday of European power coincided with a period of advanced corruption and rot in the heart of the key Asian empires.)[37]

*Another of these joint stock ventures was the Hudson's Bay Company, which opened up British trade routes in what would later become Canada and the United States of America. For an excellent history of the company, see Peter C. Newman, *Company of Adventurers: How the Hudson's Bay Empire Determined the Destiny of a Continent* (Toronto: Penguin Canada, 2005).

Whatever the role of internal decay, political systems, or naval mastery, a vital backdrop to all that followed is that the near-total collapse of both the Indian and Chinese empires opened up a lacuna in world affairs. They were the two largest economies in the world in the 1700s, and their demise created a space into which Western power would flow and from which Europe and then the New World would profit for more than a century and a half.[38]

* * *

In the late 1700s, Britain's colonial ambitions and profits were disrupted by a populist revolt in a territory it had acquired some years earlier, one that would soon become known as the United States of America. The American war served not to weaken the British Empire as a whole, but rather to refocus it on its eastern holdings.[39] On the European continent, Britain was endlessly entangled in war with the French. In Africa, a profitable slave trade continued, but in constant friction with the French, as in the Middle East, where French rivalry and local insurrections curtailed British ambitions.[40]

In the East, however, the English dominated the colonial race, in part because Portugal and the Dutch had diminished as imperial contenders, and in large part because Britain had the superior navy. The riches they plundered from their holdings and acquisitions in India were unparalleled. In the wake of their loss of the American colonies, London's appetite for eastern expansion grew, and it turned its gaze still farther in the Orient, to the uncalculated treasures of the Qing Empire in China. British victories in the Napoleonic Wars also enabled a move against French possessions in the Indian Ocean.

As the story has been carefully told elsewhere, as Britain deepened its hold on India and the Indian Ocean, the most consequential economic feature of the colonial system became the triangular trade that emerged between Britain, India, and China. Britain and Europe as a whole had developed an appetite for Chinese tea, as well as silks, furniture, and other goods. Trade in these goods started at a small scale, but grew through the late 1700s and into the early 1800s. But as Britain traded its gold for that tea, it developed a substantial trading deficit with China—to the mounting concern of London and the masters of The Company. (There are sharp echoes here of modern complaints about China's large "current-account surplus" with the United States.)

To change the equation, Britain began exporting opium, which it grew in India, to feed an incipient Chinese market for the drug. Increasing the flow of opium into China began to ease British gold losses in the triangular trade. This became a domestic problem in China, as the health effects of the opium trade began to take a toll on Chinese society. The British and European trade nevertheless deepened.[41,*] By 1828, opium accounted for more than half of the British total export value to China.[42] In 1834, the British Crown revoked the monopoly it had given to the East India Company, and an influx of private traders flowed into China. The opium trade grew still further.[43]

At this point in history, China's trade with the outside world was tightly controlled. After early, unsettling encounters with foreign traders, the Chinese court had established a careful system for limiting contact between foreigners and the Chinese. They gave a monopoly on foreign trade to a small number of families, termed the Cohong or Hongs, and forbade foreigners from entering China proper. The Qing court demarcated a small area of Canton (modern-day Guangzhou), at the opening of the Pearl River, to house foreign traders. They established "factories" there—the word "factory" not implying a production facility, but housing for the "factors," or tradesmen of the day. These were a combination of boardinghouse and warehouse for the British, French, Russian, German, and other European traders who maintained a consistent flow of goods into China. And by the mid-1830s, opium accounted for a huge portion of that flow of goods.

In 1836, the imperial court of China, together with the viceroy of Canton, started a campaign to try to eliminate the opium trade. The Qing Dynasty appointed Imperial Commissioner Lin Zexu to Canton to try to crack down on the opium trade, including destroying chests of opium, and pushing back on the British penetration of Canton.[44,†]

*Even the United States joined the trade in 1784, when the *Empress of China* became the first American merchant ship to enter Chinese waters, a mere eight years after the country became independent. See Michael Green, *By More Than Providence* (New York: Columbia University Press, 2017), 22.

†Not for the first time in Chinese history. In 878 AD, Chinese rebels defied the edicts of the emperor and massacred Arab and Persian traders who had established a trading base at Guangzhou. See William Bernstein, *A Splendid Exchange* (New York: Atlantic Monthly Press, 2008), 68.

Tensions grew; Britain was simply gaining too much profit from the trade to allow for a restriction. The British had tried for years to open up Chinese markets to deeper trade. As early as 1793, they had tried direct diplomatic appeals to the Chinese Imperial Court. Lord George Macartney undertook a famous diplomatic mission to Beijing to ask the court to further open up the opium trade. A portrait of the diplomatic mission shows Lord Macartney in his audience with the Qing emperor. A note in his diary explains what happened in the meeting: he "was received with the utmost politeness, treated with the utmost hospitality, watched with the utmost vigilance and dismissed with the utmost civility."[45] Little came of his mission. In 1816, George Staunton, the son of one of Macartney's translators, served as a commissioner on the earl of Amherst's diplomatic embassy to Beijing. This time, the British did not even manage to gain an audience with the emperor, when Staunton advised Amherst not to kowtow to the Chinese. Diplomacy failed. Then, as would so often afterward be the case, what followed failed diplomacy was military escalation.

By the late 1820s, the Qing Dynasty was using its limited naval power to block English clippers from sailing up the Pearl River, forcing them to port at the small island of Lintin, in the mouth of the river delta. In 1839, Lin Zexu's campaign to push back on the English trades began to intensify as the Chinese commissioner confiscated and destroyed chests of British-supplied opium. In September 1839 there were skirmishes off the coast, and in November 1839 a military confrontation at Cheunpi, in Canton Bay, saw two British frigates, the twenty-eight-gun *Volage* and the eighteen-gun *Hyacinth*, take on twenty-nine Chinese vessels that were blocking the harbor. The overwhelming military superiority of the British ships carried the day and the Chinese junks were destroyed with almost no casualties on the British side.[46] In the words of Bruce Swanson, a historian of Chinese naval power: "The ocean no longer served as an extension of the Great Wall."[47]

From there, the situation escalated quickly. In Britain, politicians had been arguing about the benefits and costs of demanding retaliation against the Chinese for blocking their market—but the decision to launch a full-blown fight was ultimately not made in London. On January 31, 1840, The Company's authorities in India, who had command of British forces in Asia, declared war on the Chinese.[48] The British government wouldn't pass a motion for war against China until April 1840. The purpose of the war was a limited one: to compel the Chinese to open to wider trade. Lord Palmerston was the foreign secretary in London and his name will always be associated with "gunboat diplomacy"—a phrase that captured the somewhat ironic notion of using naval force to achieve better terms in a negotiation over "free" trade. In point of fact, Palmerston long resisted deploying British forces to help the opium traders, arguing that Britain could not "interfere for the purpose of enabling British subjects to violate the laws of the country to which they trade."[49] Eventually, though, events on the ground (and strong lobbying from British opium traders) forced his hand.

As the British intensified their military operations on the Pearl River, they focused their attention on the great natural harbor of Hong Kong, some twenty miles due south from the Chinese mainland. The harbor features deep, protected, and easily defended waters with easy access to the South China Sea and beyond. Prior to the open conflict with China, the harbor and surrounding areas had been used as a location to replenish fresh-water supplies. But during the ensuing war, the British navy and traders began to use the harbor at scale. On January 26, 1841, Hong Kong island was occupied by the British with the signing of the Convention of Chuenpi (today romanized as Chuanbi), although neither side professed happiness with it; Palmerston called Hong Kong "a barren island with hardly a house upon it."[50]

Military action intensified, and what is known as the First Opium War was well underway. It lasted, at varying degrees of intensity, for two and a half years. At its peak, the British had sixteen gunboats plying Chinese waters.[51] By the summer of 1842, the Chinese recognized that they were literally outgunned, and they sued for peace. The result was the August 29, 1842, Treaty of Nanking. This ended the monopoly of the Cohongs who had controlled trade and opened new treaty ports in addition to Canton, in Amoy, Foochow (modern-day Xiamen and Fuzhou), Ningpo, and Shanghai. The Chinese paid the British off for their opium losses, and they ceded Hong Kong to Britain. In 1843, a supplementary treaty, known as the Treaty of the Bogue, reinforced the Treaty of Nanking and added further provisions. Between them, the two treaties stipulated that British citizens would be tried by British courts for any violations of the treaty or of Chinese law, and if China were to grant other rights to other European powers, they would also grant Britain those same rights.

The Treaties of Nanking and Bogue are some of the most consequential documents in modern history. The treaties effectively established the principles that form the legal heart of global trade arrangements to this day—what are known in modern parlance as the principle of "extra-territoriality" and the principle of the "most-favored nation." For all intents and purposes they sealed the fate of the late Qing Empire in China, assigning it to a subordinate status in the face of British power. Although the Qing would rule until 1912, from the 1850s onward they were progressively weakened by a combination of internal rebellion and external intrusion by the European power. This set the stage for the so-called Century of Humiliation, a period of history that the modern Chinese government still references as it deals with the West. And it solidified the three-way trade in gold, tea, and opium that undergirded British dominance of world finance for a century to come.[52]

The period that followed were the years when Britain "ruled the waves," in the words of the Gilbert and Sullivan song that became the anthem of an age.

The Great Bypass

For the rest of the nineteenth century and into the twentieth, Britain continued its dominance of the high seas. Ironically, a major boost to its dominance came in the form of an innovation by its archrival, France.

Given the critical role played in the imperial contest by sea power, and the growing importance of global trade to the coffers of both Paris and London, it was foremost in the minds of Britain's rulers to look at their long-running competition with France, in part through the question of who had greater control of the seas. France and England's endless land wars—the Hundred Years' War, the Thirty Years' War, and the Napoleonic Wars—are better known; but control of the critical seaways was a vital part of Anglo-French rivalry.[53]

In parallel to British imperial expansion in Asia was France's imperial domination of the western half of the Middle East, in particular the

Levant and Egypt.[54] The forging of the modern Middle East through imperial conquest and combat is a distinct story—but it intersects with ours, in Egypt.

In the 1830s, as part of its growing colonial presence in the Middle East, France sent a consul to Alexandria, an individual whose name would end up written into the history books precisely on the question of access to the seas. French consul Ferdinand Marie, Vicomte de Lesseps, turned into reality a dream that had long been considered by Europe's colonial adventurers. Although Egypt was a landlocked country, the formation that lay between the Mediterranean and Europe's ports on the one hand and the outer fringes of the Indian Ocean on the other was a fairly small parcel of land, the Sinai Peninsula. For years, people had considered the possibility of creating a sea passage, a canal, to link the two seas. De Lesseps made it happen.

De Lesseps began exploring the idea of a water passage across Egypt from his very first days in the country. Although an early proponent of the canal, Barthélemy Prosper Enfantin, set up a Suez Canal Study Group in 1846, the accession of an unfriendly Egyptian khedive to the throne in 1849 nixed his plans. It was not until 1854 that de Lesseps secured the permission of a more pliable khedive to form a company to begin the work with a French charter and French engineers. De Lesseps began to plan for one of the great engineering marvels of the era (despite British opposition to a project that Palmerston—soon to be prime minister—viewed as an unrealistic French dream that would only cause problems for its neighbors, including Britain). The Suez Canal Company started operations in 1858. Dug between 1859 and 1869, the canal forged a connection between Port Said in the south to the Mediterranean in the north, passing through a series of large lakes in the Sinai Peninsula, including the Great Bitter Lake (which would host a fateful encounter at the end of World War II).[55]

Thus did the French achieve an engineering marvel and an economic revolution. The Suez Canal transformed global trading relations in the heyday of the imperial age by creating a short route for sea-based trade from Asia to Europe. By digging the canal, de Lesseps reduced the distance from London to Bombay, for instance, by a whopping 6,649 miles. It cut the time for sea voyages from Asia to Europe in half, and the costs by an equal amount. And it allowed ships to avoid sailing around the Cape of Good Hope—a singularly ill-named feature, noted for the scale and severity of its storms and the number of ships that perished off its coast.[56] Avoiding the Cape and forging this new straighter path between Asia and Europe was a huge boon to trade.[57]

It should also have been a massive boon to France's clout. But for this: in 1881, an Egyptian army officer initiated a coup against the khedive, the leader of Egypt and Sudan—and together France and Britain sent warships off the coast of Alexandria in support of the khedive. After a riot in the city that killed fifty Europeans, the French fleet was recalled home. Meanwhile, the British offered an ultimatum—and when it was rejected, began a bombardment of Alexandria, on Egypt's Mediterranean coast. They went on to occupy much of Egypt and to gain effective control of the Suez Canal.[58]

The canal itself quickly became a source of tension between the two most active European colonialists, as well as their respective rivals. Neither France nor England trusted the other to allow the passage to be left open for trade. And thus, Egypt and control of this canal became a major prize in the long-running imperial contest between London and Paris.[59] Eventually, after much friction, they decided to resolve the issue by a diplomatic agreement. They met, together with Germany, the Austro-Hungarian empire, the Ottoman Empire, Spain, France, Italy, the Netherlands, and Russia—the other European imperial powers of the day—and set out some rules of the game. Their envoys eventually signed the Convention of Constantinople, a treaty that stipulated that the canal should be a source of free passage in war or peace. It was an early example of using diplomacy to set out a series of commitments about how the powers would behave on the seas—a body of convention and law that we now refer to as the "law of the sea," and was eventually encoded in an overarching treaty by that name. Like much of the rest of the law of the sea that was to come, the Convention of Constantinople was a document honored in times of comity and peace, and rapidly abandoned in times of war.[60]

Still, for the fifty years that followed the signing of the Convention in 1888, the canal was largely open, a source of the free flow of trade especially from India and the Asian colonies into Europe's markets.

World War I briefly interrupted the flow of trade through the Suez, although it reopened quickly at war's end. By this time, the Suez Canal was the most important waterway in the world, a crucial artery in the flow of global trade. Virtually all of the shipping that flowed into Europe's ports from Asia sailed through the Suez Canal. With the advent of modern industrialization and the energy revolution that accompanied it, as well as the discovery of oil in the Arabian Peninsula, the importance of the Suez grew further. From what had been a vague dream to the digging project to a vital artery of trade, the Suez Canal came to be an essential feature of the architecture of the late phase of the British Empire.[61]

Sailing to World War

For more than two hundred years, the British maintained the dominant navy on the high seas, and the global standing it allowed.[62] But by the early 1900s, it was facing a new aspirant to that status, Germany. At the turn of the twentieth century, Berlin sought to challenge London's dominance on the sea. The threat to Britain's position in the English Channel and beyond triggered London to build even larger, even more potent frigates. The arms buildup that resulted was a crucial part of the dynamic that culminated in the First World War.[63]

Historians disagree on many fundamentals about the causes of that great slaughter, or of the relative importance of specific actions and decisions taken by the European powers in the decade leading up to it.[64] But there's a surprising degree of agreement around the importance of an unsolicited memorandum penned by a relatively lowly Foreign Office official, working of all places in the registry system—essentially, the British government's filing system for the many, varied cables it received from all corners of the empire.

The official in question, Sir Eyre Alexander Barby Wichart Crowe, was what passed for an expert on German affairs in those days, when the Foreign Office was still proudly manned by "gifted amateurs." Crowe was born in Leipzig, his mother was of German ancestry, his wife was of German descent, and he spent much of his youth in Berlin, so he had some claim to at least a layman's familiarity with German culture and mindset. More to the point, he had served in the Foreign Office's unit dealing with the Africa Protectorates, and in that capacity had been privy to the negotiations between Germany, France, England, America, and the other European powers over the status of Morocco—negotiations that culminated in the Treaty of Algeciras in 1906. The treaty emerged from a German attempt to block France's efforts to establish a protectorate over Morocco and to divide the French-British entente that had occurred after 1904. German efforts failed, however, and the conference left Britain and France closer than before—and skeptical of a rising Germany. Those negotiations shaped Crowe's perception of German foreign relations in the age of Bismarck.[65] In 1907, evidently somewhat bored with his role in the registry, and mindful of the recent negotiations in Spain, he took the initiative to pen a long memo about Britain's relations with Germany, and more specifically on the question of how Britain should respond to Germany's evident desire to expand its naval capacity and commercial reach. It's a wordy, turgid text that meanders through Anglo-German history and treaty negotiations—but its core arguments about the dynamics of great power rivalry shape our understanding of international relations to this day.[66]

The Crowe Memorandum, as it has come to be known, had three essential themes. The first, almost in passing, sets out Britain's understanding of its own role as a guardian of the world's naval and trade routes. Then he spells out the implications of a theory about sea power recently published by the American academic Alfred Thayer Mahan:

> *The general character of England's foreign policy is determined by the immutable conditions of her geographical situation on the ocean flank of Europe as an island State with vast oversea colonies and dependencies, whose existence and survival as an independent community are inseparably bound up with the possession of preponderant sea power. The tremendous influence of such preponderance has been described in the classical pages of Captain Mahan. No one now disputes it. Sea power is more potent than land power, because it is as pervading as the element in which it moves.*

Second, he talks about Germany's presumed desire for a wider leadership stance in international affairs. In so doing he describes the essential dilemma of modern state-to-state relations:

Now, it is quite possible that Germany does not, nor ever will, consciously cherish any schemes of so subversive a nature. Her statesmen have openly repudiated them with indignation. Their denial may be perfectly honest, and their indignation justified. If so they will be most unlikely to come into any kind of armed conflict with England, because, as she knows of no causes of present dispute between the two countries, so she would have difficulty in imagining where, on the hypothesis stated, any such should arise in the future. England seeks no quarrels, and will never give Germany cause for legitimate offence.

All well and good, it would seem. But then Crowe describes the dilemma that carries his name:

But this is not a matter in which England can safely run any risks.

In other words, while Germany's intentions *might* be peaceable, Britain could not risk having Germany challenge its dominance in case Berlin's intentions changed. So Britain had no choice but to make clear to Berlin that Germany would pay a high price should it choose to try.[67]

And in the circles of power in London, Crowe's argument resonated, and Britain's rulers responded by investing still further in their naval power.

It is a feature of great power politics that is with us to this day: one power sees the other having an advantage, and seeks to close the gap, if for no other than defensive reasons; but then the first power, seeing this, perceives a challenge to its dominance, and moves to protect its advantage. The result is an arms race and a spiral of perceptions of threat and insecurity that can lead nations to war.

There's a strong parallel between Crowe's thinking, later adopted by the Foreign Office, and the language of German statesman Theobold von Bethmann-Hollweg, who would serve as chancellor from 1909 to 1917. In 1913, Bethmann-Hollweg argued that to be a "really Great power," Germany had to have "a fleet, and a strong one . . . not merely for the purposes of defending her commerce, but for the general purpose of her greatness."[68] And he set his sights on eroding Britain's naval dominance. Germany saw the gap between its own navy and Britain's as a threat to its ambitions and began to invest in building a more powerful fleet. Britain, of course, in turn saw that buildup as a direct threat to its own power and began to respond. In 1898, Germany had passed what was known as the First Fleet Act, which funded seven new battleships to be built over the course of the next six years. And then it put this shipbuilding program in the hands of Admiral Alfred von Tirpitz, who had campaigned for the law's passage.[69] Von Tirpitz was more aggressive still and determined to create a fleet so powerful it would make Britain feel compelled to make diplomatic concessions. Von Tirpitz's plan called for Germany to double its fleet, including building two new squadrons of battleships and ten cruisers. This became known as the *Risikoflotte*, or the Risk Fleet. It was never designed to defeat Britain on the high seas, but simply to make it increasingly expensive for Britain to maintain its dominance.[70]

Britain's response was to outmatch the Germans, and in 1906 it launched what was known as His Majesty's Ship *Dreadnought*, a new type of super battleship. The *Dreadnought*, and the class of ships that followed after her, revolutionized battleships in two primary ways: first, she had an "all-big-gun" armament scheme, meaning that she held more heavy-caliber guns than prior ships; and second, she was the first big warship to be powered by steam turbine, making the *Dreadnought* faster than any other contemporary battleships. The *Dreadnought* was so revolutionary that all earlier battleships became known as "pre-dreadnoughts," and the next dreadnoughts were built with incredible speed in Britain, which had the industrial resources to almost literally churn them out, each bigger and more powerful than the next. Germany could not match it.[71]

But Germany had another card to play, a disruptive new technology: the submarine. As the less rich of the two countries, Germany had limited resources to pour into this naval arms race, while the British could basically build and stretch out as long as it needed. Germany switched tactics to submarines.

This became important at the onset of war, when Britain's first move was to blockade the English Channel. Germany managed to poke holes in the blockade through the deployment of what it called U-boats. In August 1914, by sending a flotilla of nine U-boats into the North Sea, Germany launched the first submarine war patrol in history. Its goal was to sink British ships and reduce Britain's numerical capacity, and the Germans would come to turn the entire North Sea into a war zone. Germany's submarines went farther from its shores, sailing around Great Britain out into the Atlantic. And while this move caused London some discomfort, it ultimately backfired. Because German submarine activities in 1916 began to generate costs to a very different actor—that is, the United States. It was German attacks against US shipping in the Atlantic channel that would eventually bring the United States into the war. The American entry into the war in 1917 helped bring that continental slaughter to an end, in 1918.[72]

Britain ended the war challenged and changed, though still in command of its vast empire. Its naval strength had been sapped, and the Bank of England drained.[73] And America was rising.

New Nation at Sea

The interwar years that followed were a time of confusion. Among the odd features of the age was the passivity of the United States, which had surpassed Britain in economic terms at some point in the 1890s, but had so far chosen to limit its involvement in global politics before being reluctantly pulled into WWI. And after the war it returned to its more reticent position.

This seesaw between expansive naval appetite and reticence to use it had in fact characterized the United States almost since the birth of the nation.[74] It was not long after American independence that it found itself developing a navy. The decision was controversial: many believed that Washington, with limited resources to put into its new state military, should eschew a navy and simply rely on the long distances between its Atlantic shores and the home ports of any potential challenger, while others opposed a navy on the grounds that it would require higher taxes and allow another mechanism to suppress liberty.[75] In the first one hundred years after the founding of the republic, there was no consistent position on naval power, despite George Washington's firm belief that "without a decisive naval force we can do nothing definitive, and with it, everything honorable and glorious."[76] Naval power was not essential for deepening trade with America's backyard,

Mexico and the wider expanses of South America. And in Asia, the United States had no hope of challenging British dominance, nor did it seek to: it simply engaged in commercial activity in Asia, and contributed modestly to wider European security efforts in the region—to use today's terms, America was a "free rider" on British naval power in Asia.[77]

America's attitude started to change toward the end of the 1700s, when it began to experience in the Atlantic the harassment of American shipping by pirates operating out of the Barbary Coast of North Africa. Congress finally shifted, and formally established the new American navy by authorizing funds to build six frigates in 1794.[78] Not for nothing does the battle hymn of the American marines start with an invocation of "the shores of Tripoli," for it was to Tripoli, modern-day Libya and back then the main hub of the Barbary pirates, that America deployed its first overseas naval and marine campaign (joining a Swedish campaign already underway).* The destruction of the Barbary pirates in their home port of Tripoli echoed the Portuguese belief that you had to take the fight to the enemy's home base, and set a precedent for later American power projection in the Middle East.[79]

Then, shortly after the new nation had tested its naval and marine contingents, the War of 1812 against its old master solidified the importance of a navy for American defense and enabled the nascent navy to solidify its importance.[80]

Asia, too, was important even in these early days of the American nation. Both merchant ships and the new American navy found their way to Asia. China was the main goal, as knowledge about its collection of some of the world's most sought after commodities—tea, porcelain, and silk, for example—enticed American entrepreneurs to cross the Pacific. The voyage, however, required a network of ports that extended across the ocean, and the US sought to expand its presence throughout the region.[81]

As China and India were dominated by the British, America turned its ambitions toward Japan. US Commander Matthew Calbraith Perry

*President Thomas Jefferson's first choice to lead the Barbary Wars was a former British pirate turned American naval officer, John Paul Jones. Later in this book we'll encounter the destroyer that carries his name.

was dispatched to establish a regional foothold that would strengthen the United States' ability to pursue its interests within the Pacific. To this end, America tried to do to Japan what Britain had done to China: to use superior naval firepower to force that ancient Asian nation to open itself and its markets to foreign trade. Dutch, English, and Jesuit traders had been trying to penetrate Japan with limited success since the 1500s. But none had at their disposal the degree of naval firepower that Perry had when he sailed his famous flagships into Tokyo Bay in Yokosuka in 1853. Perry's Black Ships, as they were called, anchored four vessels in the bay for six days, threatening to use force to ensure the delivery of a letter from President Millard Fillmore. The Japanese refused to accept the letter for several days, but on July 14 it was formally received—to the sound of a thirteen-gun salute from the *Susquehanna.* In early 1854, Perry returned with ten vessels and 1,600 men to receive the response. On March 8, while three military bands played "The Star-Spangled Banner," Perry landed in Yokohama and began three weeks of negotiations that led to the opening of ports to American ships—and the opening of Japan.[82]

These growing interests required protection. Threats to the safety of American ships were not just to be found along the Barbary Coast. In 1831, inhabitants on the coast of Sumatra plundered an American merchant ship and killed several of her crew. The next year, a US frigate was sent to the island—and burned the town.[83] In 1835, the US East India Squadron was created, charged with protecting American commercial interests from China to Arabia.[84]

Once again, the history of the interactions between Asia and the West might have unfolded rather differently had not the United States shortly thereafter largely retreated from Asia. It did so as it fell into the internal, consuming drama of the American Civil War. The navy's ships were repurposed to blockade the Confederacy. And America emerged from the Civil War exhausted and looking inward, focused on the massive reconstruction process that began at war's end.[85]

Not until the late 1880s would America once again look outward, this time provoked by Spanish exploration in its near waters, specifically around the island of Cuba. (Not the last time that that island would play an outsize role in American diplomacy.) The ensuing Spanish-American War would be fought in neither country, but between the two navies in and around the coast of Cuba and off the coast of the Philippines, Spain's main colonial possession in Asia. The US Navy won two decisive victories: in Manila Bay, in the Philippines, and at the Battle of Santiago de Cuba. One result of the Spanish-American War was the establishment of America's first overseas colony, the Philippines. A second result was the shaping of the mindset of a man who had recently served as the assistant secretary of the navy and had made many of the major naval decisions leading up to the war, one Theodore Roosevelt.[86]

Although the US Navy had won a decisive victory in Manila Bay, the reality was that it won through a combination of naval tactics, planning, and luck. Its warships were less modern, less large, and less effective than those of America's peers at the time. While it fought its civil war, the US was on the sidelines as, worldwide, ironclad ships displaced the earlier generation of wooden sailing craft. US policy planners began to recognize that their navy was out of date, and with the growth in overseas markets and the importance of sea-based communications, they started a modernization program in 1883 that would help lead the country into a new era of naval engagement. In 1870, the US had the world's twelfth-largest navy—by the turn of the twentieth century, it had the fifth.[87] The Spanish-American War gave the US an idea of its navy's shortcomings, but also a taste of increased maritime responsibility.[88]

The American presence in Asia grew beyond Japan. The US established consulates in Fiji in 1844, Samoa in 1856, and the Marshall Islands in 1881 to protect its interests in way stations for the Chinese trade, and increased its presence in Hawaii in order to establish a Pacific base of operations to support that trade.[89] In each case, it was pursuing a deliberate strategy—influenced in part by the father of modern maritime strategy, Captain Alfred Thayer Mahan, and embraced by a young Theodore Roosevelt—of pushing America's defensive line ever farther west across the Pacific. American naval leaders and politicians were acutely aware of the growing Japanese naval threat and sought to build a sea perimeter from which to defend mainland United States.[90] The annexation of Hawaii in 1898—implemented while Teddy Roosevelt was serving as assistant secretary of the navy—constituted the pinnacle of this strategy, establishing a permanent American presence deep in the Pacific, and from which American naval power could readily reach out as far as Guam and Formosa (now Taiwan). It set the pattern for American defense strategy in Asia that remains with us to this day.

In this period, the United States also began to play an important role in shaping international standards and legal agreements governing shipping. For example, in 1889, the United States hosted in Washington, DC, an International Marine Conference designed to resolve important differences in how various countries mapped and charted the seas. Such variant methods made for complexity and difficulty in navigation. The conference resulted in a proposal for a permanent international commission that would help countries resolve differences in their charting—a commission that still exists in the form of the International Hydrographic Organization, headquartered in Monaco.[91]

When Teddy Roosevelt became president after William McKinley's assassination in September 1901, he entered office well aware of the United States' growing maritime potential, as well as the shortcomings of the US Navy itself. As he ascended into the presidency, he had a hunger for a more expansive international role for the United States, and the tools to administer it.[92] What he would do next would set the foundations for modern American power projection, and the acquisition of its first colonies—the start of America's entry into the perilous business of imperial competition.

Roosevelt, seeking to demonstrate growing US naval power, convened often with Alfred Thayer Mahan.* In 1890, Mahan, then president of the newly established US Naval War College, published *The Influence of Sea Power Upon History*. The classic book argues for the importance of maritime dominance, highlighting the need for both a strong navy and a strong commercial fleet. Mahan's argument starts with the notion that wealth begins with trade, and international trade depends on sea commerce—and thus, in turn, the ability of a country to accumulate wealth depends on its ability to control the seas, and is

*The two became so close that when Roosevelt left Washington, DC, to run the Rough Riders, Mahan moved into his home. Peter Karsten, "The Nature of 'Influence': Roosevelt, Mahan and the Concept of Sea Power," *American Quarterly* 23, no. 4 (1971), 589.

thus a function of the nation's sea power. He stressed building a bigger navy, building the Panama Canal, and acquiring overseas bases.[93]

Roosevelt took many of Mahan's policies to heart and began to demonstrate that to the world. The Russo-Japanese War and the launching of the HMS *Dreadnought* in 1906 helped spur a sense of urgency in growing the US fleet. Under Roosevelt's tenure, the Panama Canal's construction was initiated. And in 1907, Roosevelt sent a US Navy battle fleet across the globe to showcase America's growing naval power. Sixteen battleships, alongside escorts, and some fourteen thousand sailors took part in Roosevelt's "Great White Fleet"—so named because Roosevelt ordered that the ships be painted with white hulls, instead of the gray that most other navies were using. The Great White Fleet traveled the course of the seas, making stops in the Americas, the Mediterranean, and Asia. In particular, the voyage was meant to send a signal to the British and to Japan that the US Navy could now deploy around the world.[94]

This voyage symbolized a new age in US naval presence and global reach. Then, with the onset of World War I in Europe, the US Navy continued to grow, and not just in vessels; also in people. By the end of World War I, the US Navy had almost five hundred thousand officers and enlisted personnel—the largest naval force in the world.[95]

In 1921 to 1922, in the wake of World War I, the world's greatest naval powers met in what came to be known as the Washington Naval Conference. The meeting was prompted by a drastic shift in the world's naval balance—the Japanese navy was growing, and while the British navy was still technically the world's largest by vessel number, it was becoming obsolete as its vessels aged, and the US had demonstrated its great naval capabilities during the war. Faced with the threat of a potential conflict, representatives of the United States, Japan, China, France, Britain, Italy, Belgium, the Netherlands, and Portugal sat down to try to restrain naval competition. The primary result of the conference was the Washington Naval Treaty, a landmark agreement that tried to prevent another naval arms race by limiting naval construction. It created a tonnage ratio for the countries, outlining the maximum weight of capital ships and aircraft carriers each of the five signatories—Britain, the US, Japan, France, and Italy—could have. The US and Britain were given the largest tonnage allowances—formally recognizing that the United States navy was as powerful as the British.[96]

After the war, however, America retreated to a recalcitrant position. Apart from the absence of a wide array of colonial presences (America did have some, beyond the Philippines, especially in the Caribbean), the US ended World War I as the largest global economy. But it had not yet chosen to take on the role of an ordering power or an activist power. The result was twenty years of confusion and retribution and positioning that directly contributed to the descent back into global carnage in the late 1930s.[97]

When the German war broke out in 1939, the American reaction at first was similar to that which kept it out of World War II, with this one critical difference: this President Roosevelt (fifth cousin of Teddy) was determined not to repeat the experience of World War I. Despite the intense political difficulties he encountered in Congress, Franklin Delano Roosevelt was open from the outset to bringing America into the war effort. He worked hard to convince Congress, by scheme and by schmoozing, to help supply Britain during the early phase of its fight with Germany. What emerged first from the interplay between FDR and Churchill, and FDR and Congress, was an executive decision by Roosevelt to agree to what became known as the "destroyers for bases" deal—an agreement to lend Britain forty of America's outdated battleships, in exchange for ninety-nine-year agreements on basing rights at British installations in the Bahamas and throughout the Western Hemisphere. Later came the Lend-Lease program by which the American industrial base supplied Britain with ships and matériel for its war effort.[98]

It took a different naval power, Japan, to bring America into the war.

From the late 1920s onward, spurred in part by the shock of Commander Perry's excursion into Tokyo Harbor, Japan had been prosecuting an expansionist policy in Asia, taking Manchuria and eventually Shanghai and Nanking in a brutal campaign. Its expansionist role had put it increasingly into loggerheads with the British fleet in Asia. In the late 1930s, Britain began to blockade the Japanese resupply of both oil and rubber, critical elements for its war machine. Japan sought to bust the blockade using its increasingly powerful navy. Then war broke out in Europe and looked to spread across the British Empire. Fatefully, on December 7th and 8th, 1941, Japan launched what it believed would be a knockout blow against both Britain and the United States in Asia, simultaneously attacking British strongholds in Singapore and

Hong Kong, and US positions in the Philippines, Wake Island, Guam, and Pearl Harbor, Hawaii. While the Japanese attack on Pearl Harbor killed thousands of American sailors and badly damaged the American Pacific Fleet, it famously did not manage to destroy the three US aircraft carriers that were not in the harbor at the time of the attack. They would become the centerpiece of US naval strategy in the Pacific.

The Rise of Goliath

After the attack on Pearl Harbor, the US Navy grew tremendously as it fought a two-front war. In Europe, it proved its value, especially in marine landings in Italy and Normandy, playing a key supporting role to US and other Allied ground troops. Meanwhile, in the Atlantic it had to grapple with the challenge of anti-submarine warfare, a vital effort in protecting the flow of convoys to supply the war in Europe.[99] It was in the Pacific, though, that the navy really carried WWII, and where the advent of aircraft carriers and naval aviation took hold. The US Navy took the fight to the Japanese fleet in such famous battles as Midway, Coral Sea, and Guadalcanal, and enabled the Allies' "island hopping" campaign that eventually broke Japanese supply lines and set the stage for victory against Japan.[100]

By the end of the war, the US Navy had added nearly 1,200 combatant ships—accounting for over 70 percent of the world's total combat vessels.[101] More than that, it had practiced and demonstrated its ability (and willingness) to conduct global naval combat. Combined with the American role in the ground war in Europe, US conduct in World War II proved that it was the leading global power, on land and on water. It emerged from the war stronger than when it had entered it. America had defeated the second-most powerful navy of the day, Germany; it had also defeated the most powerful naval actor in Asia, Japan; it had done so with the help of a former naval contender, Russia. What's more, it had done so in close collaboration with what was in military and colonial terms the dominant global power of the day, Britain.

Over the course of its long dominance of the high seas, Britain had acquired a network of ports, bases, resupply depots, and fueling stations to power and support its global fleet; now it made much of that network available to the United States. The US Navy almost literally had the seas to itself. It quickly consolidated its position by solidifying its bases in Japan (Okinawa), the Philippines (Subic Bay), northern Europe (Iceland), and so on. And as it did so, it began to take over Britain's previously dominant position in the Middle East.[102] Writing in 1947, British foreign minister Ernest Bevin noted, "The US is in the position today where Britain was at the end of the Napoleonic Wars."[103] America had replaced Britain as the dominant power on the world stage.

As it did all of this, the United States—and specifically the US Navy—would take on two key roles, one inherited from the Royal Navy: as the global guarantor of the flow of trade and as the guarantor of the free flow of energy. These remain fundamental to the dynamics of American power to this day.[104]

Two events—one summit and one war—exemplified and solidified this change. Both took place in the Suez Canal. The interplay between global power and command of the seas was central to both.

Back to Suez

The first was a summit between key leaders. It took place in secrecy, received little press or diplomatic coverage when it became known, and is neglected in accounts of how international order was forged in the wake of World War II. Yet it began a relationship central to geopolitics for seventy years.[105] It shaped the fate of the Middle East, the global oil trade, and the projection of American power in the postwar world.

The date was February 14, 1945, just days after US president Franklin D. Roosevelt's fateful talks in Yalta with Prime Minister Winston Churchill of Britain and Premier Joseph Stalin of the Soviet Union. The site was the USS *Quincy*, afloat in the Great Bitter Lake in the Sinai Peninsula, part of the Suez Canal system. On board, FDR and a delegation of admirals and advisers awaited their guest. Earlier, the USS *Murphy* had steamed to Jeddah, Saudi Arabia, to fetch him. It was a sign of the limited contact between the United States and Saudi Arabia at the time that the US Navy had no up-to-date chart of Jeddah's harbor, and little diplomatic presence in Saudi Arabia to secure one. The navy had to borrow a chart from the Arabian American Oil Company, better known as ARAMCO (and the Standard Oil Company of California before that).[106]

At Jeddah, the *Murphy* boarded its passengers—forty-eight men, seven sheep, and one large, ornate throne. Just before midday on the fourteenth, the *Murphy* rendezvoused with the *Quincy*, and this throne was hoisted across. Its owner was King Abdulaziz Ibn Saud, the founder of Saudi Arabia. This was the first and only meeting between the president and the king, and the first time that the king had left his country. In Jeddah, rumors flew that the king had absconded or been kidnapped by the Americans. The ladies of his harem went into ritual mourning at the thought their protector would never return.

The meeting between the two leaders lasted for four hours. Discussion focused on the fate of Jewish refugees from Europe and whether the king would support the notion of a Jewish homeland in Palestine (he did not). The two leaders also discussed agriculture—President Roosevelt offered to assist King Abdulaziz with the technology that would be needed to irrigate Saudi Arabia and generate an agricultural industry (an offer the king politely spurned, telling the president he was too old to become a farmer). Those policy issues may not have been advanced, but international politics is sometimes about personality, not policy. Roosevelt charmed the Saudi leader. He also convinced him that the United States was not looking for a relationship of dominance in the region, but one of openness and mutual support. The question of oil was not discussed.

And yet oil was the point of the meeting. The king knew very well what the president was subtly proposing. The United States had supplied much of the oil consumed by Allied forces during World War II, but the strain had been keenly felt, despite unprecedented cooperation between government and industry to keep supplies flowing. Roosevelt knew it was important for the United States to diversify its own supply and to resist British moves to shut American oil companies out of the Middle East. Within weeks of the meeting on Great Bitter Lake, the Saudis would grant ARAMCO their preferred path for a pipeline from the kingdom's main oil fields in Dhahran toward the Mediterranean, allowing the flow of Saudi oil to Europe and later the United States. Tapline (the Trans-Arabian pipeline) was operational by 1950; American investors provided the capital and the expertise and, in early years, at least, took the bulk of the profits.[107] The United States, meanwhile, began construction of an airfield in Saudi Arabia, a visible show of its security commitment to the king.

Churchill reacted with fury when he discovered the American president was meeting the Saudis behind his back and hastily organized his own summit to re-exert control. But this went poorly after he drank and smoked cigars in the king's presence, underlining the image of British insensitivity and arrogance. King Abdulaziz was convinced that his country's future lay in partnership with a country that embraced the future, not one that was tied to a colonial past.[108]

These events represented the start of a strategic and economic partnership: an American guarantee of security for Saudi Arabia in exchange for Saudi de facto guarantees about the free flow of oil. It was a relationship that put the United States—for good and bad—at the heart of the Arab world and pushed Britain to the sidelines. The Saudis received reassurance that they would be protected from neighbors who coveted Saudi oil riches (a commitment that bore its greatest fruit when Iraq invaded Kuwait decades later). The United States gained a bulwark against Soviet influence in the Middle East, as its military provided a security guarantee to the region.[109] Saudi willingness to act as a swing producer of oil, and US determination to secure Middle Eastern supplies, were fundamental to the architecture of global economics and international security in the late twentieth century and into the twenty-first. They bound together an authoritarian and secretive kingdom and the country that led the free world. And they gave the United States a critical role in global affairs, as the guarantor of the flow of oil to the economies of the West.[110]

And then even more dramatic events in the Suez Canal would crystalize the shift from British to American hegemony in world affairs.

During World War II, Britain had closed the Suez Canal to enemy trade, and the access to the canal was a major strategic advantage for the Allied powers, hampering Germany. The canal reopened after the war, and trade resumed. But the patterns of fighting had shifted more than just the relative power of the United States. The end of the Second World War was also the beginning of the end of the system of European colonial dominance. In 1947, desirous of hastening the British

Empire's exit from India, Viceroy Mountbatten brought India's independence forward to August 15, 1947, partitioning the country along religious lines (and sparking mass violence and migration along the way) while doing so. This liberation was quickly followed by the granting of independence by their respective colonial powers to Burma (1948), Indonesia (1949), and Libya (1951)—often under immense international pressure. What British prime minister Harold Macmillan once called "the winds of change" blew through Europe's colonial possessions in Africa, Latin America, the Caribbean, and Asia. And those winds also blew through the Middle East, and into Cairo, where in 1952 a revolution overthrew King Farouk and ejected the British army, returning Egypt to its status as a fully independent nation.[111]

The Suez Canal, however, remained under international control, and still subject to the international agreements established in the Convention of Constantinople. That state of affairs held for the first decade after World War II. But as the revolutionary leader Gamal Abdel Nasser consolidated power in Egypt, the equation began to change. Nasser had been an integral part of the 1952 revolution, but only took over as president in 1954, as part of a three-year transitional arrangement. In 1956 he was elected to the presidency. And in July of that year, he announced that he had decided to nationalize the canal.

Nasser's decision sparked a full-blown international crisis. In London, Prime Minister Anthony Eden consulted with his influential foreign secretary, Baron Selwyn-Lloyd, and his parliament. Eden found that the country, otherwise divided on foreign policy, was united on the view that Egypt could not be allowed to nationalize the canal. Most fundamentally—a theme we will come back to—the closure of the canal risked interrupting the flow of oil from Saudi Arabia to London, which would in turn imperil the British economy. France, too, was affected by the risk—like England, its economy had also become dependent on the flow of oil from the Middle East, via the Suez.[112] London and Paris began to conspire on their response.

Another player in the game was Israel, newly forged as an independent nation in 1946, and already once attacked by the Arab states, literally days into its birth as a nation. Its enmity with the Arab states, and above all with Egypt, continued unabated. It saw in Nasser's nationalism and his desire to establish full Egyptian sovereignty in the canal a direct threat to its own survival.[113] In secret, the United Kingdom, France, and Israel plotted to deal with Nasser's challenge.

In October 1956, when Nasser repeated his threat of nationalization, Israel moved quickly to block his action, sending several tens of thousands of Israeli troops into the Sinai Peninsula to gain control of the eastern bank of the Suez Canal. As they had secretly agreed, the next day the UK and France called for a cease-fire. And when, within twenty-four hours, Egypt had not responded, the UK and France also moved forces into the Sinai Peninsula. Operation Musketeer saw tens of thousands of British and French troops join Israeli troops in the Sinai.[114]

What Eden had not counted on was the scale and fury of the Soviet reaction. A decade after their wartime alliance, the US and UK had already moved into a Cold War with the Soviet Union. The Suez Crisis was one of the first moments when the Cold War might have escalated into actual conflict. Soviet Premier Nikita Khrushchev had been courting a relationship with Nasser in Egypt, and he saw the UK's move as a design to block Russian advances, which it partially was. In a fury, Khrushchev threatened a nuclear response in Western Europe.[115]

The Soviet reaction meant that the Suez Crisis in turn became an American problem. The United States had ended World War II as the largest power in the world, the largest economy in the world, and with the largest navy in the world, and so it, too, had vital stakes in the Suez—as it did in deterring and containing Soviet reactions. And so the critical player quickly became US President Dwight D. Eisenhower. If Eden was surprised by Khrushchev's reaction, he was shocked by Eisenhower's. Against the opposition of the Democrats in Congress and of his own secretary of state, Dean Acheson, Eisenhower threatened to sanction the UK, France, and Israel if they didn't back down from their dangerous stance. The UK and France relatively quickly withdrew their forces. Some months later, so, too, did Israel, although only after securing Eisenhower's backing for an Egyptian guarantee that Egypt would preserve Israeli interests in the Sinai and the surrounding waters.

The episode is widely viewed by historians of the period as that moment when what remained of Britain's imperial influence collapsed, and the full weight of America's global muscle became apparent.[116] Soviet Premier Khrushchev backed down, although he did secure a UK/French withdrawal from the Sinai. At the recently established United Nations, the Security Council agreed to deploy a neutral force to the peninsula to help keep the peace—the birth of modern peacekeeping. And Egypt ended the episode with international recognition of its ownership of the canal, although also with conditionalities on that ownership.* A new international convention oversaw the deployment of a UN Emergency Force to the Sinai and guaranteed free passage in the Suez Canal.[117]

* * *

America came out of the Suez episode firmly established as *the* global power, willing and able (by dint of its naval reach) to deploy military force to the other side of the world, including to secure its interests in the free flow of oil and the free flow of trade.[118] As Lincoln Paine wrote, "As was true of Portugal in the sixteenth century, the US fleet exists to project power and safeguard trade, not to fight fleets of comparable capabilities because there are none."[119] And the US Navy inherited, bought, or borrowed (in some cases, by applying considerable pressure) several of Britain's network of bases and fueling stations—from Diego Garcia, in the midst of the Indian Ocean, to Sembawang naval facility, in Singapore.

But if the Suez Crisis solidified America's role as the hegemon in world affairs, it did something else as well. It fired a warning shot across the bows of the global shipping business and the countries that depended on it. The closure of the canal for eight months was a major blow to global trade. Restrictions not just on the flow of oil but on the flow of industrial goods through the Suez caused a major downturn in global trade during the months of the closure. Global business let out a huge sigh of relief when the canal was reopened in March of 1956.[120]

Much worse was to come.

*In this, while Egypt lost the war militarily, it won politically: not the last time this pattern would eventuate in the West's Middle East wars.

PART II

To Contain the World – 1956–2017

On the *Madrid*'s Monkey Island, Singapore Strait

The best vantage point from any ship at sea is what's known by mariners as a monkey island. In the days of sail, the monkey island was usually a small platform or basket, large enough to hold a man, lashed two-thirds up the main mast, a place from where sailors could scan the horizon by telescope or the naked eye. On modern ships, it's simply the roof above the captain's bridge, the highest point on the ship, accessed by a set of steep metal stairs off the bridge deck. It's still used for navigation, though, as this is where a ship's radar towers and radio antennas and satellite beacons are housed. When standing atop the monkey island of the *Madrid Maersk*, an ultra-large container ship, you're looking out over the oceans from a height of 230 feet, and you command an unbroken view of the surrounding seas.

At the mouth of the Singapore Strait, where the warm waters of the South China Sea mingle with those of the Java Sea, that's a view that's absolutely choked with ships. Hundreds of them, from small fishing junks to large oil tankers to giant container vessels. All of them maneuvering for space in the narrow channel of the strait, eighty-two feet deep in the shipping channel. On any given day, more than two thousand merchant vessels of all classes transit these waters.

At night, each of them displays both running and signal lights, green on the starboard side and red at port, to reveal direction; white on the masthead, to show position. From the bridge below comes a steady stream of navigational commands from the Singaporean Coast Guard, their English calm and precise, unflustered by the constant punctuation of urgent and angry calls from ship captains jostling for advantage. Far from the calm seas, it's a view more reminiscent of looking down from an office tower to the angry honking and snarl of New York City rush hour traffic. From there, ships sail past the vibrant lights of Singapore's downtown towers, northeast into the South China Sea, or southwest into the Malacca Strait. In any given hour, more than one hundred ships carrying cargo worth several tens of billions of dollars maneuver around Horsburgh Lighthouse. What the Suez Canal was to the late nineteenth century, the Singapore Strait is to the twenty-first: the most important waterway in the world, *the* critical artery of the world economy.

The transition from Suez to Singapore is the story of not one but several revolutions: in the technologies of global shipping and trade; in relations between world powers; in the geography of the world economy; and in the nature of trade itself. Along the way, these changes would bring China back into the top ranks of global economic power, transform the American economy, and start to strain the relationship between America and the world around it.

4

Western Tide Rising

Bulk Shipping and the Wealth of the West (1956–1980)

Sea power helped the British forge their empire and, with it, the nature of the modern world. Sea power was a critical feature in the articulation of America's new global role, in the wake of World War II. And it was a crisis in 1956 at that era's most important seaway, the Suez Canal, that symbolized and solidified the shift in world power from London to Washington, removing the last vestiges of more than a century of British domination of the high seas and high politics.[1] The Suez Crisis crystalized the emergence of an expansive phase of American power and its new roles of securing the free flow of energy and protecting global trade.

It also marked the onset of one of the most dangerous phases of the Cold War, when the Soviet Union widened its gaze beyond its own security and its Eastern European buffer zone to the wider expanse of Europe, and then beyond—to a global competition for allegiances and resources. Although naval competition was a part of that titanic struggle, it was not at the forefront of the US-Soviet rivalry; nuclear missiles displaced naval power as the primary instrument of great power security rivalry.

But in world economic affairs, seafaring was about to become even more crucial. For the Suez Crisis, and the year 1956 more generally, was also an inflection point in global shipping, one that would gradually and then radically transform the world economy. The changes that followed would drive the huge economic gains of the West in the 1970s, 1980s, and 1990s.

So far in this book, we've watched empires and states and navies stitch together the world around us, as well as the state-sanctioned "companies" of the seventeenth and eighteenth centuries—those semi-private entities like the East India Company, organized for trade and profit, but wielding the legal authority to make war and forge their own colonies. In the end, they proved to be extensions of the Crown, more than private interests. But in the post–World War II world, it was not only states that reshaped world trade. Private companies and entrepreneurs now played a critical role.

In this chapter and the next, we'll encounter two companies on opposite sides of the world—both family-owned, both passed from father to son, both born on the precipice of war—that exemplify a world transformed.

The first of them was born in the Baltic trade, in a Europe about to be thrust into global conflict.

Modern-Day Vikings

There is a photograph from 1837 of the International Settlement in Canton, where foreigners were first allowed to engage in structured trade with the Chinese. In the foreground are the proud flags of the countries represented there, the great trading empires of the day: Britain, of course; Holland, France, Russia, Sweden; and the United States. And one from a trading empire we haven't encountered yet—the flag of the ancient kingdom of Denmark, a white cross on a red field, recognizable even in a black-and-white photograph. In the mid-1800s, Denmark was still a kingdom of some significance, and a trading power as well.[2] Though its power would fade in the early twentieth century, the lineage survives to this day—not in the Danish state, but in the form of what became from the 1970s onward one of the world's most significant global trading companies.

Broad Street (Bredgade) in Copenhagen's historic port district is populated by antiques stores and art galleries, faced in the city's classical limestone architecture, and Lutheran churches. Nearby are the dignified courtyards and imperial splendor of the Amalienborg Palace, home to the Danish royal family since the mid-1700s. Amid the limestone, an unusual building stands out. This edifice, with its gray and redbrick facade, interlaced with sandstone, rises to a set of steeples topped by gold-plated, onion-shaped domes. This is the Alexander Nevsky Church of Copenhagen. Built between 1881 and 1883 with funds provided personally by Tsar Alexander III, it served to celebrate his marriage to the Danish-born Maria Feodorovna, daughter of Denmark's Christian IX. The marriage ties between the Russian and Danish courts, and the presence of the Alexander Nevsky Church, whose architecture mirrors that of seventeenth-century Muscovite styles, is a vivid reminder of Copenhagen's past as a hub for the Baltic trade (and Denmark's past as a buffer state between Russia and Germany), at a time when the cold waters of the Baltic Sea played a central part in the lives of empires.[3]

When the Alexander Nevsky Church was built in the late 1880s, Russia was one of the largest economies in the world, in league with Britain and Germany and the United States.[4] The Baltic Sea was the critical artery of Russia's trade with the West, served by the port of St. Petersburg, then its capital and most important economic center.[5] From the Baltic, Russian ships could sail West toward rich English markets. But to get there they first encountered the Øresund, the narrow strait between modern-day Denmark and Sweden that separates the Baltic Sea from the North Sea, home to Britain's ports. In the very coldest winters, the surface waters of the Øresund freeze over; but not solidly so, and strong currents break the ice sheet apart and push large shards up against the Danish coast, which pile together under the pressure of the waves. Each wave of ice shards push the earlier ones upward, and they crush ever closer together, pointing out at all angles, like someone shattered a giant sheet of glass across the shores. But most years, the Øresund is passable year-round.

Copenhagen sits on the Øresund and has historically controlled passage through it. Copenhagen was thus an essential hub between ports in Russia, Sweden, and Poland, and the vital port of London. Navigating this trade route was essential to imperial Russia (as well as imperial Germany).[6] The Baltic would also play a crucial role in the First and Second World Wars, as British (and later American) ships sailing out of ports in the south of England sought to limit German egress from the Baltic Sea to the Atlantic.

Trade in the Baltics had historically been conducted on sailing cutters, until in the early 1800s the advent of steamships began to transform the business. Trading ships docked and recorded their trade in the old harbor center of Copenhagen, two blocks away from the Alexander Nevsky Church. One person who worked there and saw the switch from sail to steam being made was a young Danish seaman named Peter Maersk Møller. Having sailed for twenty years on other people's cutters, he decided to take advantage of the changing dynamics of the business and strike out on his own. In 1886, he bought a British-built steamship, the SS *Laura*, and began carrying cargo across the Baltics for clients in each of the major ports. His log from the period is housed in a small modern museum in the old customs port area of Copenhagen, around the corner from the Alexander Nevsky Church, and next door to the old customs building, where Møller had his first job as a clerk. His small, precise handwriting records the locations of his trips and the details of his cargo. In 1890, the ship made sixty-nine port calls to twenty different locations, ranged across Denmark, Germany, Latvia, and Sweden, carrying grains, bran, animal forage, hemp, rapeseed, rye, limestone, and wooden railway sleepers.

By 1904, business was good enough that he and his son, A. P. Møller, incorporated the Svendborg Steamship Company, in a small town of the same name that borders the other major passageway between the Baltic and North Seas, on the southern coast of Denmark's Funen island. The company's first ship was a British-built steamer, the 2,200-ton cargo ship *Svendborg*. It was painted with what became one of the best-known symbols in international business, the seven-sided white star on a light blue background.*

Eight years later, in 1912, A. P. Møller decided to get a license to build his own ships, and incorporated the Dampskibsselskabet af 1912, the Steamship Company of 1912. That year sounds like it would have been a bad time to expand the business, as Europe was about to descend into the continental slaughter that was the Great War. But while wars disrupt civic life and many parts of the business world, they also

*According to a letter Peter Maersk Møller wrote to his wife, the symbol represented a star that had appeared to him one night amid an otherwise cloudy sky, when he prayed for her to recover from a serious illness she had at the time. Author's notes, Maersk Museum, Copenhagen, April 2018.

drive economic activity. Simply put, armies on the march consume huge quantities of energy, weapons, food, and clothes, and need to receive them in real time wherever they are located. For the businesses that supply such goods, war creates huge demand. The same is true for the businesses that transport those goods—including shipping companies. The Great War was mainly fought on the continent, but it entailed troop and goods movements around the whole of the Baltic and the coasts of Europe as far southeast as Turkey. Supplying the war effort proved to be an important part of the Steamship Company's business from 1914 to 1918.

At the end of the war, Peter Maersk Møller and his son took the bold decision to open their own shipyards. They chose a site on a canal near the major city of Odense on the same island where they had started their company. Like Svendborg, Odense is located on the sea-lane that connects the Baltic and the North Sea, on Denmark's large central island. The Odense shipyard delivered the company's first self-built ship in 1920 and their first diesel ship one year later. The shipyards would eventually help to transform what was then still operating as the Svendborg Shipping and Steamship Companies, a small family-owned business, into the global giant that it is today. Now known as the A. P. Møller-Maersk company, it's the largest shipping company in the world, with a fleet of more than seven hundred ships.[7]

The interwar years were a period of growth and territorial expansion for Maersk. In 1919, they opened their first overseas office, in New York City, which was then, and for the next half century, the key hub of global shipping and trade. World War I left London, previously the key hub of international trade, weakened; and as it recovered from the war, it also had to compete with an emerging market in New York. America had become the largest economy in the world, had the largest navy, and a stock market second only to London's. In 1923, the city also produced one-twelfth of all US manufacturing—and more to the point for a shipping firm, half of all imports and exports out of the United States transited New York Harbor. Oceangoing steamers went through the port every twenty minutes.[8] For a company with international ambitions, New York was a vital port of call.

Shortly after the opening in New York came a key breakthrough. In that era, global trade had two dimensions: the flow of agriculture and natural resources from the colonies to the "center" (the colonial powers, as well as the United States), and trade in industrial goods between the industrial powers—in Europe, especially, but also with the United States and Japan. As part of the second type of trade, Maersk managed to land a prime contract—transporting car parts for the Ford Motor Company to the port of Yokohama in Japan, where Ford had assembly factories.* It was their first set-route delivery. On the back of it, they grew the business further, and in 1928 opened what was known as the Maersk Line, operating a transpacific route through Baltimore by way of the Panama Canal. At that stage, six ships were sailing the route for the company. By 1937, that number had swelled to forty-six ships on all of their routes combined.

The years of World War II proved more complicated for Maersk than had the Great War.† A day before Denmark was invaded and surrendered to the Nazis, A. P. Møller decreed that if Denmark was invaded, all of their ships outside Danish waters were to report directly to the New York office.[9] Maersk ran their fleet out of New York for the rest of the war, and from June 1941 onward, much of the fleet served as a support element to the United States Navy, called up as the US took control of foreign ships to support the war effort. More than half of the Maersk fleet was lost during the war. But Møller also owned the largest share in a weapons factory in Denmark, and during the Nazi occupation, both the weapons factory and the Odense yard were used by the Germans. After the war, the company was fined for this, though their service to the Allied war effort was also highlighted.[10]

After the war, the Odense shipyard began a brisk shipbuilding program to bring the fleet back up to prewar levels; a mark they hit by 1956. They also expanded their tanker business. Between 1946 and 1966, it was actually tanker traffic and oil transport that led the growth of the

*It's a striking reminder that what we think of as a contemporary reality—global supply chains that cross continents—got its start well before the Second World War.

†Briefly, it looked as if the straits between Denmark and Sweden would become an early naval battleground between Britain and Germany, when Churchill asked the Sea Lord to begin preparations for a Royal Navy blockade of German ships sailing south from Sweden and Norway, carrying vital iron ore supplies. The Sea Lord explained to Churchill the substantial logistical and political difficulties involved in such a blockade, and the idea was jettisoned.

company. By the mid-1950s, Maersk tankers were among the largest fleets carrying Saudi oil into the European and American markets—in effect, realizing the deal struck between FDR and King Saud in 1944. But what really propelled the company from the ranks of a middle-tier firm to the top of the global food chain was that it was among the first to be able to apply new shipping technologies, changes to ship design, and techniques for transport that would become the cornerstone of the growth of the Western economies from the 1970s onward.

The Advent of Bulk Shipping and Containerization

Trading by sea had been underway for more than a millennium, and through that time the essential way that goods were handled at sea had barely changed. Goods were loaded by hand or pulley and later by crane into the cargo hold of a ship. Loose goods, like coal or wheat, were shoveled or troweled into the holds of cargo bays. Foodstuffs or furniture or machine parts were packed into a variety of crates transported and stored on a dock and then loaded into the cargo hold as best they fit. Crates for packing came in an endless variety of shapes and sizes, to package a bushel of tomatoes or a piano or a small truck or crates of bananas or coffee or rubber. Goods had to be carefully loaded to protect against damage during the voyage; damage to goods in transport was a major factor in shipping costs. And even before being loaded onto ships, they would be delivered to ports around the world, where they would wait at quayside for the right ship and for stevedores—often for weeks.[11] Stevedores would then work to load and unload these crates; and then began the labor of repackaging and reloading the goods for transportation on land. Modern cranes and forklifts eased the labor challenge, but in broad terms these techniques for packing a ship remained largely unchanged from what Ibn Battuta would have seen in the early fourteenth century.[12]

That was all about to change, transformed both by scale and by standardization. Just as standardization took cars from the world of bespoke European motors for the elite to Henry Ford's mass industrialization, so standardization of containers took us from a world where trade was a modest portion of the world's economic activity to a world where sea-based trade was the dominant feature of every part of our economic lives.

It was a change with many sources. The first was a technological shift so rudimentary and significant that in hindsight it is hard to comprehend why it hadn't happened earlier. It was, quite simply, a rectangular metal container; a box. In the words of the economist Marc Levinson, whose careful study of the economics of shipping first documented the huge economic impact of the introduction of containerization, this innovation was "a development that had sweeping consequences for workers and consumers all around the globe."[13]

The earliest innovations in the path toward containerization started in the nineteenth century. As early as 1837, James O'Connor, a Pittsburgh-based shipping executive, tested a kind of container that could move smoothly between train and ship; but he was blocked from developing it by interstate commerce regulators.[14] Later in the century, British and French railways tried using wooden crates to move furniture, transferring the containers from the railcars to horse-drawn carts.[15] From there, different engineers and company owners had varying ideas about how to ship most efficiently, and by the beginning of World War II, the US and many European countries had developed some partial container systems. Critically, then, the US Army began using wooden crates on trains as a technique for speeding the delivery of supplies.[16] It would experiment further with such techniques during World War II. But the real breakthrough came during the Korean War.

As the US Army continued to experiment, it developed what became known as CONEX, or the container express system—a series of standardized crates that could fit one on top of another, three high. That became its go-to technique for organizing the logistics of shipping the goods that the army needed from the United States to the Korean Peninsula, where it was fighting the Korean War (and where it was, as a consequence, establishing a large American logistical hub and base in Asia, supplied by the Korean port of Busan).[17] The American involvement in the Korean War and the troop presence that remained in Korea, constantly being supplied by the United States, became the essential first plank in the now massive trade between the US and Asia. And much of it flowed across the Pacific in the standard-size boxes of the evolving container system.

As yet, this innovation was limited to the army and did not affect commercial traffic. Shortly after the end of the Korean War, though, two sets of events occurred that began to take this from a specialized innovation to a global industrial revolution.

The first of these was the Suez Crisis, which caused shipping owners to start looking for bulk solutions that could absorb the great cost of the Suez closure. That would begin a transformation in shipping design, first in the area of bulk carriers and oil transport ships, that would over time change the economics of the transport in industrial goods. Coincidentally, at the same time, an American trucking executive, Malcolm McLean, began to agitate for commercial solutions that mirrored CONEX.

McLean was an American trucking entrepreneur and faced recurrent problems in long delays of his goods quayside at US ports. His shipments were getting held up, raising his shipping company's costs, and he wanted to get around this. His first innovation built on the CONEX concept but took it further, and he put his trucks directly onto ships that would then travel between North Carolina, New York, and Rhode Island—circumventing heavy East Coast traffic. He quickly realized, however, that that was inefficient; the trucks took more space than the goods they were carrying needed, and once on the ship his trucks couldn't be used for other loads.[18]

Instead, on April 26, 1956, he put fifty-eight trailer vans—the back part of the truck, or just the container—onto a retrofitted tanker ship named *Ideal X* and sailed it from Elizabeth, New Jersey, to Houston, Texas. His Sea-Land Service, as it came to be called, would become the first company to successfully move containers seamlessly from land to sea and back—effectively establishing the world's first container shipping company.[19] More specifically, he was the first to develop commercially feasible techniques for what became known as "intermodality"—simply, the ability to move seamlessly between two or more modes of transportation, rail, truck, and sea.

Containerization did not catch on easily, though. The shipping industry was deep-rooted in tradition and entrenched interests. Levinson, in his study of the impact of containerization on shipping costs, shows how containerization encountered significant resistance from traditional interests—from unions of longshoremen who risked losing their jobs, to port operators who were going to have to spend millions to retool their infrastructure. Some simply did not understand the innovation; others were worried about how long it would really last, and the impact it would make. Port facilities also needed to be amended—to accept containers in volume, they needed bigger holding lots, a major capital investment. Changing the industry standard wasn't easy.[20]

McLean kept on innovating. By 1961 he had taken ships that were decommissioned from transport use in World War II and refitted them to hold a larger number of containers—as many as 476 containers on a single ship. It was described at the time as a behemoth.[21]

Throughout the 1960s, containerization began to creep across different parts of the industry; slowly. An important factor was first domestic and then international negotiations about the *standard* size of the containers. If the industry as a whole was going to invest in the ships, container yards, cranes, and related adaptations necessary to adopt containerization, it was going to have to settle on an agreed size for the containers—so that every part of the industry could adapt to the same changes. But in the early days, there was no standard size of containers. Though containers were growing in use, everyone seemed to use different dimensions: in Europe, for example, the containers were usually wooden crates 4 to 5 feet tall; the US Army's CONEX boxes were steel and 8.5 feet by 6 feet 10.5 inches. Their design was different, too: some containers were meant to be moved by cranes with hooks; others had slots so they could be moved by forklifts.[22] This posed a challenge to the "intermodality" that made container shipping potentially so revolutionary: if containers couldn't be moved from one company's ships to another's rail to another's truck with ease, each company would need to have a host of sizes for each customer's needs, and they would have to pick modes of transport based on which could fit whatever container was being shipped.

It wasn't until the 1960s that standardization really began to take place. This came, first, through domestic negotiations within the United States, and then through international negotiations involving the US and the major European economies. The International Maritime Organization published global standards for containers that specified terminology, dimensions, markings, loading, and more. It helped created the version of the container we know today: eight feet wide by eight feet six inches high with a length of twenty feet. This container is now the industry standard reference, with volumes of shipping being measured in twenty-foot equivalent units, or TEUs.[23] (Though most ships now carry a majority of double-length boxes, forty feet long, that count for two TEUs.[24])

What followed was the ever-wider adoption of standardized containers. Ports began adapting their technology and their physical geography to allow for containerization. Port operators with a combination of foresight and capital made early moves in this direction and reaped handsome rewards. Rotterdam was an example. It had been decimated by German bombings during World War II, and by the 1950s was in the process of rebuilding and refurbishing its infrastructure. Betting on future trends, the managers of the Rotterdam port decided to plunge into the new container model, setting aside land and building the European Container Terminus with ten berths (and room for more). Rotterdam would quickly pass London as the top European port, and would later overtake New York as the world's largest port (by tonnage).[25] In the same year that Rotterdam received its first container ship, Hong Kong—a small port by world standards—decided to examine the option of containerization of its own port infrastructure.[26] The decision to do so would eventually help make Hong Kong the largest port in the world.

While these innovations were taking hold, there was still a way to go toward general adoption of containers. For example: in 1966 Maersk commissioned a planning study of shipping trends, and while it predicted growth in containerized shipping, that growth was not by its account so large as to warrant new investments in ships adapted to containerization. In the immediate term, the firm continued to focus on pallet-based shipping.

But then, once again, geopolitics would help transform trade.

* * *

There's an odd gap in Levinson's otherwise persuasive study of the way in which containerization, intermodality, and standardization drove the transformation in shipping in the 1960s and '70s. By the late 1960s, as these innovations were gaining an ever-larger foothold, Levinson's study notes with puzzlement that shipping costs were still not going down. But the explanation, likely, does not lie in the domain of the economics of transport, but in the essential fact that the Suez Canal was closed again, this time for years.

This second, longer closure came about more or less the same way the first one had: an Egyptian threat of nationalization, followed by a military clash with Israel. In this case, Egypt's threats to further nationalize the canal triggered the Six-Day War, which ran between June 5 and 10, 1967, and saw Israel strike deep into the heart of both Egyptian and Syrian territory, ending up in control of the Golan Heights and the Sinai Peninsula. Although Israel won the war swiftly and decisively, nonetheless the canal ended up closed, both mined by Egypt and blocked by ships sunk by the Israeli air force. It would stay that way until two years after the end of a follow-on war, the Yom Kippur War of 1973, which played out very differently. That war saw Egypt, Syria, and Jordan combining forces for a surprise attack on Israel, which caught it off guard; Israel only recovered and survived by means of a massive program of airlift and resupply by the United States. The canal would remain closed until 1975, following a two-year program of de-mining and ship-clearing led by the United States in the aftermath of the war.*

The Suez closure would drive shipping prices higher and create still more pressure on the owners of oil tankers and bulk carrier ships to develop larger, more efficient shipping designs.[27] And the OPEC oil embargo accompanying the 1973 Yom Kippur War caused a huge spike in the price of oil—the first of the major oil shocks to the West's economies.[28]

At the time that crisis hit, container shipping had spread even farther, in large part because of the second geopolitical factor: the Vietnam War.

Throughout McLean's turbulent career, he had found that a relationship with the US military was an important source of both contracts and support for his innovations. Even in the early phase of the SeaLand company, the large numbers of American troops in Germany and the need to supply them created huge logistical demands for the

*When the canal was closed in 1967, fifteen ships were caught in the Great Bitter Lake. The ships would stay there until the reopening of the canal in 1975. While the crews would be relieved and changed in and out, the ships would stay, eventually getting covered in desert sand—thus ending up with the name the Yellow Fleet. Only two would ever sail on their own again.

US Army, from which McLean profited. In the late 1960s, the Soviet invasion of Czechoslovakia led to a buildup of American forces in Europe, and they needed to be constantly supplied by goods from the United States—a growing percentage of which was shipped by container.[29] But when this relationship would really come to fruition was during Vietnam.

The huge cost of flowing goods to Vietnam led the army to be searching for solutions. McLean engaged in continuous negotiations with them to get them to adopt containerization, which they eventually did at Cam Ranh Bay in Vietnam and Subic Bay in the Philippines (one of the early prizes of the American colonial conquest of the Philippines). The large-scale use of containers by the US Army for supplying the Vietnam War made containerized shipping the go-to option for global trade.[30]

Then came a further evolution, in somewhat circuitous fashion. The first Suez Crisis had caused the bulk carrier and oil tanker industry to drive for larger ships. A 2013 report by the World Trade Organization put it simply: "Suddenly faced with the expense of transporting oil, coal, iron ore and other bulk commodities over much greater distances, the shipping industry decided to invest in huge, specialized bulk carriers as well as in the harbor facilities needed to handle these new vessels."[31] The need to find efficient ways around the Suez closure led to innovations in shipping design. Specifically, the tanker industry developed larger, more cost-effective ships.

The basic design of most ships resembles a rib cage laid flat. Most essential is the keel: a long, single beam that runs from the very front of the ship to the very rear—from bow to stern. Off the keel are a series of ribs, evenly spaced along the length of the keel, and rising up on each side—port and starboard, or left and right—to just above where the waterline will be. The ribs are then encased in a hull: wood or fiberglass or steel sheets that enclose the entire area below the water's surface, trapping air and creating buoyancy. What keeps a large, steel ship afloat is the buoyancy of the water trapped below sea level. But all of that wood or steel and air below water creates a heavy drag, slowing the ship.[32] So for most of the eighteenth and nineteenth centuries, the effort in marine engineering was to find tighter shapes for the hull—ever steeper V shapes that while remaining stable and buoyant would reduce drag in the water and allow ships to sail faster. This was true of both naval and commercial vessels.

With the Suez Crisis, that changed. The basic innovation for tanker designers after the crisis was to move away from the V-shaped hulls, toward a U-shaped hull, with wider beams—the beam being the measure of the ship from side to side.[33] U-shaped hulls made ships slower, but more stable at longer lengths; and slower was an acceptable tradeoff for the tanker industry.[34] At the time, more than 50 percent of oil imports to Europe came from the Middle East, and while a tanker could travel just 6,200 miles from the Persian Gulf to Britain through the Suez, with its closure that trip grew to 10,000 miles, as the tankers had to navigate around the Cape of Good Hope. Larger ships changed the price equation—if they carried larger loads, these ships would still be as cost-effective as shipping through the Suez, despite the longer route. A 1968 article argued that a 200,000-ton ship going around the cape could save 34 percent in costs compared to an 80,000-ton tanker going through the Suez. An oil analyst in New York wrote, "The supertankers are not going to replace the Suez Canal, but they're going to go a long way to letting the industry live without the Suez."[35,*]

In the 1960s and early '70s, the container industry, unlike the tanker industry, was still using older standards for ship design, with V-shaped hulls designed to reduce drag in the water, and therefore allow for faster speeds. But faster speeds meant greater fuel consumption. The oil price spike in 1973 hit the container shipping industry hard.[36]

What followed was a merger of two sets of innovations: the innovations in containerization and intermodality that had been driven by the US Army and McLean, and the innovations in U-shaped shipping design that had been driven by Suez and oil prices. The fusion of the two gave birth to the early antecedents of today's mega-container carriers.

*On March 23, 2021, the Taiwanese container ship *Ever Given* ran aground in the Suez Canal, where it became stuck. Several hundred ships waiting to transit the canal were kept waiting for six days, while local authorities struggled to tow or otherwise dislodge the ship. The event generated a huge outpouring of social media comments about the fragility of global supply lines.

The Size Race

Among the first to marry these innovations was Maersk. Although they had stayed away from containerization in the mid-1960s, by the turn of the decade they had changed course. In 1970, P. Maersk Møller's grandson Arnold Maersk Mc-Kinney Møller, who took over the company after his father's death in 1965, would decide to commission their first cargo ship fully outfitted to support containerization. Maersk took delivery of the *Svendborg Maersk* in 1974, after it traveled from its port of construction in Japan. It copied some of the U-shaped design of the large tankers of the day, creating more room in the hold and straighter hull walls, which eased the process of stacking containers.

The advent of fully containerized ships allowed Maersk—and the rest of the global shipping business—to expand the volume of what they could carry and the frequency of their trips. Maersk had run ships from Europe to Asia since 1926. But the new container ships allowed them to progressively and then massively increase the volume of cargo they could carry.

Container ships and trade volumes grew hand in hand. Spurred by American industrial prowess, postwar reconstruction in Europe, and these new technologies for shipping, the world economy grew quickly, recording faster growth between 1950 and 1973 than it had in the heady years before 1914.[37] Europe and the United States were the primary drivers and primary beneficiaries of this trade. In 1950, the US economy stood at almost $2.4 trillion in 2012 dollars; by 1980, when containerized trade had been fully adopted, it had grown to $6.8 trillion.[38]

A running list of the largest ports in the world, by value or by volume, shows this growth—and the near-total extent to which "world" trade was, in that period, dominated by the West. In 1969, the top container ports in the world were New York, Oakland, Rotterdam, Sydney, Los Angeles, Antwerp, Yokohama, Melbourne, Felixstowe (in southern England), and Bremen.[39] The only non-Western port on the list was Yokohama—Japan being then the only industrialized democracy in Asia. Together, these economies accounted for more than 90 percent of global exports.[40]

As Western trade grew, so did the demand for container traffic. Maersk and its competitors were in a constant race for scale. Other major shipping companies were nipping at their heels. Their primary competitors in those days were other European majors: the Geneva-based but Italian-owned Mediterranean Shipping Company (MSC); the French-owned CMA CGM, a company formed by the merger of Compagnie Maritime d'Affrètement (CMA) and Compagnie Générale Maritime (CGM); and the German-owned Hapag-Lloyd.[41] The nationality of the shipping firms reflected the legacy of the role Europe had played in the previous two hundred years in forging global trade. And they profited from the huge investment in the reconstruction of Europe after WWII and the intensification of trade with the United States.

It is striking that there was only one American company in the top ranks for global shipping firms in that period (McLean's own company, Sea-Land). Perhaps this reflected the fact that, despite its size, the American economy was in that period largely driven by domestic consumption—by goods made, sold, and used in the United States. In the early 1960s, only 5 percent of the American economy was driven by exports, and even after two decades of globalization, by 1980 that number had risen only to 10 percent.[42] Europe, on the other hand, was heavily dependent on trade—and the scale and weight of its shipping firms reflected that.

Maersk and its European competitors kept up the race for size, building ever-bigger ships. Although the company had vaulted up the ranks of the larger container shipping companies, its rivals were constantly vying to catch up. In 1977, it extended the size of its first-generation container ships, allowing them to carry 1,800 TEU.[43] In 1978, it commissioned a ship able to hold 2,124 TEU.[44] And it kept going: in the mid-1980s, it commissioned what became known as the *Marchen Maersk*, this one produced by the Odense shipyard itself, capable of carrying 5,000 TEU, fully ten times the "behemoth" that McLean had sailed in 1961.[45]

The growth in scale of the ships precisely mirrored the growth in volume of global trade—indeed, the two are all but synonymous. In 1950, when Maersk was rebuilding its shipping fleet after the losses of World War II, the total value of all global trade was $61 billion.[46] The evolution of ship design and containerization—and the standardization of inter-model containers—helped to drive large-scale growth in trade, and with it the total size of the Western economies. No other factor does as much to explain the growth of these economies in the 1970s, '80s, and '90s as the drastic reduction in the cost of transportation that large-scale shipping allowed.[47] By 1990, when the *Marchen* was plying the transpacific route, global trade had skyrocketed to $3.5 trillion.[48] And Maersk had become the largest shipping company in the world.

But by then, bigger changes were afoot. And to understand and visualize them, we need to shift our gaze back to geopolitics, and Asia. And to the second family-owned company that helped to shape the world of today.

5

Taipans of Globalization

Containerization and the Rise of Asia (1980–2012)

In the 1960s and '70s, international trade was heavily dominated by the Western democracies of Europe and the United States. But by the early 1980s, there was also growing dynamism in the capitalist countries of Asia—Korea, Taiwan, Japan—as well as in the city-state of Singapore. It's striking to look at the names and origins of the shipping companies that began climbing the global ranks in this period: Mitsui O.S.K. Lines from Japan, American President Lines from Singapore, Yang Ming Marine Transport Corporation from Taiwan. Each of these nations developed companies that built or commissioned their own container ships, each vying for a share of the burgeoning world trade market. All this was amplified by the Japanese economic boom in the 1980s, which turned Japan into the number two economy in the world.

But the largest Asian shipping firm in the 1970s and '80s was from none of these countries. It was based, rather, in that British exclave of the West, Hong Kong.

Hong Kong has played strangely important roles in the story lines of two modern global powers: Britain, which, when it encountered Hong Kong in the 1830s, was at the very peak of its might and reach; and China, which was then at the nadir of its own. Ironically, when the English East India Company first sought London's backing for the Opium Wars and held out Hong Kong as an important reward, Lord Palmerston quipped, "It will never be a mart for trade."[1] A hundred and thirty years later, it was the largest port in the world.[2]

Just as the expansion of European and Atlantic trade in the 1960s through the 1980s is reflected in the change and growth of the family-owned company Maersk, so, too, can the expansion of Asia's role in the world economy be seen reflected in a second family-owned company—this one in Hong Kong. At its peak, the Orient Overseas Container Line family of firms would become the largest shipping conglomerate in Asia.*

* * *

Part of what makes Hong Kong so important is its entrepreneurial culture. Much of this was inherited from Shanghai—many of Hong Kong's most important business families have their roots in 1930s Shanghai, at the time the third-largest city in the world and a key hub for international shipping and finance (as well as espionage and imperial rivalry).[3] One such family was the Hong Kong Tungs.

In 1922, a short story by the English novelist W. Somerset Maugham introduced Western readers to the concept of the Taipan—a figure that blends the roles of business leader, family scion, and overlord of trade.† If there's a modern-day equivalent of the Taipan, it's the Hong Kong Tungs: local business leaders, political figures, international business tycoons, and scions of the most important shipping dynasty in Hong Kong.

The founder, Chao Yung Tung (or C.Y., as he's commonly known), was born outside Shanghai in 1912—the same year Peter Maersk and his son founded their business. Like Maersk, the company C. Y. Tung founded would remain in private hands, would pass from father to

*For a time, the parent company, Overseas Orient Ltd., even owned the Port of Long Beach, before the US government forced it to sell, citing what are known as CFIUS concerns—rules issued by the Committee on Foreign Investment in the United States that authorize the US government to limit sales of American firms to foreign companies on national security grounds.

†James Clavell further popularized this notion with his novels about the establishment of what he terms "the Noble House"—loosely modeled on the oldest English trading firm in Asia, Jardines, whose main business house in China is still to be found on the famous Bund of Shanghai, and whose fifty-two-story Hong Kong skyscraper was the tallest in Asia when it was built. The Jardine building dominated the skyline of Hong Kong in the 1980s, its nautically themed porthole-shaped windows and the reputation of its inhabitants earning it the unfortunate sobriquet of "the house of a thousand arseholes."

son, and would help craft modern globalization. And like the Danish Shipbuilding Company of 1912, the company he founded was born into a world on the precipice of war.

The story of C.Y.'s company is well told in a small museum housed on the campus of Shanghai Jiao Tong University. The university was formed in 1896 as the Nanyang Public School by Emperor Guangxu, at the urging of Shanghainese leaders eager to develop the intellectual and entrepreneurial energy of the city's residents. Shanghai's merchants were ambitious and seeking to reverse the decline in Chinese fortunes that had followed the unequal treaties. They invested in education and engineering and in the industry that had so obviously and so visibly seen China subordinated to foreign powers and foreign companies—shipping.[4]

Modern Chinese universities can be brutish affairs, reflecting the ideology of their times. But the earliest China universities, Shanghai Jiao Tong among them, resemble their English redbrick counterparts, organized around central courtyards lined with yew trees and boxwoods, and populated by buildings that echo the architectural interplay of old Shanghai—with Victorian, Gothic, and Chinese styles all represented in the university's central square.

At the edge of the university is a small shikumen building—a style of gray-and-red-brick two-story architecture unique to Shanghai of the 1930s. Open the doors and you enter a cantilevered hall with a skylight that runs the entire length of the building, creating a large sun-filled chamber off of which are mounted side rooms that house the main displays. These depict the history of Chinese maritime exploration from the 1400s onward, recounting the exploits, for example, of the Shanghai sand fishermen who first ventured across the surprisingly shallow waters of the East China Sea. Pride of place is given over to Zheng He and the Chinese Treasure Fleet. Then a side staircase rises to an upper gallery, which takes up all of the second floor. This is dedicated in its entirety to C. Y. Tung.

In 1928, at the age of sixteen, C.Y. began work for a Japanese firm, Kokusai Transport Company, where he learned the basics of the transportation sector. A year later he transferred to Tongcheng Co., a Chinese bank. Tongcheng had a subsidiary, the Tianjin Navigation Company, which had the contract to service much of the fleet docked at Shanghai's wharfs—at the time, one of only a handful of Chinese-owned firms with a piece of the action of the maritime trade. C.Y. transferred to the Tianjin Navigation Company, and quickly climbed the corporate ladder. At age twenty-three, he was made the vice president of the Tianjin Shipowners Association. One of the visible features of European dominance of Shanghai at the time was the tall ships and tea clippers and steamships docked immediately in front of the Bund, Shanghai's glittering new waterfront quay. The C. Y. Tung gallery displays dozens of sepia photographs of the steamers and cruisers and cargo ships of Jardine Matheson, Butterfield and Swire, the American-owned Shanghai Steam Navigation company, and of the other European and Japanese firms that occupied the riverside harbor in old Shanghai. It was a daily reminder of the backwardness of turn-of-the-century China. On the very first day of his job at Tainjin Navigation, C.Y. would write a note to his boss, highlighting the fact that all the ships that they were servicing were European or Japanese, not Chinese: "It should never have been allowed to be like this."[5] In his diaries he would write about the need to move China out of its backwardness to refresh the memory of Zheng He and to launch China's own industrialists and entrepreneurs into the critical industry of the maritime shipping trade.[6] In 1964, he wrote, "Admiral Zheng He (known in Chinese history as Eunuch San Pao) visited the South Seas seven times from Asia to Africa. This epic-making event of 550 years ago all happened before Columbus discovered the New World." In a connected passage he would ask about Chinese industry, "How can we not continue to conquer the sea?"[7,*]

In 1941, C.Y. launched his own shipping company, Chinese Maritime Trust Ltd., taking offices in rooms 300, 301, and 303 in No. 12 The Bund, a building whose main tenant was the Hongkong and Shanghai Banking Corporation (now better known by its initials, HSBC; Asia's largest bank). The company he founded would end up a critical player in the economic rise of Asia.[8]

*Once established in a wealthy position in Hong Kong, C. Y. Tung wanted to make a movie about Zheng He, and approached a famous Hong Kong film director with the proposition. The director told him: "C.Y., you don't want to make that movie; you'll lose a fortune." C.Y. went to his deathbed with this one unfulfilled ambition. (Author interview with C. H. Tung, Hong Kong, November 1, 2019.)

But Shanghai was (and is) a city of contradictions. For all its international commercial energy, it was also here in 1920 after the fall of the Qing emperor that the Chinese labor movement grew, forged ties with the Soviets, and took form as the Communist Party of China. And in 1937, as C. Y. Tung registered his company, Shanghai was about to be torn apart by violence. Already in the late 1920s, Shanghai had been the scene of a brutal massacre at the hands of Chiang Kai-shek and his nationalist forces of the Kuomintang.[9] Much worse was to come. On July 7, 1937, Japan invaded China, and they skirmished in what later became famous as the Marco Polo Bridge Incident—on the very day that C. Y. Tung's first son was born.

Later that summer the Japanese would press further, and in August of 1937, Japanese and Chinese forces clashed on the banks of the Huangpu River in central Shanghai. By the time the battle ended three months later, what became known as the Battle of Shanghai had left as many as three hundred thousand dead—one of the deadliest battles in modern history, until World War II obliterated such records with its vast killing fields.[10]

At the outbreak of World War II, C. Y. Tung registered his company in Hong Kong, before that city-state fell to Japanese occupation, one day before the Japanese attack on Pearl Harbor. He then temporarily set up shop in Chongqing, where the Chinese government established a temporary capital. And then when the war receded, he returned to Shanghai in 1946. But China was set to see more strife, as the internal divisions that had begun to tear China apart before the war returned in full force, and China fell again into civil war. In 1949, Chairman Mao's Red Army defeated Chiang Kai-shek of the Koumintang, who was pushed into exile in Taiwan, and formed the People's Republic of China. One of Mao's first acts was to close Shanghai off from the outside world. The gilded city that had endured so much folded into itself, forced to recede from world markets and fading from the world's imagination. A red star, the symbol of the Communist Party, was installed on top of the tallest spire of the major trading house on the Bund.[11]

C. Y. Tung had already left. In 1948, seeing the growing risk of a communist takeover, he moved his business and his family permanently to Hong Kong.

* * *

Chinese Maritime Ltd. quickly became one of Hong Kong's most important companies. Understanding the importance of bold moves, C.Y. acquired the *Tien Loong*, a steamship of more than ten thousand tons. It became the first ship in modern history owned and managed by a Chinese national to sail the Atlantic and arrive in Europe.[12] In 1948, he went farther, when the *Tung Ping* became the first Chinese ship to sail to the United States.[13,*] Shipping was his life: "The sea has held my fascination since I was a child; the ship is my other self."[14]

Like Maersk in the same era, China Maritime Ltd. first developed its global business through the tanker trade. As early as 1959, just after the first Suez Crisis, C. Y. Tung ordered the construction of *Oriental Giant*, which became the largest ship in Asia when it was delivered. And in 1973 he commissioned the construction of the mega-tanker *Seawise Giant* (a pun on his initials), which lived up to its name—when delivered in 1979, it was the largest ship in the world.[15]

But what really drove C. Y. Tung's companies to the forefront of Hong Kong's role in globalization was, again like Maersk, an early move into containerization of the international trade. In 1965, C. Y. Tung converted a series of bulk carriers into semi-containerized ships. He served on the containerization commission for Hong Kong in 1966. And in 1971 he committed, commissioning two fully containerized ships, the *Oriental Commander* and *Oriental Financier*. And in 1973, just as Maersk took delivery of the *Svendborg*, he established a separate company to deepen his container investment, Orient Overseas Container Line (OOCL).

For the next decade, as Hong Kong rose, so did OOCL; or really, the other way around. In December 1966, the Hong Kong Container Committee, with C. Y. Tung on board, reported, "[U]nless a container terminal is available in Hong Kong to serve these [new container] ships the trading position of the Colony will be affected detrimentally."[16] The authorities acted on the commission's recommendations—in 1969, three initial terminals were funded by operators from Europe, Japan, and the US. In July of that year, Hong Kong received its first visit from a fully containerized ship (before the terminal was ready); in 1972, the

*Here, the word "Chinese" is referring to the ethnicity of C. Y. Tung, not his nationality.

first berths for a new facility, today known as the Kwai Tsing Container Terminals, opened; and in 1976, five container terminals became fully operational. Between 1970 and 1972, shipments out of Hong Kong rose from 3 million tons to 3.8 million, and the value of foreign trade increased by 35 percent—even before the container terminals were operating at full steam.[17]

Through all of this, the Tungs were a central pillar of Hong Kong's growth. Indeed the family is the living embodiment of the changing fate of China, with its storied past and turbulent history; of the crisis of the communist takeover of China in the 1940s; of the unique role of Hong Kong as a kind of offshore safety valve for Chinese industrial prowess; of the transformation of Hong Kong into a modern hub for finance and trade; and of its eventual reabsorption back into mainland China.

* * *

Modern-day Hong Kong is a dramatic place, where steep mountain slopes fall down toward the blue-gray waters of the harbor, only to be interrupted in their descent by a wall of expansive neon-ringed skyscrapers that line the shore. From some vantage points it seems like the skyscrapers are taller than Hong Kong's famed Victoria Peak, but in fact that natural feature still does just top out the island. From there, on a clear day (rarer than they used to be) the naked eye can see for miles, well into mainland China across Kowloon Bay. Also visible is the modern harbor of Hong Kong, fronting right up to the skyline: until 2017, the world's largest. This is the Hong Kong that these Taipans of globalization helped create.*

The central offices of the Tung business empire lie very close to the harbor—not in the glitzy Central District, where modern financial Hong Kong works, but in the more modest Wan Chai district, a nondescript office block close to the main port facility of old. The Tung offices are situated on the thirty-third floor of the Harbor Center, the marble lobby of which could be found in any commercial quarter of

*Despite *New York Times* profiles and friendships with world leaders, and the prestige as Asia's largest shipper, C.Y. still did not see himself as belonging. In the 1950s, he sent his son to school in the United Kingdom. At the time, he told him: "You cannot enter the university in Hong Kong, because it is for the elite; and we are not of the elite." Author interview, C. H. Tung, Hong Kong, November 1, 2019.

any Western city—except for the small boutique of Chinese antiques tucked away in a corner. Step out of the elevator on the thirty-third floor, though, and you could only be in Hong Kong.

When the doors open, three staff members are waiting to greet you. They escort you warmly, but quickly, to an outer office, where a receptionist takes your coat, if you have one. (Hong Kong gets quite cold in its winter months.) She offers you tea while you wait. This being China, you always have to wait; but this being Hong Kong, you don't wait long.

C.H. stands about five foot seven and is always immaculately dressed, usually in a bespoke suit, his silvering hair trimmed at the temples. He exudes the quiet confidence of a man with both economic and political power at his ready disposal. For four decades he was at the heart of Hong Kong's economic rise.

After you wait for a few minutes in his outer office, his staff invite you to go into the inner sanctum. A modern office suite with a wide desk set against a bank of large windows and a series of black leather sofas formed into a rectangle to allow for quiet conversation. On the rear wall, a montage of black-and-white photographs captures the development of the technology and the steadily growing size of OOCL's ships, ships that formed the backbone of Hong Kong's economic growth in the 1970s, '80s, and '90s.

When C. H. Tung himself enters the office to greet you, he bears a warm smile on his face. He is dressed in the Western businessman's uniform, charcoal gray suit and crisp white shirt, both impeccably tailored. Then he asks you to wait for a brief moment and disappears into a personal office. When he returns, the suit jacket has been replaced by a black fleece Mao jacket. Perhaps the change is motivated simply by an effort to combat the chills, but somehow it seems to capture the essence of the man: an avatar of globalization and of modern business, a member of the International Council at J.P. Morgan, a capitalist to his very bones—but in his marrow, Chinese.

C.H. never had the same love for the sea that inspired his father. "He was a romantic. I counted the money," he says with a rueful smile. And at first, C. H. Tung resisted being pulled into the family business. When he was away at school in England—graduating in 1960 with a bachelor's degree in maritime engineering from the University of Liverpool—his mother had sent word that he should come back to

Hong Kong to support his father. But when his father came to see him in England and asked him what he wanted to do, C.H. did not propose to return. "I told my father, 'I think you are still at a stage where you do not need my help. I'd like to stay in England and learn more about business.'" His father had other ideas, but to C.H.'s pleasant surprise they did not involve a return to Hong Kong. "He told me, 'Go to America. That is the country of the future. If you go there, you will never regret taking my advice.' And I never did." C. H. Tung spent ten years in America, several of them working with General Electric. His father visited him so frequently—sometimes up to ten times a year—that he ended up taking his own apartment, on New York's Fifth Avenue.

But duty did eventually call. In 1969, C.H. returned to Hong Kong to learn the business from the inside, and gradually take over management. When his father died in 1981, the company passed into C.H.'s hands. He recalls the period gravely: "It was not an easy time for me." Not only had he been called home from the America he had grown to love, he found the company heavily indebted, and underwater financially. "We had some financial difficulties. And it was at a time when interests rates were at thirteen or fourteen percent; and we had a lot of debt. I had to find a way out."

That way out involved support from China. A local tycoon, Henry Fok, helped arrange $120 million to save the company. Fifty million dollars reportedly came from the mainland-controlled Bank of China, and a significant amount also came from China Merchants, part of China's transport ministry.[18] It was the start of a relationship with mainland China, just at the start of its new opening to the Western world; a relationship that would shape much of the rest of the story of OOCL.

C.H. ran the company for fourteen years, and in that period he returned it to profitability. The key was not new trade routes or new ship designs or new partners: it was technology. "Business is business. And the best that you can do, the only thing you can do, is to know what role you play in the transportation chain and why you and only you are important. What can you do for your customers that nobody else can do that make them willing to pay? For years our margin was higher, but they would pay. Why? Because we were the first to be able to extensively use innovation and technology to make the difference."

Specifically, under C. H. Tung, the company became a pioneer in the marriage between containerization and computerization. Until very recently, the global shipping industry was resistant to computerization—to this day, many ports and many shipping companies do their business by faxed copies of paper forms. C.H. foresaw that using computers to track shipments would enable greater efficiency in getting customers' goods from origin to destination.

By 1983, the company was the sixth-largest shipping firm in the world.[19] It played a key role in Hong Kong's own growth—which was itself remarkable. In 1974, Hong Kong broke the international record by handling more than 3,500 TEUs in a single day. That year, Hong Kong container terminals handled a total of 726,000 TEUs; by 1989, that number grew to 4.5 *million*—an increase of more than 500 percent.[20] In 1987, Hong Kong passed Rotterdam and New York City as the largest container port in the world. The related industries of finance and commercial law also grew, and Hong Kong became the critical anchor of Western globalization in Asia.

And then, a decade later, a very dramatic change occurred: in 1997, Britain's 150-year rule of Hong Kong came to an end. Hong Kong reverted to Chinese sovereignty.

* * *

When Hong Kong reverted to Chinese control, it brought into the heart of China an economic powerhouse. China had begun its exploration of overseas markets and would, one year later, enter the World Trade Organization; having Hong Kong was a massive economic shot in the arm.

It's easy to miss the significance of this. China was trying to forge an international economic strategy with a leadership drawn exclusively from the ranks of the Chinese Communist Party, almost none of whom had lived or worked abroad. They had no experience of foreign trade, and no trading infrastructure. And then, suddenly, the world's largest trading port—with all the infrastructure, relationships, financiers, and international lawyers that go along with it—fell into their lap. Moreover, Hong Kong's return to China was the final belated nail in the coffin of Britain's overseas empire. It is one of history's great ironies that this small cluster of islands, so central to the manner in which the British Empire extracted the riches of China, was about to reverse roles.

China Opening

Earlier in this book we encountered the notion that a lacuna had opened up in world affairs when British imperial conquest had resulted, nearly simultaneously, in both the Indian and the Chinese empires all but disappearing from the world stage. Each of them had, at the time, accounted for roughly a quarter of the world's economic activity. That number fell to roughly 3 percent of world GDP each.[21] Into that lacuna flowed European trade and imperial power, and wealth. Europe (and the New World) profited for nearly a century and a half, dominating both world politics and the global economy out of all proportion to population size or intrinsic resources. That a country like Denmark, puny by global standards, could have become a significant trading empire is indicative of the disproportionate role Europe played. But with the advent of containerization, and geopolitical changes, the lacuna was about to start to close.

These changes would be manifest in the late 1990s and early 2000s. But they date back to the fall of 1967—when a former vice president and presidential hopeful, Richard Nixon, penned an article about the future of US relations with China, one that would shape the diplomacy of his presidency and ultimately the later part of the twentieth century. Nixon's thinking appeared in the October 1967 issue of the influential journal *Foreign Affairs*; he argued that the United States needed to shift its engagement in Asia and bring China back into the international fold. His logic was simple: he believed the United States needed China on its side to help balance the Soviet Union. But he argued in more elegiac terms: "There is no place on this small planet for a billion of its potentially most able people to live in angry isolation."[22]

Thirteen months later he would be elected to the presidency. In February 1969, barely one month into office, Nixon wrote a memo to his national security advisor, Henry Kissinger (later secretary of state), directing him to look into possibilities of engaging with the Chinese through private channels.[23] On June 26 of that year, National Security Decision Memorandum 17 ordered the modification of some trade controls against China that had been put in place in the context of the Korean War from 1950 to 1953; it also removed regulatory restraints on foreign subsidiaries of US firms undertaking transactions with the Chinese.[24]

Then, quiet diplomacy got underway. On December 3, the American ambassador to Poland, Walter Stoessel, passed a message to the Chinese embassy in Warsaw that Nixon was willing to have substantive talks with the Chinese. Over the course of the next two years the Americans would communicate to the Chinese through various Eastern European embassies that they were willing to meet directly to discuss a warming in US-China relations.[25] A Pakistani channel opened up in April 1971 when the Pakistani ambassador to Washington, DC, Agha Hilaly, delivered a note from Zhou Enlai, the first premier of the People's Republic of China, inviting a special envoy to a meeting in Peking.[26]

Kissinger began to prepare for the trip. Such were the sensitivities at the time that the trip was conducted in secret. Kissinger flew to Vietnam in July 1971 for consultations with leadership of the American war effort there, and then flew on to Pakistan. In Islamabad, he feigned a stomachache and then flew secretly to Peking, where he met with Zhou.* The meeting was a success: On July 11, 1971, Kissinger sent a cable to Nixon from the US embassy in Pakistan that contained a simple word: "Eureka." Four days later, on July 15, Nixon announced on national TV that he would visit China.[27]

The historic visit took place February 21 to 28 of 1972. Nixon visited both Premier Zhou Enlai and Chairman Mao Zedong, and together they negotiated a communiqué that laid out a "roadmap"—a diplomatic term that simply means a rough sketch of potential agreements—to peaceful relations between the two countries.[28]

Nixon's resignation in 1974 might have slowed the warming between the two countries; but when Gerald Ford took office, he immediately sent a letter to Chairman Mao pledging to continue the opening policy. Negotiations continued apace. Elections in 1976 brought to power the Democratic Party and President Jimmy Carter; but he, too,

*The Pakistanis employed a body double of Kissinger to further throw any observers off the scent—who got an actual stomachache when he ate six mangoes in quick succession. As a result, the Pakistanis had to find a doctor who had never heard of Kissinger so their ruse could continue. Chris Tudda, *A Cold War Turning Point* (Baton Rouge: Louisiana State University Press, 2012), 81.

continued the policy. It was Carter who in January 1979 gave China full diplomatic recognition, formalized in February 1979 with a symbolic visit by Vice Premier Deng Xiaoping to the United States. It had taken a decade.[29]

The warming of US-China ties continued through the last decade of the Cold War, although President Ronald Reagan sought to roll back some concessions Carter had made to the Chinese on US relations with Taiwan. Still, diplomatic recognition stood and the warming of relations continued. In 1989, they were temporarily set back when the Chinese People's Liberation Army was sent into Beijing's Tiananmen Square to forcibly disperse tens of thousands of student protesters assembled there to call for democratic reforms, killing thousands of civilians. The United States suspended arms sales and official visits to China. However, through private channels, President George H. W. Bush communicated that the events would not derail broader US-China relations.[30] But then another event occurred that cast the entire issue in a different light: the Berlin Wall fell.

As the wall fell, so, too, did the Soviet Union—and with it, the underlying reason for the US rapprochement to Beijing, which had been initially inspired by a desire to rebalance global political affairs against Moscow. But by then, the diplomatic process of opening up to China had been underway for two decades. And during the course of it, both China and the US had found another reason for closer ties: trade.

As the Cold War began to wind down, with the start of the opening up of the Soviet Union under Mikhail Gorbachev, decision makers in China began to worry that by staying out of the Western-led global trade and finance systems—which they had done ever since taking power in 1947—they were losing out on substantial opportunities for economic growth. In the years since Nixon penned his article, Western economies had grown steadily. In 1980, China's GDP stood at $191 billion; that compared badly to the GDP of the United States, at $2.86 *trillion*, despite a Chinese population nearly four times that of the US.[31] Put differently: the average Chinese citizen had an annual income of less than one-fortieth of that of the average American.[32]

And so the Chinese leadership did something unorthodox: it changed course. Fatefully, in 1986, China formally submitted an application to join the main trading body of the time, the General Agreement on Tariffs and Trade (which would be replaced in 1995 by the World Trade Organization).[33] They were not alone: over the coming years, the Soviet Union also applied to join under reformer President Gorbachev, though its application would take far longer to advance.[34] Eventually dozens of other countries of the "developing world" that had stayed outside of both the Western and Soviet blocs during the Cold War joined them. But it was China's bid that would prove the most significant.

* * *

Life comes full circle. By the time China entered the WTO, Hong Kong had reverted to Chinese sovereignty. And the first governor of non-British Hong Kong was none other than C. H. Tung. Their fortunes—in both senses of that word—would continue to grow together, but now their fates were intertwined with that of China, and its reentry into the world. OOCL grew, Hong Kong grew, world trade grew, and China grew. In 2003, Tung's Orient Overseas Container Line took possession of the *OOCL Shenzhen*, with a capacity of 8,063 TEU. A Chinese-owned ship was now the largest container ship in the world.[35]

6

The Great Closing

Yangshan Port and China's Return (2012–2017)

The Yangtze River, Asia's longest, is the historic lifeline of Chinese civilization, and the city that dominates its mouth, Shanghai, has long been that nation's economic heart. But for almost forty years, from 1947 to 1984, China kept Shanghai closed off from global commerce. It was as if the United States had, in the 1950s, decided to shut down the New York Stock Exchange and seal off the Port of New York.

But when China decided to change course, a decade before they reabsorbed Hong Kong, Shanghai would once again become the actual center and the symbol of China's opening to the West and to globalization.[1] In 1984, the Chinese government opened Shanghai to foreign investment. China's leader at the time, Deng Xiaoping, anointed Shanghai as the "head of the dragon"—the cutting edge of China's liberalization.[2]

The transformation that followed is best symbolized by the change to Shanghai's Pudong district—in the early 1980s, it was still parkland and farmland opposite the Bund, a place where middle-class families would come by ferry to picnic and escape the heat and bustle of central Shanghai. The decision to open Shanghai would transform its bucolic nature.

To mark the start of China's opening, the authorities launched the building of its first modern skyscraper. The Oriental Pearl Tower, with its 1,535-foot-high TV tower spiking up from two purple domes covered in neon lights and spiking mastheads, was the first major building in Pudong. But it was quickly flanked by two other skyscrapers built at around the same time, and then by a growing number of hotels and office towers.[3] The skyline became internationally known in 2005 as the producers of the *Mission Impossible* series took the unusual step (for the time) of filming in China, shooting the third episode of the franchise in Shanghai, showcasing its new commercial grandeur and the impressive high-rises that then dominated its skyline.[4] Today it's hard to make out those buildings, so fully dominated are they by the now far taller buildings of the rest of the Pudong skyline. Much as the United States at the height of its global economic clout strutted its stuff by building competing skyscrapers in New York and Chicago, so, too, has China used Shanghai's skyline to demonstrate its financial, engineering, and architectural prowess, and to symbolize its growing power on the world stage.[5]

That skyline is now dominated by a trio of remarkable buildings that abut one another in a single city block in Pudong. In 1994, Shanghai began construction of the eighty-eight stories of the Jin Mao Tower. The building is a masterpiece of modern architecture, a fusion of modernism and Orientalism that pulls the eye upward constantly as it moves between its sixteen cantilevered sections and its aluminum shell. The entire building is wrapped in filigree, like someone took the Chrysler Building and wrapped it in dragon scale. A spiking tower at its top completes the effect. When finished, it was the fifth-tallest building in the world and the tallest in Asia, a symbol of China's growing economic clout.[6] Then came the World Financial Center, opened to the public in 2008. It briefly took the title of world's tallest building.[7] Most dramatic of all is the Shanghai Tower immediately to the north. Built between 2008 and 2014, the tower is now the second-tallest building in the world. Among other engineering advances, it houses the world's second-fastest elevator—which shoots from the ground floor to an observation deck on the 108th floor in only twenty-seven seconds.[8] Along the building's immense height it twists gently as it rises, creating both an elegant design and greater functionality, a device designed to counter typhoon winds. It houses new museums, and art galleries dedicated to the young innovators of Shanghai's burgeoning art scene. In the dynamic architecture and vibrant cultural life of Pudong and central Shanghai is everything to celebrate about China's rise.[9]

* * *

From the observation deck of the Shanghai Tower, you look out over Shanghai's multiple sets of skylines, to a view of the old French Concession, the Bund, and the Huangpu River, a tributary of the Yangtze. You watch a constant flow of barges carrying coal and containers atop as they flow through central Shanghai. But you see few ships docked now at Shanghai wharf, except the occasional river cruise ship. For with the advent of very large commercial container ships, with huge hulls, the most important trading ships could no longer sail up the Huangpu to the piers of Shanghai. The city risked being left behind in the global scale race among container ports, just as China most needed trade access and the growth opportunity it provided.

So in 2005, the modern Chinese Communist Party did what it does best: it engineered around the problem. Specifically, it created a new, deepwater port seventeen miles off the coast of Shanghai, built on reclaimed land assimilating two small islands, known collectively as Yangshan. And it's in the new port of Yangshan that we can really visualize the true scale of China's economic return.[10]

The rise of China and its involvement in the WTO is an interwoven story. In 2018, a *Wall Street Journal* essay described China's accession to the WTO as "when the world opened the gates of China."[11] It helped create the giant economy that China today represents. The basic numbers tell the story. In 1999, twenty years after opening up diplomatically, China's GDP had grown to an estimated $1 trillion. A decade later, it had grown to $5 trillion.[12]

But one of China's major weaknesses is that the size of its population hugely outstrips the scale of natural resources available inside its borders. If it was going to continue to grow, it was going to have to get natural resources from outside its borders, as well as conduct trade in industrial goods. So China began to explore how to acquire resources overseas.

Now, nearly two-thirds of China's huge population lives along its eastern edges, with 96 percent living to the east of the so-called Hu Line that demarcates China's densely populated east and its sparsely populated west.[13] Of course, China has land routes into Europe's huge markets, but those routes are thousands of miles long. The trans-Siberian highway and railroad does the difficult part of connecting Beijing to

Moscow, but even then, having traversed a distance of 4,735 miles, it covers only two-thirds of the journey from Beijing to London.[14] Even with Chinese investment in transportation and trade infrastructure to its west, the easiest and fastest way for China to connect to global markets was to deviate from its long history of inland consolidation. China was, for the first time since the 1400s, about to venture out to sea.

As China began to look for huge volumes of natural resources overseas, it encountered the basic question that had constrained the British and the French in the early days of their overseas adventures: the simple cost of bringing goods back home. In China's case: to make trade with the rest of the world economical, given the distances involved for reaching Europe or the United States, required the ability to move things in very large volumes.

The still relatively new container ship technology was the perfect solution at the perfect time. Bulk shipping and containerized trade was key: it allowed for large, economical volumes of natural resources to flow into China's domestic markets, and for equally large volumes of inexpensive manufactured goods to flow out of China to developed markets in the West.

What followed was exponential growth of two types—of the scale of container shipping and of the quantity of goods these ships sailed in and out of China's ports. The pace of growth in the size of the ships almost perfectly tracks China's stunning growth between the mid-1990s and the present day. China's growth could not have been accomplished without the advent of containerized trade.[15]

The New Port of Shanghai

Driving from central Shanghai to the new port is an escapade through the drab realities of modern industrial and suburban planning. Like most exciting metropolises, Shanghai is surrounded by miles of suburban and light-industrial blight, admittedly vastly preferable for its inhabitants to the crumbling infrastructure of the late communist era, but hardly an uplifting urban landscape. Twenty miles south along Highway 52, the industrial architecture gives way to farmlands that supply Shanghai's 24 million souls—farmlands spliced through with high-voltage wires and even nuclear plants that abut the highway, their double cooling towers appearing almost within reach from the roadside rest stops.

From the end of the highway, to access the modern port, you first have to cross the Donghai Bridge. It's hard to write about China without constantly reaching for trite superlatives. At the time that it was built, the Donghai Bridge was the largest sea-crossing bridge in the entire world—until an even larger one was built north of Shanghai to connect Shanghai's markets to the trade routes to the north. (Today, another Chinese bridge, between Hong Kong, Macau, and Zhuhai, is the longest sea-crossing bridge in the world.[16]) The Donghai Bridge is yet another engineering marvel, given both its scale and its location in the East China Sea, where it is exposed to frequent typhoons. On a clear day you can see most of its twenty miles snake its way across the opening between Shanghai and the islands of the new port. It curves and twists like a dragon's tail, an engineering solution designed to defeat typhoons, and a seeming visual continuation of the shapes of the Pudong towers.[17] From conception to completion, the bridge took a mere four years.

Notwithstanding its architectural sophistication, driving the Donghai Bridge is a long way from the romance of the Shanghai Bund. The endlessly unfolding gray concrete of the bridge winds above the surrounding gray of the East China Sea. A large wind farm provides some visual interest, though only in direct sunlight can you tell that the giant spinning fans are white, not gray as well. The gray steel hulls of a couple of naval cruisers keeping an eye on the port occasionally appear before dipping back below the horizon. The immense scale and the endless drab contribute to a suffocating sense of industrial heft.

Twenty minutes later, one exits the bridge and the view scape is briefly broken by the green hills of the island and the small collection of traditional Chinese fishing junks that still dock in its original port. These belong to the few original residents of the island, the majority of whom were forced to relocate to make way for the modern port of Shanghai.

From the base of the hill, a road winds its way up the steep sides of the cliff base to the peak. Along the road are modern apartment buildings that house foreign guests who come to check on their cargoes, their shipping berths, or simply to marvel at the scale of the Yangshan Port. Cross the peak and come to the other side, and a viewing platform provides a view of the entire port; or so it seems, until you turn the corner and realize that the first part of the port is simply that—the *first* part. Beyond, an enormous forest of cranes and containers extends far beyond the original vista.

Visitors to the viewing platform are often greeted by Zhao Yaping, director, and He Caixue, deputy general manager. Responsible for the day-to-day operations of the port, they are both themselves original residents of the fishing community. Many of the island community were forcibly displaced from the island, and many of them were given jobs in the new port and are housed in the new apartment blocks at the mainland base of the Donghai Bridge. Others commute by company shuttle from eastern Shanghai, a drive of nearly two hours in each direction. The industrial gray, the scale, the forced displacement, and the tough conditions for the port workers: Yangshan exemplifies everything that's worrying about China's economic rise.[18]

The port itself was built in four phases. It was well timed to capture the economic boom that came from China's opening to the world economy and then its entry into the World Trade Organization. Already by 2002, Shanghai had become the fourth-largest port in the world by container volume.[19] Over the course of the next decade it would steadily and inexorably climb the lead tables of the largest ports in the world—and by 2017 it would top that list.[20]

The port itself is simple in its layout. A large expanse of reclaimed land lies behind the original slopes of the Yangshan hills. Along its eastern edge are arrayed more than forty container cranes, each of them almost three hundred feet in height and two hundred feet in width, and each capable of lifting a twenty-thousand-pound container onto a cargo ship in a matter of thirty seconds. Along the base of the port lie more than one hundred thousand containers—literally a day's worth of work for the industrial mass of the shipyard. What are known as "rubber tire gantries"—basically cranes on wheels, forty feet high topped by small glass and metal caves that house their drivers—maneuver around the port on eight foot wheels to shift containers from docking back to prime movers and back again, keeping a constant flow of containers from ship to port and back.

The newest part of the port, Phase 4, was completed in 2017 and at first glance looks identical to the rest. On closer inspection, a very important difference reveals itself: *there are no people*. This part of the port is the world's largest, and one of the first, to be entirely automated. The movement of containers, the unloading and off-loading from ships, all happens by the same cranes and the same trollies, but in Phase 4, they're controlled by computers. A highly sophisticated artificial intelligence and robotics system manages the entire flow, and an AI-powered surveillance system monitors the operation. With its scale, sophistication, and the displacement of human labor, Phase 4 of Yangshan Port is everything that's ominous about China's future, and perhaps the future of globalization itself.[21]

China Goes Out

With the return of Hong Kong and the trade and investment opportunities that afforded, China pushed further, encouraging its businesses to invest overseas. This helped Chinese business abroad, but it also helped domestically—as new WTO commitments accelerated the opening up of the domestic market, encouraging Chinese businesses to operate abroad helped them gain international experience that could help them keep up with foreign businesses now entering the Chinese market.

This strategy evolved through several phases. Starting in 1986, as China negotiated for global trade access, the Chinese authorities allowed its state-owned firms to start investing in overseas markets. The returns were quite limited; between 1986 and 1991 only around $1 billion in investments were made by Chinese firms in foreign markets.[22] Starting in 1991, with the Cold War now decisively in the dustbin of history, China decided to open up more, and began to allow *private* firms as well to invest overseas. This was underway when the Asian financial crisis hit in 1997, triggered by a market crisis in Thailand that quickly spread through the rest of Asia. In 1994, China had taken the important reform decision to peg its currency to the US dollar, so it, too, was affected when global financial markets were roiled by the crisis.[23] So, in 1999, just as China's negotiations to join the WTO entered the endgame, the authorities decided to formalize and deepen their overseas investment strategy, announcing a policy later described as its "go out" policy.

The focus of investment was the raw materials and natural resources that China needed for its own growth. In the first years of China's "go out" policy, state-owned enterprises were leading the effort, and focused their investment on mergers and acquisitions of foreign assets. China learned fast that this was not the most efficient way to acquire resources and shifted strategy. So then, both state-owned firms and Chinese private enterprise were incentivized to invest in natural resources and infrastructure projects—the basic logic being that if more natural resources were transported into the global market, China could simply acquire them through commercial transactions. The strategy evolved still further. Chinese authorities recognized that there was enough global supply of most natural resources that China's investments began to shift to a more straightforward focus on profit-making, and thus to investing where the profits were to be made—often by buying sizable shares of key industries. Over time, this policy would evolve into what became much more commonly known as China's Belt and Road Initiative.[24]

Containerization and bulk shipping made this possible. The raw numbers tell the story: Chinese outward investment went from $913 million USD in 1991 to $9.7 billion in 2001, to a peak of a whopping $216 billion in 2016.[25] And between 1998 and 2008, global trade in natural resources grew from $613 billion to $3.7 trillion, with money pouring into the coffers of both traditional and new commodity exporters.[26]

This is often written simply as a story of Chinese economic growth. In fact, the massive Chinese appetite for resources led to a global boom in commodity prices, a commodity super-cycle.[27] Resource-rich lower-income countries gained significant economic opportunities as a result, extracting $1 trillion in oil revenues alone during the height of the commodities boom from 2005 to '08.[28] This helped create conditions that led to this remarkable phenomenon: *every* developing country in the world grew, barring those at war.[29]

The gains were substantial. Nigeria went from $567 per capita in 1990 to $2,242 in 2008; Ghana from $398 to $1,210; the average per capita size of Latin America's developing countries jumped from

$2,500 to $7,672; and so on.[30] China's commodity super-cycle transformed the "third world."

All of this would in turn transform world affairs. From a world in which the rich countries of the north could dictate the terms of international politics to developing countries, the commodity super-cycle created a new reality. More than sixty countries grew from low-income status to middle-income status, and gained the diplomatic influence that goes along with that growth. By the late 2000s, the largest of these countries were being talked about as "emerging markets," and later as "rising powers." The countries would begin to wield substantially greater clout in global affairs. No longer could the rich northern countries of Europe and the free world simply dictate the field of play; they now had to contend with the influence of the "global south." Chinese investment was not the only factor: Western aid played a useful role in some settings, like Vietnam and Ethiopia, as did regional organizations. But it was the Chinese-led commodity super-cycle that created the basic conditions for these countries' economic rise.[31]

The rest of the story *is* all about China. It's remarkable to look at the tables of the largest ports in the world and watch China simply start to dominate. In 2001, leaving aside Hong Kong, China has one port, Shanghai, in the top five, well below Singapore and Busan, and only marginally larger than the largest European or Western port of the time, Rotterdam.[32] Fast-forward to 2005, and Singapore holds the top slot, but the next in the ranks are Chinese: Hong Kong and Shanghai. In 2010, China has six of the ten top slots—including Guangzhou, earlier known as Canton, site of China's original confrontation with the trading West. At this stage, Europe has only one slot left in the top ten, Rotterdam—and the United States has none. Both Los Angeles and New York have been booted out of the top levels of world trade.[33] By this point, more than two-thirds of the world's trade was passing through a port with Chinese investment at some stage of its travels.[34]

From there, the list of ports doesn't change much, though Rotterdam drops out of the top ten by 2013—it's just that the numbers continue to grow, inexorably. In 2002, Shenzhen was the number six port in the world, with an annual TEU throughput rate of 7,618,000 containers. By 2005, it reached 16,000,000 TEU, and by 2015 it was at 24,000,000 TEU—more than twice as large as the largest European container port, Rotterdam. But even its numbers were dwarfed by the new global champion in container ports: Shanghai, which processed more than 35 million TEUs.[35]

* * *

In 2017, Shanghai became the largest port in the world. In 2018, it was the location of over *40 million* container drops—an astonishing number when considering that merely a decade earlier, the largest port in the US, Los Angeles, serviced just over 7 million containers. Even in 2018 it serviced only 9.5 million container drops. Yangshan was not only the largest port in the world: *it was more than four times larger than its American competitors.*

From Yangshan Port, containers now flow to every major economy in the world—150 of them. By 2017, Chinese GDP had grown to fully $12 trillion, a more than tenfold growth over that twenty-year period. In the annals of modern economics, it's a story of unparalleled success. By value, the most important trade is to the United States. In 2000, the year of China's entry into the WTO, the largest trading partners to the US were its neighbors, Canada and Mexico, and its ally Japan. No longer. In 2015, China became the largest trading partner of the United States.[36]

Between the scale, the gray, the economic success, the forced displacement, the automation, the sheer engineering domination over the seas and hills, Shanghai and its new port are everything that's admirable and everything that's disturbing about modern China. Like the red star over the Bund, its fundamental contradictions are visible for all to see, its juggernaut scale intimidating by design, and its sophistication, its history, its culture numbed but unsuppressed. Shanghai looks set to be to the coming world what New York was to the golden age of American power—a dominant economic, technological, cultural, and trading giant, for good and for ill.[37]

7

Global Supply Ships

How Trade Was Remade (2017–Present Day)

Old harbors were cauldrons of humanity, bustling centers of labor and commerce, of strife and corruption, pockets of cosmopolitanism where cultures met and clashed and merged. Modern container ports, instead, are industrial operations, all but devoid of humanity—and Yanghsan's fourth bay is literally devoid of people. Yet, a residue of their past vibrancy remains, in the colors and origins of the shipping containers stacked on their shores.

There's the orange from Hapag-Lloyd of Germany; the bright yellow of Italy's Mediterranean Shipping Company; the orange-red of Japan's "K" Line; the eponymous color of Taiwan's Evergreen. The bright red of Hyundai and the reddish pinks of Kisac Global, both from Korea. OOCL's containers are red with white logos or the inverse; a plum blossom logo adorns all their boxes (perhaps evoking their early ties to Taiwan's Kuomintang). There's the creamy white of Hamburg Süd and the teal blue of Hanjin, the bright blue of Safmarine out of South Africa and the dark navy blue of Switzerland's CMA CGM. More anonymous containers in gray, brown, rust, and the occasional purple add to the visual effect. The names and logos tell the story of the truly global nature of the shipping trade. And in many ports around the world, the largest number of containers, by far, are light blue with a white seven-pointed star.

When Maersk broke into the transatlantic trade in 1936 (just as Shanghai was about to fall into violence and one year before OOCL's predecessor was opening its doors), the company owned thirty-eight ships. Global exports were worth $21 billion.[1] In the intervening decades, global trade ballooned, and so did shipping. By 2016, there were over 55,000 merchant ships registered globally, in more than 150 nations, manned by more than 1,500,000 seafarers.[2] And notwithstanding the pace of the competition, Maersk maintained its position as the largest shipping company in the world. In 2018, Maersk alone employed 88,000 people in 135 different countries and its 794 ships made nearly 90,000 port calls a year—240 per day, or one every six minutes.[3] Indeed, Maersk now sails just under one-fifth of all containers shipped worldwide.[4] It is effectively a global supply ship to the new world economy.

Maersk ships call on almost 350 ports around the world. But their largest destination by number of containers, by a huge measure: Yangshan Port. This highlights the essential fact that while China has returned to its historic place in the top ranks of world economies, its growth has not (as yet) created a separate economic sphere or a separate Asian-centered hub of economic activity. China has grown to its huge scale *within* the wider global economy.

And that in turn leads to another essential point. That containerized shipping didn't just help increase the scale and volume of trade; it transformed its nature. "Trade" is now all about the flow of components in a global supply chain—components that sail in mega container ships like the ones operated by Maersk.

The Voyage of the Madrid Maersk

Maersk claimed the top spot in largest container ships in June 1996, with the delivery of the *Regina Maersk*. It was the first ship in the world to cross the threshold of 6,000 TEU.[5,*] And in 1997, the shipyards delivered the *Sovereign Maersk*, which beat the *Regina* by topping out at 8,000 TEU.[6] In 2003, they briefly lost the top slot to OOCL. In 2006,

*When Marc Levinson wrote his landmark study on the economics of containerization, he was awed by the tremendous size to which container ships had then swelled: up to four thousand containers.

the *Emma Maersk* took back the record from the *OOCL Shenzhen*; it was capable of carrying 14,700 TEU.[7] In May 2010, the *Ebba Maersk* set the record at 15,011 TEU.[8] And then, in 2011, Maersk ordered the first of its "Triple-E" class ships, the *Maersk Mc-Kinney Møller*, which was delivered on June 14, 2013, with a carrying capacity of 18,000 TEU.[9] Within a couple of years, several other companies—CSM, MSC, COSCO—all took delivery of ships in the same TEU range. But Maersk kept the record for the top ship when it took delivery in 2017 of the *Madrid Maersk*, which became the first ship to break the 20,000 TEU barrier.[10]

It lost the top slot in 2018, again to OOCL, which took possession of the *OOCL Hong Kong*. But Maersk insists that its ship is actually bigger: OOCL measures its carrying capacity under an assumption that each container it is carrying weighs an average of five thousand pounds; Maersk assumes a seven-thousand-pound average container. By this measure, the *Madrid* is still larger than the *Hong Kong*.

One way or another, the *Madrid* is a monster of a ship.

It is so large, in fact, that the brain doesn't quite process the imagery of the ship when it's first sighted offshore. From the base of the dock of Yangshan Port, a ship the size of the *Madrid* becomes visible a few minutes after it rounds the outer harbor islands, ten miles away. When the *Madrid* is fully loaded, containers stacked twelve high above its deck, she's an awesome sight; but a confounding one. From that distance, the mild U shape of the hull almost disappears under the scale of the rectangle that sits above it, composed of all the containers above the deck and the upper stories of the hull itself. One of the factors of the post-Suez search for scale in bulk carriers was the use of much-wider-hulled ships. The *Madrid* takes this to an entirely new level, with a hull that's fully 193 feet wide. Together the wide, deep hull of the ship and the volume of boxes above produce a visual image that doesn't translate in the mind's eye as a ship: it looks more like a large city block of apartment towers or a giant factory, solid and rectangular—but confusingly, moving slowly toward you. If you took an entire city block of back-to-back twelve-story apartment buildings, two buildings deep, and floated them out to sea, the overall bulk of that rectangular block would be slightly *smaller* than the *Madrid*. Only as it gets closer does the gentle U of the hull reveal itself, and you can understand that this floating behemoth is actually a ship. The huge volume of global trade, four times the size of the American economy, is evident in the sheer visual scale of the *Madrid*.

We've become used to thinking of aircraft carriers as the giants of the ocean. The largest aircraft carrier in the world currently under sail is the USS *Nimitz*, which displaces ninety-seven thousand tons of water when at sea—displacement of water being the main way in which naval ships are compared for scale.[11] The *Nimitz* is indeed a substantial ship. But by contrast, the *Madrid* is more than twice its size, displacing fully 212,000 short tons of water when fully loaded.[12] You could take two of the USS *Nimitz*, stack them side by side on the *Madrid Maersk*, and still have room left over for the Empire State Building.

Climb the outer ladder onto the deck of the *Madrid* and what becomes apparent is that this is not just a ship; it's a floating factory. Containers are typically made of steel, with twenty-by-eight-by-eight-foot or forty-by-eight-by-eight-foot containers stacked on top of each other and held into place by bars separating each column. A typical twenty-foot container (1 TEU) has over 4,000 pounds of steel—so, if the *Madrid* were full, the containers alone would give her nearly 900 million pounds of steel, or 45,000 tons. As a point of comparison—the Burj Khalifa, the tallest building in the world, used 39,000 tons of steel in its construction.

Another way to experience the size of the *Madrid* is simply to walk the bridge. For a fit person of average height and a speedy gait it takes a full seven minutes and nine hundred paces to circumnavigate the ship's deck, a distance of three thousand feet. This is roughly the same time it takes to walk eight and a half football fields. Or: take the containers off the ship and lay them flat, stacked two high, the way they're carried on a transport train. Most people have had the experience of coming to a stop at a railroad crossing when a freight train is rumbling by at full speed. It can take up to two minutes for a cargo train with one hundred wagons to pass a crossing. But it would take *fifty* of these trains to carry the same load as the *Madrid*. Stacked back-to-back, the containers on board the *Madrid* would run for 411,360 feet, or seventy-eight miles.

But where the sheer enormity and the economic heft of the *Madrid* fully reveals itself is in the floor of the hold.

There are two different systems for stacking containers on a ship, above and below decks. Above decks, container ships feature a series of what are known as lashing towers—basically, a system of interlocking metal piping arrayed across the width of the ship and as high up as seven containers stacked one atop the other, to create a steel framework to which the stacked containers can be secured by crisscrossing aluminum poles. Each of these lashing towers is forty-four feet apart from the other, with just enough distance for an able-bodied seaman to operate in the narrow two-foot corridor thus created on either side of a forty-foot container. They're linked by a series of steel gangways and planks, bolted together between metal arches just taller than the height of an average man. Walking across these gangways, the experience is oddly like walking through an industrialized version of a cloister—the covered walkways with their arched ceilings, open on one side, that adorned old monasteries.

From the lowest level of the lashing towers, an able-bodied seaman can access the second storage system, in the hold. The U-shaped hull design means that, once the cargo floor doors are removed—an industrial operation in its own right, as each of these bay doors weighs several tons—there's a perfect rectangular shape into which the containers can be placed. Underneath the lashing towers are a series of steel walls that divide the hull into bays, also forty-four feet wide, with guide channels arrayed across their width at 8.8-foot gaps, into which the containers can neatly fit—twelve on top of one another.

To get to the bottom of one of these bays you first walk across the lowest gangway on a lashing tower to its center. From there, you swing yourself out into a porthole and, holding on to the rail, you lower your body into the ladder bay. A steep climb takes you to the first level down, below the hold but still above the waterline. Then the descent continues. Walk fifty feet to the side stair, which angles down at a pitch of sixty degrees, roughly twice as steep as normal stairs. On a ship you always walk forward as you descend, holding tight to the rails. Nine such staircases later, and you've walked down one hundred feet into the depth of the hold. Then you walk out of the arched doorways onto a metal floor—which on the *Madrid* is painted seafoam green.

And from there you crane your neck upward to the very top of the steel hull, the lashing towers and the containers above it. An immense wall of containers, twenty-four high by twenty-four wide, confronts you, twelve of the containers below and twelve above the hold, the top box towering above you at a height of 220 feet. It's just slightly higher than the spire of Canterbury Cathedral—but twenty-five times wider.

The *Madrid*, and ships like her, are the juggernauts of modern commerce, cathedrals of globalization.

* * *

Her thousands of containers are not stacked randomly; there's a complex set of calculations that goes into where they are placed on board. The variables include their weight and where they are destined to be unloaded so that containers for a specific port can be concentrated in a single bay, allowing operators at the next port to direct the effort of the cranes that load and unload these containers. But just as important: Are they carrying dangerous goods? For these containers hold not just innocuous items like clothes and TVs. They also contain critical industrial goods, from components for nuclear reactors to explosive chemicals to farm engines to lithium batteries to printer's ink. The goods inside these containers power much of American and European heavy industry.

On the *Madrid*, the job of making sure these containers are stacked safely belongs to a young Polish officer, Chief Officer Marcin Kulas. When the ship arrives in Yangshan to load and unload, the port captain comes on board to discuss the manifests and help certify contents. Marcin sits in front of a computer with a large screen running LodeStar software, in which the ship's full container stack is arrayed. Dangerous goods are marked red, safe ones marked green. A printout of the loading plan lies on the desk in front of him. It's Marcin's job to make sure he's cross-checked that the containers holding dangerous goods are properly distributed around the ship. The risk here is fire: many of these goods are flammable, and the specific contents require specific firefighting tools or chemicals. Fire in one container can easily start fire in the next, and if the chemical needed to douse the flames in the first isn't the same as what's needed for the second—or worse, can fuel that fire—you have a serious problem. So the distribution of dangerous goods containers is designed to limit the risk of a fire spreading. Officer Marcin pores over the details of this plan, double- and triple-checking the placement of every container. Like every other sailor on board, his first and often only thought is to get off the ship safely. He longs to be back home in Gdańsk with his wife and the son he adores, and the muscle cars that are his real passion in life.

Marcin is but one member of a crew whose backgrounds reflect both the international nature of trade and the history of seafaring nations. He's joined in the *Madrid* crew by Peter Bodgan Murat, a surly but ultimately charming Russian who serves as the number two engineer on board. There's Peter Paul Handrick, who started his career with Hapag-Lloyd and happily retired from a life at sea to Germany, where he bought and restored an old house—only to see it consumed by fire the next year. He went back to sea for the simple reason that he needed to make money, and found himself aboard a Maersk ship after Hapag-Lloyd was acquired by the Danish company. There's Andrew Hughes, a young trainee engineer from Manchester who started life as a banker but found it so boring that he restarted his education and took a certificate in maritime studies. The able-bodied seamen who crew the ship, from shop floor to construction bay to engine room, hail from older ship-faring nations like India, Thailand, and the Philippines. Their leader is Richard Corporalz, a Filipino from Mindanao island whose thick beard, rolling mustache, and large earrings make him look like he's been planted on board for a film shoot about old-world piracy.

The job of captaining these men and maneuvering this gargantuan ship through the troubled waters of the East and South China Seas, and later through the tangled Singapore Strait, belongs to Captain Mikkel Jensen, a modern-day Viking if there ever was one, replete with a tattoo of a dragon snaking across his muscular chest. The rest of his arms and torso are covered with the tattoos that sailors get to symbolize specific passages and voyages—an anchor to symbolize first passage across the Atlantic, a rigged ship for passage around the Cape of Good Hope, the dragon actually a marker of first passage to China. He stands five foot seven, with sandy-blond hair cut short, and eschews the formal shirt and long pants of the captain's dress uniform; he prefers khaki shorts and Teva sandals, and a white Maersk polo shirt.

Captain Jensen was born in 1975 on the Danish island of Funen, where the Shipbuilding Company of 1916 was founded. He first encountered the sea not through his family, but through school. When he was just sixteen, a local ship captain came to talk to his high school class about careers at sea, and his imagination was captured by the oceans.

He set sail for the first time in January of 1995 as a ship's cook. He hurt his back in an early accident and decided the job of a cook was not for him. He applied to seaman's school, was rejected by Maersk, but accepted by and trained through the Faroe School of Navigation, where he earned his master's license. He landed a job at Esvast Shipping, sailing standby rescue vessels near the oil rigs in the North Sea—one of the most turbulent and dangerous bodies of water on the planet.[13] It was extreme training in navigation. He did it for eight months and then applied to Maersk, and this time was accepted into the company, in April 2001. By 2012, at the ripe old age of thirty-six, he had become a captain, and in 2017 was given the command of one of Maersk's three flagship ultra-large container ships.

Captains of these mega-containers are on call around the clock when aboard, so they work in shifts of several weeks at a time before being relieved by a co-captain. This means that they share a cabin, and so can't overly personalize it when aboard. What's more, you can't have anything on a ship that can't be bolted to a wall or closed inside a cabin during rough seas. So in Mikkel's cabin there are only these bare essentials: a picture of his wife, his muscle-building vitamins and supplements, and a Danish flag.

To be the captain of the *Madrid* is to be in charge of an enormously complex floating city of metal, electronics, legal arrangements, crew responsibilities, and up to $1 billion worth of cargo. But for Mikkel, first and foremost on his mind are things that seem almost prosaic, given the volume of cargo that he is responsible for delivering. "At the start of every voyage, I have to think about two basic things first. Do I have enough fuel? And do I have enough food?"

There's also the simple but enormously important business of checking and double-checking and triple-checking the draft of the ship as it enters and exits the shallow waters of ports, whose clearance can be as little as seven feet below the hull. The precise stacking of the containers shifts the weight of the ship. The weather, tides, the total weight of the cargo, its distribution; all these variables go into a complex calculation as to whether and how the ship can enter and moor at its berth. When leaving port, the captain is laser-focused on these maneuvers, using every modern and old-fashioned navigational aide at his disposal. In some places, it gets enormously complex and fraught to move through the narrow passage of a channel approaching a dock. "It's a massive challenge; you have a couple of meters on either side, a couple of feet below you. Any mistake and you're going to end up running aground."

The minute Captain Mikkel maneuvers out of the inner harbor and heads out to open waters, his mind turns to his bigger fear.

For smaller ships, storms and the prospect of sinking at sea are an ever-present worry. But the sheer size of the *Madrid* and ships like her changes the equation. By most accounts, for a wave to sink a ship it has to rise to a height slightly longer than the ship itself. Under some circumstances, a ship that confronts such a wave may not be able to crest it and can be driven down into the hollow that forms underneath monster waves, flipped on its end. Scientists have theorized about the possibility of 190-foot waves, but no wave of that size has ever been reported in real conditions.[14] The largest wave ever recorded at sea was around 140 feet.[15] At that height a wave confronting the *Madrid* would be barely more than a tenth of the length of the ship and pose no threat to its stability.[16] A slightly greater concern is for the ship rolling on its beam. The same calculation applies. If a wave is taller than a ship is wide, it can, in theory, turn the vessel on its side as the ship rides up its face. This occurs only in very rare and extreme conditions, but it is conceivable.[17] But even there, for the *Madrid* with its beam of 190 feet, no wave ever reported would be wide enough to roll the boat onto its side. Weather is not the enemy of the mega-container ships.

When new crew or passengers board the *Madrid*, they're handed two keys. The first unlocks their cabin door in the fourteen-story accommodation tower that anchors the front third of the ship.* The second is designed to save their lives. Ships can flounder for a number of reasons. But for a modern container ship, the big fear is not breach or crash; it's fire.

Fire can start because of electrical trouble in the engine, because

*The placement of the accommodation tower in the front third of the ship was an important innovation of Maersk's Triple-E line ships. When the accommodation tower and bridge are at the rear of the ship, as is traditional, the need to have sight lines from the bridge over the prow of the ship limits the height of container stacks that are possible. By moving the bridge forward, Maersk was able to add three layers of container stacks to its ships.

the oily rags they use to clean the engine can combust when stacked together in their container bins, or because the dangerous cargo in the containers themselves can combust in the heat, which can rise as high as 129 degrees Fahrenheit when sailing through the South China Sea.[18] The ship contains innumerable firefighting devices, foams, waters, and other materials designed to put out the fires for the specific kind of chemicals or other accelerants that could be found in the engine or in containers. A complex system of fire alarms runs across the entirety of the ship and through each of the container stacks so that the fire situation can be monitored 24/7 by the captain or his chief officers from the bridge. But in the end, fire is fire and all the preventive measures don't necessarily suffice to stop it from breaking out. And if a fire gets out of control, sometimes the only option the crew has is to abandon ship.

When they do, they use a survival boat made famous in the movie *Captain Phillips*, which showed the captain escaping the MV *Maersk Alabama* in the face of a pirate attack. Maersk ships, and many like them, carry rescue crafts that look more like submarines, forged of a single, cylindrical hard plastic shell and painted vibrant orange. These ships are loaded full of safety devices, twelve days' supply of water, and old-school navigation equipment.

But before climbing into the escape craft, the crew do something else. They use the second key to unlock a large chest on the bridge beside the escape vessel that contains both life vests and ultra-modern survival suits. These are cherry-red neoprene suits that weigh almost ten pounds and are extraordinarily cumbersome to climb into. The basic procedure is to lay the suit flat on the deck, lie down beside it, and stuff yourself into it feet-first, the way you would into a sleeping bag. Pull the legs up and secure them around your feet. Make sure that there's no excess air or water in the boots. Then zip the suit up to midriff and, one by one, place your hands in the giant sleeves, working your fingers into the mitts. Then, fumbling through the thick neoprene, pull the hood over your head and zip the rest of the suit up to neck height. Now, encased in two inches of neoprene from head to toe, you can survive for up to twelve hours in 0 degree waters. Only then do you enter the escape vehicle. The hatch is closed, and the first officer pulls a lever inside the ship that releases it from an anchoring crane, and the escape ship descends at high speed along guy wires to sea level, where it's launched into the ocean. It's an intensely cumbersome procedure from start to finish, but Mikkel ensures that every crew member and every passenger is *repeatedly* drilled through all the necessary safety and evacuation procedures—especially when it comes to fire.

On calm days at sea, Mikkel revels in his job. "My favorite times are when the winds are completely quiet. The waters are still, and you can barely see a ripple. The ocean takes on a glassy quality, like you're sailing across ice. I can see every detail of the ship in the mirrored reflection of the water. For hours I can watch the sea like that, and I never get tired of it." Listening to him describe his love of the calm seas brings to mind a passage from Mark Twain's Atlantic travelogue: "There is nothing like this serenity, this comfort, this peace, this deep contentment to be found anywhere on land. If I had my way I would sail on forever and never go live on the solid ground again."[19]

Much as he thrills to his job, when it's a simple matter of him and the ship and the crew, Mikkel is somewhat nostalgic for an older time in the industry. "It used to be that when a captain came off the ship, they had to go immediately to see A. P. Møller [the old CEO], to tell him what we'd seen. To tell him of the way things were working on the front lines, how things were going in markets like Nigeria and Saudi Arabia and Brazil. But that was before we had global information. I guess it's not needed anymore. But there was something good about the old ways."

What particularly annoys him is micromanagement from afar. When a loud ping indicates a new email message from headquarters updating the course or causing him to change speeds or slow down or speed up or reroute, he'll break into a loud bout of swearing: "*For helvede!* (Goddamn it!)" He bridles against the micromanagement of route planners and technicians more than seven thousand miles away. "They have no idea what conditions we face, what it means to slow down a ship like this, the price we pay in wasted fuel. They change the times of when we arrive and when we leave on a whim, and everything we plan is blown away!"

He may rail against it, but he can't escape it. Even at night with the lights turned off, the quiet on the bridge is interrupted every few minutes by the high-pitched ping of a signal that a new message has been received. Some of these are dramatic, like a launch of new naval military maneuvers nearby; others are banal in their simplicity—an update from the company on bunkering procedures or new human resources rules. Some of the messages relay weather updates, many of them irrelevant to the ship's actual journey. The most important provide updates from ships passing through the channels ahead, or from port operators, updating plans and conditions on their voyage moving forward. Captain Mikkel may not like it, but this is a reality of modern shipping—the ever-present flow of data.

All this data flows to a series of computer terminals and VHF and satellite receivers at the epicenter of the ship, the bridge, two hundred feet above the deck. On a vessel the size of the *Madrid*, the lateral width of the bridge is simply enormous, over two hundred feet, the same width as the wingspan of a 747, with huge glass-encased wings that span out the entire width of the ship and just beyond, to allow the captain to see either side of the hull as they're maneuvering into port. In front and behind, huge windshield wipers clean each of the sixty windows, keeping them clear from rain and mist.*

In the middle of the South China Sea, that view could not be more different than the clogged Singapore Strait. The South China Sea is the most important economic sea-lane of commerce in the world, and at midday, midweek, the busiest time for shipping, a 360-degree view from the bridge shows a calm, green-blue sea, flecked with the white foam churned up by the *Madrid*'s bow—and with not a single ship in sight to the east, west, south, or north. For hours on end, the captain takes turns with the first officer, scanning the horizon with binoculars while he keeps a close eye on the radar, but no ships cross the *Madrid*'s path for long parts of the day. So large, so wide, is even this bounded sea that the vastness of the world's oceanic trade shrinks to the size of a single ship surrounded in all directions by empty waters.

At the center of the bridge is the steering console, centered around

*Captain Jensen is fastidious about cleanliness. During his first tour on the *Madrid*, he was frustrated by the frequent tracking of dirt onto the wings of the bridge. So he bought a small robotic vacuum cleaner that constantly moves up and down the floors, cleaning as it goes. But at night, it's easy to trip over the small black circular object. So now, the vacuum is adorned with a bright pink plastic pig—an incongruous feature on the otherwise pristine lines of the bridge.

a small steering wheel, a small joystick, and a throttle, much like those found in an airplane cockpit. The only old-fashioned part of the bridge is a telephone receiver that the captain can use to call specific crew members to the bridge or to sound the general alarm. Immediately in front of the steering console is a screen that shows the propulsion, direction, and drag: this gives the actual position of the ship in the water. It connects to a series of additional screens, which are in turn connected to satellite, email, and VHF, and all come together in what's called the Integrated Bridge System, which gives the captain a rich data picture of the seas around and ahead. That includes a gyrocompass, a depth sounder, a speed log, satellite navigation, radar, and the ECDIS—the Electronic Chart Display and Information System, a one-stop data-gathering system that shows the ship relative to sea features, currents, and surrounding ships. Those ships, and the *Madrid*, all continuously ping what's known as AIS data. Similar to the black box on airplanes, but more sophisticated, the Automatic Identification System constantly updates with the name, type, heading, and direction of every registered ship on the water—generating hundreds of millions of data points per minute, all computed and calculated and processed back into a real-time image of the sea traffic in front of the bridge.

This information should be enough but for this fact: most naval ships don't relay their AIS data. They are exempt, as ships don't have to share that data if doing so would undermine their security. And what's more, not all fishing ships have an AIS transponder; they're supposed to, but some don't.[20] So the AIS data would ensure that you didn't bump into another container ship or oil tanker, but it wouldn't stop you from bumping into a naval frigate, or running a fishing trawler under your keel.* So radar is still an essential tool for avoiding hitting ships in the night. This is data-enhanced radar, though: use the embedded mouse to right click on the radar signature of a ship and the screen displays a dotted line showing the ship's direction in time. The captain can see whether he's on course to pass or to intersect, at which point he'll execute a slight course correction. A slight tap on the joystick is all it takes.

*The dangers of this were recognized in 2017, when two US Navy ships collided with civilian tankers in the space of nine weeks near Japan and Singapore, respectively. See Robert Faturechi, Megan Rose, and T. Christian Miller, "Years of Warnings, Then Death and Disaster: How the Navy Failed Its Sailors," ProPublica, February 7, 2019.

To be on the safe side, Mikkel also uses an older, more traditional piece of equipment: a pair of binoculars. Walk onto the bridge at any time of day, and a second officer or able-bodied seaman is standing in front of the windows just to the left of the captain, constantly scanning the horizon for ships or their lights, and tracking those positions to confirm that there's no error in the radar or AIS data.

All this data is collected and collated at Maersk's global data management center, in Copenhagen. This center processes millions of pieces of data an hour, 24/7.

While the big numbers of the *Madrid Maersk* and the global container trade astound, their impact really lies in the contrast between these great numbers and small ones. The number twenty-three, for example. That is the number of souls, from captain to engineer to crew to cooks, who maneuver this gargantuan ship through its worldwide sail. When Peter Maersk steamed his SS *Laura* around the Baltic Sea in 1910, his ship could hold a maximum of 165,000 cubic feet of cargo, or the equivalent of 121 TEU. His ship had a crew of twenty-four. So the *Madrid* represents more than a 17,000 percent gain in the labor efficiency of cargo shipping—and that's before you factor in the huge gains of efficiency in the loading and unloading onto the ships and the transfer to truck and train of the same containers.*

Another small number: six inches by four inches by two inches deep, weighing in at eight pounds. That's the size of a locking clamp, a forged piece of metal engineered and painted yellow with two pull tabs inserted on each side. The locking clamp, as its name suggests, locks together the feet of a container box to the one below or to the lashing tower. For seven containers above the hold, the lashing towers provide a fixed metal structure to which aluminum ties can affix the containers. Above that, it's only the locking clamps that hold them together. For five stories of boxes above the lashing towers, these six-by-four metal clamps are the only thing holding together over $1 billion worth of cargo.

*And the scale keeps growing. On the bridge of the *Madrid*, the crew were gossiping about the rumors that someone was going to unveil a 24,000 TEU ship. They were right: in September 2019, MSC sailed a ship carrying 23,736 TEU out of Tainjin, China.

The critical role of the clamp is evident when the ship enters harbor and the crew prepares to unload and load seven thousand containers in the course of twenty-four hours.[21] These small metal devices are key—they are what allow the containers to fit securely on cargo trains or in the back of prime movers or transport trucks, which we now see everywhere on our roads and highways. They are what make intermodality—the ability to move seamlessly between modes of transport—a reality. In effect, this tiny metal object is what locks together modern globalization.

Beyond Free Trade

The standard conception of free trade, from Adam Smith and David Ricardo on, is a simple one. A specific country—let's say Portugal—is good at producing a specific product, either because it has a special geography or growing conditions, like those that nurture Portugal's cork oaks, the trees from which cork is harvested and then used to produce its distinctive port wine. Another country, say England, could in theory plant cork oak trees and develop a related industry. But it would be extremely inefficient for it to do so; it doesn't have the right weather or the right soil. What it does have, in abundance, is efficient cloth production. So the more efficient thing is for Portugal to buy cloth from England and England to buy wine from Portugal. Both sides save substantially by doing so and also diversify the products available to their citizens. This kind of specialization and comparative advantage giving rise to trade in agriculture and manufactured goods were the essential ingredients in the earliest forms of trade, and in the large-scale growth in eighteenth- and nineteenth-century trade, from opium to tea to spices to iron ore.[22]

This is still an important part of trade in *agricultural* goods. The Caribbean has comparative advantage in banana growing, and the Philippines in pineapples. So these countries grow massive quantities of those products and sell them to American and European markets that cannot grow them efficiently (or in some cases at all). And the market for transport in agricultural goods expanded after a further innovation in global container shipping, the refrigerated container (or "reefer," as it's somewhat oddly known in the shipping industry). Reefers allow for a huge variety of agricultural goods to be shipped around the world, in all seasons.[23]

Maersk was among the early innovators in reefer technology and it's now an important part of their business model. The fact that you can buy fresh bananas (and mangoes and pineapples) in Safeway in the US in December is because Maersk and OOCL and Hapag-Lloyd and others take huge volumes of them from ports in the Caribbean to ports across the United States.[24] Bananas are the fourth most valuable food product in the world, after wheat, rice, and milk.[25] Writing about the global container trade in 2013, Rose George noted that a single container ship (at that time, the largest of them held 15,000 TEUs) could transport a whopping 746 million bananas on board a single container vessel.[26] Now, the largest ship could carry more than 1.2 billion.

But the more important part of the global economy doesn't work like this at all. When it comes to *industrialized* goods, in fact, the whole concept of "trade" is outmoded. With containerization and computerization—and the marriage of the two pioneered by C. H. Tung in the 1980s—what happened was actually a fundamental shift in the way we produce manufactured goods the world over.[27]

Containerization together with advances in shipping design and computer technology took the concept of "just in time" production and made it global. Just-in-time manufacturing is an organizational and management theory that has its roots in Japan in the 1960s and '70s that aims to reduce inefficiencies in production systems and to improve the time from supply to delivery. To do this, it relies on producing items just as they are ordered. So, for example, instead of building a red Toyota Corolla and letting it sit in inventory until someone buys it, you wait until someone orders it and then very rapidly assemble it. And if they order a blue one, or one with a sunroof, or one with manual transmission, that's what you build. It's a way of being highly responsive to consumer demand. For this system to work, exact parts and supplies need to be delivered on short notice. The second part of this management philosophy was that it drew an important distinction between firms that built *parts* of goods and firms that assembled them into a finished product—it took specialization and moved it further up the production chain. This system was developed largely by Japanese firms for their domestic production. But with the combination of containerization and computerization, it was possible to take that model and make it global.[28] And now much of what is manufactured is produced as part of a global just-in-time process that connects the US Midwest with Stuttgart, Germany, and Hanoi, Vietnam—and above all, China.

You can see this dynamic in the cargo manifests and sailing routes of the world's great shipping companies: CSM, Safmarine, Evergreen, and of course OOCL and Maersk. The Maersk routes connect the world's manufacturing powerhouses in Asia and Africa to big consumer states in the West. Shanghai is its largest destination, by number of containers and by value of what's in them. And from there many head due east to Los Angeles and Long Beach, the twin hubs of the LA-area port. Or to Tacoma and Seattle, twin hubs of trade in the Northwest. But more of them sail south, through the East China Sea and the troubled waters of the Taiwan Strait, and into the world's most important waterway, the South China Sea.[29] From there to the choked Singapore Strait and the dangerous Malacca Strait. And then across the vastness of the Indian Ocean, past the island of Perim and up the Red Sea to Suez. From there, they sail across the Mediterranean on to the ports of Rotterdam and Felixstowe, or on to routes across the Americas. The most profitable trip goes from Shanghai all the way to the East Coast of the United States—New York, Boston, and Charleston. This constant flow of containers feeds the European and American markets with a steady flow of manufacturing inputs, as well as assembled goods—part of the worldwide network of production that economists call the "global supply chain."

A lot of what America consumes today is produced this way. Take the iPhone—the signature product of America's most valuable company. This is an American-designed product, to be sure, and American owned; but there's very little about it that's American made. Its accelerometer (used to measure movement) is supplied by the German company Bosch, but manufactured in their plants in China, Korea, Japan, and Taiwan. The audio chip comes from Cirrus Logic, an American firm—that manufactures its components in the UK, China, Korea, Japan, and Singapore. The battery is made by Korea's Samsung in plants in more than eighty countries worldwide. The camera: Qualcomm, which is based in the US, but manufactured in Brazil, Australia, Indonesia, India, and East Asia. The gyroscope comes from Switzerland, the flash memory from Japan, the touchscreen controller from Israel, Greece, the Netherlands, Belgium, or France, the Wi-Fi chip from some of the countries already mentioned or Mexico, Canada, Thailand, Malaysia, the Philippines, Germany, Hungary, France, Italy, or Finland. The iconic glass screen is designed by an established American firm, Corning—but manufactured in plants in Australia, Belgium, Brazil, China, Denmark, France, Germany, Hong Kong, India, Israel, Japan, Korea, Malaysia, Mexico, the Philippines, Poland, Russia, Singapore, South Africa, Spain, Taiwan, the Netherlands, Turkey, the UK, and the United Arab Emirates.[30] Overall, any given iPhone may have parts manufactured in more than thirty countries in Asia, Europe, Latin America, and the Middle East. And almost every component is transported by ship at some point along the production voyage.

Similar patterns are reflected even in simple products. Think of Nutella. Imported from Italy, right? Yes, but produced with sugar from Brazil, India, Mexico, and Australia; palm oil from Indonesia and Malaysia; hazelnuts from Turkey, Argentina, Georgia, South Africa, Australia, or Serbia; cocoa from Côte d'Ivoire, Nigeria, and Ghana; lecithin from Brazil, India, and Italy; and vanillin, a synthetic version of vanilla, from China. (The milk is relatively local; it comes from Switzerland.)[31] And those ingredients are put together in many different regions—five factories in Europe, one in Russia, one in North America, two in South America, and one in Australia as of 2012. So, a jar of Nutella requires imports from at least eleven countries and is distributed to some seventy-five countries for sale.[32,*]

All of this is made possible by high-volume, low-cost container shipping, which for economic purposes all but erases the comparative advantage of geography. In the past, shipping costs were a significant

*Sometimes this dynamic reaches absurd levels. A common Norwegian food is salmon. It's caught locally; but before you can purchase your meal in a Norwegian supermarket, a large amount of Norwegian salmon is frozen, shipped to China, fileted in factories there, and shipped back to Norway via Singapore or Tanjung Pelepas for consumer consumption. (It helps explain one of the strangest sights of contemporary globalization: ATMs dispensing filets of Norwegian salmon in shopping malls and hotel lobbies across Singapore.)

barrier to a producer in England competing with a producer in Pittsburgh for the Massachusetts market—but now the cost of shipping by container from Manchester to Boston is so small that it's easily competitive with the cost of trucking it across two states. And the same is true for a low-cost manufacturer in Malaysia, or Thailand, or Brazil. The Gap, a ubiquitous retailer, likes to emphasize its American identity in its advertisements and promotional efforts; the *New York Times* described it as being "as American as Mickey Mouse."[33] In fact, Gap and Old Navy clothes are designed in San Francisco but manufactured in Southeast Asia—primarily in India, Vietnam, Cambodia, and Bangladesh, using Vietnamese and Laotian cotton—and then sent worldwide for consumption, in ever-larger container ships.[34]

The sheer volume of what is imported this way is staggering. In 2018, the port of Los Angeles alone imported 579,405 TEUs of furniture; 373,934 TEUs of auto parts; 354,578 of clothing; 233,157 of footwear; and 218,554 of electronics.[35] That's only 18.5 percent of the total TEUs imported just into Los Angeles in a single year. But even those 1.7 million boxes carry an astonishing quantity of goods when you realize that a single forty-foot container can carry: two cars; 60 refrigerators; 200 mattresses; 400 flat-screen TVs; 1,500 cases of Coke; 4,000 boxes of shoes; 7,800 reams of paper; or 9,600 bottles of wine.[36]

* * *

Thus is much of what is consumed in the United States reliant on a constant flow of containers into the American market. Whether it ends up scanned through the Central Examination Station in Elizabeth, New Jersey, or in one of the other major port complexes that dominate American trade, American consumption often starts with containerized flows. And this has transformed the American economy because the container revolution has all but erased shipping costs as a factor in modern production. In the words of Marc Levinson: "Shipping costs no longer sheltered producers whose advantage was proximity to the customer. Even with customs duties and time delays, factories in Malaysia could deliver blouses to Macy's in Herald Square more cheaply than blouse manufacturers in the heart of New York's garment district."[37] And so US manufacturing, with its relatively high labor costs, started losing out to low-cost manufacturers in Asia, Africa, and Latin America, as containerization enabled those countries to sell their products into the American market. And with this development went manufacturing jobs—roughly 2.4 million of them.[38]

Containerization was a key ingredient in the Western economic boom of the 1970s and '80s, but by the 1990s and 2000s it was also a key driver in the deindustrialization of the American economy. Look at a container traveling on a train through the center of town or on a prime mover driving down Interstate 95 and you're seeing a manufacturing job that's gone to Asia, the hollowing out of western Pennsylvania and eastern Ohio, the decimation of the steel and auto industries of the northeast. This loss of manufacturing jobs in the United States is increasingly blamed on China's entry into the World Trade Organization, which was certainly a key factor, but China—and Vietnam and Malaysia and Taiwan and India—couldn't have absorbed US manufacturing jobs were it not for the connective tissue of the global supply ships that flow low-cost manufactured goods at low transportation cost into the American economy.[39]

This fact reveals the broader consequence for the United States of the containerization and shipping revolution, the worldwide spread of globalization, and the emergence of a global supply chain. But every one of those ships and every one of those containers has been accompanied by a very different kind of value proposition for the US economy, and specifically the financial firms that ring the New York harbor: nearly 90 percent of that flow in goods is traded in US dollars.[40] When China sells farm engines to India, when India sells cotton to Brazil, when Brazil sells soybeans to Germany, when Germany sells car parts to Russia, when Russia sells steel to the United States—all these goods are shipped around the world on container or bulk cargo ships, and all of them are paid for in US dollars. And as those countries grow, so do their global investments—much of which occurs in US dollars. Every single one of those dollars is processed by American financial firms, and roughly 70 percent of them are tracked by American accounting firms. And these American firms generate huge profits.

What this highlights is that containerization has helped drive deep change in the American economy. In the 1930s, global trade was a fractional part of US economic activity. In the 1960s, the same was true. By the 1980s, the US economy was roughly 10 percent driven by global trade; an important change, but still a small amount by the standards of global economies. But fast-forward to 2015, and now fully 30 percent of the US economy is driven by the flow of global trade and the investment and services that it generates.[41] In the words of President George W. Bush's undersecretary for policy at the US Department of Transportation: "The U.S. intermodal freight system—now seamlessly integrated into the global supply chain—underpins the nation's economic growth and prosperity."[42]

This is a critical part of a wider reality, which is that economic growth worldwide—whether it is recorded in China, India, Russia, Vietnam, Brazil, or elsewhere—has been matched by growth in American jobs in financing, accounting, logistics management, marketing, and design; collectively, the service industry. These are high-paying, high-education jobs. Against the 2.4 million manufacturing jobs lost to low-cost manufacturing in China and the rest of Asia, service jobs were created by the same phenomenon—just over 7 million of them.[43]

Watch a container move from rail to truck to ship and you may be watching the hollowing out of American manufacturing, but you're also watching the expansion of the American service sector, the creation of jobs in accounting, and huge net profits to the American economy. In 1947, American financial firms accounted for 10 percent of the profits recorded in the non-farm sectors of the American economy. Now, after seven decades of expanding trade, they account for fully 50 percent of the non-farm profits in the American economy.[44,*]

But—and the importance of this cannot be understated—those profits are enjoyed by a decreasingly small proportion of the American population. That is to say, globalized trade and investment and the accompanying financialization are a key driver of the growing inequality of the American economy. And that's creating tensions pushing back *against* globalization.

This financialization of the American economy, and the huge weight and power it gives to people who work within the two-mile radius of the Port of New York—and the Port of Seattle, the Port of Houston, the Port of Los Angeles—has torqued the politics of the United States. The consolidation of wealth and power of the major cities, and the financial

*Economists refer to this development as the "financialization" of the American economy.

class, versus the hollowing out of the American heartland, was a factor behind the global financial crisis, the lack of accountability from that crisis, and the rise of populist anger in America's rust belt and inland states.[45] It fed into the election of Donald Trump, the popularity of Bernie Sanders, the January 6, 2021, riot in Washington, DC, and the erosion of political support for America's expansive role in the world.[46]

After his 2016 election, President Trump was often seen carrying a map of his victory. It showed an enormous sea of red across the entire country, with a scattered set of small blue dots along the coast (and occasionally inland). Turn the map into 3-D, though, so that it reflects population concentration, and a very different picture emerges. There's Republican red across much of the country where it's largely flat, but in the forty or so places that spike up indicating large populations, the vast majority of them are Democratic blue.[47] Cities now account for 84 percent of the GDP of the United States, and the difference between urban and rural in both politics and economics is a major feature of modern-day America.[48] And the largest of these cities are closely linked to sea-based trade.

* * *

Meanwhile, America's key role in global finance and the growing spread of global trade has created a key imbalance: one that pits globalized economics against America's international security roles. Why? If containerization, globalization, and financialization opened up an economic and political imbalance within the United States, it also created a second imbalance between the role that the US Navy plays in securing the flow of trade (and energy) across the world's oceans, *and who profits from it.*

At the end of World War II, when the United States Navy took over from the Royal Navy in that critical global role, it was the US itself—then accounting for 50 percent of the world economy—and its wartime European allies that primarily profited from global trade.[49] As Japan became a postwar ally and a democracy and entered global markets, it grew as well, as did, later, the Asian democracies and Asian allies—Korea, Taiwan, Singapore. The West as a whole profited from the flow of trade goods from New York to Rotterdam to Sydney to Yokohama. In short, the US Navy was securing the trade of its allies.[50]

Those allies have grown rich during the ensuing several decades.

Their growth is critically dependent on the role of the US Navy in protecting the sea-lanes of commerce. What role do these actors play in securing the high seas and protecting the flow of trade? What share of the cost do they bear?

What's more, as the entry of China and Russia into the WTO (and the opening of India and Brazil and Malaysia and many others) changed the geography of global commerce, so, too, did the dynamics of the relationship between trade and security begin to change. Fast-forward to the present day, and the US Navy is securing a flow of trade in goods and energy that profits China and Russia—hardly allies, increasingly adversaries.[51] For how much longer will the United States agree to play the role of protecting the flow of sea-based trade for wealthy allies and potential enemies?

* * *

These issues were very much on C. H. Tung's mind in 2019. Indeed, they had been ever since US-China tensions began to flare up in the South China Sea. The trade war that started in 2017 was even worse. For OOCL, whose whole history had been about using the seas and Hong Kong to bring China back into the world and forge close ties with the West, this erosion of relations between China and the United States was disastrous, both politically and financially.

What's more, the industry was changing. The technological advantages that had kept OOCL ahead of its competitors in the 1990s and early 2000s had spread across the industry. C. H. Tung watched his father's company lose its cutting edge. It was still the largest shipping firm in Asia, and in 2018 again deployed the largest ship in the world, the *OOCL Hong Kong*. But the dynamics of the industry were not on OOCL's side. "We held our lead because of our technology. But when Maersk caught up with us in technology, they were so much bigger in scale, there was no way we could compete. I discussed it with our colleagues internally. We decided that over time there were only going to be five or six genuinely global shipping companies. And to compete at that scale, we were going to have to put in a huge amount of capital. I decided to sell instead."

And sell he did, to COSCO Shipping Lines, out of Beijing. There are multiple ironies here. Tung's father fled Shanghai for Hong Kong to escape the takeover by the Communist Party of China. He turned his company and with it the Port of Hong Kong into the critical node of Western globalization in Asia. The return of Hong Kong to China critically aided China's penetration of the global market, and its economic rise. And the same factors that generated China's growth led to changes in the shipping industry that ultimately compelled OOCL to sell itself—to a company ultimately under the direction of the Communist Party of China.[52]

To C. H. Tung's generation, the quest for stability trumps all in international affairs—and that stability is essential, too, to Hong Kong's financial and commercial fortunes.[53] It's a stability that, for many decades, was maintained by Beijing's respect for Hong Kong's separate system; it's now badly eroded by China's crackdown. And it was maintained by a broader stability in US-China relations.

Peace was the underlying condition for Hong Kong's growth. But peace is not where the United States and China are headed.

PART III

The Flag Follows the Trade

From the clogged Singapore Strait, at the southern end of the South China Sea, the shipping lanes flow north to the wide Vietnamese waters. The Malay Peninsula lies to the west, beyond visible range, and the storied island of Borneo to the east. The traffic and the congestion ease. Here, and for two to three days steaming north, by all appearances the South China Sea is an open, flowing body of water. Containers and tankers cruise the main channel with room to spare. For all of the volume of sea trade through this sea, its scale is such that, at many moments, only three or four vessels can be seen within a fifty-nautical-mile range. The dark blue waters are lightly flecked with white as gentle breezes blow across its expanse (except in typhoon season), and ships sailing its channels are chased by seabirds, mostly streaked shearwaters and white terns, that glide above the bow waves, occasionally diving into the waters to catch the fish churned up by the movement of the ships. From the bustle and claustrophobia of the Singapore Strait, the wide sea imparts a sense of space and calm.

Appearances can be deceiving.

At 01:58:27 in the morning of August 24, 2019, the quiet on the bridge of the *Madrid Maersk* was broken by an incoming message on what's known as the worldwide Enhanced Group Call system, broadcast through Inmarsat satellites. The header was "Urgency EGC Received," and it was titled NAVAREA XI WARNING: JAPAN SEA. It read, "North Korea probably launched ballistic missile from North Korea, on 24 Aug. The launched ballistic missile estimated [*sic*] landed outside of Japanese EEZ in the Japan Sea. Vessels are requested to pay attention to further information and to keep clear when recognizing falling object. Vessels are requested to report related information to Japan Coast Guard."*

*Author's notes, *Madrid Maersk*, August 24, 2019.

There was an immediate domino effect across the seas along China's eastern coast—what it calls its "Near Seas." Later that morning, a further EGC message warned of new naval maneuvers by the Philippine navy in the area off the coast of that country's archipelago, in the easternmost waters of the South China Sea. The Japan Maritime Self-Defense Force (Japan's navy) was put on high alert in the East China Sea. And in the early afternoon came warning of live-fire exercises by Taiwan's navy, just south of the narrow strait between the Chinese mainland and the island of Taiwan. At midday at Lat 22*37, Lon 119*44, west off the southern tip of the Taiwan Strait, five Taiwanese frigates, equipped with ship-to-ship missiles, raced across the bow of the *Madrid*, steaming at thirty knots in the direction of the Philippine Sea.

And later that day, at a distance of two miles, an Aegis-class destroyer of the US Navy sailed northwest of the *Madrid*'s position. It was shadowed by a Chinese frigate, equipped with ship-to-ship "harpoon" missiles, keeping a careful eye on the American vessel. Far from the expansive calm of the prior day, for the better part of an afternoon the *Madrid*, and two other container ships sailing nearby, found themselves uncomfortably positioned between the American and Chinese ships as they maneuvered to maintain close watch on one another.

And beneath the waters, a plethora of submarines—Chinese, American, Japanese, and Russian—maneuvered for position.*

* * *

In recent years, the South China Sea has been the subject of a lot of discussion of US-China tensions. To be sure, for the Chinese navy to be actively patrolling in those waters and going nose-to-nose with the American navy represents a huge change in Chinese strategic thinking—a break with a nearly five-hundred-year tradition in Chinese foreign policy. It's a change that's reshaping the world as we know it.

But it goes well beyond that sea. The instant response to the communication of the North Korean missile test by Asian navies across the Japan Sea, the East China Sea, the Taiwan Strait, and the Philippine Sea tells us immediately that the dynamics of major power tension in Asia

*In 2019, it was estimated that more than two hundred full-size submarines were operating in the East and South China Seas alone. Zhenhau Lu, "US and China's Underwater Rivalry Fuels Calls for Submarine Code of Conduct to Cut Risk of Accidents," *South China Morning Post*, March 21, 2019.

is not limited to the turbulent south. Rather, the whole of the Western Pacific is in play. The Western Pacific is becoming to today what East Germany was to the Cold War: the front line of tensions between the world's leading military powers.[1] Its deep waters have replaced the European heartland as the fault line of geopolitical tension.

Some of the competing players, like Japan and Russia, are former imperial naval rivals in Asia. As is the United States, in effect: although the US has only had a global blue-water navy since the end of World War II, it has a far longer history in Asia's waters, where it has been sailing continuously since the mid-1820s, when US Navy schooners followed American merchant ships across the Pacific.[2] And tensions are not limited to the Western Pacific: the Indian, Arctic, and perhaps even Atlantic Oceans are once again the site of great power rivalries. Not only countries with a long naval tradition are vying for influence; the stakes are such that even India, which resisted developing its naval power through its long imperial and recent modern history, now finds itself scrambling to compete in the game of ports and bases.

The most important new factor, of course, is China itself. Not since the mid-1500s has China been a power at sea. But in two short decades, it has rapidly changed the balance of naval power in Asia, and threatened it beyond. And in so doing, it's forced a critical debate in the United States—not just about how our navy should respond, but about what risks we are willing to take to defend the open seas and flow of trade worldwide.

* * *

The US Naval War College, the institution over which Alfred Thayer Mahan presided and which trains the US Navy's elite officers, sits on Coasters Harbor Island in Narragansett Bay, in Newport, Rhode Island. Nearby, the town's historic wooden warehouses and colonial dwellings carry the legacy of its history as a major hub for whaling, and its Ocean Drive still sports the sprawling mansions that housed the Vanderbilts and the Astors and others of the country's wealthiest families during America's gilded age. The war college itself is more modest, though Luce Hall, built in 1892, carries something of the grandeur of the surrounding town.

For several years, the Naval War College has hosted a biannual gathering of officers, commanders, and scholars designed to undertake a high-level assessment of its primary adversary. Throughout the Cold War, the focus of the college was the Soviet fleet. More recently, its focus has been China's People's Liberation Navy (PLAN).

In May 2019, the conference convened with more than two hundred officers and scholars attending. There were frontline sailors from the US Korea fleet; from the American base in Yokosuka, Japan; from Pacific Fleet headquarters in Oahu—all in crisp white uniforms—and commanders in the greens and blues of navy headquarters. The major think tanks and universities of the United States were represented there as well. They were gathered to answer one question: Was China trying to build a genuinely global blue-water navy? And if so, were its purposes defensive or offensive?

In the corridors, the trappings of modern life were amply present in the iPads, laptops, and iPhones that everyone used to check on their home offices or home lives. But when the formal proceedings of the conference began, security rules required all concerned to store their electronic devices in nearby lockers. Inside, pen and paper replaced tablets. And between the setting, the uniforms, and the older mode of writing, the room was redolent of the history of the much older naval conferences that sought to shape the balance of power between imperial rivals.

The question in front of the conference was simple: As China had developed into a global commercial power, with a network of commercial bases around the globe, would the Chinese navy follow? To the Pacific Fleet leadership in the room, the answer was obvious: absolutely, yes, China was trying to build a global navy, and challenge US supremacy. But for the careful scholars of the Naval War College's China Maritime Studies department, the answer was not so obvious. There was evidence in favor of that conclusion and against it. Their job, as they saw it, was to sift the evidence, challenge the obvious assertions, and let the data take them to a clear conclusion. Their methods were meticulous, involving detailed study of Chinese Communist Party documents, satellite analysis of Chinese shipyards, and an economic study of the cost to the Chinese treasury of building and maintaining an expanding fleet.

Mahan, when he was president of the college, argued that a genuine maritime power had to have a full array of assets in the form of maritime commerce, naval ships, and a network of naval bases. That China had developed as the world's leading maritime commercial power was obvious. As we'll see in what follows, equally obvious was that it was developing an ever more effective fleet of surface ships and submarines. But what about basing? Did China have the intention, or the capacity, to build out a network of mutually reinforcing bases across the Indian and Pacific Oceans, let alone farther afield? The scholars and naval officers in the conference debated fiercely how to interpret China's growing list of port acquisitions—from the east coast of Africa to the western Levant—and what would come next.

To listen to the Naval War College debate was like watching the British Foreign Office write the Crowe Memorandum (see chapter 3) all over again, in real time. For as they debated over two days the question of China's motives, the following, fateful reality loomed: whatever China's current capacity, it would grow; and whatever China's current motives, they could change. China's current intentions *might* be limited to the defense of its sea-based trade; that stance would challenge the US Navy's conception of its own role in maintaining freedom of navigation around the world, but not necessarily core American interests. But what if Chinese intentions changed? What if China's and Russia's navies worked more closely together to challenge the US? And as the discussion continued, the inevitable conclusion began to emerge. To adapt the words of Crowe, "This is a matter in which the United States cannot safely run risks."

* * *

In what comes next, we'll first follow China's foray back to sea in the early 2000s, when it joined international efforts to counter a new version of an old threat to trade: piracy. Its efforts then seemed to presage the prospect that China would focus on cooperating with the established powers. But as its standing grew, so did its confidence, and so did its unease. And thus it turned to more expansive claims and naval ambitions, initially in its surrounding seas. As it deepened its network of ships and "bases" in the waters off its eastern shores, its ability to project power across the "Near Seas" grew. But in the inimitable, escalatory logic of military affairs, as China's security deepened in the Near Seas, its vulnerability in the Far Seas became a greater preoccupation. And so, island by island, sea by sea, China's sense of its first line of defense crept outward—until it crossed into waters that the US Navy still sees as central to its own interests, and to America's defense. And what began as a tense but limited contest in the South China Sea has become a near-global naval arms race—a spiral of escalation that risks taking the world's two most important powers to war.

8

Pirates of the Twenty-First Century

Securing Global Trade (2005–2009)

As soon as human beings began transporting valuable goods via ship, you can be sure there were criminals scheming to intercept those vessels and run off with the loot.

—Steven Johnson, *The Enemy of All Mankind*[1]

At the eastern edge of the island of Singapore, a large jetty juts out into Changi Bay, the deepwater harbor that lies between that city-state, its Malaysian neighbor, and the Batam Islands of Indonesia—all abutting the Singapore Strait, ten miles to the east. Strung along the jetty are the gray hulls of the Republic of Singapore Navy, its frigates and corvettes docked in close formation.* Singapore is known for its highly efficient government, its key role in Asian finance—and for the frequent visitor, its Peranakan cuisine. It's also the location of the world's most advanced counter-piracy operation.

*They are not there alone, though: they are moored beside warships of the US Navy. And nearby is Sembawang Terminal, formerly a base of the Royal Navy, now headquarters of the innocuously named Logistics Group Western Pacific—in reality, a unit of the powerful Seventh Fleet. While there is officially no American base in Singapore, Sembawang Terminal in effect serves as an important forward station for the US Navy, and carries with it the rich legacy of America's presence in Asia: it's the direct descendant of the Yangtze Patrol, America's first naval deployment into China in 1854.

Singapore is another of those small locales, like Hong Kong, that has played an outsize role in the texture of modern history. It became a British colony in 1824 as part of London's effort to deepen its base of operations in Asia. In the 1920s and '30s it became a key transport hub for oil and rubber from the Malay Peninsula just to its north—both goods essential to the galloping industrial development of that period. Its role in the oil and rubber trade made it a key target when the Imperial Japanese Navy moved to outflank the 1941 British and American blockade of its imports, and in February 1942 Singapore became the site of the first major British defeat in Asia.

After the war Singapore reverted to British colonial rule. In 1966 it declared independence from Britain together with Malaysia; and then two years later, it separated from Malaysia to become an independent country. It developed quickly, helped along by a highly efficient (although nondemocratic) government system, and a huge investment in the education of its population. By the 1980s, Singapore had turned itself into a significant hub for finance and trade in Asia.[2] It managed to grow at a sustained pace over the next four decades and by 2019 had an average per capita income of just over $64,000, making it the eighth-richest country in the world.[3]

All this was deeply to the credit of Singapore's postwar leaders. But they were aided by geography. Singapore was almost destined to ride the wave of Asia's economic growth, for it sits adjacent to Asia's sea gate to the Middle East and Europe: the Malacca Strait.

The Strait of Malacca runs for over six hundred miles, connecting the South China Sea to the easternmost part of the Indian Ocean. With the reentry of China into the global economy, it outstripped the Suez Canal as the most important economic choke point in the world.

The Malacca Strait has long been contested. Between 605 and 1025 CE, the Srivijaya empire, a kingdom that stretched over much of the Indonesian archipelago, dominated the trade in ivory, tin, camphor, nutmeg, and sandalwood through the strait to India and China.[4] As the spice trade flourished in the 1400s, Arab and Omani merchants took control of the strait and fortified several trading towns around it. Then it fell to the Portuguese.[5] Just over a century later, the Dutch wrenched it away and held it for one hundred years. At which point, inevitably, the British got into the act. They established a base at George Town, at the western edge of the strait (in what is currently Malaysia), and from there sought to dominate the Malacca trade.[6]

Unusually, the British didn't try to force the Dutch out of the region. They found they faced a common threat: pirates. So pernicious was the effect of piracy on the spice trade that the two bitter European enemies put aside their differences to combat the threat together. They signed the Anglo-Dutch Treaty, establishing what was called the British Straits Settlement and demarcating British and Dutch parts of the territory, each agreeing to patrol their part of the strait in a joint effort to weaken the damage caused by the pirates.[7]

Fast-forward to the turn of the twenty-first century, and little had changed except the size of the ships and the number of countries involved in the counter-piracy effort. As container traffic out of Asia began its steep growth, shipping in and around the Malacca Strait began to experience a surge in piracy, which for many decades had been somewhat dormant. The United States was so worried about the potential of a large terrorist attack in the strait that it proposed sending its own ships there.[8]

The Malacca Strait has three features that make it especially vulnerable to pirates. It's narrow: at its widest point, it's only twenty-five miles. It's shallow: for large stretches, it's merely eighty-nine feet deep and, at the edges, much shallower still—which means there are very narrow passages through which ships must sail, making it easy to target them. And it's remote: it is bordered by states that are made up of archipelagos, with distant capitals whose sovereign control on outlying islands is loose at best. Indonesia, the largest of the three border states, is comprised of literally thousands of islands, and its central authorities have long been comparatively weak and extremely remote. From Malacca Town to Indonesia's present-day capital city, Jakarta, for example, is a distance of over 621 miles by air, and half that again in nautical miles. In the vacancies and spaces thus created, piracy flourished.

The costs of piracy were potentially very great indeed. There's the immediate cost to any given shipowner whose vessel is detained, or whose crew is kidnapped by pirates—to say nothing of the risk of loss of life. But the economic costs go far, far beyond the individual ship at risk. The cost of piracy is hugely amplified by the effect on one of the oldest forms of international finance—maritime insurance.

Modern-day shipping firms have to worry about insuring their ships and cargoes against modern forms of loss—mostly accident, but also, suddenly, twenty-first-century piracy. That is, they have to pay premiums to the world's large shipping insurance agencies—the most important of which is Lloyd's of London.

Just as car insurance companies charge different premiums depending on crime and accident rates in the neighborhood in which you live, so do Lloyd's and other maritime insurance agents charge a premium for accident-prone shipping routes. And even more for sailing in areas where there is a risk of war damage. And when piracy spiked in the Malacca waters in 2005, Lloyd's declared Malacca to be a "war risk zone." This led to a spike in insurance premiums.

This was no trivial problem. Shipping is an intensely competitive business, with low margins, so costs like insurance premiums can have a major effect on profits and losses—and on the price of traded goods. And the spike in prices affected not only the small number of ships that actually encountered pirates, but all ships seeking to sail through the passage. And that was half the world's ships, carrying half the world's trade.[9]

It's not straightforward to project outward what it would mean for the world economy as a whole had insurance rates remained at "war risk zone" levels. But at the very least it would have added a premium to the trade that passed through those waters—which, again, was half of all world trade. If sustained, the economic consequences would have been in the hundreds of billions of dollars, perhaps more.[10]

That was certainly the view of governments worldwide, who rallied to tackle the Malacca piracy problem, hoping to convince Lloyd's to remove the war risk designation. Much like the British and the Dutch came together to tackle the scourge of piracy in the nineteenth century, governments joined forces—literally—to confront their twenty-first-century counterparts in the 2006 Regional Cooperation Agreement on Combating Piracy and Armed Robbery Against Ships in Asia (ReCAAP). Under the lead of the Singaporean navy, they formed what's known as the Maritime Security Task Force in 2009—a coalition of the littoral states. They increased patrols, shared information about pirates, and mounted joint raids—all designed to respond quickly to pirate attacks, especially kidnappings, and help deter new ones.[11]

As they worked together, they discovered that modern states can wield a weapon that individual pirates cannot: big data.[12]

Tucked away at the rear of Changi Naval Base is a nondescript building; seen from the outside, it might be a conference facility, or a training center. In fact, it hosts the Information Fusion Center, where Singaporean naval officers gather and integrate global shipping information and turn it into action items, especially for the three navies that actively patrol the straits. The heart of the Information Fusion Center is a war room, familiar from movies and TV shows, replete with multiple large screens conveying real-time global data and a bank of computers manned by Singaporean naval officers tracking the flowing information in real time. That data comes from companies, global databases, international institutions like the International Maritime Organization and NATO, and the commercial fleets of the two dozen countries that now form part of this coalition.

In their offices, the leadership have their own personal maps of their area of operations, a huge screen full of global incidents data, and details of the ever more sophisticated efforts to use information technology and AI algorithms to track the flow of containers headed to the Malacca Strait. From the office windows, you can see the hulls of several dozen container ships of all sizes, from the modest to the massive, queued up, waiting for clearance.

The volume of information processed at Changi is astonishing. At any given minute, the Information Fusion Center can pinpoint the location of any one of the ninety thousand ships that transit the Malacca Strait yearly—ships that between them carry millions of containers, millions of opportunities to smuggle terrorists, weapons of mass destruction, human beings, and other illicit goods into ports around the world.

The war room and data flow into the Information Fusion Center is one-half of its operation; the other half is a simple conference room. In that conference room sit naval attachés from the now twenty-four nations that have joined the effort. This is no small group of nations, either: together the twenty-four countries around the table represent almost 70 percent of the global GDP and global military spending. However, unlike, say, the naval war room of NATO or the EU, these nations are not allies; many of them are sharp rivals—India participates, for example, alongside Pakistan. (One of the more recent participants: China.)[13]

This was the initial coalition to counter piracy; and it was highly successful. In 2006, just one year after it deployed it, Lloyd's removed the war risk designation. But the Malacca Straits, critical though they are, are a comparatively tiny piece of geography. Just as the Malacca piracy was coming under control, a far larger problem spawned—a new breed of pirates threatening a far larger swath of the world's oceans.

Pirates of the Indian Ocean

The Indian Ocean is smaller than the Pacific or the Atlantic, and yet even its scale is hard to envisage. At its narrowest point, it's just over six thousand miles wide, more than twice the entire width of the United States. It covers 27 million square miles of the Earth's surface and laps out at the edges of four continents: Asia in the north, Africa in the west, Australia in the east, and the Antarctic in the south (after it blends into the littoral Southern Ocean). Two billion people live along its coasts. Even a modern, high-speed ship takes nearly five and a half days to cross to the African or Middle Eastern coasts. During that period of time, it's exceedingly unlikely that it will encounter a single other ship or spot any form of human activity other than the people on the ship itself.

That changes when ships get within a thousand miles of the coast of Zanzibar. And then, mile by mile, the odds of encountering another ship start to climb. And that is not a good thing.

To stand on Zanzibar's Indian Ocean coast is to be transported back to an earlier time. Zanzibar's soft white sand and its temperate waters, turquoise bleeding into aquamarine, rival the most spectacular of the Caribbean islands. Everywhere the scent of clove permeates the air. Clove trees were planted in Zanzibar in 1818 by the sultan of Oman, seeking to break the Indonesian monopoly on that most lucrative part of the spice trade.[14] And the vibrant red of peppercorns covers field after field of inland farms.

Like almost every other territory we'll encounter in this book, the east coast of Africa has been the locus of fights between empires for control of trade.* The most successful empire in the history of East Af-

* Readers interested in the history of the Omani empire should read Robert D. Kaplan's sweeping (and foresightful) account of the Indian Ocean, *Monsoon: The Indian Ocean and the Future of American Power* (New York: Random House, 2011).

rica is perhaps the least well known—the Omani Empire, which from the early seventeenth century held sway over a swath of territory that stretched more than one thousand miles north and a similar distance south from its base in Muscat, Oman. From the Arabian Peninsula, the Omanis developed advanced seafaring technologies that allowed them to impose their presence and expand their trade in spices and slaves as far north as modern-day Iran, Gwadar port in Pakistan, and south across modern-day Somalia down through Kenya and Zanzibar (in modern-day Tanzania). So significant was the Omani Empire in the nineteenth century that the private secretary of the sultan of Oman, Ahmad bin Na'aman Al Kaabi, became the first Arab emissary to visit the United States, sailing from Zanzibar to New York in 1840, where he met with Vice President Richard Mentor Johnson.[15]

Having defeated the Portuguese in Mombasa (then East Africa's major port city) in 1698, the Omanis established a new capital in the fabled city of Zanzibar in 1832, and moved the center of their operations from Muscat to Stone Town, on Zanzibar Island.[16] To this day, Stone Town still largely reflects the architectural and cultural legacy of the Omani occupation. A maze of narrow, high-walled streets are enclosed by the three-story gray-stone houses that dominate the inner byways of the city. Anchoring the center of town is the Palace of Wonders, home of the second Sultan of Zanzibar, with its high clock tower—best viewed from the rooftop of the nearby Emerson Hotel, a favorite of western tourists in the early days of Zanzibar's development.* Huge mahogany doors, intricately carved, mark the entrances to the city's more important civic buildings. Its markets are festooned with kikoys woven in every color under the tropical sun, imports from India, as well as cheap plastic and polyester trade goods imported from China of the kind that now dominate every market in the Middle East. The ruins of Omani fortifications are still to be found on Zanzibar's east coast, from where dhows, still built on Omani designs, ply the fishing trade off East Africa's productive waters.

The German East African colony of Tanganyika gained indepen-

*As this book was being finalized, the Omani government began a restoration of the Palace of Wonders, which went badly wrong; the clock tower and much of the original facade of the former Sultanate collapsed.

dence in 1961, and in 1964 joined with Zanzibar to form the modern nation of Tanzania. It's been largely at peace ever since. It's one of the poorest countries in the world, though, and for decades labored under a socialist government that married equal parts corruption and inefficiency. It gained a form of democracy in the 1990s, and by the mid-2000s had begun to develop economically. Its mainland port of Dar es Salaam (House of Peace) is now the second-largest on Africa's eastern coast.[17]

But anyone navigating a large container ship past the island of Zanzibar into the Dar es Salaam port is not focused on Tanzania's growth. From the mid-2000s onward, the Zanzibari coast became famous once again, for a different kind of danger. This time, it was not a distant empire threatening the fishing dhows, but modern-day pirates threatening ocean liners and container ships.

One of the more dramatic and consequential attacks off the Zanzibari coast came in 2011 when seven pirates in a small skiff attacked an oil and gas exploration ship, *Ocean Rig Poseidon*, owned by Brazil's Petrobras. It was part of a major Brazilian joint venture with Tanzania to explore new gas fields in Tanzania's territorial waters in the Indian Ocean. The attack, which injured several, was eventually repulsed by security guards on the ship and a Tanzanian rescue crew was quickly dispatched to the scene, eighty-two nautical miles off the coast from Dar es Salaam. In total, authorities had arrested eighteen pirates for attacks in Zanzibari waters that year—all of them Somali.[18]

The Malacca pirates may have long tradition on their side, but today's most sophisticated pirates are Somali. They ply that ancient craft along a route that has almost exactly the same reach as the Omani Empire. From towns on the Somali coast, often using the ruins of Omani fortresses as their hub of operations, they sail in small dhows fitted with outboard motors, up and down the white-sand coasts of Somalia, Kenya, Tanzania, Yemen, and Oman, and as far across as the waters off the coast of Pakistan. Since 2008, they've conducted thousands of documented attacks.

For Western audiences, Somali pirates made their popular debut in the 2013 movie *Captain Phillips*, based on a real incident. On the morning of April 8, 2009, the *Maersk Alabama* was en route to Mombasa, Kenya, when it was hijacked by pirates off the Somali coast. What this crew had going for it that the pirates' previous targets did not was that its captain, Richard Phillips, was American. This was the first time in one hundred years that the US needed to rescue an American aboard a ship seized by pirates. The pirate crew that tackled the *Alabama* had to deal with the world's largest and most powerful naval force, the modern US Navy. On April 9, the USS *Bainbridge* intercepted the ship. Shortly thereafter, the *Bainbridge* crew boarded the *Alabama*, capturing most of the pirates and rescuing the crew. The captain escaped on a lifeboat, only to be tracked down and boarded by pirates again. On April 12, US Navy SEALS raided the lifeboat, freeing the captain, killing three pirates, and capturing the fourth, Abduwali Abdukadir Muse.[19] Muse became the first pirate in a century to be tried in an American court.[20]

Seen through a historical lens, this was a remarkable act by the United States—projecting naval power and protecting nationals from pirates half a world away from home shores.

Still, although the largest navy in the world by a substantial measure, even the US Navy cannot single-handedly patrol the entire breadth of the Indian Ocean. And so, just as the Royal Navy in its heyday had sought the help of the Dutch to tackle Malacca piracy, so the US Navy sought the help of its allies. And of some interesting partners.

Counter-Piracy Coalition

In 2005, the UN's International Maritime Organization, from its headquarters in London on the banks of the Thames, started warning of an increase in piracy attacks in the Gulf of Aden, which opens out into the Indian Ocean.[21] There had been a handful of attacks in the previous decade, but then there was a sharp rise in 2005, to more than ten. That year, and in each of the subsequent two years, there were roughly a dozen attacks. Concern about them was amplified by the fact that Yemen, on the northern shore of the Gulf of Aden, was home to an Al Qaeda affiliate. A second Al Qaeda affiliate, Al Shabab, was gaining a foothold on Somali's anarchic soil.

From 2007 to '08, the situation got worse. The number of attacks spiked to 51 in 2007 and then to 111 in 2008.[22] The attacks spread from the Gulf of Aden out into the Indian Ocean. And in 2007, Somali pirates attacked a ship that was part of a World Food Programme convoy bringing food to relieve the crisis in Somalia—where an estimated 2 million to 3 million Somalis were facing starvation.[23]

Governments moved to respond, starting at the UN Security Council, where they issued a collective call to take swift action to protect the World Food Programme's ships and to tackle the mounting problem of piracy.[24] This had international lawyers scrambling to figure out one of the oldest domains of international law, the law of piracy—largely a series of legal arrangements between the European powers from the eighteenth century, barely updated since the nineteenth.[25]

To update the rule book for twenty-first-century piracy, the lawyers took two consequential steps. One of the bedrock principles of contemporary international law is that state sovereignty extends into the seas—that is to say, every state with a coastline is granted a twelve-mile zone of exclusive sovereignty into what are called its "territorial waters." Other countries can sail through those waters through a provision known as "innocent passage," which (unusually for an international legal concept) actually explains the principle at stake: other states' vessels can pass through a sovereign state's exclusive waters if their presence in no way threatens or harms the state in question. What this meant, though, is that foreign navies couldn't legally sail into the territorial waters of Somalia to tackle the pirates because their actions weren't "innocent." So all the pirates had to do was retreat to that outer band of territorial waters twelve miles off the coast to be free from chase. For the fight against the Somali pirates, the UN Security Council waived that provision, giving any state willing to participate in the fight against piracy the right to enter Somali territorial waters to tackle the pirates. And it gave those states the right to use "any and all means" to repress the pirates—that is, the right to use force.[26]

As it happened, there was already a set of ships patrolling in the Gulf of Aden. In the wake of 9/11, the United States had established what was known as the Combined Task Force 150 to guard against terrorist activity in the gulf. It drew together navies from core NATO allies like Germany and the UK, with other American security partners.[27] Part of this unit was repurposed into Combined Task Force 151, with a counter-piracy mission focused on the Gulf of Aden.

The Somali pirates' response was agile. Far from retreating from attacks in the Gulf of Aden, where CTF 151 was patrolling, they simply spread out their range of threat, moving farther into the Indian Ocean, south to Zanzibar, and north toward Oman and Pakistan. Pirate attacks continued to climb, as did the economic costs.

The European Union stepped into the breach, deploying its own naval task force, Operation Atalanta (or Combined Task Force 465). Twenty-six European nations participated in Operation Atalanta.[28] And then, to further extend the reach of patrols, NATO created a third task force, Operation Ocean Shield. Five NATO allies made up the core of Operation Ocean Shield: the United States, Denmark, Italy, Turkey, and the United Kingdom. Other countries—Ukraine, for example—participated in the force through alliance partnership arrangements.[29]

But what really made the maritime operations off the coast of Somalia interesting is that several unusual partners joined in: the Republic of Korea and Turkey in Operation Ocean Shield; the United Arab Emirates, Bahrain, and Pakistan in Combined Task Force 151. And the navies of China and Russia started to patrol alongside NATO forces.[30]

It was a striking display. During the Cold War, the Western powers patrolled together and shared intelligence among themselves, but not beyond. And in the first period after the end of the Cold War, the Western powers took on a broader, global role. Now a series of non-Western powers were growing in influence—gaining power for the first time, or regaining it. What relationship they would have to the West, and to the established international system, was a key question. Here, they seemed poised to cooperate with the West.

At first, there were problems in coordination, and debates about what to do with the pirates once they were captured.[31] These details were ironed out, however, and combined with on-land efforts—including the UN and African Union helping to maintain security in Mogadishu's port, and EU naval patrols on Somali rivers—piracy began to drop off.* The counter-piracy effort began to work. Attacks fell slightly in 2010, and then dramatically in 2011.[32]

*The European powers sailing in Operation Atalanta didn't want to jail the captured pirates in their own countries because of the high cost of doing so. The British special envoy for the piracy problem, the feisty Karen Pierce (later UK ambassador to the United Nations and then to the United States) had a simple if dramatic proposal: sink their ships. In the end, the Western powers decided on a different course, offering expanded aid to Kenya, the Seychelles, and Mauritius if those countries would try the

This was more than an economic success. It seemed to hint at a world in which the shared interests of the United States, Europe, and the "rising powers"—China, Russia, Turkey, India, Brazil, and others—would trump the historic instinct for competition among them. All these actors were participants in a single, integrated global economy forged by sea-based trade. It presaged a world where the major military powers could put aside older patterns of rivalry and cooperate for mutual economic gain.

Or was it too good to be true?

* * *

Over time, the role of China in the counter-piracy operations began to be seen in a different light. Western naval planners worried that the Chinese were using these operations for a different purpose: to train the People's Liberation Navy to mount operations far from China's shores. The operations gave China extensive practice in mounting sorties, navigating through the tricky Malacca Strait, and testing their capacity to maintain effective communication between their ships and other parts of their defense apparatus, across the entire width of the Indian Ocean.* All of which was useful to the counter-piracy effort, to be sure. But in the minds of the West, the question began to arise: Was China's expanding role really only about protection of trade? Or was it developing naval capacity as part of a wider effort to project power—contemplating, in fact, a more forceful return to the seas?[33]

Somali pirates in their courts and jail them in their territories, with the bulk of the trials and imprisonments happening in Kenya. See Jay Bahadur, *The Pirates of Somalia: Inside Their Hidden World* (New York: Vintage), 2012.

*Fast-forward, and China's role has grown—and grown. As of 2018, China had conducted no less than thirty separate task groups (sorties), each involving multiple frigates or destroyers—including advanced ships like their Jiangkai II class guided-missile frigates—to patrol the Gulf of Aden and the western edge of the Indian Ocean.

9

The Near Seas

China's Return to the Ocean (2009–2015)

"Historical experience tells us that countries that embrace the sea thrive, while states that spurn the sea decline."

—Xi Jingping, speech to the Chinese Politburu, 2013[1]

In the modern period, each of the nations that has stood atop world affairs has faced the world from a capital on or near the seas. Venice forged its maritime empire from a lagoon within the Adriatic Sea. The Ottomans competed for power from the banks of the Golden Horn, separating the Bosphorus from the Marmara Sea. Portugal dominated the high seas from the port city of Lisbon, set on the westernmost ledge of the European continent and protected from the Atlantic currents only by the headlands at the mouth of the Tagus River. London is arrayed along the tidal flows of the Thames and lies a mere thirty miles from where the river opens to the English Channel and thence the North Sea. And even when America's first independent leaders moved the US Congress from the great port city of Philadelphia, it chose a site on the Potomac River merely twenty-five miles from Chesapeake Bay,* one of the world's great inland waterways, its brackish waters flowing swiftly out into the western Atlantic.

*And once home to several notorious pirates. See Jamie L. H. Goodall, *Pirates of the Chesapeake Bay: From the Colonial Era to the Oyster Wars* (Charleston, SC: The History Press, 2020).

Not so for China. Since the 1200s, the various dynasties and republics that have ruled the Middle Kingdom have placed their seat of governmental power in the city that evolved into modern Beijing.[2] Over time, China's rulers fortified the city, its defensive walls, and its moated innermost compound: the Forbidden City. Until the Chinese civil war in the 1920s, China ruled its Middle Kingdom from this highly defended bastion inside a walled city one hundred miles from the nearest coast.

When the Communist Party under Mao Zedong completed their "Long March" and took Beijing, Mao stood in Tiananmen Square, across the road from the Forbidden Palace, to declare his victory. And although the essence of the Communist Party's movement was to overthrow the power structures of the imperial rulers of China (and the short-tenured republics that succeeded them), as a government it nonetheless installed itself immediately beside the Forbidden City—in the former imperial gardens and lakes, known as Zhongnanhai.[3]

The formal entrance to Zhongnanhai, the Gate of China, is located opposite Tiananmen Square, but rarely used; it is opened only for the most formal and prominent of state visits. Visitors below the status of head of state enter the compound from the rear, off the back wall of the Forbidden City. The whole compound is set along the banks of a series of small lakes in central Beijing—the most proximate of which has the slightly confounding name "the Middle Sea."

Entering the compound, visitors are ushered inside to a large reception area. Here, there are several rooms that can be used to greet and entertain visiting ministers, dignitaries, CEOs, and the occasional scholar. Many of these are modern variants on older styles of greeting halls, furnished with cream-white carpets and plush leather armchairs, and with large paintings in the antique style adorning the main wall behind the leaders' seats. An inner room that can seat a maximum of twelve in each delegation is reserved for "private" talks between the top leaders. Nearby are the official offices of the Party's leadership.

The most lavish building, reserved for use by the chairman and vice chairman and the other senior-most leaders of the Party, lies in the East Building Compound. It manages at the same time to convey the modern authority of China's central government and to appropriate the long history of the rulers they overthrow. A two-story building in the traditional style, with sloping ceramic tile roofs supported by curved beams and adorned by wood carvings, it was built originally by the Ming Dynasty and restored by the Qings. There are no modern decorations here. Intricately carved wood screens set off the main reception area from the rest of the hall. Wood columns painted in the traditional Chinese red, with vibrant yellows and blues as well, support the ceiling of the main hall. Chinese ancestor paintings are hung on several walls, adding to the sense of history. The only concession to modern style is the row of comfortable chairs made available to modern delegations. Officially known as Ziguang Hall, it also has an older, more redolent name: the Hall of Barbarian Tributes.

To understand the evolution of China's relationship to naval power, it helps to put yourself in the mindset of one of its top leaders, contemplating China's place in the world from the highly secured compound of Zhongnanhai. From the boardwalk that flanks the offices of the most senior leaders of the Chinese Community Party, you look out over the gardens and the Middle Sea lake to the outer walls of the Forbidden City—and it's easy to feel the weight and solidity of one thousand years of continuous Chinese rule from this location.

But as you look farther afield, all is uncertain. You find yourself—from the 1980s onward—seeking to grow and to develop in a world whose global economic activity is dominated by the United States and its Western allies (all the more so since the end of the Cold War). You are trying to grow in a world in which you have become deeply dependent on the flow of mineral resources and energy resources from overseas and the sale of your manufactured goods to foreign markets. And as you worry about the security of that flow of sea trade, you confront the following, confounding geography.

When Chinese leaders journey from Beijing to Shanghai or Guangzhou or the other major Chinese coastal cities, they look out from them not to unbroken waters as the Portuguese, the English, or the Americans do. Rather, like the Germans, they look out to a set of highly constrained passages to the high seas.

China's modern economy is organized around three major economic zones. There's Beijing and the area around it, the Bohai Economic Rim, where Tanjin Port serves as Beijing's gateway to the Yellow Sea.[4] There's the Yangtze River basin, where Shanghai serves as China's financial, technological, and export hub, and where Shanghai's Yangshan Port complex opens up into the East China Sea. And there's the Pearl River Delta, where Guangzhou (formerly Canton) and Hong Kong anchor China's economic activity in the south, exporting and importing its trade through the South China Sea. But on the other side of those seas are the Korean Peninsula and what China calls the "first island chain"— Japan, with its long string of islands from its southern coast almost the whole way to the Taiwan Sea; then Taiwan itself; and then the Philippine archipelago.

That peninsula and this string of islands fundamentally constrain Chinese maritime space. All the countries on those islands are American allies, or security partners. And all of them provide bases or basing rights to the US Navy—bringing what China calls "the powerful enemy" right to its maritime doorstep.* The resulting sense of constriction has profoundly shaped the evolution of Chinese strategic thinking.

As China consolidated itself in the 1980s and '90s, it began to have both sufficient confidence and wealth to reorient its security concepts beyond a posture of coastal defense. China's long, northern border with the Soviet Union (the "near enemy") was more complicated, although its geopolitical rivalry with the USSR would soon ebb, leaving China with more resources to devote to naval activities. Indeed, on its eastern and southern shores, China began to believe that it could halt a potential foreign intrusion at the coastline. And over time, it began to have confidence about defending itself in the Near Seas—and even project its own power farther into those seas.[5]

*Chinese scholars tend not to refer to Singapore as part of this first island chain, but it does bound the South China Sea at its southern end, and also provides the US Navy with the equivalent to basing rights, completing the encirclement of China's Near Seas.

The Enclosing Seas

Governments of major powers are big, unwieldy things, shaped by heavy institutions that compete with one another for space and attention—almost as much in authoritarian systems as in democracies. But sometimes an individual can make an outsize difference in these institutions, and to the country's trajectory. One such man was Liu Huaqing, who served from 1982 to 1987 as commander of the Chinese PLAN, and for more than two decades worked from various positions of power to reshape China's naval strategy, leadership, personnel, and organizing concepts.[6,*]

His thinking, perhaps oddly, drew heavily from the scholar who had shaped Roosevelt and the British admirals of the late 1800s—the aforementioned Alfred Thayer Mahan.[7]

What Carl von Clausewitz is to ground war, Mahan is to maritime strategy and naval conflict. In his classic text, *The Influence of Sea Power Upon History*, Mahan spelled out his theory of sea power. Mahan's insight begins with the centrality of geography and the notion that control of key choke points on the global map is indispensable to sea power and trade, and hence ultimately to a seafaring nation's livelihood. He highlights the importance of a network of bases and the ability to sail securely between them, establishing what he calls "lines of communication"[8]—now often referred to in naval parlance as the "sea-lanes of communication."[†]

> *This combination of useful harbors and the conditions of the communication between them constitute, as has been said, the main strategic out-*

*He did not do so in isolation. Those not familiar with modern China might assume that because the regime is communist (and now increasingly authoritarian) that it supports no debate about its policy. In fact, China has for years allowed a fairly free-ranging debate about naval strategy within its services, academies, universities, and think tanks.

†Mahan is also credited with coining the phrase "the global commons"—the notion of a shared sea, available to all nations; this is a central tenet in modern American naval strategy. (See Michele Flournoy and Shawn Brimley, "The Contested Commons," *Proceedings*, July 2009, https://www.usni.org/magazines/proceedings/2009/july/contested-commons.)

lines of the situation. The navy, as the organized force linking the whole together, has been indicated as the principal objective of military effort.[9]

In short, national power depended on being able to control the key sea-lanes that connected a nation's commerce to overseas trade (the very opposite of China's situation in the 1990s). For Mahan, peacetime commerce was the true path to national prosperity and greatness. "Military considerations are simply accessory and subordinate to other greater interests."[10] Naval competition, he argued, was a by-product of the efforts meant to generate national wealth and greatness. The purpose of a navy was to secure maritime commerce—in his view, the sine qua non of a nation's wealth and intrinsic power.

That is not to say that Mahan's strategy wasn't martial, for it certainly was. He highlighted in particular the importance of forward naval stations and fleets and competition among nations for control of key geographical points. What's more, Mahan argued that a powerful nation had to have a *string of bases* across the geography it sought to protect, each within range of the next, so that its forward bases could be reinforced in times of war from bases within striking distance. It was similar concepts that underpinned much of America's expansion in the Pacific—from the annexation of Hawaii to the acquisition of Wake Island, and then the Marshall Islands, and Guam. These were the stepping-stones across the Pacific to America's ultimate forward naval bases in the Philippines and Japan.[11]

In the US, Mahan's influence had waned in the decades after World War II. The writings of Halford Mackinder posited that "continental power"—the economic productivity of controlling an industrial heartland—was more important than maritime power.[12] This seemed to match the dynamics of competition between two massive land powers—the United States and the Soviet Union. China is a continental power, too, of course, and controls a large industrial heartland. But its growth strategy was dependent on trade, and that meant that it was dependent on the seas. As China's maritime trade grew—and grew ever more central to its overall national economic strength—Mahan's thinking about the relationship between growth and naval power began to shape Chinese naval strategy.[13]

Among the most important concepts that emerged at this time:

Chinese planners began to refer to their desire to have a "string of pearls"—a network of reinforceable bases that they could use to protect their overseas interests. But for China to have a "string of pearls," it had first to be able to mount effective naval operations within the first island chain. And it had to begin by developing a capacity to match the US Navy and its allies in the Near Seas.

And so China began to develop its naval muscles. Liu Huaqing laid out a seven-element plan to create a navy capable of defending Chinese interests in the near waters. It involved training of personnel; scientific education; acquisition of ports, logistics, and maintenance capacity; weapons modernization (over a twenty-year timeline); development of a nuclear submarine force; and eventual acquisition of an aircraft carrier.[14]

At the time, some critics within China dismissed his program as too ambitious. Looking back, it's striking to note that China accomplished every aspect of his program. And in doing so, he enabled China not merely to mount a defense of its coastline, but to project power across the expanse of the Near Seas—together, roughly 2 million square miles of ocean territory.

As it did so, China encountered not only its own geography, but its neighbors'.*

The Cow's Tongue: China's Expansive Claim

In March 2008, Zhang Zhenhua, a policy planner in China's Ministry of Foreign Affairs, met with staff from the US embassy in Beijing. His purpose: to explain the basis of his country's claim in the South China Sea. He brought with him a printed statement that read: "The dotted line of the South China Sea indicates the sovereignty of China over the islands in the South China Sea since ancient times and demonstrates

*The material that follows concentrates on the areas of largest Chinese deployments over the last decade, namely the South and East China Seas and the Taiwan Strait. Readers will remember that we already encountered the last of the Near Seas, in chapter 2, when we covered sanctions-busting operations in the Yellow Sea, off the North Korean coast. The seventy-thousand-personnel-strong navy of the Republic of Korea (South Korea) is a factor to be reckoned with in those waters, and one that China must deal with as it crafts its Near Seas strategy.

the long-standing claims and jurisdiction practice over the waters of the South China Sea."[15]

The context was that the following year, 2009, was an important year for maritime issues. Ten years earlier, the UN Convention on the Law of the Sea had been adopted by many governments worldwide and come into force. At that time, the UN set a ten-year deadline for countries to file claims under the law for ownership of maritime territory. The rules allowed for countries to claim a twelve-mile exclusive zone along their continental shelf, and a two-hundred-mile economic zone (where they were granted privileged fishing and energy exploration rights) extending outward from their sea borders. Where states had outlying islands, those same rules would apply, but states had to show that they had meaningful control over those islands. As the clock ticked down toward the deadline for claims, an open question was: How would China portray its claims in the Near Seas?

When China made its claim, America's China watchers were stunned. For the dotted line presented by Zhenhua—quickly circulated from the embassy to Washington—represented the oceanic version of a vast land grab by China. The dotted line depicted on his map has come to be known as the Cow's Tongue, for its shape. It represented a claim of some 1.4 million square miles of ocean.[16] And within that huge expanse, China claimed specific sovereignty over a whole series of rocks, semi-islands, and "land features" (things too small to count as an island) within the South China Sea.

China's vast claim focused on land features in the Paracels, the Spratly Islands, and the Scarborough Shoal. These three features together comprise a kind of lopsided triangle encompassing the heart of the South China Sea. The Paracels lie some 250 miles off of central Vietnam's coast, 220 miles south of the Chinese island of Hainan, and stretch as far as a tiny feature known as Woody Island (which lies at 16.8366 degrees north, 112.3368 degrees east). The Spratlys lie southeast, off the northern coast of the Malaysian Peninsula. And the Scarborough Shoal lies roughly four hundred miles from China's shore, but just west of the main Philippine islands.[17] By claiming these three sets of features, China was claiming the whale's share of the sea, and land features that together encircled the shipping lanes—the key Mahanian "sea-lanes of communication."[18]

China was not alone in making claims in the South China Sea. Five other states had filed claims for some combination of those land features, and their surrounding maritime space: Taiwan, Vietnam, the Philippines, Malaysia, and Brunei. The other states' claims, though, were substantially more modest and more targeted to island features close to their shores.

China's claims were not particularly compelling.[19] But then again, neither were those of its competitors. In the modern era, none of these islands had been meaningfully occupied in ways that common sense would say meant that they "belonged" to one state or another. Competing states tried to buttress their claims with a whole series of creative steps—building maritime research stations in disputed areas, putting up lighthouses, locating meteorology stations and satellite control posts on the features—and even building a so-called "special bird-watching stand."[20] However, in the words of one prominent legal scholar, "in a sense these occupations and related activities can be viewed as being symptomatic of the shortcomings in the claimant states' cases" and the states "give every appearance of operating on the basis of the old adage that possession is nine-tenths of the law."[21]

But possess them they soon did. And as China asserted these claims, it backed them up—with a steady tempo of deployments of frigates and cruisers and destroyers of the PLAN.

The East China Sea—and the Old Enemy

Soon after its move to claim territory in the South China Sea, the Chinese gaze swept northward to the East China Sea. But there it encountered a more powerful obstacle than geography—the Japanese navy.

In the postwar period, we've become accustomed to thinking of Japan as a pacifist power. Japan's Basic Law—the constitution drafted for postwar Japan by the American occupation authorities after World War II—explicitly forbids Japanese rearmament for offensive purposes and explicitly commits Japan not to engage in warring activities. Even its armed forces, such as they are, are known as the Japan *Self-Defense* Force. Japan has been reluctant to engage even in such modest international security activities as UN peacekeeping.[22] Japan's anti-militarism, a reaction to its own excesses in the days of the Japanese occupation of Korea and Manchuria and to the horrors of Nagasaki and Hiroshima, is now deeply embedded in Japanese political culture.[23]

There's a crucial exception: defense against China is not considered to be a warring activity. It's explicitly a function of self-defense and so it falls outside of the prohibitions in the Japanese constitution. Japan's capacity to defend itself against Beijing is *substantial*.[24] That's particularly so when it comes to its navy.

Operating from numerous bases across the Japanese archipelago, the Japan Maritime Self-Defense Force is the world's fourth-largest navy and one of its most effective. It encompasses 45,800 personnel with a total of 114 ships. That surface fleet is accompanied by around twenty submarines, as well as other support ships.[25] All of this is complemented by a highly effective Coast Guard of fourteen thousand personnel.[26] And in 2006, it decided to turn two large destroyers into what it euphemistically called "helicopter destroyers," but was really the next step toward an aircraft carrier.[27] In 2018, the Japanese government announced that it would turn its larger Izumo-class "helicopter destroyers" into "multi-purpose operation destroyers" that would happen to be capable of launching jets. For all intents and purposes, these vessels would serve as aircraft carriers, marking the first time since World War II that Japan has possessed that particular naval weapon.[28]

Japan deploys that force along the breadth of its archipelago, which encloses the East China Sea. As such, it encloses China at its most productive zone: the eastern seaboard, where lies the delta of the Yangtze River, just east of Shanghai. The East China Sea is also rich in resources (especially oil and gas—as we'll see in Part IV), adding to the competitive pressure between the two countries.

All of Japan is an archipelago. Its major islands run from Hokkaido in the northeast to Kyushu in the southwest. But even farther south and west, a string of small islands stretch from the Osumi islands of Kyushu's coast via Okinawa to the Senkaku Islands, a mere eighty-seven miles off Taiwan's coast. And it was there that in 2010, the Chinese and Japanese nearly came to blows.

Initially, there was a degree of ambiguity as to whether or not US treaty obligation to Japan covered these Japanese-administered but essentially uninhabited islands. President Obama removed that uncertainty in 2014 when he explicitly declared that the Japanese-administered territory was covered by the treaty.[29] And when China declared that the airspace out from the Chinese coast just below Korea's island of Jeju to just north of Taiwan, an area that includes the Senkakus, constituted an "air defense interdiction zone"—i.e., a zone in which China would exclude foreign planes from flying—Obama ordered two nuclear-capable B-52s to fly through the airspace.[30]

Because unlike the situation in the South China Sea, the East China Sea comes with a twist—Japan is not only a treaty ally, it is an ally with whom the United States has a mutual defense commitment. Article 5 of the Treaty of Mutual Cooperation and Security Between the United States and Japan commits the United States to come to the defense of Japan if it falls under attack. This is no mere formality, either, for Japan also houses the largest overseas American naval presence in the world, at United States Fleet Activities Yokosuka in Tokyo Harbor. Together with Fuchu Air Base, Yokota Air Base, Sasebo Naval Base, and Marine Corps camps on Okinawa, Torii Station Army Base, and smaller encampments throughout Japan, over one hundred thousand American personnel and families from all the services are present, as well as tens of thousands of Japanese personnel.[31]

All of this makes Japan a serious obstacle for China's Near Seas activities, let alone its wider ambitions.

While the Senkaku standoff did not ultimately escalate into direct confrontation, nor did the Japanese and American reaction cause China to back down completely. Instead, China has continued a high tempo of activities that fall in the gray zone between legitimate commercial and Coast Guard activity, and military harassment.[32] For example, in 2010 a Chinese fishing trawler (part of its maritime militia*) collided with a Japanese Coast Guard patrol boat near the Senkakus. Japan arrested the Chinese captain, sparking protests in China and a diplomatic crisis.[33] In December 2012, a Chinese government aircraft entered Japanese-controlled airspace for the first time since 1958, when such records began to be kept.[34] One defense official told reporters, "I think . . . neither side has an interest or an intention to escalate

*Which Japanese defense officials call "little green fishermen," reminiscent of the "little green men" that Russia sent into Crimea.

the conflict at this point, although there's a lot of air and naval activity on a small confined space, so there's always potential for something."[35]

But the Senkakus presented the United States with a rather acute dilemma. What if China called its bluff? Or gambled on the idea that an American president would not actually commit to war with a 1.2-billion-strong China over what amounted to a distant pile of rocks? Few American politicians or security analysts doubt that the United States would live up to its security obligations to Japan should the main body of that country come under attack. But a pile of rocks occupied only by a small herd of goats? The situation seemed absurd.*

Far less absurd is the question of America's security relations with the next island down the chain—Taiwan itself.

Flash Point Formosa

The Taiwan Strait divides mainland China from the island of Taiwan, running along the island's 245-mile length. At its widest, it is 110 miles; at its narrowest, 81. It's also fairly shallow, with the vast majority of the strait less than 490 feet deep.

Taiwan has a complex history. The indigenous population were largely displaced by mass Han migration in the seventeenth century, and then the island fell under Dutch rule when the Min Dynasty in turn expelled the Han rulers. The island was annexed to the Qing Dynasty in 1683, but a hundred and some odd years later ceded to Japan during the first Japan-China war in 1895. Japan used Taiwan during World War II as an important industrial base and as a key set of ports. After the war and the surrender of Japan, the Republic of China, which was founded in the mainland in 1912 and replaced the Ching Dynasty, took control over the island of Formosa. When, during the Chinese civil war, the ROC lost the mainland to the Chinese Communist Party, the core of the ROC government fled to Taiwan in 1949. Over time, it

*It has since been described as "the Senkaku Paradox"—because the United States couldn't afford to back down, but also couldn't credibly commit to launching a war with China over such small triggering stakes. See Michael E. O'Hanlon, *The Senkaku Paradox: Risking Great Power War Over Small Stakes* (Washington, DC: Brookings Institution Press, 2019).

transitioned from a one-party dictatorship to a multiparty democracy, and thus, is two thorns in the side of the Chinese leadership. They see it as a physical loss of formerly Chinese-owned territory and as an ideological threat to the mainland.[36]

Its relations to the United States have also been complex. Although the US recognized the Kuomintang government of the ROC in 1950, it explicitly ruled out engaging in the Taiwan Straits. Truman, though, did send the Seventh Fleet to the Straits of Formosa during the Korean War. In the 1950s, Taiwanese deployment on the islands of Quemoy and Matsu, among others, sparked the First Taiwan Strait Crisis. Rather than engage militarily, the United States upgraded its legislative standards, adopting the Formosa Resolution, which gave Eisenhower the authority to defend Taiwan. Beijing backed down.[37]

Then Taiwan and the United States signed the Sino-American Mutual Defense Treaty, which held from 1955 to 1979, and would have brought the United States to the defense of Taiwan if and when it came under attack. In 1972, the Shanghai Communiqué, which followed Kissinger's negotiations for the diplomatic recognition of Beijing, recognized that the PRC was "the sole legal Government of China." Simultaneously, the United States, partly through the urging of Congress, adopted what's known as the One China policy. Under this policy, the US did *not* officially recognize Chinese sovereignty over Taiwan. Instead, in a diplomatic sleight of hand, Washington acknowledged the Chinese position that Taiwan was part of China. It thus has formal relations with the PRC and unofficial relations with Taiwan.[38] The Mutual Defense Treaty lasted until 1979, when President Jimmy Carter formally cut off relations with Taiwan and abrogated the treaty. But that same year, Congress adopted the Taiwan Relations Act, which allowed the United States to conduct unofficial diplomacy with Taiwan, but even more critically to sell them defensive military equipment.[39]

The sale of defensive military equipment is the key point. Sales of new equipment and of refurbished American ships and aircraft have allowed Taiwan to develop into a substantial naval power in its own right. By 2018, its naval force comprised 38,000 personnel, 28 aircraft, and 117 ships—and all of that capacity is dedicated to defending a narrow strip of Taiwanese territorial waters. That included a small submarine fleet, but more importantly four destroyers (formerly US destroyers), and about two dozen frigates, built based on licensing agreements with the United States.[40] Ships bought from France round out the combat fleet. The Republic of China's navy also has a missile boat, a dozen patrol ships, minesweepers, and up to nine amphibious ships that allow for tank landing and personnel movement across the Taiwan Strait. In addition, auxiliary ships like fast combat support ships, research ships, and rescue and salvage operations round out their naval capability. Most recently, they have commissioned a large amphibious ship and have begun to develop their own diesel submarine fleet.[41]

All of this still leaves Taiwan facing a stronger, more sophisticated force across the Taiwan Strait, but Taiwan has invested in "asymmetric operations"—basically, David versus Goliath tactics—like laying large quantities of mines in the waters, or having the capacity to lay large quantities of mines, and using small fast attack boats and truck-launched anti-ship cruise missiles to weaken the Chinese advantage.

All of this still probably leaves China with the upper hand should it come to direct conflict between China and Taiwan, but a far more equal conflict than would be normal for a country with the size and population of Taiwan, relative to a country the size and population of China.

There is no legal requirement for the United States to involve itself in Taiwan now, but there are a whole series of political and other reasons why it might. It's a former ally, and a current defense partner. Taiwan plays a critical role in the American supply chain in high technology, especially in computer chips. And not just technology: Taiwan was the first country to supply surplus personal protective equipment to the United States after the outbreak of COVID-19.[42] There's anti-China sentiment to factor in, and seen from the vantage point of Washington's national security establishment, there's American prestige on the line. Above all, Taiwan is a democracy threatened by a country that many in the United States have begun to perceive as America's most important adversary.

And there's this: if China were to reintegrate Taiwan into the core of the Chinese political entity, it would suddenly gain naval bases beyond the first island chain. The southern coast of Japan would be far more vulnerable to the Chinese PLAN, and America's defenses in the rest of the Western Pacific more exposed to Chinese power. Taiwan has become a major feature in the debate about American power and prestige in Asia, but it's also China's key to unlocking the first island chain. And therefore critical to America's forward posture.

So if China was to contemplate a military operation to retake Taiwan, it would have to be prepared to stop the US Navy from reinforcing the Taiwanese fleet (and its own forces) inside the Near Seas. In other words, it would have to be able to mount what it calls a "counter-intervention" operation beyond the Near Seas—out past the first island chain, into the wider waters of the Philippine Sea, perhaps as far east as Guam. This required a substantial toughening of the PLAN.

Hardening the Seas

That the Chinese have to think about the presence of the US Navy in the Near Seas is an artifact of three distinct but reinforcing American concepts. There's the alliance system, and the notion that the United States would come to the defense of smaller powers that have chosen to ally themselves to the US. There's America's long naval presence in Asia, stretching as far back as the 1840s. And there's a deeply embedded view in the US Navy that one of its core functions—inherited from the Royal Navy—is to protect the freedom of the seas.

This is an important part of what's meant when American diplomats these days refer to a "rules-based international order." The "rules" in question are the UN Convention on the Law of the Sea—an international law the United States has not ratified in Congress, but in practice both implements and enforces.* Those rules stipulate the right of any state to sail through the territorial waters of any other state so long as the purpose of their sailing is "innocent"—the concept of "innocent passage" we encountered in chapter 8. Only the state that has the territorial claim can fish its waters or develop its seabed resources, but any state can sail through. This makes it, among other things, a way of pushing back against any one power operating a naval sphere of

*It may seem ironic that the US Navy should focus on enforcing an international law Congress has refused to ratify. Yet this has been how the United States has approached many such treaties, like the Comprehensive Nuclear-Test-Ban Treaty.

influence off their coast. Which is a very comfortable set of rules if you're the only global power able to operate off everyone's coast, and a somewhat less comfortable set of rules if you are a rising, aspiring power like China.

The essential mechanism by which the United States enforces the law of the sea is what it calls freedom of navigation operations (which go by the clumsy abbreviation FONOPs). That is, the US Navy deliberately sails its ships directly through waters that it believes are permissible for open navigation even if another power has claimed them as part of their territory, daring the other power to push back.[43] To its credit, the United States has undertaken such freedom of navigation operations in the territories of allies and adversaries alike, living up to its claim to act as an impartial arbiter of the rules.* But it has placed particular emphasis on freedom of navigation operations in waters now claimed by China.

Even assuming that the US Navy's presence in the Near Seas is only to defend the Law of the Sea Convention (and the US no longer even really maintains that stance), these "freedom of navigation operations" put US warships in a position to substantially impede China's military options in the Taiwan Strait, and across the South and East China Seas.[44] And so, from the late 1990s onward, China focused its energy and effort on building out its capacity to push back, to defend its interests in the Near Seas, and frustrate or limit USN freedom within those waters.

A UN tribunal eventually ruled on the expansive claim by China and rejected large swaths of it. But China's reaction to this was essentially to shrug—it simply ignored the law and went about its business.[45] And as time progressed, it became increasingly clear that part of its business was to transform these island features into bases for the PLAN.

A key to understanding the dynamic of the Near Seas is that large reaches of them are exceedingly shallow. The large container ships

* In April 2021, the USS *John Paul Jones*—which we will shortly encounter—conducted a series of freedom of navigation operations in Indian waters, to howls of protest from the Indian media.

that ply its route stick to narrow passages where the depths plummet to more than two miles. But even they frequently sail through subchannels that are no more than two to three hundred feet in depth, carefully watching their draw. As they sail, they closely watch charts that show a plethora of sand cays, banks, reefs, and other features of extremely shallow waters. This is very useful for such activities as fishing and oil exploration. But it's also helpful for land reclamation—for taking minor "island features" and turning them into larger tracts of low-lying land.

And so began an initial phase of Chinese militarization of these waters. It dredged and reclaimed and built out from its claimed land features, eventually creating new, usable land in the South China Sea, especially around the Spratlys. Two of the main features around which China built out their land seemed particularly aptly named: Fiery Cross Reef, and Mischief Reef. These were built up with docks, large metal sheds, and, in some cases, landing strips. And then Beijing took a step it had repeatedly promised not to: they put military equipment on those reclaimed lands. Starting on Woody Island in the Paracels, China placed missile batteries, built airstrips, established docks, and in several other ways militarized their outposts in these disputed waters.[46]

These developments extended the range of the PLAN Air Force, especially its main fighter jets (the Russian-designed Sukhoi 30 MKKs, core of its fighter fleet), and enabled China to pose a threat to US Navy ships much farther away from the Chinese mainland. It was all part of the more ambitious vision of the Chinese leadership.

One such leader was Admiral Wu Shengli, who took command of the PLAN in 2006. From the start, he pushed for two key reforms. First, he built up the sophistication and fighting capacity of the core Chinese fleet, and continued the effort to militarize its positions, building out still larger fortifications in the reclaimed islands. And he began to agitate for the PLAN to aim farther than the Western Pacific. As he drove modernization of the fleet, he updated its doctrine. His explicit instruction to the Chinese PLAN: to use its counter-piracy missions in the Malacca Strait and in the Indian Ocean to train for far-seas operations—and to interact with foreign navies to gain knowledge. In his writings to the Chinese fleet, he was explicit that the purpose of this effort was more than defensive: it was to bring to an end the "Century of Humiliation."[47,*] His vision seemed designed to give China the capacity to reach out to the "far seas"—to develop that symbolic and persuasive instrument of global power, a blue-water navy. That meant extending the PLAN to the Pacific, Indian, and Arctic Oceans—in short, the precise area of operations of America's largest naval force, stationed out of Hawaii.[48] And on the very waters that have been at the heart of American power projection since the end of World War II.

*Foreign critics of China often argue that the regime uses the "Century of Humiliation" purely as a propaganda device. It's striking, though, that Chinese PLAN commanders, writing in Mandarin and in specialized naval journals, also invoke the memory. In their authoritative account of Chinese-language sources on doctrine, *Red Star over the Pacific*, Yoshihara and Holmes cite Admiral Wu's articles in the Chinese-language magazine *Qiushi*, which invoke this concept.

10

America's Lake

Naval Warfare in the Western Pacific and Beyond (2010–2017)

When an "Urgency EGC Received" warning about a North Korean missile test flashes into the bridges of commercial ships worldwide, they are not the first to receive the message. The test would have been detected first by satellites orbiting the area, and by American and Japanese long-range radar mounted on ships patrolling the adjacent waters. Then American signals collectors would relay the information to the US Naval Computer and Telecommunications Area Master Station Pacific on Wahiawa, Hawaii—the largest telecommunications station in the world.

Master Station Pacific is an essential hub in the flow of sensor and satellite information and data that forms a critical part of modern naval war fighting. But Master Station Pacific itself is but one part of an array of American defensive assets deployed across the Hawaiian archipelago. Hawaii is the last line of America's Pacific defense, and its first line of action for projecting military power across Asia.

America's forward naval positions in Japan and Korea, and its defense arrangements with Singapore, bring the US Navy to the very edge of the Near Seas. Those forward positions are then vitally supported by America's own "string of pearls"—a chain of islands that run across the width of the Pacific at intervals that allow each one to be reinforced by the next.[1] Basing agreements in the Philippines (where once the US held the mighty Subic Bay) start this island chain. From there, the navy can fall back to the American territory of Guam, 1,500 miles east; from there to the Marshall Islands and Micronesia (one thousand miles farther east), where the US has permanent basing rights; and from there, the last one thousand miles to the Hawaii archipelago. By dint of Hawaii's location, America's rear base for dealing with Asia is more than three thousand miles closer to Japan and China than it would be if California were still the western edge of American territory.*

Hawaii was of course the site of the December 7, 1941, attack by the Imperial Japanese Navy Air Service that sunk the USS *Arizona* and damaged twenty other American surface vessels at the American naval port that carries the same name as the small town at the mouth of its inlet, Pearl City. One of the more surprising features of the Japanese attack on Pearl Harbor is how little damage was done to the base itself. Notwithstanding the large loss of life, the Japanese bombing runs inflicted little damage to the base facilities.† That meant that the US Navy was able quickly to restore what was then called Naval Station Pearl Harbor to operational use. It became a critical part of American operations in the Pacific through the rest of World War II. In the aftermath of the war, it served as the base headquarters for what was then known as Commander in Chief Pacific, or CINCPAC—a role held by such famed naval commanders as Admiral Nimitz.

These facilities have grown and evolved. CINCPAC headquarters was moved up the hill to Camp Smith, originally the site of the Aiea Naval Hospital. In April 2004, it moved into a newly built facility, the Nimitz-MacArthur Pacific Command Center, a six-story building encompassing almost 250,000 square feet of office space for the senior leadership. From the offices and conference rooms of the three- and four-star admirals, the building looks down over banyan trees, red mangroves, and bungalows that slope down along Halawa Heights, to nearly the entire southern coast of Oahu, from Diamond Head to

*For a commanding account of America's long-unfolding presence in Asia, readers should turn to Michael Green's *By More Than Providence: Grand Strategy and American Power in the Asia Pacific Since 1783* (New York: Columbia University Press, 2017).

†Historian Craig Symonds, in his account *World War II at Sea*, notes that Admiral Chuichi Nagumo, commander of the First Air Fleet during the attack on Pearl Harbor, took the fateful decision not to launch a third wave of attacks on the base, which had originally been envisaged as a strike designed to take out headquarters and maintenance facilities, oil tanks, and dry dock facilities.

Waikiki to the light blue waters of Mamala Bay. The sweeping view echoes the growing responsibilities of the command, which were evolving to meet new Chinese (and Russian) activity. In 2018, at the order of Secretary of Defense Mattis, this evolution was formalized in a reconfiguration that gave it the designation Indo-Pacific Command, adding the entire Indian Ocean basin to its already extensive area of operations.

* * *

Pearl Harbor also is the home port of the USS *John Paul Jones*—a guided-missile destroyer. It's at the very heart of American defenses in the Pacific and Indian Oceans. The ship forms part of Destroyer Squadron 9, which comprises six other destroyers built to the same design—the so-called Arleigh Burke–class destroyers that form the backbone of the American fleet.* The destroyer group in turn is assigned to Carrier Strike Group 11, which sails together with the aircraft carrier USS *Nimitz* out of Naval Base San Diego, the largest base in the Pacific. Both are supported from naval installations in Everett, Washington.[2] Aside from Carrier Strike Group 11 and four others like it, the US Pacific Fleet also comprises Naval Submarine Forces Pacific, the Naval Air Forces Pacific, the famed Seventh Fleet (which encompasses Task Force 73, a logistics unit, in Singapore), the Third Fleet, US Naval Forces Korea, and US Naval Forces Marianas (Guam). And, crucially, it incorporates Fleet Activities Yokosuka—diplomatic wording for what would otherwise be known as a base, in Tokyo Harbor (almost exactly where Commander Perry anchored his Black Ships in 1853). Yokosuka hosts the USS *Ronald Reagan* together with Carrier Strike Group 5 and Destroyer Squadron 15—the only American aircraft carrier homeported outside of US territory, and a highly visible symbol of America's treaty obligations to defend Japan from attack.

All of this amounts to 120,000 personnel under the command of the Pacific Fleet. But even this huge machinery is only one part of

*It is the US Navy's tradition to name both specific ships and classes of ships (specific hull designs) after famous admirals—like the Nimitz, the Arleigh Burke, and most recently the Zumwalt-class frigates. The Arleigh Burke class has a hull design that simultaneously improved its sea handling and generated a smaller radar footprint than destroyers with a similar displacement.

Indo-Pacific Command—the integrated command structure responsible for managing the deployments of up to 380,000 naval, air force, army, marine, and Special Forces personnel, almost one-quarter of the entire US armed services.

The officers of the wardroom of the *John Paul Jones* are fully aware of the bureaucracy above them. But equally, happily, uninvolved in their day-to-day tussles. For the ship is at the fighting end of this large complex of military arrangements.

They are also steeped in naval tradition—on this ship, particularly. It is named after one of the most famous officers in the long history of the US Navy, often referred to as the founder of the service.* Jones fought for the fledgling nation during the Revolutionary War, before the United States actually had its own naval forces, sailing under orders from George Washington.[3] In 1779, his most famous engagement, still one of the most storied in American naval history, occurred just off the coast of England. Jones had evaded the British blockade of its rebellious colonies and crossed the Atlantic to approach English waters. There, he then encountered HMS *Serapis* and the *Countess of Scarborough*. Early action saw him raked with gunfire and seeming to face certain defeat. The captain of the *Serapis* called over for his surrender. It was then that Jones reportedly uttered his famous phrase, "I have not yet begun to fight!" Through a series of skillful maneuvers and a substantial degree of luck, Jones proceeded to defeat both ships and to capture the *Serapis*. The flag flown by Jones during his defeat of the *Serapis* flies to this day on board the modern destroyer. (As does a second flag, which shows thirteen American stars and thirteen stripes, but with the sixth, tenth, and twelfth stripes rendered in blue rather than red or white. The flag was sent to Jones by Ben Franklin, then serving as ambassador in Paris, who had it rapidly commissioned by a seamstress. Clearly Franklin's explanation of the flag's design left something to be desired.†)

*Jones was an early advocate of a standing American navy, and an agitator for major naval action to deal with the Barbary pirates. Indeed, Thomas Jefferson turned to Jones to lead the campaign into Barbary—but by the time his orders reached him in Paris, Jones had died.

†As told to the author by the XO of the USS *John Paul Jones*.

Jones's "I have not yet begun to fight" is the better-known (and probably apocryphal) quote, but the crew of the modern ship prefer to cite his other famous saying: "I wish to have no connection with any ship that does not sail fast, for I intend to go in harm's way." Harm's way is exactly where the *Jones* sails. Although its specific mission details are classified, it's not hard to determine that Carrier Group 11 spends much of its time deployed to the Western Pacific, engaging in operations designed to defend Guam, to patrol the Philippine Sea, and to defend Japan. That puts it on the front lines of most potential confrontations with the Chinese navy, and potentially Russia's fleet as well.*

The modern *John Paul Jones* is a fearsome piece of war-fighting machinery. A crew of thirty officers command the ship with a crew of around three hundred men and women. It's 505 feet long and displaces just over nine thousand tons. Four gas turbine engines, each operating 26,000 shaft horsepower equivalents, allow it to sail at a top speed of over thirty knots. Her surface is thoroughly bristling with radar, sonar, and weapons systems. On her upper decks and rigging, she carries search and control radar, navigation radar, surface search radar, target illumination radar, and fire control radar.† That's in addition to a suite of sonar tools, including bow-mounted sonar, and towed array sonar. She has a whole series of countermeasures and jammers as well, including decoy systems, and towed torpedo decoys. Above all, she sports the Aegis radar—the most sophisticated radar system in the world.

All this hardware is designed to support a battery of weapons. That includes a five-inch gun; two radar-equipped 20 mm Gatling guns; two seventy-five caliber Bushmaster guns; four machine guns; two sets of torpedo launchers; and eight harpoon missiles for ship-to-ship defense. The word "harpoon" conjures an image of old-school whalers firing large, tied arrows from crossbows. The harpoons aboard the *Jones* are fifteen-foot missiles that fire from tubes on her deck and skim along the surface of the water at a speed of Mach .75 (equivalent to 556

*Indo-Pacific Command ranges as far north as the Arctic, so the *Jones* might also be deployed near where Russia has recently reinforced its Northern Fleet. It also covers India's coastline, where the *Jones* conducted FONOPs in 2021.

†More technically: the Lockheed Martin SPY-1 3D search weapons and control radar, the Raytheon AN/SPS-64 navigation radar, surface search radar, the Raytheon AN/SPG-62 target illumination radar, and an MK-15 Phalanx fire control radar.

mph) before exploding their five-hundred-pound warheads against the target.[4]

The core of her weaponry, though, is only partially visible on deck. Both at the foredeck and the rear deck of the ship stand two arrays of flat doors with heavy hinges, clustered together in blocks of eight. The doors are similar in shape to those atop the plastic recycling containers that dot America's driveways, but these are made of a heavy metal painted naval gray. They conceal the deadly weaponry within: vertically launched missiles.

The *Jones* can fire several types of missiles from those bays. That includes the SM-2, a medium-range anti-aircraft missile (that can also be used for short-range ship-to-ship fighting); the SM-3, which travels into the outer atmosphere; the VLA (Vertical Launch Anti-Submarine Rocket), used to launch torpedoes against submarines at a longer range than ship-based torpedo tubes; and the Evolved Sea Sparrow Missile, short-range anti-air missiles. The *Jones* also carries Tomahawks—indeed, she was the first ship to fire them into Iraq after the launch of the Gulf War. And crucially, she also carries what is known as Standard Missile 6. This is a multi-mission missile, initially used primarily for long-range air defense, and in other configurations for high-speed anti-ship fighting. But it is also used for what's known as "terminal ballistic missile defense," the latest instrument in the information technology–fueled arms race between the US and China.

Dynamics of "Informatized" War

In previous eras, the pulsing heart of a warship was the bridge, from where the captain and the leading officers would both navigate the ship, control its engines, maintain surface watch, and command the fire of the guns. The smell of ocean air, the scent of cordite, the sounds of gunfire—these were all part of the sensory experience of ship-to-ship battle at sea.

No more. In the world of modern war fighting, the heart of the *Jones* is a dark room known as the CIC—or the Combat Information Center. It's as far removed from human sensory experience as the ship designers can make it.

To access the CIC, you descend a series of steep metal ladders four decks down from the bridge. Quarters on a naval ship are exceedingly tight, and the dark gray paint of every surface increases the sense of enclosure as you descend these spaces. Walk the long, tight corridor of the main deck of the ship, and you arrive at the outer doors of the CIC, which can only be accessed by secure keycode.

Inside, the room is roughly thirty feet square, with an eight-foot ceiling. The walls and ceiling are painted black, which helps absorb the heat from a huge amount of computing power (plus up to two dozen bodies crowded into this small space) and keeps things dark. Though there are a few overhead blue fluorescent bulbs, most of the light in the room comes from the computer screens in front of the firing crew.

At the front are mounted three huge screens, displaying geographical, tactical, and targeting information. Immediately facing these screens is a station reserved for the captain or his XO. The rest of the room is organized around twenty workstations, arranged by type of warfare or weapon: there's a station for anti-aircraft fire, for sonar control, for anti-submarine fire, electronic measures, missile defense, naval surface fire, and air control. Some stations are equipped with joysticks to control on-deck guns. Hived off on their own, secured even inside the CIC, are the strike warfare controls for the Tomahawk missile launches—which are still one of the most closely guarded secrets in the US Navy.

Most consoles have computer terminals with a bank of three screens. These screens in turn relay specific targeting information, allowing the officers to communicate with one another, with the Tactical Action Office, or if necessary, with the captain. Some stations have classic radar with a green circle and a glowing radial arm. Others can display high-resolution topographical maps.

The firing controls for these systems are decentralized; the captain sets the overall tone of any given encounter, but decisive action is delegated to the officers managing each station. With the speed at which their targets move and the speed at which information is processed, every station has to act at a fast pace—so they have to be able to fire at their own discretion. Every station is trained on a range of scenarios and has specific orders as to how to respond to unfolding situations. From there, the ship operates by what's known as "command by negation." That is, an officer can initiate defensive actions without prior permission. Their responsibility is to alert the tactical action officer, or if necessary, the XO or captain, to their imminent actions. One of those senior officers in turn can then order them to stop—to negate their action. In the absence of an order to stop, they have a green light to act. This allows them to move with the speed of combat.

Tradition dies hard in the navy. One thing that naval officers like to do when plotting their firing positions is to scribble their targeting calculations as they make them. Historically, they would write calculations on the glass panel where map and ship information was displayed. As the glass panels were replaced by computers, naval officers still used wax pens to scribble their calculations directly on their screens. But the *Jones*'s computer systems were recently upgraded to touchscreens, making it impossible to scribble onto the monitors. That didn't stop the crew. On top of the new terminal screens, several officers have Velcroed plastic blue light screens onto which they can scribble their calculations—a $50 solution on top of what was roughly a $50 million upgrade.

Strung across the ceiling of the CIC are a large number of thick, black cables. These link the room to the on-deck radar. On-deck receivers are also pulling in data, at a rate of 128 bursts per second, from what's known as the Joint Tactical Information Distribution System. This is a complex set of radio, satellite, and internet-based systems that link US tracking and targeting systems on land (among other places, in Alaska, Greenland, and the UK), in aircraft like AWACS, satellites, and ships into a seamless, global flow of tactical and targeting information. The Aegis software integrates that data and its own sensory information into targeting options for the tactical action officers. This is crucial; for what actually makes the *John Paul Jones* a vital part of the American defensive array is not actually her missiles, or even her radar; it's her software.

The *John Paul Jones* was the first ship in the American fleet to receive what's known as Aegis Baseline 9, the latest software upgrade to the Aegis radar system. It represents the culmination of more than forty years of continuous innovation in radar design.* It improves the ship's ability to engage in the extremely complex business of shooting down a ballistic missile while simultaneously engaging in more traditional air defense actions.

Ballistic missiles are small, fast, and travel at heights that exceed the Earth's atmosphere. On descent, they are moving at speeds up to Mach 10—that's ten times the speed of sound, or nearly 7,700 miles per hour.[5] The challenge of tracking a small missile moving at those speeds is substantial. The challenge of using radar to guide a second missile to intercept it is epic.

Many of the details about Aegis radar are secret. One is very visible, though, the device itself. It looks nothing like the rotating device familiar from airport radar towers or cops' radar guns or similar. The Aegis radar appears to be a simple metal plate, roughly the same shape as a stop sign, though much larger; two of them are mounted on the forward part of the ship's superstructure, and two aft. Up close, you can see that it's actually comprised of more than one thousand "windows," or radiating elements.

In some ways, it is surprising that in a world of nuclear weapons and artificial intelligence and massive aircraft carriers, radar is still a critical technology. Yet it is a fact that continuous innovations in radar are a major part of what gives the United States its technological edge in modern battle. **Ra**dio **d**etection **a**nd **r**anging, aka radar, basically entails pulsing radio waves out into the air and recording the signal when they bounce back off of solid objects. Since radio waves move at the speed of light, or 186,000 miles per second, that happens near instantaneously. The signal, frequently repeated, can reveal both location and speed. What's known as the Doppler effect, a slight curve in the radio wave as it bounces off a moving object, shows direction.

There are lots of things that can limit radar or diminish its effectiveness. First there's the question of the frequency of the pulse. You

*In some senses, more than seventy-five years of innovation; for some of the engineers most deeply involved with the innovations that ultimately became Aegis got their start at England's Bletchley Park, de-encrypting the German Enigma machine.

have to get a signal back before the next one is emitted. Normal radar is sufficient to track ships and airplanes. But when you move out to atmospheric distance and you're dealing with missiles moving at three miles per second, traditional radar can't cope. Then there's what's known as signal noise, in other words, random variations internal to the pulse itself—irrelevant in short bursts but increasingly problematic over long distance. Also, the longer the distance between a radar array and the object it's trying to track, the more likely that simple clutter will interfere—random other objects that might be in the line of sight. Weather matters, too: rain, snow, cold, and wind can all interfere with radar over distance. And of course your adversary can deliberately jam or try to deceive your radar by sending out counter signals. Finally, short-range and long-range radar work rather differently because different energy pulses are more effective at the two different distances, and so it's hard to combine the two—but combining them is absolutely necessary if you're going to shoot down a fast-moving missile as it approaches its terminal destination.

Most important, there has to be a line of sight between the radar pulse, which moves in a straight line, and the object it's detecting. Line of sight is not a problem for old-fashioned ship-to-ship radar or from a ground-based station to the air above it. But its more complicated when you're trying to detect a long-range missile that's being launched out beyond the curvature of the Earth's surface. For ballistic missile defense, tracking a missile through its launch requires multiple sensors (radar arrays) on ships, in ground-based stations, and in satellite orbit, communicating with one another in real time.

To overcome these obstacles, the American navy does two things. First, the Aegis-class ships operate what's known as a phased array—far more precise than traditional radar. This allows it to compare information from different signals and sort out what is noise. It also allows it to track multiple targets simultaneously, a key asset. Second, it takes inputs from Master Station Pacific, satellite stations in the Arctic, and multiple other feeds—from ships, stationary positions, and satellites—and integrates them into a single, integrated tracking picture. Then, exceptionally powerful software that forms the Baseline 9 system draws together several different radar, sensor, integration, and firing control packages and prepares decisions for confirmation and action by tactical action officers.*

All this is described in the stilted language of the US Department of Defense as "an advanced automatic detect and track multifunction, three-dimensional passive, electronically scanned array radar." The navy has a more descriptive term: "shield of the fleet."

Ballistic Missile Defense

One of the people who is expert in this is Captain Rob Watts. The navy has been part of his life from early childhood in Norfolk, Virginia. Although he was not born into a navy family, he grew up surrounded by naval life. To this day, he recalls spending an early birthday in the wardroom of an aircraft carrier, an outing arranged by a family friend. He read a lot of Tom Clancy novels in middle school, and also *Jane's Fighting Ships*. By high school, he realized that he wanted to join the navy. That took him to the University of Virginia, and then into the service.

He was soon deployed into Operation Iraqi Freedom, aboard the USS *Raven*, a minesweeper patrolling the Persian Gulf from its base in Bahrain. He was then stationed aboard the USS *Oscar Austin*, homeported in Norfolk, on which he gained his first experience with the Aegis system. He learned about deeper oceans when the *Oscar Austin* was deployed to the Indian Ocean as part of the counter-piracy operations there (described in chapter 8). He spent a tour on the navy staff at the Pentagon, and then in the Protocol Office, working for the vice chief of Naval Operations.

It was service in the Pentagon that turned his career toward Asia. He had already been interested in the country, spending a semester in Beijing in 1996, and returning to spend six months studying the Mandarin language in Chongqing in 2001. Working with the vice chief of Naval Operations, he helped to plan the first visit to the US by the

*Specifically, the AEGIS Weapon System (AWS), comprised of AN/SPY-1 radar (similar to the better-known land-based THAAD, which stands for Terminal High Altitude Area Defense), a fire control system, and a suite of command and control software packages.

PLAN's new chief of operations, none other than Wu Shengli. And his expertise in Asia deepened when he was deployed to a ship based in Yokosuka, in Tokyo Bay.

Tall and fit, but bookish with glasses, and always with a quick intellect, Watts has kept up his focus on Asian security questions. He enrolled at Princeton to earn a master's degree in public policy and international security studies, and focused on the question of US strategy in Asia. He's also developed something of a career specialization in ballistic missile defense. That makes him particularly well suited to the command of the USS *John Paul Jones*—a commission he received in July 2020. Because of the continuing US spread of COVID-19, his ceremony was limited to senior crew and family only and broadcast on the ship's Facebook page.

In his period first as XO then captain of the *Jones*, one of the focus areas for the ship's training was on what's called "terminal defense." In an essay for his master's degree, Watts explains: "Regional defense employs a range of sensors and weapons to defend deployed forces and allies against shorter-range threats in the midcourse and terminal phases of flight. Midcourse defense involves intercepting missiles while they are outside the atmosphere. Terminal defense means intercepting a ballistic missile *as it descends toward its target*."

The United States has tried on several occasions to shoot down a ballistic missile, and results are spotty. The USS *John Paul Jones* was part of some of those early trials. On November 1, 2015, it participated in a test operation off of Wake Island (some 2,300 miles west of Honolulu), but failed to intercept a medium-range ballistic missile launched from a C-17 transport plane. Watts says of ballistic missile defense, "Sometimes the weapons exceed what our sensors can see." But that is the job Aegis Baseline 9 was designed to solve.

On August 29, 2017, with the new operating system installed, the *Jones* was the anchor ship in a new trial, designated Flight Test Standard Missile-27 Event 2. A ballistic missile was fired from the Pacific Missile Range Facility on the island of Kauai, at the western edge of the windward Hawaiian islands. A video of a similar event is stored on Watts's computer, and shows the huge plume of smoke and fire that accompanied the launch of a missile from the front vertical launch bays. The AN/SPY-1 radar component of the Aegis system tracked the incoming missile as the SM-6 flew to meet it, flying at a speed of over 2,600 miles per hour. Overhead, satellites detected the launch, and radar tracked both missiles, communicating to the *Jones*'s radar through the Joint Tactical Information Distribution System. ("Ballistic missile defense is a team sport," Captain Watts quipped.) Between the operation of the *Jones* and the various involved commands and the dummy missile, that single test cost an astonishing $200 million. But it had the desired result: the *Jones* intercepted and destroyed the ballistic missile as it descended from exo-atmospheric space.[6]

It was, to its proponents, a key element in the wider American response to China's evolving strategy.

The Battle of Networks: Air-Sea Battle vs. A2/AD

When Admiral Wu Shengli took over the PLAN in 2006, he developed a new doctrine for its "far seas" activities. But he also hardened its Near Seas deployments. That involved increasing the focus on land reclamation and installing facilities in the Near Seas. And it involved putting missile systems on those islands. For in 2010, China became the first country in the world to announce that they had within their arsenal a new type of weapon: an anti-ship ballistic missile. That is to say, a theater-range missile that could target American frigates and possibly even American aircraft carriers, at a range of at least nine hundred miles (the DF-21D missile). Soon after, China revealed that it had also developed (though not yet tested) a missile with a much more powerful range, out to 2,500 miles (the DF-26).[7] These missiles can be fired from ships, aircraft, and surface batteries, and can increasingly reach US forces stationed beyond China's immediate offshore waters.[8]

The missiles were not China's only new advance. They were designed to be deployed in tandem with a suite of systems whose purpose is to interfere with American radar and targeting. This included anti-radiation systems that jam or incapacitate enemy sensors, weaponry that specializes in attacking the airborne sensors and electronic warfare assets that the US relies on. In a best-case scenario for China, this would paralyze the US ability to win what China started to call "informatized wars"—what American planners call "systems war."

The purpose of China's advanced systems is plainly stated: to destroy US or allied ships and facilities inside the first island chain, and to threaten and deter US ships or aircraft carriers if or as they try to enter that zone, or even to approach it.[9] It added up to a major blow to American naval dominance in the Western Pacific.

In military circles, this combination of island reclamation, military installations, forward deployment of aircraft, and above all the anti-ship missiles became known by the somewhat unwieldy acronym A2/AD. That stands for "anti-access/area denial." Anti-access means making it impossible or prohibitively costly for an adversarial navy to gain access to the waters in question—in this case, the Near Seas. Area denial means keeping that adversary force at bay over long periods of time, preventing them from gaining a foothold from which to expand their force.

But as China evolved its forces, so did the United States. In the first decades of the post–Cold War era, the US had focused on far-range land operations—the long wars and high-impact Special Forces operations in the Middle East, above all. Those were operations that focused on Special Forces command, and the marines. But now the US turned back to the navy—and the air force. Because what emerged from early US thinking about how to respond to China's growing naval prowess was the concept of Air-Sea Battle—or ASB, as it is known in the acronym-clogged world of national security.[10,*]

In an earlier era, when confronted with advances by another peer competitor, the Soviet Union, the United States had looked to offset those advances with developments of its own. The first of these came in confronting the sheer size of the Soviet conventional force; the US offset the Soviet advantage by developments in its nuclear weapons program. It became known as the "first offset."[11] When the Soviets caught up in the nuclear arena, the United States looked to innovations in information technology and connectivity to provide the "second offset," improving what's referred to as the "qualitative edge" of American military performance—basically, cutting-edge information and communication

*The Department of Defense later decided that the phrase "Air-Sea Battle" was too provocative, and replaced it with "Joint Concept for Access and Maneuver in the Global Commons." Then, deciding that was too inelegant, replaced it in turn with "Multi-Domain Operations" or "Joint All-Domain Operations," or even "Joint All-Domain Command and Control." The original "Air-Sea Battle" does a much better job of conveying the point.

technology. It has sought to maintain that edge ever since. And in 2010, confronting China's launch of anti-ship ballistic missiles, the United States began to seek a "third offset." Air-Sea Battle was the answer.[12]

Air-Sea Battle comprises a lot of acronyms and concepts and technical complexities, but its core is simple: to blunt the power of the Chinese missile systems, to allow the US to depend on its better ship design and higher-quality radar and communications technology for the edge in ship-to-ship combat. This can be done in three ways: by disrupting Chinese targeting; by destroying missile launchers in their bases; or by intercepting the missiles in flight.

The first is conceptually straightforward, but technologically complex. Unlike missiles, ships—especially aircraft carriers—are large and very slow (by the standards of radar detection). Without sophisticated countermeasures, targeting of the ships is relatively straightforward. Of course, the US does engage in substantial countermeasures, using counter-radar, cyber offense, sending out counter-information, and other means to inject uncertainty into China's targeting. By these means, the US tries to confuse the Chinese picture of its naval assets in the Western Pacific—disrupting the sensory picture. And every time China tries to track and target an American ship, it is revealing valuable information—for any use of active sensors gives away the presence and identity of the user at a much greater range than what the sensor itself can detect. Still, as China develops its satellite and naval radar technologies, it's more and more likely that American ships could be successfully targeted. Disrupting targeting is not a sufficient measure to reduce the threat of China's anti-ship missiles.

The second option—destroying the missiles in their bases on island features in the Near Seas or on the Chinese mainland—is both complex and dangerous. It involves the United States deploying either long-range strike fighters, long-range missiles, or forward US air fighters; penetrating Chinese airspace; evading Chinese air defenses; evading or surviving combat with the (very sophisticated) Chinese air force; and successfully targeting and striking Chinese assets on land. Now, striking targets on land is easier than hitting them at sea, but it is far from foolproof. As one expert in this field notes, "Getting a weapon to the right place at the right time is just the last step in a long chain of inference." China would take substantial measures to shield its missiles, to confuse American tracking, and to stop American jets from successfully flying over Chinese territory. Most analysts believe that ultimately the United States would be successful in its efforts to take out the missile launchers. But that necessarily involves hitting targets on the Chinese mainland, which takes what might once have been a limited encounter between two navies at sea right to the edge of full-blown war with the Chinese PLA.

And so the third option—shooting down Chinese missiles in flight—is a hugely preferable option. If it can be done reliably. If the United States can successfully, repeatedly, shoot down Chinese missiles, it limits the game-changing feature of China's anti-ship system. And we go back to ship-to-ship competition, where the US Navy has a vital technological and qualitative edge over its Chinese competitors.

* * *

This approach has its skeptics. Some of them are former Department of Defense officials closely involved with the original arguments around Air-Sea Battle, who argue that to defeat American anti-ballistic missile defenses, the Chinese (or even the North Koreans) could simply barrage American ships with "garbage missiles" until the American supply of SM-6 missiles was exhausted—and then target American ships with higher-quality munitions.

For this reason, the navy's research establishment is experimenting with weapons that can be fired more frequently, like high-powered microwave, electrical, and laser weapons. That sounds like a sci-fi novel, but there's long been research on such weapons, and new tests are advancing the capacity for missile-targeting with lasers. One senior defense official originally involved in the Air-Sea Battle concept argues that "We need to be doing a Manhattan Project on electronic weapons; and we're not."[13] Others are focused on railguns.* Watts himself is more skeptical of those: "It's the technology of the future, and always will be."[14] But there have been recent breakthroughs in laser weapons tested at sea.

* * *

*A railgun looks like a large, square cannon; it uses parallel metal conductors (they look like railroad tracks, hence the name) and an electrical current flowing down one side, to generate electromagnetic force that launches a projectile at very high speed. Most railgun projectiles do not contain explosives, but rather rely on the speed and kinetic energy to inflict damage.

Whatever weapons systems are involved, Air-Sea Battle also requires something that sounds very mundane but is in fact equally hard: the integration of combat services. The core idea behind the concept of Air-Sea Battle is that tight communication between air force and naval operations, with each service playing an enabling role for the other, can substantially extend the range, accuracy, and punch of the other.*

In real terms, integrated air and naval operations would give the United States the ability to do the following (very difficult) things. The US Air Force could conduct "counter-space" operations—basically, attacking Chinese satellites—to blind China's space-based ocean surveillance systems; that would improve operational freedom for the US Navy. The navy's Aegis ships could then sail forward to supplement ground-based missile-defense assets to improve the security of US Air Force bases in Japan and elsewhere along the Near Seas perimeter. Navy submarines and carrier-based strike groups could then conduct attacks on Chinese missile outposts in the South and East China Seas, enabling further US Air Force strikes. Then the air force could conduct long-range strikes designed to destroy PLA maritime surveillance systems, and to destroy ground-based ballistic missile launchers. That would again expand the navy's freedom of maneuver and reduce strikes on US and allied bases. The navy's carrier-based fighters could then launch a wave of attacks against what's known as the Intelligence, Surveillance, and Reconnaissance platforms of the Chinese forces—their tracking and targeting instruments—thereby enabling air force tankers and support aircraft to move deeper into the Near Seas. And finally the air force could support anti-submarine warfare through offensive mining by stealth bombers.[15] All this effort would enable the US to roll back PLAN positions across the breadth of the Near Seas.

But once launched, this "battle of networks" or "systems war" likely becomes a full-blown war between the American and Chinese armed forces.

*All of this is still conceptual, and much debated, and so there are as many versions of Air-Sea Battle as there are analysts working through its details. The following paragraphs represent the core of what many analysts see as the principal elements of Air-Sea Battle, but there are also lots of skeptics about the ability of the navy or the air force to actually pull this off—let alone of Congress to adequately fund the necessary purchases of equipment.

America's Hard Choices

Unsurprisingly, there's been a heated debate within the American strategic community about the feasibility (and the cost) of the Air-Sea Battle plan.[16] But it's also about the wisdom of even contemplating it.

At the end of Part I, we highlighted the fact that the United States pays the bulk of the costs of securing the freedom of trade even as other nations profit handsomely from it. Skeptics ask the question this way: Why should the United States pay for the security of trade when countries like Japan, the third-richest country in the world, profit so hugely from it? Going further, a growing body of skeptical opinion in Washington asks: Why should the United States put itself at risk of war with China to secure the Western Pacific, when all of its allies in that region profit from freedom of the seas there? During his term, President Trump made this question explicit in his negotiations with the Japanese: at the very least, he argued, Japan should pay the full cost of the American forward presence in its waters.

But the issue is a difficult one. If the United States chose to pull back from its commitments to the security of Japan (and perhaps similarly Korea), there are two distinct possibilities of what would happen next. One is that Japan and China could find a way to get along, despite a long-running rivalry. They are, after all, each other's largest trading partners and despite mounting strategic tensions, they continue to deepen their economic ties. But that's no guarantee of peace. It's also possible that Japan and China could end up in a hot war at sea—pitting the world's second- and third-largest economies against each other, massively disrupting the global economy and roiling the most important shipping lanes in the world—shipping lanes on which the American economy now vitally relies. That conflict would also roil the entire North Asian region. Defense of the freedom of commerce in Asian waters has been central to America's security concept since the middle of the nineteenth century, and its importance has only grown in the modern era.[17] And the wider the Chinese naval reach grows, the more reasons the United States would have to blunt it.

* * *

By around 2016, many observers in Southeast Asia warned that China was gradually gaining the upper hand in the Near Seas. Certainly, China had increased its capacity to impose *substantial* costs on the US Navy in times of war. But to military observers, China had also gained "escalation dominance"—that is to say, it has the ability to prevail at several different levels of conflict, and ratchet up its response if need be. To countries like Singapore and Japan, who rely on the protection of the US Navy, this was a deeply worrying development.

At one level, it's also deeply unsurprising. After all, we are talking about a series of bodies of waters immediately off the Chinese coast, and at least seven thousand miles from the Pacific border of the United States (excepting Hawaii). A fast cruiser steaming at a sustainable speed of twenty knots would take about fourteen days to reach Woody Island (in the South China Sea, site of China's first reported missile installation in those waters) from the US Naval Base in San Diego. China could take myriad types of actions within comfortable range of its shore before the United States could even seriously start to reinforce its presence.

But for American strategic planners, the deeper concern was in the inexorable, escalatory logic of military affairs: the sense that, as China improved its capacity for integrated operations in the Near Seas, and its capacity to defend those operations from "counter-insurgency" by the US Navy in the Western Pacific, it was in effect giving itself the building blocks of a genuinely global blue-water navy. By roughly 2015, China was showing every sign of moving in that direction—engaging in port visits, long-range ship trials, and weapons developments that many believed could only be explained by an ambition to deploy naval capacity far beyond the Western Pacific. And at the same time, the costs kept growing for the United States to maintain a sufficient fleet in the Near Seas and address China's relentless strategic escalation. And so US thinking turned to two new tactics to confront the Chinese. One was to turn back to a key instrument of American military superiority during the Cold War: the nuclear submarine. The other was a tactic to hurt the Chinese at lower costs—by blockading Chinese ports.

11

To Conquer the Seas

Confronting a Global PLAN (2017–Present)

"How should we not continue to conquer the sea?"

—C. Y. Tung, 1954 Entry, Personal Diaries, C. Y. Tung Museum

Mahan described maritime power as involving commercial reach, adequate ships, and a network of ports. By 2015, that China had acquired the first two measures of power was beyond doubt. But for the officers and scholars at the Naval War College debating the question of Chinese intentions, the question of China's access to global bases remained. Without them, China could pose only a limited, regional threat to American strategy. This helps explain why the officers and scholars were so focused on a striking development in a region that otherwise attracts limited attention from the United States—the Red Sea, off the Indian Ocean, lying between Asia and Africa.

* * *

Perim Island is a small, crab-shaped island in the Red Sea, two miles deep and three miles wide. It has limited plant life and no animals. Nor does it have a single source of potable water, and hence no long-standing human settlement. And yet, Perim has been the source of an amazing amount of political tension over time. It was written about by Pliny the Elder, the Roman historian who in 77 BCE published the *Naturalis Historia*, under the name of the island of Diodorus. Not much is known about its history during the Dark Ages, but in 1513, as part of their effort to dominate the spice trade, the Portuguese seized Perim. They controlled it until the mid-1700s, when the Red Sea became again a zone of contest, between the French and Ottomans. And in 1799, the island was briefly occupied by the British East India Company. The British did not sustain their presence, but fifty years later would resume it, when they got wind of the French construction of the Suez Canal. During the First World War, British forces in Perim came under attack by the Turks. The British maintained control of Perim and nearby Aden until 1967, when the island became part of the independent nation of the People's Republic of South Yemen. In 1971, the Marxist government of South Yemen allowed a Palestinian terrorist group, the People's Front for the Liberation of Palestine (PFLP), to use Perim as a base for an attack on an Israeli commercial vessel sailing up the Rea Sea to Aqaba/Eilat. And during the Cold War, Perim and Aden were a base for the Soviet navy.

Why should this barren isle be fought over so prodigiously? The simple answer is: geography. Perim Island lies right in the middle of the Bab el-Mandeb, or the Gate of Tears—a narrow passage that lies at the opening of the Gulf of Aden to the Indian Ocean. Put differently: it's the key passageway between the Indian Ocean and the Red Sea, which buts up against the Sinai Peninsula and the Suez Canal, the choke points from which empires and states have sought to patrol and control the flow of goods between the European and Asian worlds.

And so it provoked more than a few raised eyebrows when a new sea power chose to take over a port and build out a logistical hub, not on Perim itself but on the eastern coast of Djibouti, just eight miles away from Perim. In August 2017, China opened what it termed a "Chinese PLA Operations Support Base"—China's first overseas military installation, and the first time since the 1450s that Chinese naval ships had been based in the Indian Ocean.

China argued that it was simply expanding its capacity to support the counter-piracy operations and to protect its overseas interests. In 2015, it issued a government white paper that spelled this out: "The security of overseas interests concerning energy and resources, strategic sea lines of communication (SLOCs), as well as institutions, personnel, and assets abroad, has become an imminent issue."[1] In essence, Beijing was arguing that the Djibouti installation was simply designed to protect China's economic interests. But it's hard to deny the significance of the location.[2]

Strategic Strong Points

The United States came out of World War II with a world-dominant navy, a network of allies, a long history of naval deployments in Asia, and access to many of the Royal Navy's far-flung network of bases, logistical facilities, and fueling stations. China had none of these. But what China has built, in spades, is economic and commercial ties. And one of the world's largest and most extensive infrastructure lending programs. Over the past several years, China has turned those assets into an important network of ports—not quite the same thing as bases, but an important step in that direction.[3]

Much of this has been developed through its infamous Belt and Road Initiative, a network of infrastructure investments, port investments, and political relationships with countries at the terminus of key sea-lanes of communication. Among them was the commercial port of Hambantota, Sri Lanka, to which China was given a ninety-nine-year lease after the Sri Lankan government struggled to pay back the debt on Chinese loans it had used to build the port; Piraeus, Greece, just across from the Suez Canal; Haifa, Israel, also close to the Suez and very close to Russia's base in Tartus, Syria; in Gwadar, Pakistan, relatively close to the Strait of Hormuz; Curitiba, Brazil, Brazil's most profitable port terminal; Bruges, Belgium; and Casablanca, Morocco. Some of these are self-evidently commercial, and have no clear strategic function. But others are certainly amenable to "dual use."

Rush Doshi, who had plumbed a unique archive of Chinese Communist Party sources, notes that China had also officially adopted a doctrine to allow those economic hubs to be rapidly reinforced by China's marines, to serve the function of protecting Chinese citizens overseas and Chinese economic interests.[4] Of course, that's entirely legitimate and consistent with an overarching strategy of defense of trade; but could it be the thin edge of the wedge in a militarization of China's network of ports?

One concept that seemed to square the circle between China's commercial approach and its military potential is the notion of what's known as "strategic strongpoints."[5] These are foreign ports that hold special value for their economic functions and are operated by Chinese firms. There are at least seventy global ports in which Chinese firms have equity or operating leases.[6] With its network of China-friendly or Chinese state–owned enterprise-run commercial facilities, Chinese forces operating abroad could stop at these ports to receive supplies and other services and thus help extend China's projection capabilities by shortening resupply time and by providing a Chinese presence.[7] And if Djibouti is an example, they could be rapidly expanded from commercial installations to naval ones. In December 2016, PLAN commander Admiral Wu Shengli spoke about these ports during an event commemorating the eighth anniversary of China's anti-piracy operations off the Horn of Africa: "We must give full play to the supporting role of the overseas support system to carry out larger scale missions in broader areas and the shape the situation."[8] That's China's bureaucratic-speak for preparing to fight wars in the far seas.

China appears, in fact, to be following the model of the English East India Company. When the East India Company received its charter from Queen Elizabeth I at the dawn of the seventeenth century, its focus was on building trade relations. But the flag soon followed. China seems to be pursuing a similar model, with trade leading the way—and, potentially, the military not far behind. Or as two China scholars put it: "The flag lags, but follows."[9]

China is already flexing its military muscles at some of these overseas strong points—especially with its submarines, which have been spotted at ports far from the Near Seas. In 2016, a Chinese submarine made a port call in Karachi, Pakistan, China's most important ally.[10] In 2017, Chinese attack submarines conducted port calls in Sepanggar, Malaysia. Chinese subs have also been increasingly spotted in the Indian Ocean—in 2013, China confirmed that a nuclear attack sub would make its way across the ocean to carry out anti-piracy missions in the Gulf of Aden.[11] And China tried but ultimately failed to get Sri Lanka to host a port call in Colombo, in the heart of the Indian Ocean.[12]

These PLAN moves, and the mounting distrust of Chinese intent, have caused America to contemplate the aforementioned countermeasures of blockades and submarines.

Blockading the Chinese

Blockades are a tested tactic of naval warfare. The British blockaded France continuously from 1773 to 1802, and again from 1804 to 1814, ultimately helping Britain to defeat France in the Napoleanic Wars. Britain also blockaded the United States during the Revolutionary War, and again during the War of 1812. (With less favorable outcomes for London.) During the Civil War, the Union mounted a naval blockade of the Confederacy both to impose shortages and to prevent reinforcements from European powers. And Britain and the United States blockaded Japan in the 1930s in response to its invasion of China, and then again after it allied itself to Nazi Germany.

China is quite vulnerable to a potential blockade. In 2018, trade made up 38 percent of China's GDP,[13] and 64 percent of that maritime trade went through the South China Sea. Add the Yellow Sea and the East China Sea and the numbers go up still further.[14] So if the United States and its allies could actually succeed in stopping shipping from reaching Chinese shores, it could cripple the Chinese economy.

What would a blockade look like? Historically, there have been two kinds. First is a *close blockade*, which takes place close to the coasts of the target country. That involves placing warships just off of an enemy's shore to search all incoming and outgoing merchant ships (as the British did with the United States before the breakout of the War of 1812). The second option is a *distant blockade*, which involves stationing warships farther away from the coasts, along sea-lanes, and then choking off trade in a similar manner—by searching all incoming and outgoing merchant ships. The trade-offs are simple: the farther away you are from the target nation's coast, the less exposed you are to counterattack; but the more you risk allowing ships to route around you or slip through the blockade.

Several American think tanks and defense contractors have undertaken studies about how a blockade could be implemented. A major study by RAND looked at how the US could close off the Malacca Strait, as well as the nearby straits of Sunda and Lombok (mostly used by oil tankers).[15] A study led by Jan van Tol, a former naval captain who served as a special adviser in the vice president's office and as a military assistant to the famous Pentagon strategist Andy Marshall (known as "Yoda"), argued that distant blockade operations could require disrupting Chinese undersea telecommunications lines; and seizing/destroying Chinese undersea energy infrastructure.[16] And studies of potential blockade scenarios were published in the navy's semi-official journal, *Proceedings*. Chinese planners tracking the American navy saw a surge of such writings in the 2010 to 2014 period.

The history of blockades suggests that they have been most successful when they differentiate between neutral and enemy shipping and consistently block enemy shipping.[17] This creates trade-offs. Consistent blocking is easier with a close blockade, but it would involve putting American assets at risk close to China's shores. The US could diminish the risk to its assets by mounting a distant blockade. These assets could neutralize shipping—but they couldn't differentiate between Chinese and neutral shipping, thus infuriating neutral parties whose ships were disturbed. And that includes countries like Japan, whose support of a blockade would be essential for success. So American planners are exploring the notion of a "two-ring" blockade: an inner ring, which would be a close blockade that aimed to neutralize vessels bound for China, and an outer ring to solve the differentiation problem.[18] The inner ring would be declared an "exclusion zone" that is off-limits to commercial shipping and enforced by firepower (essentially a "sink-on-sight" policy) as close to China's shores as operationally possible. It would be principally enforced by submarines, backed up by long-distance airpower, and mines. By avoiding the use of surface ships, the US could limit its exposure to Chinese anti-ship mines. The outer ring would allow for differentiation and "non-lethal neutralization"—i.e., seizure, or redirection—by setting up checkpoints and closing or limiting traffic through a number of key passageways (though that may very well violate international law). The US could also establish an inspection regime here, trying to determine merchant vessels' ultimate destinations and reviewing their bills of lading—in an extreme circumstance, by boarding the ships, but perhaps also by exchange of electronic information.

All this has the advantage of avoiding American strikes on the Chinese mainland. But there are serious difficulties with this idea as well.

First, there are the economic challenges. China is a far bigger player in the global economy than Germany was on the eve of WWI—

Germany accounted for slightly under 15 percent of global manufacturing production in 1913; China now accounts for more than 25 percent of global manufacturing value added. Impeding the economy of China would rebound into the economies of Japan, Australia, and the United States—the key actors that would have to implement a blockade. (To say nothing of European allies.) And rewiring around China would take years, and might not really be possible—at least not without the kind of costs that societies are only willing to bear in times of war.[19]

There's an additional, modern problem: the nature of what's on commercial vessels. One of the more spectacular early German attacks against British shipping in WWII came in 1939 when a German U-boat sank the *Doric Star*, a Blue Star Line ship carrying wool and mutton from New Zealand to UK ports. It was a major blow against British food stocks. But the modern equivalent would be far more complicated. If an American submarine sank a ship sailing to Chinese harbors, not only would it likely be sinking a non-Chinese vessel, it would be destroying cargo ultimately bound not just for Chinese consumption, but for Chinese intermediate manufacturing designed ultimately to end up as part of the supply chain of American and European goods. By imposing costs on the Chinese economy, the US would be imposing costs on Japan, Australia, Europe—and itself.

And there's a third problem—China could counterattack.*

Most historians agree that it was the British and American rubber and oil blockade of Japan that triggered its military incursions into what it called the East Asian Resource Zone (Singapore and Hong Kong, principally) to gain access and sea routes to Indonesian and Malaysian rubber and oil supplies. To deter America from interfering with this move, Japan also attacked Pearl Harbor.[20]

The lessons of that episode clearly inform China's thinking about blockades.

*Germany used a counterattack in response to the British blockade, sinking some 11,153,000 tons of Allied merchant shipping by the end of WWI, mostly through submarine attacks. And in WWII, Germans responded to a blockade with commercial warfare against the British and later Allied maritime trade, sinking more than five thousand Allied merchant ships. This also delayed supply chains, since convoys had to move slowly and were substantially rerouted. In short, blockades can lead to major escalation, rather than the opposite.

China has threatened to respond to a blockade by sinking American aircraft carriers, and exploiting other American weaknesses. "What the United States fears the most is taking casualties," said PLAN Rear Admiral Luo Yuan, commenting on a possible attack on US aircraft carriers.[21] And others have noted that over time Beijing could adapt its anti-access, area denial tactics to implement a form of "economic warfare with Chinese characteristics." That could involve conducting strikes against economic targets in nearby nations (like ports, ground transportation nodes, communications facilities, manufacturing, and energy infrastructure), or other moves to disrupt global supply chains.[22] All this could result in a two-sided naval war on trade.

Still, faced with the alternative of an attack on the Chinese mainland, possibly provoking all-out war, blockades could be a lower-cost way to confront China's navy.

The second countermeasure is a lot more expensive. It involves some of the most advanced technology in the American arsenal: submarines.

* * *

The job of keeping the US Navy at the forefront of submarine technology belongs to the labyrinthine set of research stations and labs that report to the Naval Research Center—ranging from testing and development sites in the Hawaiian archipelago, in Alaska, Florida, Virginia, and Washington State, to a sonar testing facility in, of all places, central Idaho.* At the heart of this, though, are two "echelon commands"—the Naval Undersea Warfare Center in Newport, Rhode Island, and the Naval Surface Warfare Center in Carderock, Maryland.

In the post–Cold War era, the American focus on submarines waned. But there's been a full reversal. A recent report from an Australian university put it succinctly: "As the environment above the surface becomes more deadly because of Chinese deployments of cruise missiles, hypersonic technologies and anti-air defenses, America's enduring advantage in undersea warfare will become increasingly important in the regional balance of power."[23] That argument is echoed

*For new sonar and other undersea detection technologies, the open ocean creates too many complications and variables for initial testing; so the navy operates its Acoustic Research Department in the 1,150-foot-deep waters of Lake Pend Oreille in northern Idaho.

by the leadership of the US Indo-Pacific Command: Admiral Philip Davidson told Congress in 2019 that submarine activity by America's adversaries had tripled since 2009.[24] He said, "Continuing to build submarines is critically important. It is our most significant advantage in all domains right now."[25]

It is not just American and Chinese submarines at play. Former US assistant secretary of defense for Asian and Pacific security affairs David Shear has said, "The region—particularly the western Pacific, and particularly within the first island chain on the American front perimeter—is filling up with submarines."[26] Those waters are now replete with Korean, Japanese, and even Malaysian and Vietnamese submarines.[27, 28] This has led to calls for a kind of underwater code of conduct, since there are so many submarines in the Indo-Pacific now and the risk of accident has risen dramatically.[29,*]

The United States currently operates the world's most sophisticated fleet of submarines, about seventy of them. They are built to several different classes, or hull designs. Most powerful are the Ohio-class boats, which are classified as SSBNs—that is, submarine ships ballistic nuclear, in other words, submarines capable of launching ballistic nuclear missiles. Each of the Ohio-class submarines can fire twenty-four such missiles armed with nuclear warheads. Those subs that don't carry a nuclear payload are designated SSGNs—they carry submarine launched cruise missiles, including up to 154 Tomahawk missiles.[†] Then, the US has a number of attack submarines designed to engage in ship-to-ship combat and to support and defend the carrier strike

*It's not the first time that political leaders have called for a code of conduct to regulate submarine warfare. So brutal were the effects of submarine warfare in the First World War that in its wake, Britain's King George VI floated the idea of an outright ban on submarines, likening them to other classes of weaponry that "civilized nations" had chosen to forego. But King George got little traction with his proposal, and submarines played a critical role again in World War II. Then, as in World War I, their critical function: to attack trade. And that's what makes them theoretically critical for a blockading operation. For submarines' role in World War II, see Craig L. Symonds, *World War II at Sea: A Global History* (New York: Oxford University Press, 2018), chs. 6, 12, 17.

†Many submarines are nuclear-powered; others are powered by diesel or electrical batteries. A subset of nuclear-powered submarines also carry and can launch nuclear weapons. Nuclear-powered submarines are designated SSN; those that can launch nuclear weapons are designated SSBN. The *SS* signifies submarine; the *G* denotes a guided missile; and the *N* tells us that the submarine is nuclear-powered.

groups. These include the Los Angeles–class, the Seawolf-class, and the Virginia-class boats. Variants on these boats are also used to insert Special Forces units onto enemy shores. (It's an oddity of maritime convention that whereas destroyers, frigates, cruisers, and the like—the surface fleet—are referred to as "ships," their submarine cousins are referred to as "boats.")

They are powerful weapons. And they are expensive, especially in large numbers. But the United States is investing heavily in its submarine fleet. In December 2019, the USN awarded its most expensive shipbuilding contract *ever*, allocating $22.2 billion over several years for nine nuclear-powered Virginia-class attack submarines.[30] (These are huge boats, displacing 10,200 tons—compared to just over 9,000 tons for the Arleigh Burke–class destroyers like the USS *John Paul Jones.*)

A key technological edge that the United States holds is that all of its submersible boats are nuclear-powered. That gives them the ability to travel for months at a time; to operate without having to surface for oxygen; and to roam freely across the world's oceans, and under surface ice. And it gives them this critical advantage: they are quiet. And thus very hard to detect.

China's boats are not. Its fleet has been growing fast, but it still faces an important technology gap with the United States. According to a US Defense Intelligence Agency report, in 2019 China was operating six nuclear attack subs, four nuclear-powered ballistic missile submarines, and fifty diesel attack subs.[31] Its nuclear-powered ballistic missile submarines are what's known as Type 094 Jin-class, believed to have been developed with help from Russia, and which can fire missiles with an estimated range of 4,600 miles. That's a critical measure, because if China can reliably deploy those boats at the eastern edge of the Philippine Sea, they could hit the continental United States.* And China

*According to the US Defense Intelligence Agency, China also operates what are known as Type 092 Xia-class boats, which fire short-range missiles for use in regional combat; and nuclear-powered fleet submarines combat Type 093 Shang-class. That's in addition to four classes of conventionally powered submarines: the Type 039A Yuan-class, AIP-powered (one of their quietest), which can launch anti-ship cruise missiles; the Type 039 Song-class, their first indigenous design; the Kilo-class (Russian-made), providing a long-range anti-surface warfare capability of about 120 nautical miles; and the Type 035 Ming-class, its most dated boat.

is expected to begin producing more powerful submarines similar in quality to the US Virginia class.[32] These would extend China's missile range considerably.

Though over time their technology has improved, noise remains a key weakness for the Chinese submarine fleet.[33] Quiet submarines can stay hidden from anti-submarine detection and anti-submarine warfare. In most conditions, ambient sea noise is around ninety decibels; to avoid detection, submarines need to be able to power themselves with engines that do not make much more noise than that. Western submarine design hit that mark around thirty years ago; China still lags behind. The US estimates that the newest Chinese submarine (the Type 093) operates at about 110 decibels; far better than its predecessors, but still far easier to detect than the quieter American boats.

On the other hand, Chinese submarine-detection technology is advancing. Chinese boats already have passive sonar arrays on their sides and retractable towed array sonars that go behind them, similar to American boats. This allows them to operate anti-submarine reconnaissance with roughly the same sophistication as the US Navy.

And China is pouring resources into new technologies to improve its undersea targeting and detection. A key question is this: Will advances in artificial intelligence—where Chinese science is very close to that of the United States—allow China to close the gap? To put it in more technical terms: Has China significantly advanced its capacity through autonomous data analysis, inference, and decisional controls?

By far the most common technique for submarine tracking is acoustic detection, using sonar—a technology that relies on what's known as the "acoustic tomography" of the oceans (basically, its sound patterns). Readers who have watched movies like *The Hunt for Red October* will recall scenes of sonar operators listening intently to pinging sounds picked up by sending out microphone signals, which bounce off the other side's submarines (or whales or rocks; they have different sounds). In the contemporary period, human ears have been replaced by automated signal-processing algorithms—one of the earlier forms of artificial intelligence introduced into modern warfare.

In theory, there are other ways: tracking the effect of the submarine's movement on bioluminescence; measuring its effect on surface waves, or internal waves; magnetic resonance; measuring for temperature changes in the waters around the boat; and what's called "lidar" (essentially, laser radar). But all of these technologies suffer from two inescapable physical realities: the chemistry and currents of the oceans, and the sheer size of the marine environment versus the ultimately puny size of the target. This generates a fundamental problem for all detection methods: a low ratio of signal to noise.

Slightly more promising is the detection of downstream wakes. As we'll see in Part IV, the ocean's waters are actually quite stratified, with density, salinity, and temperature changing continuously, but largely quite different in the deep waters below one thousand feet, versus surface waters. When a submarine moves through those stratified layers, it disturbs them and creates a turbulent wake. This can be observed, inter alia, by laser beams.[34] Still, the large distances involved and the huge volume of water that would need to be covered for such technologies to reliably detect submarines pose considerable logistical and financial obstacles.

So difficult are these obstacles that during the Cold War, the US Navy developed a plan for an alternative method to defeat the Soviet submarine fleet: to use depth charges, but depth charges tipped with nuclear warheads. These would explode with sufficiently forceful waves to disrupt the Soviet boats as much as fifteen miles from the blast radius. Of course, even fifteen miles is only a useful distance if you have some knowledge of where the target is sailing. In the extreme—detection of a large-scale Soviet submarine launch without subsequent tracking of specific boats—the US planned to use the air force to engage in an oceans-wide "nuclear barrage" to defeat the Soviet submarine fleet.

The Chinese appear to have learned a lot from American anti-Soviet tactics—and the use of nuclear-tipped anti-submarine depth charges is now a part of the PLAN arsenal. It is now a Chinese option to use these nuclear devices against the American submarine fleet, although probably on a much smaller scale—barraging only the Luzon Strait in the Philippine Sea, for example, to prevent the US Navy from reinforcing Taiwan. American naval planners believe that the Chinese view is that the use of nuclear weapons undersea would not constitute a violation of the key international norm against the use of nuclear weapons, or generate an American nuclear response; instead, the US might choose to use conventional munitions to strike a Chinese communications base or missile installation near the coast. Still, the notion of the use of subsea nuclear weapons is a deeply disturbing one.

As the US and its potential adversaries return to a focus on antisubmarine warfare, an important question is whether advances in artificial intelligence and computing power fundamentally change the dynamics of submarine detection. Tom Stefanick, who did some of the earliest work for the US Navy in applying artificial intelligence to submarine warfare, thinks the application is limited. "There's simply no way around the fundamental problem of tracking small boats in huge waters: a low signal to noise ratio. All the AI in the world can't overcome that problem."[35]

The bottom line: the US submarine fleet remains, for all intents and purposes, indestructible. China's only reliable option to destroy the US submarine fleet is an incredibly risky one—to attack the boats in their bases, on the Pacific and Atlantic coasts, using intercontinental ballistic missiles. From what we know, China has developed the capacity to deploy such missiles, but has not done so yet. And it would have to think very carefully before taking this step, for here the planned American response is absolutely clear: nuclear strike on China.

Chinese Friends?

Short of such dramatic outcomes, a key question for China is this: If it ended up in some more limited form of naval warfare with the United States, could it count on support from any other power? It's a question most germane to Russia. For while China is now the clear number two defense spender in the world, and now has the second-largest navy by displacement, it is actually not China that has the number two navy in the world measured by sophistication and global reach. That dangerous designation belongs to Russia. And in recent years, Russia has been using its navy in ways that are very helpful to China.

That's a new development. Russian naval capacity has waxed and waned. At no point during the Cold War did the Soviet navy match the US for quality, though it did eventually match it for size. (And as one Soviet naval analyst quipped at the time, "Size is its own quality.") The Soviet navy, along with the Soviet economy, collapsed with the fall of the Berlin Wall. But it's been partially rebuilt since, under President Putin's tenure. In the past, the Soviet submarine fleet was of very high quality—coming close to matching US technology. Russia has retained the technological legacy of that period of investment and continues to operate a world-class submarine fleet.

Some of Putin's most aggressive moves against the West over the past decade have been in areas where important Russian naval bases were at stake. Russia's move into Syria in 2012 had multiple motives, but central among them was to make sure that Russia retained access to its only Mediterranean naval base (technically, it's Material Technical Support Point), in Tartus, Syria. And its annexation of Crimea, in Ukraine, again had multiple logics, but vitally included regaining its historic Black Sea base in Sevastopol, on the Crimea peninsula.[36]

Russia has also reactivated what was an important strength during the Cold War: its submarine fleet. By 2017, Russian submarine activity was at its highest point since the end of the Cold War, and particularly active in North Asia (the Western Pacific/Yellow Sea), and the North Atlantic. Russia has also repeatedly sailed its ships through the Kattegat, past Copenhagen, and into Scandinavian waters. American sailors have tracked Russian submarines as far away as Maine. When America's acting secretary of the navy was asked, in 2020, why America needed to expand its navy, his answer dwelt on China—but it started with Russia.[37]

Its submarine fleet also poses a threat to America's reliance on undersea cables. In 2015, what was technically classified as an "oceanographic research vessel," the Russian submarine *Yantar*, probed a cable route to Cuba. Then it positioned itself off a US submarine base in the Gulf of Mexico. Since then, Russian submarines have been detected along cables in the Atlantic and the Pacific, in increasing frequency. It's unclear whether submarines can tap underwater cables the same way that spies can tap fiber-optic cables on land, but it is apparent that these vessels can do serious damage.[38] And the Russians might not just be looking at cables—but also military underwater sensing equipment that is used for detecting submarines. Rear Admiral Frederick J. Roegge, the commander of the US Navy's submarine fleet in the Pacific, said in 2015, "I'm worried every day about what the Russians may be doing."[39]

Most worrying to American naval planners, Russia and China have undertaken joint naval exercises in the Mediterranean in 2015, in the South China Sea in 2016, the Yellow Sea in 2018, and the East China Sea in 2019. They are not, at this stage, an allied force, but they are certainly deploying in ways that complement each other's strengths. If China can deepen its engagement with Russia, it can gain access to at least some of Russia's network of bases and capabilities—these are not of the same scale as the combined British-American network, but they would meaningfully extend China's global reach.

China-Russia relations are complex, and it is unclear how Russia would behave in an outright conflict between the United States and China. But given its simmering tensions with the West, and its distaste for Western sanctions, it is certainly possible that the Russians would help China get around an American blockade.

But America would also try to bring in others.

America's Friends at Sea

Were this book being written at any previous point in the last four hundred years, a focus of any global naval assessment would have been the navies of Europe—Britain above all, but also France, Holland, Italy, Spain, and even Germany. These are now all shadows of their former selves. At times, some of them have fallen to a level of capacity and readiness that calls into question their basic effectiveness.

Paul Kennedy, the celebrated historian of the rise and fall of empires, has noted with concern that Europe has allowed its navies to decline just as the Asian powers began to build theirs.[40] This is both a matter of operational concern, and part of a pattern of the shift in the balance of economic and military power away from Europe, toward Asia. Kennedy recalls the advantage gained by Europe, in the 1400s to 1500s, as China withdrew its exploration of the high seas just as the Portuguese were sailing into the Indian Ocean. We may be seeing now something like the reverse; a naval counterpart to the closing of the eighteenth-century economic lacuna.

Still, Europe's decline can be exaggerated. The major European navies are roughly as large, each of them, as Japan's, and have a suite of ships and a network of former colonial outposts that give them global range—from French possessions in the Indian Ocean to British bases in East Asia. Britain continues to operate bases and fueling stations left over from the days when the Royal Navy spanned the globe and makes the majority of those bases available to the US Navy—a key asset. London and Paris and Madrid can also work together through the European Union. Taken together, the EU powers retain a sizable force, operating three aircraft carriers, two dozen destroyers, a submarine fleet including nuclear-capable submarines, and roughly 150,000 personnel. From a Chinese perspective, that's a serious factor to contend with.

America has other friends in the Indo-Pacific region as well. Fastest of those friends is Australia. And while Australia has to balance its large economic stakes in trade and investment with China, its navy has continuously exercised and sailed in the South China Sea. Under a $62 billion program, Australia is set to double the size of its fleet, building more than fifty vessels, including twelve new attack-class submarines. Australia's navy and combat troops are well tested, having served alongside the US in Iraq and elsewhere. The Australian navy has joined Japan, Britain, France, and India, among others, in the conduct of "freedom of navigation" operations in the Pacific and Indian Oceans.[41]

And in several scenarios, the US Navy would also potentially have substantial help from Japan. That includes scenarios involving submarine warfare. Indeed, one of Japan's great contemporary strengths is its submarine fleet. It operates one of the most effective submarine fleets in the world, a diesel electric fleet that is quiet, efficient, and exceedingly well maintained—no small feat in the world of metal machines that live under water.[42] It uses that submarine fleet to patrol its long archipelago of islands, down to the Ryukus, which extend to within 250 miles of China's shores. And in 2018, responding to Chinese developments in the East China Sea, Japan created an amphibious rapid deployment brigade based on submarines to defend some of the more remote islands in its own archipelago. And that is no mere passive force: in 2018, the Japanese Air Self-Defense Force scrambled nearly one thousand times—64 percent of which were to respond to Chinese aircraft largely flying around the Senkakus and the East China Sea.[43] That's nearly two sorties responding to Chinese aircraft a day. The

Japanese are almost literally building a wall, with defensive installations along Japan's southwestern island chain. The result is what one Chinese naval officer called a new "impassable maritime great wall"—more commonly, simply the "Japanese Wall" of fortifications to block Chinese naval expansion.[44]

Theoretically, the Korean navy would contribute to an American response to China as well. It is, of course, a US ally. But of late, it's an unhappy one, and it has increasingly strong economic ties to China. Already, American naval planners are reassessing whether they can rely on access to Korean ports should they face a wartime scenario in the Near Seas.[45] The point is: China's strategy for improving its ability to operate freely in the Near Seas isn't only a naval strategy—it's a multifaceted strategy of naval pressure, commercial ties, and diplomacy designed to weaken the string of American alliances that surround it.

On the other hand, there's a new entrant to the game of ports and naval power, and while it has traditionally maintained a neutral posture in global affairs, its mounting tensions with China are increasingly pushing that power toward the United States. At the very least, its new, growing navy is playing a role that looks set to complicate China's maritime life.

The India Question

The body of the Indian subcontinent lies precisely between the western end of the Malacca Strait and the eastern openings of the Suez and Hormuz. From its home ports, India has uninterrupted access to the key sea-lanes of trade and what Mahan called the "sea-lanes of communication"—the islands and choke points that abut those trade routes. In short: India is a great thousand-mile dagger thrust into the heart of China's Indian Ocean ambitions.

As China sails out past the Near Seas, it can go in one of three directions: north through the Korea Strait to the Arctic (about which we'll see more in Part IV); east to the Pacific, where it confronts the US Navy; or it can sail along the main shipping lanes, past Singapore and out through the Malacca Strait into the Indian Ocean. If China wants to be able to defend its trade against an American blockade, it has to be able to secure those shipping lanes. But when it looks toward the Indian Ocean, past the Malacca Strait, the first obstacle it encounters is the Indian navy, at Port Blair in the Andaman Sea.

The simple fact of India's geography makes China's job immeasurably harder. So, too, do its relations with India, with whom it has fought three wars since independence. Granted, those wars were all along its land border with India, in the Himalayas, and as a consequence India has privileged its land and air forces over its navy. This, despite the fact of its extraordinarily long coastline and its heavy dependence on fishing and sea-based imports.

Until very recently, India had never developed as a serious naval power.* India's limited navy has long kept its focus narrowly on India's own ring of small islands that surround it—Mauritius, Seychelles, Maldives, and above all Sri Lanka. It has also had to focus on operations against Pakistan.

India's naval ambitions began to rise, along with its economy, in the post-9/11 period. At the end of the Cold War, India, like China and Brazil and others, opened its economy to globalization and began to grow, fast. By 2010, India had overtaken France to become the sixth-largest economy in the world (and is projected to become the third-largest economy in the world by 2050). Like China, and like Britain and America before it, it has developed far-reaching foreign policy interests to match its new economic status—though not yet the capacity to match.[46]

After 9/11 and the Al Qaeda attacks on American territory, the United States decided—echoing its experience with the Barbary pirates—to launch a land invasion of Afghanistan, to rob this new set of non-state actors of a base of operations in their home territory. This caused the United States to pull resources away from functions like protecting the Malacca Straits, to deploy to the Afghan operation.

*The earliest "Indian" navy was actually part of the British East India Company. In 1612, a company vessel fought a Portuguese contingent and managed to win, but combined with the threat of the Portuguese and of pirates, they convinced the Company to establish the East India Marine. Britain controlled India until its independence in 1947. After, India developed a small navy. In a twist of fate, the first engagement of the newly independent Indian navy was also against Portugal, during India's fight to liberate Portugal's last overseas colony, Goa, in western India (in 1961).

India volunteered to carry some of the burden and took on a role in escorting ships through the Malacca Straits, freeing up American resources.

The most important focus for Indian foreign policy is the long-running alliance between its two principal adversaries, Pakistan and China. For much of its history, this kept it focused on its northern land borders. But as China's PLAN has grown global sea legs, this alliance has spilled out into the Indian Ocean.[47] During a tense India-Pakistan standoff in 2017, China sent a submarine to the area to "monitor" the situation. This so angered the Indians that it set off a wave of Indian naval purchases and deployment. Already India had an aircraft carrier, and a nuclear-capable submarine. In 2019 it started to expand its fleet—aiming to have three carrier groups, with two hundred ships, twenty-four conventional submarines, and five hundred aircraft by 2030.[48] (Though in 2019, reeling from the economic impact of the COVID-19 pandemic, it trimmed its budget aspirations.)[49]

India has used its geographical advantage well; by 2019, it had ships visiting and practicing in every one of the Indian Ocean sea lines of communication. And unlike China, India has good relations with virtually all of its neighboring countries. It has used this—and shared concern about China—to forge new maritime agreements with Singapore; a defense agreement with France for access to its Indian Ocean properties; a base-sharing agreement with Oman, near the Strait of Hormuz; and to deepen ties with the United States. This gives it access to ports and bases across the sweep of the Indian Ocean. There's even growing naval cooperation between India and Vietnam in the South China Sea, much to China's distress.*

*In all of this, India's geopolitical relations are, well, eclectic. Despite long-running tensions, China is India's largest trading partner. It is actively deepening ties with Japan and has recently joined Japan, Australia, and the United States in a mechanism called the Quad, a defensive semi-alliance against China. It is increasingly friendly to and mission-aligned with the US. And throughout all of this, it's maintained friendly relations with its largest arms supplier—Russia.

A Naval Arms Race

All of this activity amounts to a growing, near-global naval arms race—pitting the United States and China against each other, and pulling in European and Asian powers, including Russia and India. It's made the world's oceans—and particularly the Pacific, the Indian, and the Arctic—the front lines of geopolitical tensions. There's even growing Chinese and Russian naval activity in the Mediterranean, and a growing Russian presence in the northern Atlantic.

And tensions continue to mount. In June 2016, China sent a warship to the Senkakus for the first time, with a frigate sailing in the islands' waters.[50] In January 2018, the PLAN kicked off the new year by sending a nuclear attack submarine into those waters.[51] In the north, a new Russian icebreaker was built to be able to carry Kalibr cruise missiles, and with Russia—and China—increasingly active in the Arctic, in May 2020 the US Navy sent naval surface ships to the Barents Sea for the first time since the Cold War.[52]

As the US Department of Defense continues to prepare for various scenarios of escalation with China, it's recognized that it needs tighter integration between the navy and the marines. That was, of course, how both services were born—at the time of the fight against the Barbary pirates, and building on the British tradition, these were inseparable forces; the marines had no separate existence apart from life aboard and campaigns launched from naval ships. But as advanced air transport has allowed the marines to get to its battles without the navy, many countries' marines have developed ever more as a separate service—and in the case of the United States, that's especially been true as the marines become the de facto lead service in fighting America's long wars in the Middle East. But by 2019, the commandant of the marines recognized that if America's principal potential adversary is the Chinese PLA, then it has to get back to the concept of fighting together with the navy, and with a focus on the first island chain. His directive to the marine service that year called for it to prepare for pre-positioning contingents of marines out in the peninsulas and islands surrounding the first island chain.[53] It would also mean pre-positioning weapons supplies at bases and locations throughout those waters. And in a neat twist of history, one of the proposals that's been floated to accomplish this is to "containerize" missiles—literally to use what the army still refers to as CONEX boxes to ship large numbers of missiles out to American forward positions.[54] Malcom McLean, the man who popularized this technique in the 1950s, would be pleased.

To summarize, then, China's "Malacca Dilemma" spurred it to develop a naval capacity to defend the Near Seas; and then to defend that capacity out to the Western Pacific. At the same time, America has been responding, ship by ship, missile by missile, submarine by submarine, to advances in Chinese capacity. The interplay between these two dynamics is pulling the Chinese PLAN and the US Navy into an arms race; and that, in turn, is pulling the two nations toward war.

As we saw in the Combat Information Center of the *John Paul Jones*, it's a form of war that could start in the information space, and play out with almost no human-to-human contact. Indeed, with no human sensory information at all—until the first missile hits a destroyer. It might be kept limited, but it could also rapidly escalate to American attacks on the Chinese mainland—and in the extreme, Chinese missile attacks on America's mainland bases.

This dynamic shows no signs of lessening. That's both because of the seemingly inexorable escalatory logic of military affairs, and because as China has continued to grow, it has faced a deepening problem—what former Premier Hu Jintao once referred to as China's "Malacca Dilemma." Because the US Navy dominates in the Singapore and Malacca Straits, all of the trade and energy goods that flow across those waters into China's economy depend on US protection. As Jintao noted, the more China's economy grew, the *more* it depended on the US Navy. When he first articulated that concept, some 30 percent of Chinese trade flowed through those Straits; now closer to 70 percent does.

When the Chinese first made their play for sovereignty and naval power in the Near Seas, American analysts fretted about their resulting ability to choke off that vital sea-lane of communication. But that was always the wrong concern: China has never had any intention of closing off that flow of trade, on which its economy hugely relies. It wanted to deny America the capacity to do so; and for all intents and purposes, it has achieved that objective. The South China Sea has been the gateway to the flow of trade between Asia and the West for four centuries. It looks set to remain that way.

But power has its own appetite; and as China's strength in the Near Seas has grown, so has its ambition to project powers beyond them. What's more: as China has developed it has, like every industrialized nation before it, increased its appetite for energy. Throughout the modern period, there's been a 1:1 relationship between economic growth and energy consumption—and that's been true for China as well. But China—unlike Russia or the United States—is not well-blessed with its own energy endowment.

So China has had to find an ever-larger set of energy sources abroad. Some of that flows into China's factories by pipeline, across the Asian steppes. But much, much more of it flows to China by sea. And as we will see next, the quest for energy sources is yet another way the power of the seas themselves intensifies the dynamics of geopolitical rivalry.

MAERSK LINE

PART IV

The Power of the Seas

Seen from the bridge on the *Madrid*, maneuvers of the region's navies and of the American fleet are little more than a distraction. Short of the outbreak of full-blown war or the imposition of a blockade, the presence of the competing navies barely registers on the mental radar of Captain Jensen or his crew. Indeed, for much of the voyage through the South and East China Seas, the *Madrid* sails on the nautical equivalent of autopilot while its leadership focuses on more pressing concerns like fuel ratios, port timings, and brewing storms.

But there are dangers in these shipping lanes, to be sure, and plenty of them. The most visible come from the fishing fleets that ply these waters. If the commercial traffic outside Singapore resembles a busy New York avenue, the passage through the Chinese and Taiwanese fishing fleets plying the strait that divides them more closely resembles the snarl of motorbikes, tuk-tuks, and diesel-spewing cars that fuel the pollution and gridlock of the nearby cities of Jakarta and Manila. Sailing through that strait, the sea is crawling with trawlers, literally thousands of them on any given evening. And many of them don't carry the Automated Identification System transponders—ships' equivalent to airplanes' black boxes—that they're supposed to. For the *Madrid*'s crew, hitting one of the trawlers is a nightmare to be avoided at all costs. The small boats would barely dent the hull of the *Madrid*, but the huge ship would crush the trawler underneath her, causing loss of life—and a massive insurance fight with the Chinese authorities.

The fishing fleets are far from the only obstacle to shipping. On a chart of these seas, the sea-lanes are crisscrossed by dotted lines that indicate the placement of a growing profusion and entanglement of data cables. They're often bundled, too, not allowing just one cable, but huge chunks of them to straddle key passageways. The bundles coming into Hong Kong, for example, are huge, providing a clear choke point on the map of global data. In the primary sea-lanes, they pose no concern to shipping. But these are shallow waters, and as ships turn from the main channels toward the littorals and toward harbors, they keep a careful eye on the locations of cables as they rise from the seafloor to meet the coastlines.

Those same charts show a growing profusion of oil rigs and oil fields. These belong to China, Vietnam, Indonesia, the Philippines, Brunei, and even India (through joint ventures). All throughout the area of China's nine-dash line, large oil and gas fields are marked out all along the coastal waters, but also out into the farthest reaches of the seas. There is no longer any route through the South China Sea that does not traverse a claimed oil or gas field. In 2009, when the Chinese began their far-reaching play for control of these waters, rigs were few and far between. But even then, initial estimates of the sheer quantity of energy underneath the seabeds were astounding.

* * *

So far in this book, we've looked at transactions and competition, commercial and naval, on the surface of the world's great waters, only dipping below the surface briefly to encounter submarine fleets. But there's much more to the seas than what lies atop their waters. Both the seas and the seabeds are also a vast natural resource—a resource to be tapped, fished, farmed, drilled, and mined. And competed over. In much of modern life, we've become used to thinking of the world's oceans as part of the global commons, shared by all nations. Granted, there's always been competition over fishing rights, and the hunt for whales—the earliest source of oil for lighting—pitted the world's major empires against each other. But this was limited, and fluid; neither fish nor whales respect political boundaries, or legal ones. But in the contemporary period, with new abilities to probe the seafloor and suck resources out of it, the dynamics of extracting the oceans' bounty have changed. Oil and gas are increasingly found in the world's deep offshore waters.

This seabed energy, in turn, connects to the vexed question of climate change. Energy and climate aren't always viewed as two sides of the same coin, but they should be: the one is about the extraction and burning of concentrated carbon; the other about its reabsorption, and the effects of that reabsorption of carbon on our climate, our oceans, and our weather.

12

The Salt of the Oceans

For the past hundred and fifty years, the main story of energy was the story of oil, and the story of oil was mostly a story of land—of finding oil beneath the rocks of Pennsylvania and Texas, and the sands of Iraq and Saudi Arabia, and of the transportation of that oil by pipelines over land. As Richard Rhodes wrote in his *Energy: A Human History*, "The history of liquid energy is a history of pipelines."[1] But over the last sixty years, that has changed. The business of oil and gas has become a business of the oceans.

Few places have been as profoundly affected as Houston, Texas. There—and specifically in the Houston Ship Channel—we can see the major evolution in energy dynamics: the growth of the city and of the American engineering industry through the first oil boom, the change from the early years when Texas was a hub for the export of oil, to the postwar years when it became a key hub for *imports*, the development of technologies for offshore drilling, and the resulting shift in flows of oil by sea, as America regained its status as a net exporter of oil—and China claimed the dubious mantle of the world's largest importer of oil—much of it, again, by sea.

The Houston Ship Channel, Texas

The use of petroleum is most commonly dated to the discovery of large fields in Titusville, Pennsylvania, in 1859. But by the end of the century, it was the sands of Texas that generated the volumes of oil that made the United States the largest oil producer in the world.

Unlike Copenhagen or New York or Singapore or Hong Kong, the critical feature of the Port of Houston is not its natural structure; it's a man-made channel. For much of the nineteenth century and into the early twentieth, the major port on the southern coast of the United States was not Houston, but Galveston. An island city outside of Houston on the Gulf, Galveston was a natural choice for exports, having been the world's top cotton shipping port after the Civil War. Its history might have been much different, had it been able to take full advantage of the Texan oil boom. But nature had other plans. In 1900, a massive hurricane (known in the region as simply the "Great Storm") swept through the city, damaging every dwelling in the city. The highest point in the city was only 8.7 feet above sea level—the storm surge alone was nearly double that. It left nearly one-third of the population homeless and, with at least six thousand fatalities, is still the deadliest natural disaster in US history.

Ironically, Houston would benefit from the disaster. A small channel had been used to move goods from Houston to the sea since the early 1800s. But in the wake of the hurricane, fearing another direct hit, planners made the decision to create the Houston Ship Channel, a fifty-mile waterway that would be completed in 1914. President Woodrow Wilson would mark the occasion by pushing a button in the White House that sent a telegraph to Houston to trigger a cannon that officially opened the channel and its deepwater port.

Now large ships could make their way up from the Gulf of Mexico to Houston, where they were safer from storms. They moved safely, but not smoothly: large ships transitting the Houston Ship Channel have to perform what's known as the "Texas chicken" maneuver. As two large vessels approach from opposite directions, they both turn starboard, so that water displaced from their bows pushes the ships away from each other (and from the center of the channel). Once they pass each other, the suction of the displaced water flowing in behind the ships then pulls them back toward the center of the waterway.

Along this channel is the infrastructure necessary for the import of large volumes of oil. In the early years of Houston's growth, the port was an exporter of oil. It's often forgotten that in the years prior to World War II, the United States was the world's largest energy producer. Although it consumed most of that oil domestically, and moved much of it by pipeline, energy exports also formed part of Houston's early development. This was critical during World War II: according to Daniel Yergin, over the course of World War II the US and the European allies consumed seven billion barrels of oil and the US supplied six billion of those seven billion barrels, most of it shipped from Texas.[2]

But in the years after the war, with its reserves gone and US industry growing rapidly, the US became a major energy importer, and continues to be one to the present day. That being said, Houston also contains the largest concentration of refineries and petrochemical plants in the world.[3] It's also home to a large infrastructure for energy *export*. In 2018, the Texas Gulf Coast accounted for 80 percent of the nation's crude shipments.[4] Even more striking: in April 2018, the Houston-Galveston port region exported more oil than it imported for the first time since the end of the Second World War.[5] That shift reflects the underlying reality that the United States has recently returned to the position of a net exporter of energy—that is, the US produces more oil and gas than it consumes, and exports the balance.*

Some of that shift has to do with new technologies for exploration and drilling that have led to the discovery and extraction of oil from shale rock, and the extraction of what's known as "tight oil"—smaller pockets of residual oil in the rocks surrounding what were once large pockets of trapped oil. The United States has been the technological and engineering leader in both shale and unconventional oil, though now those techniques have spread worldwide—in part through foreign contracting of US firms. But what's also changed the picture is the large role of the waters off of Houston's coast—the Gulf of Mexico, which now produces nearly 20 percent of all the oil in the United States.

The story of how the Gulf of Mexico became the world's most important source of innovation in offshore oil is a story of entrepreneurship and engineering (and, to a degree, of corruption).[6] But it is also, importantly, a story about how the US Navy drove the science and engineering that has allowed us to plumb the oceans' depths, and to penetrate the ocean floor.

*The issue is somewhat confusing, as the United States still imports a large quantity of oil. That's because oil comes in several different varieties, and the US needs to import volumes of oil of types that it does not produce domestically. When people point to the fact that the US is a net exporter of energy and say that it is now "energy independent," they are glossing over this critical detail.

Drilling Deep: By-products of the Cold War

Walter Munk, of the Scripps Institution of Oceanography, was probably the most influential oceanographer of the American century. (He died in February 2019, at the age of 101, still conducting influential research and shaping the careers of generations of students.) Munk's most famous studies relate to the ways in which the wind, currents, and chemistry of the oceans shape the movement of the seas (and thus, much of our weather). He was, in this, a frequent collaborator with the US Navy's powerful Office of Naval Research (of which we'll see more in the following chapter). But the strangest collaboration between them was not in the realm of oceanography at all, but in a somewhat capricious effort to drill into the Earth's crust.

During the heart of the Cold War, the navy's star was fading as the nuclear arms race and the space race became the dominant forms of competition with the Soviet Union. The ocean sciences community was worried they were being left behind, along with the navy. But providentially, the United States had gotten wind of the notion that the Soviets were planning a project to drill into the Earth's mantle. That required an American response.[7] Munk, in a meeting of the National Science Foundation, made the surprising and bold proposal that an American project to drill into the Earth's crust should be launched—and launched from sea. His essential observation was that if the first several thousand feet of drilling involved feeding pipe through water, it would be far easier than drilling through an equivalent amount of land. He proposed aiming for what's known as the Mohorovičić Discontinuity, or the Moho—the layer that separates the Earth's crust from its mantle—at a location northwest off the coast of Hawaii.

Thus was born the cleverly named Project Mohole. It was approved by the National Science Foundation. The project attracted excitement and attention—in part due to the lyrical writing of a journalist assigned to cover the story for *Life* magazine, a young John Steinbeck. And it was carried out by the American Miscellaneous Society—a whimsically named informal group of scientists headed by Gordon Lill, at the time the director of the geophysics branch of the Office of Naval Research.

Lill's contributions were multiple, but importantly included his advanced knowledge of sonar technology, and what is known as bathymetry—the measurement of the depth of the water in oceans, seas, and lakes. He had pioneered new techniques for bathymetry while on a training stint away from the US Navy at the famed Woods Hole Oceanographic Institute. And he was closely connected to the world of the Navy Experimental Diving Unit, which had trained divers for underwater salvage.

Industry was also built into the project from the start. The Gulf Oil Corporation chaired the Project Mohole subcommittee of the American Miscellaneous Society, and a Louisiana company that had been leading innovations in offshore engineering, Global Marine, was contracted to do the actual drilling for the project. Global Marine deployed its dedicated drilling ship to the project—one of the first in the world capable of conducting drilling from open waters—and began testing off of Guadalupe, Mexico, in 1960. And Brown and Root—one of the world's largest engineering management firms, and the first ever to build an offshore platform—was contracted to run the work.[8]

From the outset, though, the project was ill-managed. The various parties had disagreements, from the engineering and scientific goals to simple personality clashes. And while the first phase of the project had a relatively modest cost, the costs for drilling into the Moho grew and grew. The mismanagement of the project became public, with *Newsweek* describing the expedition as "Project No Hole."[9] And after repeated inquiries and mounting expenses, and in the face of considerable political and scientific opposition, Congress defunded the project.[10]

But not before the project recorded some important achievements. It succeeded in extracting core samples from the Earth that penetrated through Miocene-age sediments for the first time (that's from some twenty-three million to five million years ago). But the more lasting effects of the project were the advances in deep-sea engineering.

First, the project's drilling itself was unprecedented. Five holes were drilled into the Earth's core, with the deepest being 601 feet below the seafloor. And that hole was dug from a drilling ship operating in 11,700 feet of water. It was—by far—the deepest drilling ever conducted by an untethered platform afloat at sea. That success came in large part from a related engineering advance. The project was the first to develop techniques for stabilizing ship platforms at sea, using a series of thrusters to keep the ship in place against the swell of waves and tides. The technique of "dynamic positioning" would prove key to what was to follow.

There were several follow-on projects that came out of Mohole, the most important being the Joint Oceanographic Institutions for Deep Earth Sampling program, which ran from 1968 to 1983 and provided the first comprehensive sets of data about the sub-seafloor.[11] This project discovered that evidence of salt domes in core samples positively correlated with the likelihood of the presence of oil fields. But realizing the potential of that discovery required a second project—again a collaboration of the US Navy, the national security community in Washington more broadly, and the oceanographic and engineering communities. Once again it was a by-product of the Cold War.

Project Azorian

In 2010, the US Central Intelligence Agency released to the public a declassified version of a remarkable document written in late 1985. Originally classified top secret, it was downgraded to secret/noforn ("no foreigners") when some of the project details leaked to the *Los Angeles Times* and then to the *New York Times*. As journalists filed Freedom of Information Act requests to learn more, the CIA refused to either "confirm or deny" the existence of the requested documents—a famous and oft-repeated non-reply that came to be known as the "*Glomar* response," after the name of the ship involved. Fully two decades after the collapse of the Soviet Union and after multiple leaks, the CIA deemed that it was finally safe to release their version of the story. Even so, the report is heavily redacted, including several whole pages that have been blanked out. Still, between the leaks, an eventual documentary, and the CIA's own document, most of the salient details of what the CIA had termed "Project Azorian" can be gleaned.[12]

Even the redacted version of the story in the CIA's document reads like a nautical version of the movie *Argo* about the CIA's (real) use of a fake film as a cover story for their rescue of the escapees from the Iranian embassy hostage-taking. Except that in this case the agency wasn't trying to rescue someone, but to recover something—specifically, a Soviet nuclear submarine, K-129, lost at sea in 1968 and found by the US Air Force and US Navy off the west coast of Hawaii, under some 16,700 feet of water.

This remarkable project was marked by intrigue and creative engineering. To create a plausible cover story, the agency contacted the eccentric billionaire Howard Hughes, known for his cars and his experimental wooden airplane, the *Spruce Goose*, and convinced him to agree to launch a marine mining voyage, complete with press release and accompanying stories. For the (fake) voyage, a specifically designed ship, the *Hughes Glomar Explorer*, was built by Sun Shipbuilding out of Pennsylvania, then the largest shipbuilding firm in the country, at a cost of over $200 million. Intelligence officers and nuclear technicians were quietly embedded onto the ship as part of the engineering crew contracted for the project—Global Marine, whose prowess in deep-sea drilling in Project Mohole had captured the US Navy's attention. To get from the shipyards south of Philadelphia, in the working-class city of Chester, to Hawaii, the ship, which was too wide to go through the Panama Canal, had to transit around South America, through the Strait of Magellan at the tip of the continent. They docked at Valparaiso, Chile, to resupply—on the very day that General Pinochet was ousted in a coup. They then sailed to Long Beach, where the ship ended up stuck ashore by a strike of longshoremen that rocked the California harbor. When they arrived at the recovery site, their voyage was waylaid by one of the largest typhoons ever recorded in the eastern Pacific. And when they eventually arrived at their destination, they found a Soviet ship patrolling the area, which deployed a helicopter to take photographs of the vessel. Every conceivable natural and political obstacle appeared set against their task.

After myriad tests, systems trials, misfires, and delays over four years, the project eventually recovered a thirty-eight-foot portion of the Soviet boat. What the navy gleaned from that small portion of the six-hundred-plus-foot boat is presumably the subject of the redacted portions of the 2010 document. But as with Project Mohole, the more lasting legacy of the project was its engineering advances for offshore drilling.

These were several. It was the deepest marine salvage operation in history, bringing up a portion of the Soviet sub from more than three miles below the ocean's surface. The project advanced the techniques for dynamic positioning, for keeping the ship stable in the water as it conducted drilling operations. They experimented with hydraulic/pneumatic systems that could prevent the ship's heave from affecting the string of pipes lowered down to the ocean floor—a major problem in earlier deep-sea efforts.[13] Given the complexity of drilling at such depths, this was a critical advance. Even the *Hughes Glomar Explorer* continued to be used after the recovery and played an important role in deep-sea exploration advances.

Unlike Project Mohole, which came at a time when the US was focused on the space competition with the Soviets and when the international oil supply was plentiful, Project Azorian came at a very different moment. The 1973 Suez Crisis and oil price shock that had so impacted the container ship fleet also shook up the oil industry—just as Azorian was underway. And then in 1979 the Shah of Iran was deposed, and oil prices spiked again. They stayed high for years, as both Iran and Iraq became embroiled in a long, extremely bloody war. The flow of oil was increasingly important for the United States as well. Oil tankers entering the port of Houston as well as Los Angeles and elsewhere and unloading cargoes of fuel from the Persian Gulf became the critical symbol of energy insecurity in the United States. Just as geopolitical developments had helped transform containerized shipping, so they began to reshape the energy business. And the pressure mounted to find new suppliers of oil. Part of the answer would lie in the Gulf of Mexico, using all of this new technology.

Offshore Oil: Of Salt and Carbon, Take 1

It had long been understood that the salty chemistry of the oceans' waters meant that it absorbed carbon from the atmosphere. The modern study of this phenomenon concentrates on the question of how much excess carbon—carbon produced by the burning of fossil fuels—has been absorbed by the oceans. But carbon is of course also a naturally occurring chemical in the atmosphere, essential to the formation of plant life through photosynthesis, with oxygen as the by-product of that interaction—and so, fundamental to plant and animal life on Earth, including human life. Carbon is emitted naturally into the atmosphere by volcanoes and hot springs, and released from rocks when they come into contact with groundwater, ice caps, and seawater—all naturally occurring processes. Some of this carbon sinks to the seafloor and is buried in sediment—and after millions of years, some of it is transformed into oil.

In a similar fashion, and over similar time, salt in the water settles to the bottom and forms a crust. This crust is not static, though; it is pushed around by the currents. Depending on currents and the specific salinity of the water, this salt can get trapped in mountains, or pockets. What the Integrated Ocean Drilling Project discovered is that sometimes those formations emerge as "domes." And just as pockets of oil can be "trapped" by specific geological formations beneath land, so, too, it can be trapped by sand domes or similar formations on the seabed.[14]

The search for energy at sea has a long history, much of it unproductive.* As early as the 1890s, the search for oil led some entrepreneurial spirits to experiments in the lakes of Ohio, and in Baku, and then to piers off the coasts of California, Texas, and Louisiana. This was not really offshore exploration, though; these locations were all close to land, either on piers or in very shallow waters accessible from land. It wasn't until 1947 that a truly offshore oil well was drilled, out of the sight of land—some ten miles off the coast of Louisiana.

The cost of these early platforms and drills was prohibitive. On land, you can cheaply and easily drill hundreds of test wells. Not so at sea.

*Petroleum is not the first fuel that industrialized societies have extracted from the oceans; that distinction belongs to the oil that comes from rendering the fat of sperm whales—which were hunted almost to extinction by British, French, American, Japanese, and Russian whaling fleets at the dawn of the industrial age. (Nathaniel Philbrick's intimate account of whale hunting, in *Into the Heart of the Sea: The Tragedy of the Whaleship Essex* [New York: Pengiun Books, 2020], vividly conveys the scale and the drama of that enterprise.) Notably, whaling fleets also sourced large quantities of guano from the Chincha Islands off the western coast of Peru, and later off the southwestern coast of Africa. Guano was the main input to the first industrial fertilizers in the Western world. It may also have been the source of a blight that caused the potato famine—a reversal of the process that saw the European world bring disease to their colonial possessions.

Making a very well-informed estimate of where oil might be found is absolutely vital to economically viable drilling at sea. Here, what came into play was a different set of technologies, some developed by the US Navy, others by industry. The first part of this was sonar mapping, which emerged from the work of the navy in tracking submarines, and further developed by the navy and oceanographers at Woods Hole and elsewhere in the early part of the Cold War. The second part was seismic mapping. This field owed less to the navy than to the oil industry itself. In particular, advances by Shell Oil and Mobil Oil in the late 1960s generated what was known as "bright spots" mapping. Earlier seismic mapping could identify locations where oil *could* be trapped. The new technology showed off "amplitude anomalies" (or "bright spots"), which were far more likely to be a reflection of the presence of oil itself. This dramatically reduced the risks of drilling a dry hole.[15]

Finding is one thing, drilling is another. The Gulf of Mexico emerged as a key site for development of offshore drilling for several reasons. One was politics: as Clyde Burleson quips in his history of offshore oil exploration, "Oil and water do not mix. Oil and politics, however, seem made for each other." The Louisiana legislative and pork barrel campaign to open up drilling of the Gulf tidelands was, by his account, "one of the longest, most brutal, and intense political battles ever waged in Washington, DC."[16] Politics can be overcome; geology is harder. Bright spot seismic technology only works with certain kinds of rock formations, and the deltaic rocks of the Gulf of Mexico (which are highly porous) were the perfect kind of rock sample for the new technologies.

Geology was one advantage; geography was another. The transition from land to the ocean depth does not happen immediately. Every continent and every coast has an underwater shelf, a land formation that extends outward under the water. This continental shelf is important for fishing and also for drilling. But these shelves vary in width and in slope. Off the southern coast of the United States, the Gulf of Mexico has one of the gentlest shelves in the world. In some parts of the Gulf, the water depths were less than 600 feet as far out as 140 miles. The Gulf of Mexico—with its proximity to the headquarters of energy majors in Texas; its long, gentle, sloping sea shelf; and the permissive politics of Louisiana—had the exact right conditions to enable expansive testing.[17]

Drilling a salt dome involves several steps, all of them complicated. To find an oil pocket, you start by conducting seismic surveys (using sonar equipment) to determine where oil is most likely to be. Then you use a mobile offshore drilling unit to dig an initial well. These come in four main types: *submersibles*—usually barges that rest on the seafloor, with steel posts on the deck that extend above the waterline; *jackups*—rigs that sit on a floating barge, with legs extended to the seafloor; *drill ships*—like those used for Mohole and Azorian, with a drilling rig on the top deck working through a hole in the hull; and *semi-submersibles*—drilling units that float on the surface on top of submerged pontoons. At the seafloor is a pair of hydraulically powered clamps that can close off the pipe leading up to the rig in case of a blowout. At the drill site, drill pipes are connected to form a drill string, which is used to reach deep into the Earth's crust. The drill string is then connected to a device that spins it around, and using a drill bit connected at the bottom of the drill string, the pipes grind into the Earth's surface. Putting this all together can take weeks to months. When it works, you then have to replace the temporary rig with a permanent one to capture the oil. All this while navigating the high waves and powerful storms that regularly sweep in from the Caribbean and churn up the shallow waters of the Gulf.

Understandably, these efforts are easier in shallower waters than in deep. Early offshore drilling was literally just offshore, still in very shallow waters where platforms could be tethered to the ocean floor or by cables to land. But with the development of technologies for dynamic positioning, platforms were stable without having to be tethered to the ocean floor. And with the new technologies for drilling at depth, further horizons opened up.

Step by step, consortiums of companies—energy firms like Shell and Texaco combining forces with engineering firms like Global Marine and Brown and Root—steadily pushed the boundary outward. Success at one thousand feet taught them more about the technology, and gave them more experience, including in managing and mitigating the risks associated with these amazingly complex projects.

By the late 1990s, the combination of techniques for sonar and seismic mapping, for dynamic positioning and for deep-sea drilling, had turned the entire Gulf into a giant oil field. By 1999, the cost of finding and producing oil was 60 percent of what it had been ten years prior.[18] And in 1998, the ship used by Project Azorian—the *Hughes Glomar Explorer*, on contract for Chevron and Texaco—set a world record by spudding a well 7,718 feet below the Gulf of Mexico.[19] By the mid-2000s, there were more than four thousand platforms connected to thirty-five thousand wells in the Gulf. And the US waters of the Gulf of Mexico were accounting for almost 20 percent of US crude oil production.[20]

But even greater depths were about to be plumbed, outside of US continental waters.

Offshore Goes Global

In all of this, the United States had an advantage: its major engineering firms were private, as were the firms in some of the major European countries. In the rest of the world, and among the biggest energy players in the world, this was an exception. In Russia, Saudi Arabia, Indonesia, Qatar, Iran, and Iraq, oil was dominated by state-owned and state-operated firms. By the 1980s, fully 85 percent of the world's oil reserves were held by state-owned firms.

David Victor, a colleague of Walter Munk's at Scripps, conducted a detailed study of innovation by state-owned firms and private firms.[21] His data is compelling. It showed that although there is some variation across firms, it was only under rare conditions (and mostly in democracies) that state-owned firms could develop the entrepreneurial instinct and the managerial competence for the risk-taking required to drive the kinds of advances in offshore engineering that American firms could develop. So it was overwhelmingly Western firms that developed the technology, the engineering, and the management capacity to shoulder the multifaceted scientific and engineering challenge of offshore drilling. Other countries had to contract in Western expertise, often US expertise, if they wanted to develop offshore projects. When state-owned firms did try to compete without Western firms, they quickly discovered they could not handle either the sophisticated engineering or, in particular, the management consequences of undertaking these extraordinarily complex projects. This was true of Venezuela, and of Qatar.. Even the Soviet Union was forced to call in

Western expertise when it tried to develop an oil field in the Tengiz section of the north Caspian, and ended up triggering a blowout that raged for 365 days.[22]

But, of course, American engineering can spread and US companies (and similarly capable European firms) became involved in partnership with other countries seeking to develop offshore projects. Qatar and the UAE were earlier movers in developing these relationships. As was Brazil. Its state-owned enterprise, Petrobras, had stuck its toes into offshore waters in the 1980s, but hesitantly. Still protected by a monopoly and skeptical of international investors, Petrobras was limited in its exploration of Brazil's offshore potential. This continued until the 1990s, when Brazil transitioned to a democracy and, at more or less the same time, liberalized its economy—including the oil sector.[23] International companies, with their diverse expertise from other projects, began to enter the market, partnering with Petrobras to develop the offshore industry.[24]

Just as in the Gulf of Mexico, it was not just politics that animated drilling off the Brazilian coast, but geography—specifically, the nature of its eastern shore on the Atlantic Ocean. For several miles off the coast of Brazil, where the Amazon empties into the Atlantic, Brazil's continental shelf slopes downward at a very gentle pace. As with the Gulf of Mexico, the gentle slope of Brazil's shelf allowed its state-owned enterprise to develop the capacity to manage complex engineering projects step-by-step.

Brazil started in shallow waters, with simple rigs, then moved to floating platforms as it progressed into deeper sea. This not only meant that they could innovate bit by bit, but that earlier and shallower projects could help fund the deeper, more complicated wells.

In all of this, Brazil opened up two horizons. They chartered the deepest offshore wells yet drilled and, along the way, found some of the largest oil reserves in the world. One is in the Brazilian fields of Mero (formerly known as Libra), in the Santos Basin, about 125 miles off the coast of Rio de Janeiro. The field is almost 600 square miles wide and more than 16,500 feet deep. To drill it, Petrobras contracted with several international partners—including Shell, BP, ExxonMobil, and Statoil (the Norwegian state-owned oil company, the only such entity that operates like a private-sector firm). The drilling was incredibly complex. First, there was the depth of the waters themselves. More complicated, the biggest oil deposits weren't just below the first layer of salt, but deeper still, in what's known as the "pre-salt formation"—a geological feature left over from the era when the continents split apart. The oil sits underneath a layer of salt that can be more than 6,500 feet thick in some areas. For the Mero fields, that meant a total drilling depth of twenty thousand feet—far deeper than anywhere else in the world. And drilling through the salt layer is tricky, as it is made up of different types of salt, which interact differently with drilling fluid, leading to clogging drill holes and other problems known as "salt creep."

But the Mero fields proved vast. Its Lula oil field alone, off of the southeast of the country, is believed to hold up to 8.3 billion barrels of recoverable oil.[25]

* * *

What happened in Brazil didn't stay in Brazil. Over the past decade, wherever there are continental shelves gentle enough, new drills have been tested and deployed.

That includes the shallow waters of the South and East China Seas, where the estimates of oil and gas reserves are driving ferocious expansion and competition. There, it's not just the seas themselves that are hotly contested; it's also the estimates of what lies beneath them.[26] At the conservative end, in 2013 the US Energy Information Administration estimated that about 11 billion barrels of oil and 190 trillion cubic feet of natural gas were held in those shallow waters.[27] Even that's about the same as oil reserves in Mexico and about two-thirds of the proved natural gas reserves in Europe (without Russia).[28] But an earlier estimate by the US Geological Survey estimated total discovered and undiscovered reserves at 28 billion barrels of oil and 266 trillion cubic feet of gas.[29] (China's National Offshore Oil Corporation estimates that the South China Sea contains a whopping *125 billion* barrels of oil and *500 trillion* cubic feet of gas in undiscovered areas—but this hasn't been confirmed by other, independent studies.)

The search for these potentially massive finds has added literal fuel to the fire of oceanic competition in the region. An example: Chinese and Vietnamese ships were at a standoff for four months beginning in June 2019 around a drilling rig in one of Vietnam's oil and gas blocks. On June 16, a China Coast Guard ship began harassing the rig and offshore supply vessels servicing it. Over the course of four months,

China Coast Guard vessels sailed in and out of the field to keep up the harassment.[30] In the meantime, China has also developed a gigantic ten-story oil drilling platform that can dig up to five and a half miles deep, potentially for use in waters that are disputed with Vietnam.[31]

In the East China Sea, there are also potential spots for conflict. The Energy Information Administration estimates that the sea has some 200 million barrels of oil and 30 to 60 billion cubic feet of gas; not large by international standards but meaningful for import-dependent Japan.[32] But these fields are in exactly the waters that both China and Japan contest. And China has moved in, installing oil and gas platforms in contested waters over Tokyo's objections.[33]

Offshore oil discovery also includes the long (though narrow) continental shelf off the Bering Sea, in the high north. And here, warming seas have made the area far more accessible than was previously possible. Indeed, the combination of new technology, warming seas, and Russia's drive to retain its position as an energy superpower has made the Arctic and its littoral seas one of the most adventuresome places for offshore exploration.

Once again, the scale is huge. Numbers are hard to come by in the Arctic, in part because it's hard to access, but in 2008 the US Geological Survey estimated that the Arctic Circle held *90 billion* barrels of recoverable oil—at the time 13 percent of the world's estimated undiscovered oil resources. The USGS also estimated that it held nearly 1,700 trillion cubic feet of natural gas–of which 84 percent is offshore.[34] Just as in the South and East China Seas, there is debate about how far the exclusive economic zones extend between the Arctic countries: Canada, Denmark (through Greenland), Finland, Iceland, Norway, Russia, Sweden, and the United States. In 2007, Russia famously planted a Russian flag at the ocean bottom at the North Pole, prompting concern among the other countries.[35] Russia, Norway, Denmark, and Canada have all made claims to the seafloor beyond the exclusive zones awarded by the United Nations Convention on the Law of the Sea.*

*Russian offshore drilling isn't limited to the Arctic: indeed, the largest offshore platform in the world is the Berkut oil platform, located off Russia's Pacific coast. It's illustrative of the dynamics of the energy industry that, notwithstanding the tensions between the countries in question, this platform was financed by a consortium of companies from Russia, India, Japan, and the United States.

China has also entered the arena, gaining observer status at the Arctic Council, the body that coordinates discussions among Arctic countries, and helping Russia to fund oil and gas projects in the region. As one expert summarized the Chinese position, "We know that we don't have claims in the Arctic, but if there's anything in the Arctic that we can get, we don't want to be left out."[36]

In fact, the Arctic has become one of the more confounding areas of Russia-China relations. On the one hand, supplies of Russian gas from the Yamal Peninsula (on the Barents coast) are designated for China, usefully adding to the diversity of its energy supply. On the other hand, China stands to gain much more, commercially, from the flow of shipping across a warming Arctic than does Russia, so China looks warily on Russia's increasing militarization of the seas. And in June 2020, with tensions between the two countries already running high around the COVID-19 crisis, Russia accused China of spying on its Arctic activities, fingering a Russian national for having (reportedly) supplied China with documentation about Russia's work on hyrdoacoustics in the Arctic—work vital for undersea energy exploration, as well as for monitoring submarine activity.[37]

And offshore drilling has expanded in the Persian Gulf—not the sands of Arabia or Iran that flank it, but the waters of the Gulf itself. Here, though, the offshore play is not oil, but gas. The region has long known of huge offshore fields of gas. But for most of the history of the fuel, it's been limited by the need to tie the extraction of gas to pipelines. As a result, for many years, natural gas has been a *regional* fuel, shipped from extraction fields to neighboring countries by pipeline—and thus with limited markets, and limited reach.

Technological development changed that. Liquefied natural gas (LNG) is natural gas that's been cooled to –260 degrees Fahrenheit, the temperature at which it becomes a liquid. The volume of this liquid is six hundred times smaller than the gas.[38] This allows LNG to be pumped into container vessels, then transported by sea. Just ten years ago, less than 30 percent of gas moved by sea. By 2018, almost 50 percent of the world's gas trade between regions was moved by LNG tanker.[39]

These are, once again, huge ships. The first modern natural gas tanker—which had the somewhat on-the-nose name of the *Methane*

Princess—was 908 feet long and capable of carrying 9,532,912 liquid gallons of gas. Fast-forward to the present day, and Qatar's *Mozah* is capable of carrying 70,269,765 liquid gallons of gas. (And in the still bizarre, semi-regulated world of shipping, the *Mozah*—named after the consort of the former emir of the country, and owned by the state of Qatar itself—flies under the flag of the Marshall Islands, where it registers its "flag of convenience.")

Much of this gas flows to Asia, including to Japan, which has long been a major importer of natural gas, especially from Indonesia. As Indonesia's gas fields have dried up, Japan is on the hunt for a new supply—perhaps from Myanmar, by pipeline, but also from the Persian Gulf, by sea. Japan is still thirsty for imports of gas; but by 2018, China had become the world's second-largest importer of natural gas; and its thirst is growing.[40] From 2016 to 2018, the global supply of LNG increased by 28 percent, and China absorbed half of that increase.[41]

Oceans of Energy

With the liquification of natural gas and its shipment by sea, we complete the story of the growing dominance of the oceans in the world of energy.

It's long been *part* of the story, of course. In the years after World War II, Saudi production, as well as Iranian production, transformed the global oil markets. But of course, the oil had to get from the Gulf to the markets, and then it had to get there by oceans, and thus began the story of oil tankers. The world's first oil tankers carried their cargo in barrels. New tankers emerged from the Suez Crisis of 1956, and the oil price spike that followed.[42] Just as with containerization, the subsequent Suez Crisis in the 1970s spurred the development of much larger oil tankers.

And as the scale grew, so did the pressure for standardization, much as it did with containerization. Indeed, it was tanker shipping that was the driving element in the growth of scale of modern bulk shipping. For Maersk, overseas-oriented tanker traffic was in fact the larger part of their corporate growth in the 1950s and '60s. OOCL's first truly large ship was not a container, but the *Seawise Giant*, which they ordered in

1974. They took delivery of the ship in 1979, just as the container revolution was gaining steam. The ship displaced 81,000 tons unloaded, and a whopping 564,000 tons when filled with oil.* It was 1,500 feet long—making it the longest ship ever constructed. In his epic account of the tanker industry, Noel Mostert wrote: "These are the biggest ships that have ever been, their dimensions being one of the technological audacities of the century."[43] In the 1960s and '70s, Maersk made more money delivering fuel from Saudi Arabia to Europe and the United States than from any other part of its shipping business.

So the flow of oil by sea has, for the past several decades, been an important part of the energy story. Add to this the huge expansion in offshore discovery and production of oil, and then the flow by sea of gas. As of 2016, more than a quarter of the world's oil and gas supply was produced offshore, mostly in the Persian Gulf, the Gulf of Guinea, the North Sea, Brazil, the Gulf of Mexico, and the Caspian Sea.[44] And this flow shows no sign of slowing: since 2010, more than half of the volume of energy discovered globally has been found offshore. In 2018, there were fifty-five such discoveries, representing 70 percent of the volumes of liquids and gas discovered. And the International Energy Agency predicts a rise of 24,720 billion cubic feet of offshore gas production by 2040. Similarly, the US Bureau of Ocean Energy Management in 2016 estimated that 90 billion barrels of undiscovered, recoverable oil and 327 trillion cubic feet of undiscovered, recoverable natural gas lay just in the US continental shelf.[45]

The bottom line is this: the vast majority of the world's supply of oil and gas is either found at sea or moved by sea to its destination. The story of the role of oceans in global energy trade is rarely told, but they are vital to the overall picture. Almost 80 percent of all oil consumed worldwide moves by sea at some point. And as of 2018, so does nearly 50 percent of natural gas.[46]

All of which is profoundly problematic for China.[47]

*This ship was actually ordered by a Greek shipping owner, at a smaller original size; but when early trials of the ship revealed problems with its stability, he refused to take ownership. C. Y. Tung made a deal to take over ownership of the vessel, and had it lengthened to its eventual full size. The ship was sunk during the Iran-Iraq War, but then resurfaced and was repaired to use as a fuel storage vessel.

Energy Security and Choke Points

Energy is bought and sold now as if it were a market good, like any other product on a container ship or bulk carrier. But governments don't treat energy the same way they do sneakers, or TVs, or any other elements that fill container ships. For this simple reason: blockage of their supplies of energy would cripple their economies. (These supplies also fuel the major powers' navies and armies. Indeed, the United States armed services is the largest single energy consumer in the world.) For the governments in question, energy is a strategic, not a commercial, good.

This reality is reinforced by the role of national companies in the energy space. The media, when covering issues of energy, tends to focus on the role of the American independent majors, like Shell or Exxon-Mobil, and sometimes the European independents, like BP. A common refrain of American critics of the energy sector is that these companies are too close to government and often gain preferential treatment. But by the standards of the rest of the world, they're quite distant from government; because in the rest of the world, oil companies are actually owned or controlled by governments. That's true for Russia, for China, for Brazil, India, Saudi Arabia, Qatar, Norway, Indonesia, Venezuela, and Japan. Fully 90 percent of the world's oil and gas reserves are held by nationally owned companies. The trade and flow of energy is the business of governments and semi-government entities far more than it is of the working of the marketplace.

Why does this matter? Because energy powers literally every other part of human activity. From agriculture, where energy is a vital input into fertilizer, as well as a source of fuel for the machinery used to harvest crops on an industrial scale; to industry, where the burning of fossil fuels is a necessary ingredient in the manufacture of steel and iron and other metals; to transportation, the largest single source of the consumption of oil; to heat, which is generated in most countries by the burning of oil or gas or coal; and even to modern industries like technology or finance, which require huge quantities of electricity that in most countries is generated primarily by the burning of oil or coal.

Nearly all projections of the world's energy use have oil and gas still accounting for the largest share of the world's energy through 2050. Indeed, the world's demand for oil and gas has been growing in the past three decades, as sea-based trade has allowed new countries to participate in globalization. Demand for energy in the world grew by 50 percent between 1990 and 2008.[48]

So ensuring a steady flow of oil (and now gas) by sea is a vital concern for governments worldwide. It's why the US focused on the Middle East in the postwar era, and one reason why it has stayed involved—by many accounts, too involved—ever since. For as the Malacca Strait is the great, vulnerable choke point of container trade, the Strait of Hormuz is the great, vulnerable choke point of energy flows.

In the postwar period, the US Navy has deployed in ways designed to secure key choke points for the flow of oil—especially the Sixth Fleet in Haifa, and the Fifth Fleet in Bahrain, in the Persian Gulf. But as the US deploys to be able to defend key choke points, that also means that it can close them off.

All this reinforces China's Malacca Dilemma. Indeed, Daniel Yergin, in his epic account of the modern energy industry, *The Quest*, notes that Chinese premier Hu Jintao began to focus on the Malacca Dilemma just after the Iraq War—which China at the time assumed was a US move to tighten up its control of Middle Eastern energy supplies. And Beijing's focus on the Malacca Dilemma helped drive China's "Going Out" policy of encouraging overseas investment in the oil and gas sector.

The Strait of Hormuz, which channels the Persian Gulf into the open ocean, carries about one-third of all global seaborne oil trade. Furthermore, more than 25 percent of global LNG trade goes through the strait.[49] Much of what goes through is oil from Saudi Arabia, Iraq, and Iran to importers in Asia, Europe, and Africa. Closing the strait entirely would block around 17 percent of the global oil supply—and send prices skyrocketing.[50] And China's vulnerability is particularly acute: in 2018, about 40 percent of China's crude oil imports came through Hormuz.

Hormuz is not the only energy choke point. The Malacca Strait is also key for the delivering of energy to Asia. It currently carries about 19 million barrels per day of crude oil and oil products—and is important for fuel storage, fuel blending, and ship refueling.[51] There are no easy options to avoid Malacca. The Sunda Strait, between Java and Sumatra, is the nearest option, but is too shallow and narrow for large vessels. The Lombok Strait (between Bali and Lombok islands) is the most viable alternative, but doesn't have adequate infrastructure and it would increase voyage times, causing delays and adding costs.

(And often neglected in accounts of choke points is the Bosporus Strait—but if you're Russian, it's a key fact. As Yergin notes, "Every day more than three million barrels per day of Russian and Central Asian oil pass through it, right down through the middle of Istanbul."* Remarkably, the flow of Russian oil and shipping through this channel is still governed by the relevant parties in compliance with the Treaty of Dardanelles, signed in 1809.)

The dependence on these straits isn't going to change anytime soon. The International Energy Agency estimates that by 2040, nearly 26 million barrels per day of oil will pass through the Strait of Malacca and 20 million through the Strait of Hormuz.[52]

China's not alone in this, though. Japan is equally dependent on imports—indeed, to China's 40 percent of imports that come through Hormuz, Japan's equivalent number is 80 percent. And India is increasingly dependent on oil and gas from the Persian Gulf. Just as China's energy growth has been the major story of global oil and gas markets in the past two decades, India's will dominate the next two decades. At current rates, India's growth in energy consumption up to 2050 represents fully 40 percent of the expected total world increase in consumption.[53] And already by 2030, India will be about 90 percent dependent on oil imports, most of it flowing through the Strait of Hormuz. When the US Navy contemplates energy blockades of China, these facts substantially complicate the picture.[54]

* * *

Back in Houston, these changes are visible in the major new oil and gas *export* terminals now built up along the Houston Ship Channel, as well as in nearby Louisiana. The American return to a position of net energy exporter has been widely celebrated, both by the American

*From Daniel Yergin, *The Quest*, 283. For a vivid account of the changing dynamics of energy security (and insecurity), see also Daniel Yergin, *The New Map: Energy, Climate, and the Clash of Nations* (New York: Penguin Press, 2020).

media and by political elites in Washington, DC. Indeed, it's become fashionable to argue that because the United States is now a net energy exporter, it's "independent" from the frailties of the Persian Gulf, and no longer has to worry about energy insecurity; that the United States itself is effectively immune from the vulnerabilities in Middle Eastern choke points.

It's a two-part confusion. First, it ignores the fact that the United States still imports huge quantities of oil; its level of imports is dropping, to be sure, but in 2018 the United States still imported 7,900,000 barrels of oil, just shy of China's 8,400,000. Less of that oil comes from the Persian Gulf than before, but since the four largest sources of American imports after Canada are Mexico, Saudi Arabia, Russia, and Colombia—with Iraq and Nigeria not far behind—the US is hardly in a position not to worry about stability of any sources of oil supply. Second, it ignores the fact that oil is priced globally: disruptions in one market instantly affect prices in another. So if major producers like Saudi Arabia are cut off from selling their oil overseas, prices will spike. And countries like Russia and Saudi Arabia can still very effectively manipulate the world price of oil.

* * *

And then there's a very different American vulnerability, tied to a very different dimension to the extraction of carbon from the seas. Wherever it's burned, oil and gas release carbon and that carbon reenters the atmosphere, and—as we increasingly understand—reenters the seas. And in so doing, it affects the salinity, the temperature, and the volume of the world's oceans—and that, in turn, is driving changes to our weather and our overall climate. These are changes that the United States can't insulate itself from, no matter how many walls it builds, how secure it feels, or how hard it tries to extract itself from globalization.

Which takes us to the second part of the story of the salt of the oceans—and to very different kinds of engineering and ocean sciences associated with a very different set of questions about power in the modern world.

13

Oceanography and Power

For most of this book, we've moved chronologically through history. Now we need to peer into the future. To do so, it's worth a brief look backward, to the founding of the science of oceanography by the US and Royal navies in the mid-nineteenth century. For the surprising fact is that just as the US Navy played a critical role in amplifying the technologies needed to extract carbon from the ocean floor, so, too, has it played a key role in understanding the consequences of what happens afterward, when that carbon is emitted into the atmosphere. Much of modern climate science owes its roots to early studies sponsored by the US Navy. And a focus on those studies does three useful things: it gives us an angle into the otherwise vastly complex world of climate science; it highlights that the essential facts about the way carbon emission was dangerously warming the planet were known to policy makers at the highest level—including American presidents—as early as the 1960s; and it points us to what the current science suggests are some of the most consequential dynamics in a changing climate, in the Arctic and Southern Oceans.

Of Oceanography and Power: The League of Extraordinary Gentlemen

The iconic structure of the Scripps Institution of Oceanography is a modernist glass and redwood building whose windows open to a sweeping view of the Pacific. The building, in La Jolla, California, dates only to 1964, but the institute has its roots in a Marine Biological Association set up in San Diego in 1903 by the philanthropy of the Scripps family, notably Ellen Browning Scripps. It was renamed to honor Scripps in 1912 and became part of the University of California. It was the first independent American center for the study of the oceans, and still one of the world's most preeminent.*

The foundations of oceanography are often most associated with the British Royal Navy and the Royal Society. In particular, we think of the voyages of the HMS *Beagle*, which in the 1830s brought Darwin to South America, and the HMS *Challenger*, which in the 1870s sailed purposefully to learn more about the deep seas. Between them, the two ships collected vast quantities of biological, zoological, and oceanographic science. Their reputation as groundbreaking voyages is well founded. The *Challenger*, in particular, generated findings about the ocean's floor that undergirded much of the science to come, as well as the laying of the aforementioned ocean cables upon which our digitized world relies. Other competitors for global power, from Spain to Russia, also participated in the study of the oceans. Germany's *Meteor* in the 1920s traversed the southern Atlantic no less than thirteen times, collecting a wide swath of data from salinity levels to samples of the ocean bottom. Ocean sciences become one of the symbols of international prowess in the competitive nineteenth century.[1]

But more than thirty years before the *Challenger*, the US Navy, seeking to deal itself a hand in the great game of oceanic exploration, launched its own, large-scale scientific voyage.[2] The US Exploring Expedition, comprised of the USS *Vincennes*, the *Peacock*, the *Porpoise*, the *Sea Gull*, the *Flying Fish*, the *Oregon*, and the *Relief*, sailed from 1838 to 1842. The expedition ended in infamy and the court martial of its controversial leader, Captain Charles Wilkes. Yet it brought back to the United States sufficient scientific material to form the basis of the Smithsonian collection.[3] The Smithsonian's own account of the voyage conveys something of its scale and ambition:

> *The vast crisscrossing track of the [Exploring Expedition] still takes one's breath away: first south to Cape Horn, with a side trip from there to the Antarctic, to the west coast of South America, then to Tahiti and the Fiji*

*Along with the Woods Hole Oceanographic Institution, on the other side of the country, off Cape Cod, which was established in 1930.

> *Islands and Australia, and from there a more extended exploration of Antarctica. The expedition then backtracked to Australia and New Zealand, to the Fiji and Hawaiian Islands, and from there to another of its prime objectives, the Pacific Northwest, in order to explore that coast and strengthen American claims to the Oregon Territory and the San Francisco Bay. Next, the ships sailed to Manila, Singapore, around Cape Town, and to New York, concluding the last all-sail circumnavigation of the world.*[4]

The voyage contributed 241 charts of the seas it sailed, as well as countless specimens, artifacts, drawings, and journals. Arguably, though, the most important contribution was the work it did in charting the contours of the Antarctic, providing much of the evidence that went into the recognition that Antarctica is a separate continent. And in identifying its contours, the scientists of the Ex-Ex—as the voyage was commonly known—also did much to map the contours of what we now know as the Southern Ocean.

By the turn of the twentieth century, the United States, in the wake of the Spanish-American War and under the influence of Roosevelt and Mahan, had begun to engage more expansively in the research, expedition, and exploration that characterized imperial competition at the time. As America gained colonies in the Caribbean and the Pacific, its sense of internationalism grew. The spirit of the age was embodied in people like Isaiah Bowman, who led expeditions to chart large parts of South America, founded the American Geographical Society, and advised Woodrow Wilson on Europe's new borders during Versailles negotiations.[5]

The sponsorship of science played an important part in that growing internationalism—and that prominently included the oceanographic sciences.* The most consequential oceanographer of the age was not British, but an American, Matthew Fontaine Maury. Among other distinctions, he was superintendent of the newly established Naval Observatory (which now serves as well as the residence of the American vice president). Maury conducted a series of studies of the

*For a rich account of the role of exploration and geographical research in the formation of American internationalism at the turn of the century, see in particular Neil Smith, *American Empire: Roosevelt's Geographer and the Prelude to Globalization* (Berkeley: University of California Press, 2003).

movements of the oceans, and charted them carefully, and for many decades his magnum opus, *The Physical Geography of the Sea*, was the seminal text used by mariners of all stripes and all nations to aid their navigation and their science.

Scripps was founded at this heady time. It quickly managed to attract some of the leading oceanographers from around the world, innovate a teaching program, and launch several research vessels, including one capable of deepwater oceanography. In 1936, the research director from Roald Amundsen's famous expedition to the North Pole, Harald Ulrik Sverdrup, became its director. And then, like the rest of the world, Scripps was pulled into the vast, all-consuming enterprise of World War II. The war saw a further deepening of the interaction between the national security establishment in Washington, the navy, and the oceanographic community.

Walter Munk, the Office of Naval Research, and the Science of Surfing

The business of waging a world war fought across two oceans—and beneath them—would prove to be a huge boon to ocean science. Among its effects was the establishment of a powerful unit for research in the US Navy. As the war came to a close, the navy created an Office of Naval Research to keep up its support to the ocean sciences, and the ONR would emerge as the major sponsor of science in the United States and retain that role for two decades after the war.[6]

It's unsurprising that the navy should want to understand the oceanic domain, or that the world's largest navy should emerge as a major driver of the ocean sciences. But the scale of impact of the US Navy in driving basic science research is truly far-reaching. Even the Royal Navy's infrastructure for research was but a minor fraction of that developed by the Office of Naval Research. One of the biggest players in this collaboration was Walter Munk, whom we encountered in Project Mohole. His first, and in some ways most consequential, interaction with the navy came twenty years earlier.

Munk had just joined the Scripps Institution as a PhD student, at the invitation of its storied director, Harald Sverdrup, when the war broke out. Like the rest of his colleagues, Munk joined the US Armed Forces. He was initially assigned to the US Army at Fort Lewis, but Sverdrup requested his recall to Scripps in 1941 to help with a new joint venture between Scripps and the US Navy Radio and Sound Laboratory. It was the week before Pearl Harbor. Munk worked at the new lab developing techniques for "acoustic tomography"—understanding how sound waves move through the ocean's waters, and using those sound waves to map their flow. While there, he learned of upcoming Allied landings in North Africa, but was struck by the paucity of the Allies' knowledge of local wave conditions. Munk took it upon himself to begin to work through some theories about wave formation and timing—what he would later refer to as the study of waves, wind, and swell. It would influence a generation of scholars afterward. At the time, its most important use was to help plan the timing of the D-Day invasion.

After the war, oceanographic scientists enjoyed ample resources, largely funded by the ONR. The 1950s head of the geophysics branch of the ONR, Gordon Lill (who led the American Miscellaneous Society, together with Roger Revelle), would later describe it: "The sky was the limit. We were very adventuresome. Lots of stuff, equipment, was available as left-overs from World War II. You could get trucks, you could get jeeps, you could get airplanes, and you could get ships. Almost anything you wanted, there was some surplus store of it somewhere. You could get this stuff, and ship it out to the universities, and let the scientific community use it."[7]

Munk and his colleagues at Scripps were among those who made use of that support. He continued studying how waves are formed, and how they travel and change as they move across the length of the oceans. Waves, of course, are shaped by local wind conditions, as well as the precise formation of the coastal shelf where they are formed. But what Munk saw in his research is that these local conditions shaped only a small part of how waves traveled; that their movement across huge distances was explained more by the currents of the ocean—that a single wave might begin with dynamics more than a continent away from where it would ultimately crest.

This line of Munk's research culminated in a famous 1956 study that was the first to show in detail how ocean dynamics in the Southern Pacific, six thousand miles away from Scripps, affected wave formation as distant as the California coast. It became the basis for Munk's most popular application—the ability of surfers to predict wave swells around the world. But not just that: Munk's work on wave transmission did much to illuminate the way that sound waves, moving across the ocean, were affected by the temperature and density of the water. Because sound waves are constant, this became an important mode for measuring the changing temperature of the oceans—what Munk would later call "the sound of climate change."[8]

This important interplay between national security decision makers and scientists in the formation of climate science has attracted its own study at Scripps, most notably by David Victor, who is an adjunct professor of Climate, Atmospheric Science, and Physical Oceanography. Victor, whom we met in the preceding chapter, has an unusual pedigree for an energy and climate scholar. His PhD from MIT is in the political, not the natural, sciences, and for many years his primary academic affiliation was with Stanford Law School. The University of California in San Diego lured him away from Stanford to run a research lab on climate and energy policy. He's also a student of the ways in which national security authorities, elite scientific institutions, and governmental funders have interacted over the decades to shape the course of climate science.[9,*]

The collaborations between the navy and Scripps deepened in the 1950s. By then, Woods Hole, founded in the 1930s on the other side of the continent, near Cape Cod and facing the Atlantic, was also doing important work with the navy, especially on sonar technologies and the ways that sonar could be used to track submarines hiding beneath the different layers of water that characterize the ocean depths. But by dint of geography, Scripps was more fully pulled into the next critical phase of naval science—atomic testing in the Pacific.

*He also surfs. A peripatetic character, David is often found flying himself from conference to briefing to speech on his own twin-prop airplane or on the red-eye out of San Diego. But when he's at Scripps, he likes to take advantage of the location and indulge his real passion: surfing. He's not alone: many of his colleagues also get out onto the breakers regularly. Walk through the corridors of Scripps and many of the offices have a surfboard tucked in amid the computers and scientific papers, and drying wet suits often adorn the gates and racks of the seaside campus.

In the mid-1950s, the United States began live testing of nuclear weapons, by exploding them on small islands and atolls, mostly in the Western Pacific. Munk was among a team of scientists tasked with studying the wave effects from those vast explosions. He worried that the explosion of nuclear weapons underwater could trigger tsunamis, and the work he did to measure their effects laid the early foundation for what is now the important work of the US National Oceanic and Atmospheric Administration (NOAA) and others to provide early warnings of tsunamis. Munk also realized that the atomic tests represented an opportunity to study wave dynamics, and the communication of force and of sound through the waves, under unique circumstances. David Victor recounts, "Ironically, the tests—incredibly controversial at the time—proved to be very important to climate science. Basically, they put a layer of radiocarbon in the water that had only one possible source—thermonuclear weapons. So when you saw that layer, you could tell the age of the water parcels you were examining. It's like you're an archaeologist in the oceans and suddenly you've been handed this very powerful tool to be able to know the age of the water parcels that allows you to piece out what the currents are."[10]

These studies were motivated, too, by an effort to understand a phenomenon that had fascinated Harald Sverdrup and others since the 1930s: how the chemistry of the oceans affects their currents. They knew that salt water absorbed carbon from the atmosphere. How much, how quickly, and with what effect was an item of scientific curiosity, not of central study, in this generation of oceanographers. But its exploration by Scripps scientists would prove to be one of the most consequential lines of scientific research.

From the early days of oceanography, one of the central preoccupations had been how currents and wind patterns in one part of the sea affected movements in another. This is the great puzzle of the oceans. For at the same time, the oceans and their seas exhibit highly localized and specific variations, and yet all oceanic waters ultimately flow into one another. Empty a can of paint into the Southern Ocean at Wilkes Point or into the Pacific Ocean at Hawaii, and eventually some trace of that will be found in the North Atlantic, the Norwegian Sea, or the far reaches of the Indian Ocean. Climate models now suggest that a complete circulation of the oceans' water occurs over roughly one thousand years.

At the time of the early nuclear testing, most scientists believed that the majority of carbon dioxide released by the industrial burning of fossil fuels remained in the atmosphere. A study in 1957 by Munk's colleagues Roger Revelle and Hans Suess challenged that conclusion.[11] The study is brief, merely nine pages long, and most of the text is taken up with mathematic equations and tables that recount their effort to measure the carbon captured in the shells of bicarbonates (mollusks, limpets, cockles, and the like) as well as seaweed—much as scientists measure the carbon captured in preserved wood and rocks. They take note of earlier studies of sea-level rise that estimated that most of the rise observed by then could be accounted for by naturally occurring glacial melt. But they began to worry about what's known as "ocean mixing"—the chemical process by which the colder, denser, saltier water of the deep ocean mingles with the warmer waters on the surface, impacting wave patterns. They reached the startling conclusion that "most of the CO_2 released by artificial fuel combustion since the beginning of the industrial revolution must have been absorbed by the oceans."[12]

The paper concludes by describing the "large scale geophysical experiment" that human beings were involved in: by burning industrial quantities of fossil fuels, they noted, "[w]ithin a few centuries we are returning to the atmosphere and oceans the concentrated organic carbon stored in sedimentary rocks over hundreds of millions of years."[13]

To Revelle and Suess, this was less a concern about what would later come to be known as global warming than it was a scientific curiosity. Much of the conclusion of the study is given over to a call for more research. They noted that the coming decades were likely to see large new quantities of carbon released into the atmosphere.[14]

The turning point in the study of climate change came in 1957 to 1958, which had been deemed the International Geophysical Year. The brainchild of several American scientists, the year was a grand experiment in scientific cooperation—made all the more remarkable because it coincided with one of the tensest moments in the Cold War. Yet dozens of Soviet scientists joined their American and international colleagues in the first global study of the oceans. "Suddenly," David Victor recounted, "you had all around the world these coordinated ships and ground stations doing systematic measurement of the atmosphere and the oceans." The research transformed the understanding of how the oceans and the atmosphere interacted in managing carbon. Among other things, it highlighted the importance of measuring temperature not just in a few discrete places, close to human habitation, but across the breadth of the oceans.*

Scripps scientists were also involved in studies of the interplay between carbon and the atmosphere. The most famous study was conducted by the Institute's Charles (Dave) Keeling at the Mauna Loa Observatory in Hawaii, where he installed measuring equipment, as well as in the South Pole. In Hawaii, he began systematic, regular testing of levels of carbon concentration. He observed what he described at the time as a possible worldwide rise in carbon concentration. Over subsequent decades, the steady upward rise in carbon concentrations measured at Mauna Loa has become known as "the Keeling Curve," and is foundational in atmospheric studies of climate change.

Briefing the President, and Climate's Wrong Turn

Looking back, it's astonishing to realize how much Munk and Revelle and their colleagues understood about the workings of carbon in the ocean and climate change by the late 1950s. Also astonishing is that even in those peak days of the Cold War, with its great anxiety about the Soviet Union, the signs of climate change and its consequences made it to the desk of the president of the United States.

The connections came through the scientific advisory committees

*The scientists of the International Geophysical Year were not the only ones doing important measurements. The US Navy itself was undertaking important studies and measurements as it found itself patrolling virtually every eddy of the world's oceans. For example, as it chased Soviet submarines under the Arctic sheet ice, the navy's submarine fleet took careful, repeated measurements of the thickness of the ice. That was designed to inform its tracking of the Soviet fleet, but would prove consequential, too, in the study of climate effects of warming seas.

of the National Science Foundation and the president's science council. These linked the scientific community to the national security community and its decision makers. And in 1965, several of the leading Scripps scientists—including Munk, Revelle, and Keeling—would join a who's who of climate scientists in authoring a 1965 Presidential Scientific Advisory Council report on the oceans and climate that was briefed to President Johnson. It described a looming environmental crisis caused by the growing pattern of carbon emissions, and argued that unless there was a change in direction, "measurable and perhaps marked" climate change would likely occur by the end of the twentieth century.[15] It was a remarkably prescient warning. But little came from it. Johnson was fixated that year on the escalation of the Vietnam War and on his Great Society social reform legislation and programs.

In the 1970s, each of the presidents of the United States were further warned of the consequences of a changing climate. The oil price spike of 1973 might have concentrated presidential focus on the topic, but for the fact that by then the United States was wholly absorbed in extracting itself from the Vietnam War. After the 1976 election, Jimmy Carter's key presidential advisers, James Schlesinger and Gus Speth, warned in 1977 that the environmental problem was growing worse; perhaps Carter would have listened were his presidency not about to be torqued around the axle of the 1979–81 Iranian hostage crisis.

Then, in the 1980s, seen from the vantage point of climate policy, the US split off from the world. Internationally, there was growing focus on the problem. Even Ronald Reagan's great friend and great conservative, UK prime minister Margaret Thatcher, focused on the climate issue:

> *The threat to our world comes not only from tyrants and their tanks. It can be more insidious though less visible. The danger of global warming is as yet unseen, but real enough for us to make changes and sacrifices, so that we do not live at the expense of future generations. Our ability to come together to stop or limit damage to the world's environment will be perhaps the greatest test of how far we can act as a world community. No-one should under-estimate the imagination that will be required, nor the scientific effort, nor the unprecedented co-operation we shall have to show. We shall need statesmanship of a rare order.*[16]

Unfortunately, President Reagan provided no such statesmanship. The most important moment of climate policy of his presidency came near its end, in 1988, when NASA scientist Jim Hansen provided startling testimony about the likely effects of climate change to the House of Representatives.[17] The response of the White House was to try to edit his statement (which served only to draw more attention to it). But Reagan did little or nothing to advance serious climate policy.

Briefly in the 1990s, American politics shifted to a more constructive position. As Reagan's vice president, George Bush—that careful analyst—had always taken climate science seriously. In his presidential campaign, he committed himself to acting early on the climate issue. Although he never did host the major climate conference he once promised, he did agree to attend the landmark 1992 Earth Summit in Rio. That meeting kick-started deeper negotiations within what's known as the UN Framework Convention on Climate Change, the eventual result of which was the negotiation and signing in 1997 of the Kyoto Protocol on climate change, which mandated that industrialized nations would cut their emissions to 5 percent below the levels they had recorded in 1990. President Clinton signed the Protocol, the first global treaty designed to address reductions in carbon emissions.

Seen with hindsight, though, climate diplomacy took a wrong turn in Kyoto; it exempted the major developing countries. That fact seemed eminently fair—of the total excess carbon in the atmosphere in 1997, 90 percent had been put there by the industrialized nations; only reasonable, then, for the same nations to have the lion's share of responsibility for dealing with the problem. But it failed to account for what was about to happen, as Chinese industrialization began to take off. As thousands and then tens of thousands of bulk ships began taking raw materials into China and bringing industrialized goods out to Western markets, the process of industrial consumption of fossil fuels began to shift from the West to the East. Fast-forward, and by 2012 Chinese carbon emissions accounted for 73 percent of cumulative global emissions growth.[18] Essentially, the West had outsourced its carbon emissions to China.

So, the Kyoto diplomacy left a giant loophole. And then came the second wrong turn: Bush's son, President George W. Bush, unsigned the Kyoto deal. Eventually, President Obama would return the United

States to the UN climate arrangements, by signing the Paris Climate Accords in 2015; but a mere two years later, President Trump would announce America's withdrawal. His successor, Joseph Biden Jr., restored America's participation in the accords.

In short: between 1965, when the Scripps scientists warned President Johnson that we were facing an environmental catastrophe, and 2020, the world saw exactly four years when energy and climate policy was governed by a treaty that encompassed the United States, Europe, and China—far and away the world's largest energy users and thus carbon emitters.

And so, inexorably, emissions rose, and rose, and rose.

Dismayed by the lack of policy action on their findings, one part of the ocean sciences community reacted by flirting with geoengineering—of deliberately manipulating the chemical interactions between the atmosphere and the oceans to manage the rate and the effects of carbon absorption by the seas.

It was at this time that David Victor first came to Scripps, at the invitation of then director Roger Revelle. He recalls his first dinner with Walter Munk at Scripps, in 1990. It was a gathering of the type that happened in that period, but rarely now, when several of the giants of a given field get together simply to work together on whatever projects are on their mind. The conference happened to occur at the same time as the Iraq War, and more specifically that moment in the conflict when the retreating Iraqi army set fire to the Kuwaiti oil fields. That action had turned the Kuwaiti oil fields into a hellscape of spewing flames, fire gushing from oil geysers seemingly unstoppably. American scientists and engineers were rushed to Kuwait to help figure out how to stop the fires. And at Scripps, it occupied the dinner conversation of the gathering of scientists, who were among the first to turn to the still-controversial question of whether it was possible to manipulate the climate to mitigate the effects of a warming planet. Later, David would recall the session:

> *Lots of the people at the meeting were calculating the climate effects of the Kuwaiti oil fires. But most of the meeting was spent on questions about how to manipulate the climate; geoengineering it got called later. Roger [Revelle] had a crazy scheme in mind to float Styrofoam balls in*

the ocean and make the dark water brighter (and thus more reflective). That plan failed on several obvious grounds. But other people had other ideas. One guy wanted to dump iron in the oceans—someone did a calculation over lunch to show that might work, with the right other kinds of nutrients that would allow algae to bloom and suck CO_2 from the water (and thus from the air). Wally Broecker was often at Scripps too—along with Walter, he was one of the best oceanographers of the last century. That was Scripps at the time—a gathering place for some of the most productive oceanographers of this century, free to exchange ideas. Including some pretty wild ones.[19]

None of this went far, though, in part because the science was simply too unwieldy, and the potential risks of getting it wrong very great. To take just one example, a later study of the possibility of deliberately introducing cooling into the atmosphere acknowledged that one of the potential side effects was . . . worldwide nuclear winter.

Two other strands of work were more serious and more sustained: a deep study of marine biology, and a large-scale effort to develop data-rich computer models of the climate.

Marine Biology, or the League of Extraordinary Women

The first was the start of a serious and sustained effort in marine biology—a detailed, large-scale effort to chart the effects of changing ocean chemistry on the fish, mammals, and plant life supported by the oceans. Although figures like Jacques Cousteau are most famously associated with this phase of work, it was also driven by what we might describe as a league of extraordinary (and not so gentle) women. Most famous of these was Sylvia Earle, whose lifelong attachment to the oceans, willingness to break down gender barriers, and dedication to the careful documentation of ocean biology would ultimately see her become the first woman to serve as chief scientist to NOAA—which, by the time she served there, had become at least as important as if not somewhat more important than the navy's Office of Naval Research as a sponsor of oceanographic and climate science. Earle was also the first modern oceanographer to become a media celebrity, largely on the back of her risky diving expeditions. She agitated for and succeeded in establishing worldwide a number of marine sanctuaries. And she famously convinced the leadership of Google to add an oceans dimension to their groundbreaking mapping app, Google Earth.[20]

Earle was herself inspired by another important marine biologist, Rachel Carson. Carson would become better known for her book on chemical pollution on the land, *Silent Spring*. But her first and arguably more important work was *The Sea Around Us*—an elegant, even elegiac book about the science of the ocean domain. Although much of the science the book documents has been outstripped, *The Sea Around Us* still stands as one of the most compelling accounts of the scale, the sense, and the importance of the world's oceans; what Sylvia Earle, who wrote the introduction to the reissued 2018 edition, called her "lyrical descriptions of the grand processes that underpin the existence of life on earth"—for indeed, that is what the modern study of marine biology has revealed is at stake in the health of the oceans.[21] Consider the opening passage of her account of the interplay between the surface waters and the deeper waters below:

> *Nowhere in all the sea does life exist in such bewildering abundance as in the surface waters. From the deck of a vessel you may look down, hour after hour, on the shimmering discs of jellyfish, their gently pulsating bells dotting the surface as far as you can see. Or one day you may notice early in the morning that you are passing through a sea that has taken on a brick-red color from billions upon billions of microscopic creatures, each of which contains an orange pigment granule. At noon you are still moving through red seas, and when darkness falls the waters shine with an eerie glow from the phosphorescent fires of yet more billions and trillions of these same creatures.*[22]

Her book is perhaps the single best, most accessible account of the science of the seas, and in particular of the way the swirling, undulating currents of the deep waters of the oceans play with the surface waters, in what she calls "a series of delicately adjusted, interlocking relationships,"[23] to create the photosynthesis, and thus the plankton, and thus the oxygen and the protein that sustain much of human life. (Though her account contains no warnings about climate change.)

Somewhat less famous, but arguably the most influential marine biologist of the modern era, was Jane Lubchenco. After getting her PhD at Harvard, Lubchenco moved to Oregon State University, serving as the chair of the Department of Zoology. Although her research has been wide-ranging, her work on near-coastal marine ecology has proved particularly influential. In 1993, she was given the prestigious MacArthur "genius" award.[24] And then in 2009 she served as the first marine biologist to be president of the NOAA, as part of President Obama's "Science Dream Team."* In 2021, President Biden appointed her to a top-level position, coordinating science and climate issues within his White House's Office of Science and Technology Policy.

Lubchenco and other marine biologists like her helped the scientific community, and the public, start to understand the effects that climate change was having in real time on the world's environment. It was an endeavor focused on the highly local, the visible, the tactile; on the features of the oceans that can be felt on a human scale. Another part of the oceanographic community was going in an entirely different direction.

The Modelers

If the marine biologists dwelt on the detailed, lived effects of changing ocean chemistry in specific, real-world locales, another part of the oceanographic community went in an entirely different direction—seeking to model the oceans and the climate as a single, complex system. Ocean and atmospheric scientists started constructing mathematical models of the overall oceans—what became known as global circulation models.

Just as the world of naval warfare was transformed by the evolution of large-scale information technology, so were the climate sciences. This was a story of increased access to computing power, and of big data. To operate a mathematical model of a geophysical system of

*Lubchenco also led the White House team that dealt with the huge environmental fallout from the *Deepwater Horizon* disaster in 2010—a fire and breakdown of one of the world's largest oil rigs, in the Gulf of Mexico.

any complexity requires very large amounts of computing power. And just as part of the ocean sciences community was turning to mathematical modeling, powerful computing capacity became an accessible tool. For many years, the largest single users of computing power were those in the scientific and national security communities who were running simulations of nuclear weapons tests. But next were the climate modelers.

Yet there was a lack of data. Until the early twenty-first century, the measurement of the temperature of the oceans was still incredibly episodic. When the *Challenger*, and the ships of the US Ex-Ex, sought to measure the temperature of the water, they would lower a bucket into the ocean, pull it up, and stick a thermometer into the water. Later, scientists realized that even the nature of the bucket mattered—leather, wood, and metal buckets all affected the temperature of the sampled water in different ways. The science got considerably more sophisticated in the 1980s and '90s, which saw ships sampling water in carefully constructed thermoses. But still, it was episodic and localized.

That changed, starting around 2000, with the launching of what became known as the Argo system, a program, launched out of Scripps, that fields nearly four thousand remotely operated floats across the globe. These floats dot the world's oceans, providing near-live feedback on temperature and salinity. Once a float is dropped off by a delivery ship, every ten days, an internal battery pumps oil between a reservoir inside the float and an external bladder, making the float descend 1.24 miles. As it returns to the surface, it collects measurements of ocean properties. Once back on the surface, it uses satellites to relay the information to stations onshore.[25] In a second phase, Argo also deployed a number of autonomous submarines, which could dive to depths of around two thousand feet, generating for the first time a stream of consistent temperature data from the deeper waters.

With large-scale computing power and big data now available to them, modelers could really get to work on what's called a "general circulation model."

Imagine a single square mile of surface water, perhaps one hundred feet deep. It has a specific chemistry and a specific salinity. It has waves and tides and current. It's interacting with sunlight, sometimes refracted through the clouds, and with the atmosphere as a whole. Simply to depict the dynamics of that single square mile already requires the interplay of multiple variables over time.

Now dive down. At two hundred feet, the chemistry and density are similar, although the temperature is dropping. The water here does not have surface waves, but it is moved by the waves above it, and the current below. Similar patterns hold if you capture a slice of the ocean at three hundred feet, at four hundred, at five hundred.

By around six hundred feet, the density and chemistry of the waters start to change. What's known as the thermocline layer has its own specific dynamics. Colloquially, it's called the "twilight zone," because although it's substantially darker than at the surface, some light does still penetrate these waters. Now go deeper still: to three thousand feet; to twelve thousand feet; to eighteen thousand feet; and in some places where the ocean floor gives way to trenches, to as much as thirty-three thousand feet. You're measuring the denser, darker dynamics of the deep bottom waters, all the way to the ocean floor.*

You also need to go *up*; to incorporate the interaction with the atmosphere, general circulation models also need to "map" the atmosphere *above* the surface waters of the ocean.

Now you have an extraordinarily detailed and rich depiction of this one square mile of depth. It involves hundreds of thousands of pieces of data conveying a complex picture of that single slice of ocean, from the surface to the deep. But you need to repeat this exercise for every square mile of the ocean—all 139,434,000 of them. And now you have billions of pieces of data going into your model. But you're not done.

You need to make the data *move*. The oceans are not static. Every part of them is in constant slow motion. Surface winds create what are known as "ocean gyres," which move large sections of the oceans around in a circular motion (the phenomenon first charted by Walter Munk). River runoffs change the chemistry of the water at its edges, as does glacial melt. There's also interaction with seaborne animal and plant life: phytoplankton is formed on the surface by a complex chemi-

*The scientific terms for these layers are: the epipelagic zone (where sunlight penetrates, mostly along continental shelves); the mesopelagic zone (some light penetration); the bathypelagic zone (along the continental slope); the abyssopelagic zone (colloquially, the abyss), along the ocean basin; and the hadalpelagic zone, in the deep ocean trenches.

cal process born when the deep, cold waters of the ocean bottom mix with the sun-warmed waters of the surface, giving rise to plankton blooms. Fish and sea mammals eat this plankton, and generate what biologists call "marine snow"—basically fish poop—which gradually sinks to the bottom, pulling with it large concentrations of chemicals. The middle layers of the oceans absorb this marine snow and become heavier and sink to the bottom. The sinking of the bottom waters pushes huge volumes of currents in every direction, creating what Rachel Carson called the great continental circulation.

Now you have a model of the oceans and of their interactions with the atmosphere, and you can start to tinker and to test. Most important, you can test what happens if you keep adding carbon to the atmosphere at the same rate we are doing now, or if you slow or accelerate those emissions. You can model the effect on ocean salinity as it absorbs that carbon, and on temperature, and on its volume—for warm water takes more volume than cold.

And if you add all this up, and add to it the detailed findings of marine biology, what do you learn?

What the Science Tells Us

First, that the oceans are complex. They're also not a single system, walled off from the rest of the world; they are in constant chemical interaction with the atmosphere, and the cryosphere—what scientists call the world of ice. They also interact with waters from rivers that run off from land and into the surrounding seas. All of this affects the chemistry of specific bodies of water—their temperature, their salinity, and the mix of carbon and other chemicals in the composition of surface waters.

They also are in constant motion—not just at the surface, but in the deep currents. And the currents and the surface move at different speeds, and with different densities. This interplay between the chemical composition of the deep and the surface waters is key. The general model here is what's known as "thermohaline circulation"—*thermos* referring to temperature, *haline* to salt. As a human being watching the seas and the oceans from the surface, we see wind moving waves, and the earliest study of the oceans focused on the interplay between waves, wind, and swell. But we've learned that the circulation of these great currents is far more important for the patterns of waves and swells and storms, and also, more consequentially, for the overall salinity of the ocean and for sea-level rise.

When warm air in the atmosphere mingles with the surface waters of the oceans, CO_2 in that area has a chemical reaction with the seawater molecules, generating carbonic acid. This immediately causes the CO_2 to be absorbed into the oceans—basically sucking CO_2 out of the air and into the seas. The CO_2 capacity of the oceans is much higher than that of fresh water because of its saltiness. In the deep sea, also, large reservoirs of calcium carbonate sediments neutralize large amounts of that CO_2 by partially dissolving it. Over time, literally over centuries, the mixing of this cold, salty water on the bottom and the less salty waters on the top changes the overall balance of salinity, temperature, and carbon concentration in the water. And the ocean's cold, salty water is heavier than the warmer, less salty surface waters, so it sinks to the bottom, forming cold, mineral-rich "bottom waters." The force of that sinking of waters, billions of cubic gallons of it, pushes other waters around the world, causing the circulation of waters—a phenomenon known as convection.

This phenomenon is most powerful in the polar regions and in the North Atlantic. Off the coast of Maine and Canada, the surface waters sink to a depth of around 6,500 feet. There they meet a deepwater layer from the Arctic that has flowed south. Before that surface water sinks, it absorbs vast quantities of heat and carbon and other gases, pulling that down to the bottom waters and then to the seafloor. (Over millions of years, that will turn into oil and gas that we're now drilling from the ocean floor.) But in the time frame of a millennium, to penetrate the deep waters, that sinking carbon-rich water has to mix with the bottom waters, a chemical process known as abyssal mixing. All of this pulls the dense, cold waters of the polar regions southward.

Take all this together, and the effects are profound.

For reasons that are not exactly apparent, the number *90* recurs throughout this book. Nearly 90 percent of trade flows by sea. Just over 90 percent of global data moves by undersea cables. And here's another: what the now massive climate models of the oceans and the atmosphere show us is that since 1970 the global ocean has taken up more than 90 percent of the excess heat in the climate system.[26] Over historical periods of time, the carbon concentration in the air and the carbon concentration in the water have to move into equilibrium. This can take centuries, but in the shorter term, there's an unfortunate effect. As we have increased the volume of CO_2 put out into the atmosphere by the burning of fossil fuels, the rapid rate at which that CO_2 is absorbed by the oceans means that the two bodies have come into disequilibrium and at present the oceans cannot absorb CO_2 gas as rapidly as we're admitting it into the atmosphere.

* * *

While American politics have so far failed to develop a serious reaction to these findings, the US Navy—original sponsor of the underlying research—has not. The navy's leadership is well aware of its double exposure here. First, it's the frontline service that will have to deal with conflict in the world's energy choke points. Second, it has to worry about its own energy security—it's the largest energy consumer in the US Armed Forces, which is in turn the largest single energy consumer in the world.

The navy has taken several steps to respond. In 2009, the secretary of the navy announced the creation of what it called the Great Green Fleet—an homage to Roosevelt's Great White Fleet. The navy committed itself to using 50 percent less petroleum by 2015 and pledged that at least 50 percent of all the energy it consumed would come from non–fossil fuel sources by 2020. That year saw the maiden voyage of a carrier strike group using this mix of fuels and other energy conservation methods to demonstrate its potential.[27]

The navy has also supported policy research aimed at identifying the risk posed by climate change in its various mission areas. Admiral Samuel J. Locklear III, who served as the commander of what used to be simply known as Pacific Command (from 2012 to 2015), called climate change the threat most likely to "cripple the security environment, probably more likely than the other scenarios we talk about."[28]

And in 2019 the Department of Defense conducted a study of US naval bases' own exposure to rising sea levels. (The previous year, Camp Lejeune and Marine Corps Air Stations Cherry Point and New River had been hit hard by storm surges and flooding during Hurricane Florence.) In February 2019, it released the report showing that of seventy-nine mission-essential installations it reviewed, 67 percent were under *current* risk of flooding, with that number rising to 76 percent under the likely conditions twenty years out.[29]

Even an institution as storied and steeped in tradition, though, can't entirely escape the pressures of politics, and in late 2019, under pressure from President Trump's White House, the navy closed down its climate change task force.

Still, the navy and NOAA between them continue to support and sustain a complex of oceanic, atmospheric, and climate research centers that continue to model the changing climate and its effects.

This study of the oceans, and of their interplay with the atmosphere, has become an extraordinarily sophisticated enterprise—one of the most consequential artifacts of modern American power arrayed across a network of more than two hundred institutions, offices, and collaborations on every coast of the country. It's a collection of scientific capacity that would have been unimaginable to Captain Wilkes and the sailors of the US Ex-Ex.

But despite the navy's and NOAA's excellence in this domain, the overall dominance of the US in the ocean sciences has begun to wane. A 2017 study showed the strongest growth in scientific output was in China, Iran, India, Brazil, the Republic of Korea, and Turkey, with China counting as the major new source of publications. Thus, not only are nations competing on the oceans and for their resources, but the origin of scientific study of the sea's properties now reflects the shifting dynamics of world power. Several of these nations, as we've seen, have stakes in naval competition; all of them have stakes in a changing climate.

14

Hot Waters Rising

If oceanographic study has begun to spread beyond the West, so, too, have the locations of interest. One of particular consequence for two powers gaining their sea legs, China and India, is the Andaman Sea—which lies east of the Bay of Bengal, separated from those shallow waters by the Nicobar Islands, and bounded to the east by the long arc of the tropical forests of the Malay Peninsula, where our narrative started.

Thant House, Rangoon

Thant Myint-U, the noted historian of modern Burma, has documented the myriad ways in which these two Asian giants compete for resources and influence in what he's termed "the new crossroads of Asia."[1] A peripatetic soul, in normal times Thant is hard to pin down, racing back and forth between Rangoon and Bangkok, with frequent trips to Singapore, New York, London, and Washington (usually clad in a bespoke gray suit seemingly cut from the same tailor that dresses C. H. Tung). Like most everyone else, Thant was grounded by the coronavirus pandemic, which hit Myanmar early in the Asian cycle.

Thant spent much of the pandemic period in a small apartment overlooking downtown Rangoon. Most days, he would walk the three miles down Rangoon's central boulevard to the colonial bungalow and four acres of gardens that comprise Thant House, which belonged to his grandfather, U Thant, an educator, historian, diplomat, and minister in Burma's first independent government, who became the first secretary general of the United Nations from the developing world.

Thant carries something of his grandfather's legacy—an air, not quite of noblesse oblige (for political lineage in Burma does not come with landed wealth), but simply of a depth of comfort in his own skin, and a deep love of his country. Thant was the first "outsider" to deal with the secretive SLORC regime, which ruled Burma with an iron fist, in its waning days. That time showed him the reality of the intense competition between India and China, which used both their money and savvy diplomacy to curry favor with the regime in Rangoon. (During COVID-19, Rangoon was an early recipient of Chinese supplies, advice, equipment, and financial support. India, for its part, plays to a shared history and cultural heritage, including during a much-publicized visit to the country by Indian prime minister Narendra Modi.)

The features that make Myanmar attractive to both China and India are two: large estimated reserves of energy, both onshore and off; and the country's long Andaman Sea peninsula. From China's position, access overland to Myanmar's coast would give them a new opening to the Indian Ocean, one that bypasses the Near Seas and the Malacca Strait—and the US fleet. But should China secure such a route, it would put India's navy on the front line of dealing with the PLAN. The Nicobar Islands are India's farthest outpost and the place that the Indian navy first encounters their Chinese counterparts as they sail out through the Malacca Straits. But both nations face a challenge in developing Myanmar's geography for strategic purposes—because both Myanmar and the Nicobar Islands face potential devastation from the changing climate. Of all the places in the world most likely to be profoundly harmed from rising sea levels and increased frequency of storms, the Bay of Bengal and the Nicobar Islands are the most likely to face sustained, wrenching change.

One such storm struck on May 1, 2008, when what was officially known as an "Extremely Severe Cyclonic Storm Nargis" blew across the Bay of Bengal, swamping several of the Nicobar Islands, and gathering speed. It hit the western shore of Myanmar on May 2. The US Navy/Air Force Joint Typhoon Warning Center estimated its maximum wind speeds at 130 miles per hour. Hitting the low-lying delta of the Irrawaddy River, it pushed a storm surge an unimaginable twenty-five miles inland. By morning, 138,000 people had been killed.

It was not the first time the Bay of Bengal had been wrecked by a cyclone.[2] Nargis was not even the deadliest cyclone to visit the bay in recent times; in 1970, the Bhola cyclone swept through the Bay of Bengal, made landfall in eastern Bangladesh, and killed an estimated five hundred thousand souls. Still, the scale of devastation caused by Nargis was immense, and changed the course of Burma's history. In the wake of the devastation, the regime had no choice but to open the country to the hundreds of NGOs and dozens of UN agencies clamoring to help. It opened the floodgates of Western money and influence.

Among other effects, it caused Thant to focus his attention, and that of his NGO, on a different kind of vulnerability that Myanmar faced; not just the new "imperial" competition from its giant neighbors, but from climate change.

Sea-level rise and storm surges are bad enough; but with advanced warnings, planning, and adaptive measures, the effects on human life and economic infrastructure can be mitigated. But Thant saw Myanmar experiencing a different phenomenon as well, a change in the patterns of the monsoon rains and alluvial flooding, one of the effects that arises from a complex, but by now well-mapped, interplay between melting sea ice in the world's poles and changing temperatures and salinity of waters worldwide.

Throughout Myanmar's recorded history, monsoon flooding predictably hits what's known as the "dry zone" during the months of June through September. Moisture blown in from the Andaman Sea and the adjacent Arabian Sea accumulates in the highlands of the Himalayas and Myanmar's northern mountain ranges. Then the winds change course and pull that moisture down through Southeast Asia's great floodplains, the Ganges and the Irrawaddy, in normal years flooding as much as 40 percent of Myanmar's landmass. This creates the necessary conditions for growing rice—the primary source of caloric intake for 2.7 billion people in Asia, supplying as much as 58 percent of the energy intake of several of the region's populations. But the patterns of rain appeared to be shifting.

Myanmar was feeling the effects of a series of interlocking oceanic phenomena unraveled by a remarkable piece of oceanographic detective work undertaken by researchers at the Bigelow Laboratory for Ocean Sciences in East Boothbay Harbor, Maine, and at the Naval Postgraduate School, in Monterey, California, just up the coast from

Scripps. At the Bigelow lab, a scholar named Joaquim Goés had funding from NASA to use satellite observations of chlorophyll and sea-surface temperature readings to develop a map of nitrate concentrations in the oceans—part of NASA's contribution to global circulation modeling. His mapping found unusually large blooms of phytoplankton in the Arabian Sea (on the other side of the Indian subcontinent from the Bay of Bengal and the Andaman Sea). That led to the discovery that the Arabian Sea had been cooling, affected by changes in the upwelling of cold bottom waters. Careful forensics showed that increased upwelling was related to wind patterns over the ocean, themselves a function of changing patterns of the Asian summer monsoon. Further research showed a strong link between snow patterns in the highlands of Europe and Asia and monsoon patterns—a link that had been theorized as early as the late 1880s, but never demonstrated.[3]

Using advanced climate modeling, the team found a clear set of patterns: a decline in snow coverage in Europe and Asia from the early 1990s onward meant warmer air over these continents, which was affecting glacier formation in the Himalayas, which was affecting rain concentration in the Asian highlands, which was affecting the timing and strength of the monsoon rains. And leading to increased flooding. In a normal year, up to 40 percent of the Ganges and Irrawaddy river deltas flood from the monsoon rains, and over centuries, the local populations have built up their farming and infrastructure around that predictable floodplain. But in flood years, up to 70 percent of the deltas can flood, with devastating effects. And in the last decade, the timing of the monsoons has been increasingly unpredictable, and floods increasingly common.

For the rice farmers who depend on the predictability of the monsoons to prepare their rice fields, these fluctuations were debilitating. And so many of them left the dry zones and decamped to other parts of Myanmar—becoming, in effect, internal climate refugees. They ended up at the edges of parts of Myanmar historically dominated by different ethnicities, and recently torn by more than fifty years of civil war. Myanmar's fragile young democracy was already coping with increased frequency of cyclone and storm-surge damage, dramatic global fluctuations in energy prices, and intensifying competition between China, India, and the West. Adding in a loss of productivity in the rice crop—the production and trade of which accounts for nearly half of Myanmar's GDP—as well as large numbers of internal climate refugees, and Thant was becoming worried that Myanmar's political system might not be able to cope. "I'm worried that Burma could become the world's first climate-induced failed state."*

The effects would not be limited to Myanmar's population of 56 million. On the western side of Myanmar, China has begun to invest billions of dollars in Rakhine State, to build both an oil pipeline and a deepwater port at Kyaukphyu, at the northern tip of Ramree Island. Kyaukphyu has a natural harbor and has long been an important outpost for the trade in rice between Myanmar and India. If fully operationalized, the port would realize China's bid for an equivalent to the Suez Canal—a passageway that would connect Chinese rail and trade directly to the Indian Ocean, bypassing the Malacca Straits. But instability on land and rising sea levels threaten the viability of the project.

All of this is impacted by oceanic dynamics playing out as far away as the North Atlantic and the Antarctic. In the largest sense, the oceans are one, as the Royal Navy used to say, and so is climate change. It's for this reason that climate change is usually viewed as a "we're all in one boat" problem that will logically drive cooperation between governments around the world. But what's equally true is that every sea, and every shore, is distinct; and climate change is playing out very differently in different waters of the world. That reality of variation is not driving cooperation, but rather adding to the competition over command of the seas.

The Oceans and the Climate

The vastness of the oceans has served as a place to operate navies and a global trading system, and they are a resource—for fish, for minerals, for energy. What we're coming to understand, and have increasingly confirmed through oceanographic and atmospheric observation, is that the oceans also play a pivotal role in human ecology, as a criti-

*This was before a coup in January 2021 added a further man-made crisis to the already volatile situation.

cal stabilizer of the climate. For this reason more than any other: the oceans store more heat in the top ten feet of their surface waters than does the entire atmosphere.[4]

That's germane to weather patterns in many more places than the Bay of Bengal. The great ocean currents move warm air around the world, affecting weather patterns from northern Europe to the southern cone. The oceans also help distribute rain across the globe: ocean water is constantly evaporating, increasing the temperature and humidity of the surrounding air to form rain and storms, which are then carried by the trade winds across the world. Almost all rain that falls on land begins in the ocean.

This matters most when it comes to the dynamics of El Niño and La Niña—the major patterns of rainfall and temperature that sweep across the Pacific, best known for bringing rain to the West Coast of the United States, but also vital to rain patterns as far away as the northern Sahara. Climate measurements show that both have become more variable and more intense over the past several decades.[5] El Niño occurs when water temperatures in the central and eastern equatorial Pacific are warmer than average for an extended period of time (now typically three to five months). This warm water shifts eastward, moving the strongest tropical thunderstorms to the central Pacific. This storm shift changes jet-stream wind patterns, creating warmer-than-normal winters in parts of North America and elsewhere bringing unusually heavy storms. As the storms move across the US, the South faces wetter-than-average winters. El Niño also impacts other locations across the globe, causing droughts and wildfires in Australia, floods in South America, below-average rainfall in Indonesia, and other effects as far away as in East and Central Africa.

For the past one hundred years or so, extreme El Niños have occurred about once every twenty years—but, for the next century, they are predicted to occur once every ten years. The increase is due to the fact that more water in the eastern equatorial Pacific is warmer, thanks to climate change—so it warms up more quickly, accelerating El Niño. Its effects are also anticipated to expand to a wider area: extratropical storms are projected to move toward the poles, with consequent changes in wind, precipitation, and temperature patterns.[6]

This new pattern doesn't just matter for weather; it matters for agriculture. For example: one of the things that El Niño affects is how much rain and cool air get blown across California, and along with it the central plains of the United States. It therefore also affects the average annual temperature. And on current patterns, that's set to rise somewhere between .5 to 1 degree over the next twenty or so years, and another 1.5 to 2 degrees in the fifty years after that.

Before America was the world's financier, it was the world's factory; and before it was the world's factory, it was the world's farmer—the largest and most important producer of food in the world. America's first source of wealth was the vast fields of wheat and corn and cattle and hogs that dominate the American Midwest. Adding California to the mix, with its verdant black soil that gives up five crops per year, only added to the bounty. This massive agricultural venture not only feeds America's 330 million citizens, but is also exported to every corner of the globe and forms the bulwark of food supplies provided to global counter-poverty efforts.

Why is America so productive agriculturally? Because in the California plain and the American Midwest, the average temperature between April and October (and longer in California) fluctuates between 69 and 82 degrees Fahrenheit in an average growing season. Some years are hotter, some are cooler, but on average, that's the temperature band. And that happens to be the precise temperature band at which crops like wheat and corn and barley do best. (Other crops like bananas need hotter temperatures, which is why they mostly grow in the Philippines and the Caribbean.) Now, bananas can serve as a staple if you have ready access to some protein, but to build a modern economy and a modern agricultural system you need crops that can be grown in bulk, stored in bulk, and turned into feedstock for cattle and hogs. In short, you need wheat and corn, which the United States has in enormous quantities—it's the world's largest producer of both crops. So what happens if the average temperatures in the United States rise by a couple of degrees? Simply put, a falloff in the productivity of field crops. Just a shift from an average temperature band of 73 to 82 degrees to an average temperature band of 78 to 87 degrees will cause the productivity of grain and corn to drop.[7]

There are still further effects.

The absorption of carbon by the oceans, and their subsequent warming, are also driving more and more marine heat waves—days when the daily sea-surface temperature exceeds the local ninety-ninth percentile of the last roughly forty years. These have doubled in frequency and become longer-lasting, more intense, and more extensive. The difference in density between the ocean's surface and the deep ocean is also growing—which means that less heat, salinity, oxygen, and carbon and fewer nutrients are exchanged vertically in the ocean. The ocean, meanwhile, has lost oxygen.[8]

The oceans have also become 30 percent more acidic over the last two centuries.[9] This has two effects. First, it becomes harder for animals to thrive, especially those with shells, as they have a harder time producing and keeping calcium carbonate.[10] If these animals aren't thriving, that can change the broader overall structure of the ecosystems—ultimately affecting fish populations. Some of this loss can be compensated for by fish-farming close to the coast, and in some geographies by shifting fish farms to land.

The second effect of rising acidity in the oceans is that it affects the rate at which cold bottom waters mix with the warmer surface waters. That's because it changes the salinity of the oceans. Salinity's effect on the density of water is especially important in the western tropical Pacific and far North Atlantic. Rain reduces water's salinity and evaporation increases salinity. This denser, saltier water sinks. So all of this could affect the dynamics of thermohaline circulation—though only over a very great deal of time. The likely consequence of the changing chemistry of the oceans takes us back to where modern oceanography got its start—to the Antarctic Ocean.

The Intergovernmental Panel on Climate Change's seven-hundred-plus-page "Special Report on the Oceans and the Cryosphere," published in 2019, is a monumental work of international scientific cooperation, drawing together studies from several hundred scientists in more than sixty countries for the fullest account ever of the role of the oceans in our changing climate. Its language is ponderous and bureaucratic, reflecting both the rigors of science and the politics of navigating the text through the concerns of dozens of governments. Even its summary for policy makers is clogged with jargon. But amid the technicalities lies the conclusion of a growing, foreboding consensus among the burgeoning field of ocean scientists—that the key to understanding our changing climate lies in the oceans; and the signals are not good. The IPCC's message is that much of what sustains human life comes from the interplay between the surface and deep waters and sea ice; an interplay affected in turn by the interaction between the surface waters and the atmosphere—and that delicate balance is increasingly threatened by a warming planet. The most worrying part of this complex picture is what's happening to the sea ice.

Of Glaciers That Speak with Tongues

The science of a topic as vast as the oceans proceeds with hundreds of studies, many operating in parallel, some that rarely see the light of day, some that attract attention but prove ephemeral in their scientific impact. Then there's that rare study that both attracts attention at the time and stands the test of revision, review, and reexamination. One such was a short, 2001 article by Wally Broecker with the whimsical title "Glaciers That Speak in Tongues and Other Tales of Global Warming."[11] In it, he charted the loss of glacial ice in the Arctic and Antarctic. He noted that the place that this loss was by then most pronounced was where the glacial formations licked out beyond the continental landmass into the oceans themselves—what are known as glacial tongues. There, glaciers were receding and losing mass even more quickly than on the main Arctic ice sheet, or on the Antarctic continent. In subsequent studies of what scientists call the "cryosphere" (the world of ice, at sea and in glaciers), the importance of this phenomenon has grown.

From 1902 to 2015, the global mean sea level rose some six inches—and the rate of that rise, from 2006 to 2015, was .14 inches per year, the highest rate over the last century, and about two and half times the rate recorded between 1901 and 1990.[12] This rise is generated by two phenomena. First is the simple warming of the waters, as they absorb more carbon from the atmosphere. Warm water takes up more volume than cold—just think of filling a pot to two-thirds height and leaving it on the stove; even before boiling over, the hotter water fills the pot. Just so, warmer oceans take up more space than colder ones; and globally, the mean global ocean level is rising. Although the estimates here rely on extraordinarily complex calculations from the global circulation models, the contemporary estimate is that atmospheric warming accounts for about 40 percent of sea-level rise, globally.

The other 60 percent comes from the melting of the sea ice, at both poles. This has been well documented and well covered in the Arctic. We've long measured the Arctic ice—in part because the Arctic ice sheet was where the Soviet fleet would park their submarines, to try to avoid detection from the US Navy. Tracking the Soviets became one of the most complex and dangerous parts of the Cold War, and involved the US Navy measuring the changing levels of surface and subsea ice. Much of this science was released to the public in the 1980s, in part as an effort to spur more serious attention to climate change. It forms an essential baseline. But even more important is the interplay between the oceans and the glaciers in the south.

The Great Southern Warming

On February 6, 2020, Antarctica hit its highest temperatures ever recorded: 18.3C/64.9F—which was about the same temperature as Los Angeles that day. The warm temperatures arrived February 5 and continued until the 13th. The ice melt in just those eight days was notable, and evident. Satellite pictures taken from Eagle Island, near the Drake Passage separating Antarctica from South America, tell the story: on February 4, the island was mostly white, with a few green areas in the satellite image near the coasts. But on February 13, white spots were patchy, and concentrated only in the middle. In just four days (February 6 to 11), Eagle Island lost four inches of ice.[13]

The size and the cold of the Southern Ocean plays a key role in the world's climate system, and Antarctic bottom water is crucial to global convection. This heavy, salty water is so dense that in sinking to the seafloor it pushes billions of gallons of water northward, up into the North Atlantic on one side of the Americas, where it originates the Atlantic Meridional Overturning Circulation, which plays a key role in regulating the temperature of both North America and Europe; and on the other side of the Americas, originating the Humboldt Current, and the rains it generates, which hit the Andes and flow down off of them into the Amazon, watering the entire Amazon basin and much of the South American landmass. Overall, more than one hundred quadrillion gallons of water (that is, 100 followed by fifteen zeroes) are moved through circulation by the sinking of this Antarctic bottom water.

The bottom water is also fantastically productive. Neil Mostert, a scholar of global energy trade, notes, "The layered cold-warm-cold Southern Ocean contains the biggest, most abundant, and the most important of these areas. It is highly productive over much of its area. . . . Indeed, several of those pockets of high productivity elsewhere are directly influenced by the Southern Ocean, notably the west coast of South America from Horn to the equator, and the west coast of Africa from Good Hope to the equator. The Antarctic richness is carried up the South American coast by the Humboldt Current, and along South West Africa by the Benguela Current. . . ."—naming several of the world's most productive fisheries.[14]

Even before it performs these critical roles, the Southern Ocean captures far and away the largest volume of CO_2 anywhere in the world and keeps it on the seafloor for up to one thousand years. It's the largest carbon sink in the world.

So much so in fact that it now becomes clear that the Southern Ocean has absorbed more heat and more CO_2 from the atmosphere than all other marine regions of the world combined, perhaps significantly more so. So the research showing a steady rise in the temperatures of the Southern Ocean is worrying.[15]

Every model of the global climate predicts the same phenomenon, namely that the world's two poles will warm more and warm faster than the rest of the world. This is due to a change in the way that snow reflects sunlight and heat into the atmosphere. In a region covered year-round by snow, what's known as the albedo effect occurs, when light surfaces reflect more heat than dark surfaces. On Earth, the snow reflects about 80 percent of the sunlight back into the atmosphere. By contrast, the open waters of the ocean, despite their vast size, reflect only 7 percent.[16] The exception is the poles, where the ice caps and the sea ice are (until recently) covered with snow year-round. As the atmosphere warms, some of that snow cover melts, exposing the terrain, much darker than the snow. Thus, the poles start to reflect less sunlight, and the surrounding seas are made warmer, and melt more adjacent sea ice; and the cycle deepens, creating a feedback loop. It's this process that has caused the Arctic ice sheet to melt by nearly 40 percent in forty years.[17]

Even more worrying is the situation in the Southern Ocean. Unlike the Arctic, where there's more sea than land, the Antarctic is the opposite, there's more land than sea—so there's a greater albedo effect. Another concern is the melting of the portion of the Antarctic known as the West Antarctic Ice Sheet, which appears to be reacting to climate change like the glacial tongues.

As these tongues encounter warmer water, they start to melt, and in so doing they wick the warmer water farther up the ice sheet, weakening the sheet itself. The narrower, lighter, and shorter these once-massive ice tongues become the more this phenomenon amplifies and they become weaker still, threatening the core of the ice sheet itself. The main ice sheet is constantly pushing outward toward the ocean, and these glacial fields, now weaker, cannot resist, and eventually break off. What's more, warm water is also present in the deep chasms and shells that are underneath the ice sheet, weakening its connection to the seafloor and to the main body of the Antarctic continent.

We are watching now the beginnings of a destructive chain reaction. Large portions of the West Antarctic Ice Sheet rest on land that's below sea level and slips downward. So as the Southern Ocean warms up, it comes into direct contact with ice mass and melts it, causing further rise of the seas.

Human beings have lived with sea-level rise and fall before, but never so fast and never when so many human beings lived, worked, and produced industry close to the edge of the oceans. According to the *World Ocean Review* of 2019:

> *But a glimpse into more recent climate history also reveals that since humankind began to settle down, sea level has never risen as fast as it is rising now. . . . This disturbingly sharp increase is primarily due to two factors. On the one hand, the ice sheets and glaciers of the world are losing large amounts of ice, and the resulting water either enters the ocean directly or is carried in by rivers. On the other hand, the temperatures in the world's oceans are rising, and warmer water expands and takes up more space than cold water.*[18]

How much sea-level rise will this generate? We don't precisely know. Every model has an "error band"—a numerical band that spans the distance between the best- and worst-case estimates. As Arctic and Antarctic ice sheet melt has been added to climate models, these error bands have *grown*. That's not so much a measure of scientific doubt as it is of the scale of the potential effect. At the lowest-level assumptions, loss of the Greenland and Antarctic ice sheets would contribute to a modest rise in global sea levels by 2100, of roughly four inches—a manageable rise, although still a level of rise that will exacerbate storms and storm surges, at substantial cost. But at higher estimates, the ice sheet loss would contribute something more like two feet by 2100—a rate never experienced in the modern world, and one that would pose vast challenges to the huge populations that live along the coasts.[19]

Adaptation, Engineering, and Competition

What does this all mean for geo-economics and geopolitics?

The world of climate change is generally understood to fall into two major policy streams—mitigation and adaptation. Mitigation is the world of climate diplomacy and industrial policy—the business of trying to limit the emission of carbon, methane, and other critical gases into the atmosphere, to limit the potential damage. Climate change mitigation is generally understood to be a world of cooperation—driven by a sense that, in the long term, we're all in this together.

But adaptation is another story. Even if CO_2 emissions went to zero today, the heat already stored in the oceans would continue to have effects well past the next century. The sea levels will continue to rise—what's unknown is by how much and how it will play out unevenly around the world.

Take the way the warming oceans impact fish stocks (already dangerously thinned out by overfishing*). Generally speaking, colder wa-

*The cold upwelling of the bottom waters of the Atlantic, off the Grand Banks of Newfoundland, has long generated one of the most productive fisheries in the world, particularly important for the cod that dominated fish supply in the Atlantic in the eighteenth, nineteenth, and twentieth centuries. By 1992, long before oceanic warming had a chance to affect fish productivity, the estimated biomass of the Canadian cod

ters are more productive for fishing; cold, mineral-rich waters are ideal spawning grounds for phytoplankton, the first chain in the nutrition ladder that leads to large fish stocks. The great fisheries of the world—the Humboldt, the Grand Banks—occur where cold bottom waters are pushed up to cool the surface waters, or where the waters themselves are made colder by glaciers and sea-ice melt.

If the seas are warming, then the productivity of the oceans should decline—and globally, that's estimated to be true: the IPCC believes that global net fish potential will decline as much as 24 percent in the coming decades.[20] But there are important differences in where it plays out. The already warm and shallow waters of the South and East China Seas look to be hard hit. But off the Arctic, the melting of Arctic ice is cooling those waters, leading to a substantial increase in the productivity of what was already one of the great sources of phytoplankton in the world. The melting of the sea ice in the Arctic, by cooling the nearby waters in the short term, has *increased* what the IPCC calls the "net primary production" of the Arctic—that is, the total quantity of phytoplankton blooms, generating more fish life. In warmer waters, the opposite is occurring, generating less.[21]

One of the most powerful images in the IPCC special report on oceans is a global map that overlays two measures. The first, the maximum fish catch potential; second, the relevant population's diet—with shades of orange (from light to dark) indicating how dependent on fish a country is for its animal-sourced food.[22] Overlay these two sets of data and a clear picture emerges: the sparsely populated Arctic regions are likely to see the biggest net gains in fish productivity, with small nearby populations to draw from them, turning the Arctic into one of the most attractive grounds on which to compete for fish stocks. By contrast, the South China Sea emerges as a flash point of a very different kind: it's one of the seas most likely to face substantial warming and declining fish stocks. Several hundred million Chinese, Japanese, and Southeast Asians as a whole live within one hundred miles of the East and South China Seas, and they look to the fisheries there to provide one of the

---

population had fallen to 1 percent of its earlier levels as a result of overfishing. Globally, industrial-scale fishing has depleted an estimated 90 percent of open-water fish stocks. See: Brian Fagan, *Fishing: How the Sea Fed Civilization* (New Haven, CT: Yale University Press, 2017).

most important sources of protein. For the governments in question, ensuring that they have access to those fish stocks becomes a matter of huge political import. There's a *reason* that the first time a Chinese naval vessel used force to detain another ship off its coast, it wasn't a US Navy frigate or Japanese cutter—it was a Filipino fishing vessel.

So, in the short term, the changing climate is creating winners and losers, and incentives to compete—over who can best adapt to the short-term effects of climate change.

Differential Effects

Climate change will not only impact the food that coastal nations depend on, but the very lives of those who live on the coasts. Approximately 680 million people (nearly 10 percent of the 2010 global population) live on coastal land that is less than thirty-three feet above sea level. This number is projected to reach more than 1 billion by 2050.[23] Their livelihoods will be deeply impacted—when combined with sea levels rising, increases in tropical cyclone winds and rainfall and increases in extreme waves will likely exacerbate problems caused by rising sea levels, especially on coastlines.[24] Research has suggested that a four-inch rise exposes an additional 10 million people to flooding.[25]

We can easily imagine rising seas and increased storm volatility and frequency impacting the land and infrastructure—just look at the damage that hurricanes have recently wreaked in Mississippi, Florida, Texas, and elsewhere. But recurrent coastal flooding can also increase the risk that infrastructure for drinking water and wastewater will fail—putting people at risk of coming into contact with pathogens and harmful chemicals.[26] Standing water in streets and houses can also bring in disease-carriers like mosquitoes.[27]

Furthermore, climate change will likely hasten the loss of coastal wetlands, which help protect the coastline from storms and erosion and help buffer the impacts of sea-level rise. They're also important for storing carbon—and yet nearly 50 percent of these wetlands have been lost over the last one hundred years, as a result of human pressures, sea-level rise, warming, and extreme climate events.[28] This loss of wetlands worsens the feedback loops. One effect is that areas with mostly smaller glaciers (like Central Europe, the Caucasus, North Asia, Scandinavia, the tropical Andes, Mexico, eastern Africa, and Indonesia) are projected to lose more than 80 percent of their current ice mass by 2100.[29] That will add to the albedo effect, and increase overall warming.

The US East Coast is particularly vulnerable to climate-induced sea-level rise, because it has low elevations and sinking shorelines.[30] Flooding is already becoming more frequent along the US coastline, and as of 2016, more than $1 trillion of property and infrastructure are at risk of damage from coastal flooding.[31] Since 2010, Wilmington, North Carolina, has flooded most often—forty-nine days per year, with Annapolis, Maryland, not far behind at forty-seven days per year.[32] Wilmington, Annapolis, Sandy Hook, and Atlantic, New Jersey, experience floods ten times more often now than in the 1950s.[33]

And then storms make it worse. "Extreme sea-level events" (like major flooding) are historically rare, occurring about once per century. Even with climate mitigation, they are now projected to occur frequently (at least once per year) by 2050, especially in tropical regions.[34]

* * *

But how damaging all this will be depends heavily on a different factor: the wealth of the population in question. Will the great economic, energy, and naval powers of our time choose to care about the consequences of climate adaption for the poorer nations and peoples of the world? Or will they focus only on adapting *their own* coastlines, engineering *their own* coastal protections, and extending *their own* fisheries, operating on the mentality of *sauve qui peut*, or every country for itself? Or will they look further, caring for the devastating effect of warming seas, changing wind and rain patterns, and growing sea-level rise on the livability, the agriculture, and the viability of the world's poorer nations? Will they provide the "statesmanship of a rare order" that Margaret Thatcher called for, now more than three decades ago?

It's a question that takes us beyond the realm of power, to wider questions of leadership, and of how we think about the relationship between power and the world around us.

Conclusion – Come Hell and High Water

Even in the long dark of Arctic winter, the Norwegian city of Tromsø teems with maritime activity, as scientists and fishermen and leisure boats ply its waterways. Tourists come not just for the Northern Lights, but to participate in the world's northernmost film festival, set in the town's central square and taking advantage of the blue night to screen outdoors at all hours of the day. Perhaps some of the advance crew of the Research Vessel *Polarstern* took the chance to participate before their ship launched in September 2019. It would, after all, be more than a year before they would next see terra firma.

They set sail in a world of tensions; they docked in a world in crisis. By the time they had completed their voyage, the world had been roiled by the first two rounds of the global COVID-19 pandemic. Even a ship sailing the high Arctic couldn't escape its reach; the crew had to quarantine when a helicopter pilot bringing in supplies tested positive for the disease. Yet, while the world churned, they completed a scientific marathon.

Their voyage was the core of a collaboration known as MOSAIC, or Multidisciplinary drifting Observatory for the Study of Arctic Climate. For more than a year, the RV *Polarstern* drifted in the polar ice, close to the North Pole. During the age of exploration, the HMS *Terror* and *Erebus* plied those waters as part of Sir John Franklin's ill-fated search for the Northwest Passage; and Norwegian scientist Fridtjof Nansen famously drifted his wooden sail ship *Fram* across the Arctic waters. But no ship in history had drifted so long, so close to the North Pole, as the RV *Polarstern*. During its drift, the crew planted remotely operated measuring devices in locations spanning out over a radius of fifty miles from its hull, at varying depths in the ice cap itself, and took measurements in the surrounding waters. Planes took frequent temperature readings in the air above the ice. Monitoring continuously over the course of the year, the expedition generated the closest, most detailed, most carefully measured look ever at the nature and evolution of the Arctic sea ice—its depth, chemistry, and most important, its rate of melt.

The project was the result of a scientific collaboration involving more than twenty nations, which supplied icebreakers, support ships, aircraft, helicopters, satellite bandwidth, computing power, and the research crew. In its scale and ambition, MOSAIC carried with it something of the legacy of Cold War–era global research collaborations. But this effort was not led by the United States; indeed, though some of the research crew were drawn from the Scripps Institution, America played no leadership role at all—probably the largest global scientific exploration since the 1940s *not* led by the United States.

It was led, rather, by a commercial power, one that had long since abandoned its ambitions for naval prowess: Germany. When the *Polarstern* docked, in October 2020, in Bremerhaven, it was met by Germany's science minister, who hailed its contributions to climate research. At its launch, German foreign minister Heiko Maas had set out the country's intentions: "We want to preserve the Arctic as a largely conflict-free region and use the available resources responsibly," said Maas.[1] It was a part of a wider German bid for leadership roles in international affairs—but leadership defined in diplomatic, scientific, and collaborative terms.

Germany's peaceable objectives were in stark contrast to the motives of other players simultaneously upping their stakes in the great new game of oceanic competition.[2] The most striking development was an agreement that brought full circle the story of the Royal Navy's role in Asia: the conclusion of a UK-India naval agreement in the fall of 2020. The agreement gave India—Britain's most important colonial possession during the long eighteenth and nineteenth centuries—the right to access the still substantial British naval infrastructure in the Indian Ocean.[3] Not content to rely on shared resources, India also commissioned a new naval base in the Andaman Islands, three hundred miles north of Port Blair.[4]

Beijing reacted furiously. But it, too, was deepening its naval alliances. Earlier that year, it mounted its largest naval exercises ever, sailing jointly with Russia as well as with Iran (which operates a sizable fleet, one that sometimes harasses Western shipping in the Straits of Hormuz). The Western powers matched this in turn, hosting the largest naval exercises since the end of the Cold War, anchored by the US aircraft carriers *Reagan* and *Nimitz*, and joined by Australia's HMAS *Canberra*, an amphibious assault ship, and the JS *Teruzuki*, a destroyer from the Japanese Maritime Self-Defense Force. India also deepened its ties to those three navies, through a diplomatic mechanism known simply as "the Quad."

The sense of a world reconsolidating into military blocs began to deepen. And back in Tromsø, the Olavsvern naval base officially reopened for operations. Immediately thereafter, the United States concluded its "status of forces agreement" that allowed it once again to dock in the mountain's hidden caverns. American nuclear submarines were back in the high north.

It all signaled the end of an era: the end of a period of relative calm in great power relations, and perhaps of American dominance of global affairs.

Sailing into a New Age

And so we find ourselves, now well-entrenched in the twenty-first century, reliving some of the dynamics of the nineteenth. We find ourselves at the start of a new age in world affairs. But what comes next?

This book's voyage with pirates and naval ports and polar ice caps reveals a coming age of contradictions, shaped in the swell of the world's oceans. A period of duality in America's approach to the world, torn between coastal centers tied to sea-based trade and the investment flows and financial profits it undergirds, and a non-coastal population disconnected from that global enterprise—indeed, both displaced by it and politically disenchanted by those who sustain it. An age in which we are still profoundly tied together in natural and economic terms, but increasingly chafe under a sense that we are *too* connected—a sensibility sharpened by the experience of COVID-19.

It's a coming age that will be shaped by China's bid for a global naval presence and America's reaction, a dangerous dance. Naval power was the handmaiden to American hegemony. China's bid may not yet be for true global power, for world hegemony as the United States has enjoyed; that is not an achievable objective in the near to medium term. But China is certainly engaged in a bid for counter-hegemony: a bid for the capacity to be able to stop the United States from imposing its will and its model on Chinese affairs and Chinese clients. And China is fast becoming a fuller maritime power than the United States, in that it has invested in the ships and dockyards and commercial underpinnings of its rising maritime power—which America has largely neglected of late. The remaining question is whether it can forge a network of bases to support the logistics of a global navy. Its alliance with Pakistan, growing coordination with Iran, and its "concert like" arrangements with Russia, combined with its far-flung network of civilian- but potentially dual-use ports infrastructure, are laying the physical and diplomatic foundation. Captain Alfred Thayer Mahan would recognize the world that China sees.

The coming age of contradiction and rivalry seems likely to have no clear hierarchy of power of the kind that were familiar in the Cold War and post–Cold War eras, and that infuse the American conversation about preeminence (or, more politely, "leadership"). China will soon be the largest economy in the world, by GDP, but the United States will have the more powerful military for some time to follow. Russia is a puissant military and energy actor, but an economic welterweight. Japan's military capacity is modest, but for the vital exception of its submarine fleet and marines, which pose a major first barrier to Chinese expansionism. The European Union, anchored by Germany, is a smaller commercial and financial power than the United States, but only by a modest degree, while its naval capacity badly lags its commercial weight, as does that of Britain. India is a *potential* powerhouse in every domain, but its power is yet fully realized in none.

Indeed, the decisions that India makes in the coming decade loom surprisingly large. Perhaps "surprising" is the wrong word; after all, it is the world's most populous country and will likely soon overtake the UK to be the fifth-richest. How India chooses to manage the next phase of its energy growth will be *the* central question in the world's efforts to combat climate change.[5] India has begun to make its presence felt in naval affairs; if New Delhi continues to deepen its naval cooperation with the West, then from the Bay of Bengal onward, the Indian navy will be a major obstacle in China's putative search for a global blue-water presence. Yet it is striking that for all of the scale of the Indian economy, if you list the world's top ports, there's no Indian entry in the top ten—nor even in the top twenty-five. It's an indicator that India has not yet genuinely chosen to open its economy to the world. If it does, it will open up new options for the remaking of globalization.

Conflict or Coexistence?

At the onset of the COVID-19 pandemic, the media, always hungry for an angle, shaped a narrative that COVID-19 would change everything, that nothing would be the same afterward. But that argument only holds if one believes that the world going into COVID was a world free of tension, carefully managing its interconnections. This book reveals something very different. More than a year into the pandemic, it seems quite wrong to say that COVID will change everything. Will US-China tensions ease? Will China, Japan, India, and the other Asian powers find new comity and calm in their relations? Will political distrust of globalization fade? Will climate change reverse itself, and the seas settle? Far from it. COVID has not changed things, so much as it has amplified the core tension of today's world—the sharp contradiction between deep economic and natural interconnection, and mounting geopolitical distrust.

The West also discovered that one of the things that container shipping brings to its markets is most of the world's supply of personal protective equipment (PPE)—the bulk of which is manufactured in China. It heightened a latent political interest in the West in moving away from globalized supply chains dependent on Beijing—what is referred to as "decoupling." But COVID also showed us how costly decoupling will be, if taken beyond small, focused measures like medical equipment. At the onset of the pandemic, racing to close their borders and spooked by early experiences of cruise ships serving as "super-spreaders," countries around the world refused to allow the crews of container ships to disembark while in dock. As closures endured, it generated a sustained crisis in global shipping, as crews were living for months at a time isolated on their ships. It caused major slowdowns in the global economic supply—experienced in the US largely in the form of inconveniences, like the shortage of paper towels and bicycles in the spring of 2020. But it also affected the supply of Apple iPhones and other high-tech products imported in bulk by container ship, as well as automotive parts.[6] Elsewhere, it was more serious—in Germany, knock-on effects from constrictions in global shipping brought the country to within days of serious interruptions in the food supply. It was all, of course, intensely illogical—the tiny crews of giant container ships, isolated at sea for days or weeks at a time, are about as quarantined as it's possible to be. But, dispiritingly, COVID showed us that even when confronted by a genuinely shared global challenge, fear and distrust will rapidly drown out logic and cooperation.

* * *

The huge benefits of globalization and the great cost of reversing it, combined with the reality that all countries' fates are tied together, make it tempting to hope that logic rather than fear will prevail when dealing with the epochal challenge of climate change. To believe that we will be led by women and men of responsibility who will find new, less dangerous ways to navigate this new era; that the issues that divide us can be managed by diplomats more than by destroyers. Tempting, too, to note that as the pressure mounts to find alternative, renewable sources of energy, a move away from fossil fuels will actually help the United States and China, and others, rediscover a sense of common interest in co-patrolling the sinews of global trade, just as they've sailed together to protect trade from piracy.

Perhaps. But the exposition in this book reveals, and the response to COVID reminds us, of older patterns of fear and distrust, powerful forces through history, unfolding once again. From our shared globalization and shared exposure to global climate change, we are sailing into new waters; but the likelihood that they will be calm waters seems remote. We may find our way to effective decarbonization, but along the way we'll have to manage decoupling and spiraling distrust.

The great fear must be that the fraught, ongoing arms race playing out among Chinese, American, and Russian submarine fleets and missile systems will spill out from below those waters to pull these competing powers into active war, and erode the prospects for collaboration on climate change. So far, we've not seen great power tensions rise to the level of direct military confrontation; but the tidal pull that precedes a tsunami is gaining strength.

How Should America Respond?

For decades, America was able to take for granted that it could dominate world affairs; no more. If the United States wants to compete from a position of strength, there's going to have to be a national conversation about several *existing* realities. We have to acknowledge, frankly, that globalization has been very good for the US economy, but quite bad for the US polity. The status quo cannot be sustained. Either we pull away from globalization, at fantastic cost, or we remake it—both internationally, and in terms of who benefits, domestically.

We have to be clear-eyed about the fact that we are already deeply mired in an arms race with China, and a global naval arms race—that is not *ahead* of us; we are already in it. It's a race profoundly infused by questions of computational capacity—a race that could be won or lost in satellite bursts, subsea sensors, and AI algorithms just as much or more so than in hull-to-hull combat. And it's a race that could easily trip into a war that would be fought with devastating cost, with nuclear anti-submarine warfare once again in the mix. So far, US-China/Russia tensions have not spilled into outright hostilities, but we are but a wavelength away from worse outcomes. And we have to confront the devil's dilemma posed by Taiwan.

Finally, we have to recognize that climate change is not a future threat; it's a present reality. We should focus, to be sure, on reducing our national emissions as rapidly as feasible. But we also have to confront the challenge of climate adaptation, which is already upon us, and will continue to get worse for years to come—perhaps much worse.

All this suggests that the grand challenge of American statecraft is to squarely confront the tension between globalization and geopolitics. One option, in the face of internal contractions and rising risk, is simply to retreat. To leave Asia's waters to China, to sit back while China builds a network of bases and relationships for global power projection. Those who argue along these lines do so on the basis of several untested assumptions: that the result will be a peaceful Asia, or that conflicts in

Asia will be limited and not impact the rest of the world; that the pathway to that state of affairs can be reached without crisis; that China's ambitions end in the western Pacific. All of these are theoretically possible outcomes. But the evidence casts doubt about this scenario. It is just as likely that the outcomes would be sustained tension and crisis in North Asia (source of 50 percent of world GDP), an intensification of Chinese global ambition and reach, and sustained loss of commercial and diplomatic advantage by the United States, and the wider West.

Which is not to say that if the United States seeks to retain the advantages that come from an ability to profoundly shape world affairs it can do so free of great risk, and at low cost. Those days are now behind us. The US has no easy choices ahead. But it does have strengths, and advantages. And it can build a national strategy around them.

That starts with forging a new naval and computational "alliance," building on but not limited to the Quad. In the Near Seas, some version of a "mutually assured denial" arrangement could stably cover the flow of trade. Beyond, tighter collaboration among the main Asian navies is an important element in constraining China's expansion and Russian aggression. NATO, retooled, can be a useful buttress to American power in the Arctic and the Atlantic. If China continues to expand its reach and ambition, the United States will have to forge a kind of "alliance of alliances" that links that capacity of NATO, the EU, the Quad and others—all of whom profit from the free flow of trade and energy—to keep the peace in the Pacific, the Arctic, the Indian Ocean, the Southern Ocean, and beyond.[7]

Among the critical tasks—protect undersea cables. That's a task both for submarine and surface patrols, and for technology cooperation. And such cooperation is going to be vital if the West is to stay competitive in the AI race and the "systems warfare" that characterizes the new maritime battlefied (as well as the cyber one). The Biden administration, though it has not used these terms, certainly seems to be oriented to try to forge some version of this new alliance dynamic—no accident that President Biden's first international meeting (held virtually) was the inaugural summit-level meeting of the Quad.*

*In a four-leaders op-ed that replaced the traditional summit communiqué, the Quad said that it was open to participation by other like-minded states. Already Can-

The United States will also have to push its allies to think hard about how they would respond in a scenario where China launches a military bid to reclaim Taiwan. Direct response by the United States is still a possibility—but as China deepens its hold on the Near Seas, the cost of that kind of response rises, and the likelihood of success diminishes, even with new iterations of the multi-domain operations or Air-Sea Battle plans. Better to plan for "multi-geography" responses—to use America's continuing global reach, and that of its allies, to deter China by creating risks and costs for Beijing far from its shores. Building on the idea of distant blockades, the US and its allies can highlight a new China dilemma—the more its global reach grows, the more it has far-flung vulnerabilities. Putting pressure on those vulnerabilities—from its fishing fleet in Angolan waters to its oil interests in the Strait of Hormuz to its naval base in the Red Sea—may be lower risk than confronting China in its own maritime backyard. Presenting the Chinese with *credible* scenarios for American and allied response is an important deterrent—for the overall objective of American policy here should not be to win the war, but to avoid it occurring in the first place.

At the same time, the United States has to tackle the question of winners and losers from globalization. Here, too, retreat is a theoretical option—one that President Trump tried, with his trade tariffs on China. It was a largely unsuccessful strategy, which did more to impose costs on the United States than on Beijing.* And it only takes one visit to the Centralized Examination Station in Elizabeth, New Jersey, to reveal how much of its own economy the United States would have to remake if it wanted to unwind sixty years of global economic trade. Rather, the US should reanimate its engagement with globalization, and look to domestic policy to broaden the profit-sharing from America's continued vast financial stake in the operation of the global economy.

On climate change: the crucial task obviously is to adopt the kinds of plans needed to abate carbon emissions, and sustain global cooperation

---

ada has conducted naval exercises in a Quad+ format, and South Korea has been exploring a range of forms of collaboration with Quad navies.

*Would that Trump's advisers had told him the story of King Canute (familiar to Maersk's employees)—an apocryphal Danish king who sat on his throne beside the beach and commanded the tide to stop flowing. When it did not, he told his courtiers, "Let all men know how empty and worthless is the power of kings."

on climate mitigation. But in addition, the United States should focus squarely on the issue of adaptation. And here, the United States should mobilize one of its key advantages—its world-class capacity for maritime engineering, exemplified by deep-sea energy exploration, heavily concentrated in Texas. Very soon, both the US itself and the rest of the world are going to need a great deal of advanced engineering to deal with sea-level rise. Only two nations, so far, are equipped to supply it at scale: the United States and China, with the US holding a sizable technological and managerial edge. Who leads this industry, and on what terms, may prove as consequential to the next set of global developments as the current battle over China's Belt and Road infrastructure—an investment closely tied, of course, to its huge stake in global sea-based trade. And in the US, an emphasis on maritime engineering has the advantage of cutting across the blue/red state divide on trade and globalization; Alaska, Texas, Florida, and Maine would be important beneficiaries of such an approach, in addition to California, Washington, and Virginia.

In all of this, the United States should sustain, celebrate, and where necessary revitalize one of its most important, but unheralded, advantages: its world-leading network of institutes and installations for the ocean sciences. Whether in the naval domain, on the sustainability of the oceans' biodiversity and fisheries, on the threat to that sustainability from a mounting challenge of microplastics in the ocean, to new opportunities in deep-ocean minerals mining, or on the fundamentals of climate change, the ocean sciences remain a bedrock capacity for international leadership, as they were at the height of the imperial age.

* * *

Once, oceans were the boundary of our existence; now they are the front lines of the new rivalries that will shape the twenty-first century. All but the tiniest fraction of humankind resides on land, works on land, interacts with other humans primarily on the land. It is entirely possible to live a rich life and never once set foot in the world's oceans; a substantial portion of humanity lives their entire existence without even ever setting eyes on them. And yet the seas shape the world around us. It is on the oceans that the great struggles of our day—for military power, for economic dominance, over our changing climate—are playing out. Our security, our prosperity, and our environment hang in the balance.

Acknowledgments

When I first began work on this book, it was little more than an impulse, a sense that by shifting perspective to the oceans I could help illuminate the huge changes in world affairs unfolding around us. I had always been drawn to the sea. I spent much of my youth on the beaches of the Caribbean, in the pounding surf of the Atlantic's Gulf of Guinea, on trips across the cold Baltic, and in the warm turquoise waters of the western edges of the Indian Ocean. Later, professional travels took me to the Mediterranean, the East China Sea, the Norwegian, the Red, the Black, the North, and the Japan Seas, across the Pacific Ocean, and to the Persian Gulf. I eventually settled in Washington, DC, near the shores of the Chesapeake Bay, playground of sailors, great inland fishery, and home of the US Naval Academy. Of the world's storied bodies of water, only the Southern Ocean, the Arctic, the Andaman, and the South China Sea had eluded me—until the research for this book took me to two of them.

I decided, after some reflection, to structure this book as a kind of voyage, both narrative and intellectual. Doing that required a physical voyage as well, to the many ports of call depicted in the text. And that, in turn, required help from many different groups of people. My deepest gratitude is to the captains who gave so generously of their time and knowledge to help inform my study: in particular Captain Watts of the USS *John Paul Jones*, Captain Tama of the US Coast Guard, and Captain Jensen of the *Madrid Maersk*.

Many other people supported informative visits. In Norway, the Wilhelmsen team facilitated my trip to the remarkable Olavsvern naval facility: my thanks to Brigadier General (ret.) Stener Olstad; Commander (ret.) Geir Bentzen; Rune Danielsen, CEO at Olavsvern Group; and, above all, Vidar Hole, CEO of Wilnor Governmental Services. In Shanghai, it was through the good offices and gracious hospitality of Weng Jiyi, Founding Partner, Shanghai Ivy Investment Company, that I was able to visit the vast container yard at Yangshan Port on Donghai Island; my thanks as well to Cheng Li and Ryan McElveen. In Copenhagen, Graham Slack of Maersk was both a terrific intellectual interlocutor and enormously generous in facilitating access to the company's museum and records, meetings with the leadership team, and my trip on the *Madrid*. I'm grateful also to Robert M. Uggla, CEO of A.P. Møller Holding A/S; Søren Skau, CEO of A.P. Møller-Maersk A/S; Henning Morgen; and Zhu Shuang Lim, for their time and interactions over the course of the project. The Customs and Border Protection offices in New York graciously facilitated my site visit to their inspection facility in Elizabeth, New Jersey. In Hawaii, Stephen Frano of the INDOPACOM headquarters staff graciously arranged talks with the command leadership. In Singapore, Lynn Kuok, of the International Institute for Strategic Studies, used her formidable network to get me access to the Changi Naval Base, where Col. Raymond Ong briefed me on Singapore's vital counter-piracy coalition effort.

Other people gave generously of their time or their scholarship. They include: CDR Brendan Stickles, USN, special adviser for defense in the office of the vice president of the United States; Robert O. Work, senior counselor for defense, Center for a New American Security; Thomas C. Ramey, former chairman and president of Liberty Capital, and avid fly fisherman; Michael Butt, OBE, cofounder of AXIS Capital and formerly of Lloyd's of London; my friend Carlos Pascual, now senior vice president for global energy and international affairs at IHS Markit; Captain Michael Lachowicz, Coast Guard Atlantic Area; Adam Tooze of Columbia University; Vivian Tan and Annie Ho from C. H. Tung's office in Hong Kong; and the staff of the C.Y. Tung Maritime Museum at Jiao Tong University.

The voyage was the narrative; but the substance behind it was learned mostly from my colleagues in Washington, DC; New York City; and Palo Alto. Most important were those at the Brookings Institution. I'm very grateful to Strobe Talbott and John Allen, the two presidents of the Institution under which I've served, for their unstinting support to my research. Deep thanks are owed also to Ted Gayer, as well as to John Thornton, David Rubinstein, Suzanne Nora-Johnson, and Glenn Hutchins. I owe a particular debt of gratitude to Martin

Indyk for supporting my career at Brookings and encouraging me to undertake a major writing project even when my day job lay more in management than research. As I do to vice president Suzanne Maloney, for her long support of my work at Brookings, for her leadership, and for her deep intellect and fierce commitment to principle; and to Michael O'Hanlon, research director, for his unstinting collegiality, sharp book sense, and relentless intellectual energy—and helpful suggestions on the first draft of the manuscript. My colleagues in the project on international order and in the Center on Security, Strategy, and Technology played a particularly important role in shaping my thinking over many years—a warm thank-you to Tom Wright, Bob Kagan, Tarun Chhabra, Tanvi Madan, Vanda Felbab-Brown, Fiona Hill, David Victor, Tom Stefanick, and Frank Rose; as well as colleagues in the Asia centers, particularly Lindsey Ford, Ryan Hass, Mireya Solis, and Cheng Li. I owe an additional debt to Rush Doshi both for his scholarship and for helping me navigate the fierce debates that surround the question of Chinese naval ambition. I am also grateful to two anonymous reviewers for their helpful comments and to Joshua Meltzer and Samantha Gross for comments on the draft. Additional thanks to Peter Fitzgibbons.

It goes almost without saying that none of these people are responsible for errors of omission or commission in the book; those are my responsibility alone.

Throughout my time at Brookings, I have also been fortunate to enjoy the support of the Foreign Policy Leadership Council. I'm especially grateful to the three individuals who served as Chair or Co-Chairs of the Council during my tenure: Benjamin Jacobs; Jonathan Colby; and David Weinberg. Each of them in their own way encouraged, challenged, and supported me.

Several other colleagues either played a critical role in helping me with this book, or in keeping me sane in other parts of my work, thereby freeing up some part of my brain to begin piecing together this puzzle. I owe a multidimensional debt of gratitude to Emilie Kimball, Andrew Moffat, and Will Moreland. Interns are the unsung heroes of scholarship and writing; I was fortunate to draw on help at various stages of the project from Samantha Diaz, Kizzy Dhaliwal, and Nikita Salgame; Holly Cohen and Tim Holman provided additional support. Kendrick Foster took time out from his undergraduate studies to help me in the late stages of the project, including with the laborious effort of fact-checking and compiling the bibliography. As the project was moving through production, Adam Twardowski and Leah Dreyfuss provided invaluable support. But above all, I relied on the support, research assistance, prodding, and occasional pointed (and well-deserved) critiques from Katherine Elgin, without whom I could not have completed the text.

Chris Peters is a Brookings photographer, and a huge asset to any project. Two of his photographs adorn the interior of the book, and his stunning drone videos of my trip around New York Harbor and of the arrival of the *Madrid Maersk* in Tanjung Pelepas do much to illustrate the simply enormous scale of sea-born global trade; they can be viewed on the Brookings website. I'm grateful to him, and to Emily Horne, Anna Newby, Andrea Risotto, Suzanne Schaefer, Rachel Slattery, and Ted Reinnert for their support along the way.

Words on a page are one thing; a book is quite another. When I gave Bridget Wagner Matzie, of Aevitas Creative Management, a list of possible projects that ranged in degree of somberness and scholarly merit, I listed this project last, realizing that it was the most ambitious. That she could immediately see both that this was the project I was passionate about, and that it had potential, is testimony to her book smarts; I'm grateful to her for her confidence and excellent support along this process. As I am to Colin Harrison, vice president and editor in chief at Scribner, who didn't throw me out of his office when I naively asked him whether it was possible to market a book that married the techniques of narrative reportage and scholarly research—and then did much to help lift the text and make it more accessible than I could possibly have managed without him. My thanks also to Emily Polson and the rest of the excellent team at Scribner and Simon & Schuster, including Brian Belfiglio, Clare Maurer, and Zoey Cole.

Anyone who has ever written a book knows how profound is the contribution from immediate family members. My wife, Elizabeth, inspired me, gave me ideas, and supported my long travels and longer bouts of writer's temper, despite the demands of her hectic job, a job that became even more demanding and more crucial with the outbreak of the COVID-19 pandemic. My son made his contribution—after firmly declaring that when he grows up he has no intention of spending so much time in front of a keyboard ("that's so boring, Dad")—by using his innate creativity to take photographs of me while I worked—one of which graces the book jacket. I love them both fiercely.

I thought about family a great deal while reading naval and imperial histories for this book. In particular, I thought about my father's ancestors, who lived part of their lives in India, early in the period of British rule. I had known from childhood that my paternal family's roots lay in the union—in fact, if not in law, and in sharp violation of the norms of the time—of a young "second son" from England and an unmarried Indian woman from the northern provinces. Growing up, I heard often about the scion of the family, but also about his more famous brother, who was best known for the scientific discovery that carries his name, the temperature of absolute zero, which is measured in kelvins. But it was only in doing the research for this book that I discovered that Lord Kelvin had a different distinction, too: when he was still simply known as William Thomson, it was he who helped lay the first undersea cables across the Atlantic, first aboard the HMS *Agamemnon* and then the SS *Great Eastern*. He also made vital contributions to the physics of submarine wave detection, still relevant to anti-submarine warfare. Truly, it seems, what's bred in the bone will out in the flesh—or in the writing.

It is to my paternal grandparents, descendants on my grandmother's side from the Thompson clan, that I dedicate this book, in memory.

Notes

Part I: News from the Future

1. Simon Winchester, *Atlantic: Great Sea Battles, Heroic Discoveries, Titanic Storms, and a Vast Ocean of a Million Stories* (New York: Harper Perennial, 2010), 64–66.

2: The Outer Perimeter; or, Pushing the American Border Out

1. Fort Tompkins is located within the larger boundaries of Fort Wadsworth, the longest continuously operated military facility in the United States.
2. Port of New York & New Jersey, "2018 Trade Statistics," https://www.panynj.gov/port/en/our-port/facts-and-figures.html; "World | Top Export Data," World Integrated Trade Statistics, 2018, https://wits.worldbank.org/CountryProfile/en/Country/WLD/Year/2018/TradeFlow/Import/Partner/by-country#.
3. Port Authority of New York and New Jersey, "Capital of Commerce," accessed April 17, 2021, https://www.panynj.gov/content/dam/port/customer-library-pdfs/port-capabilities.pdf.
4. Adie Tomer and Joseph W. Kane, "The Top 10 Metropolitan Port Complexes in the U.S.," Brookings, July 1, 2015, https://www.brookings.edu/blog/the-avenue/2015/07/01/the-top-10-metropolitan-port-complexes-in-the-u-s/.
5. Quoted in Michael Donner and Cornelius Kruk, *Supply Chain Security Guide*, Transport Research Support program, World Bank/Department for International Development, http://documents1.worldbank.org/curated/en/862601468339908874/pdf/579700WP0SCS1G10Box353787B01PUBLIC1.pdf, p. 27. The World Bank report provides exhaustive detail on CSI and other mandatory and voluntary trade protection programs globally.
6. "USCG extracts NOAD information from SANS to assess risk to vessels arriving or departing from a U.S. port and to identify vessels, as well as individuals associated with those vessels that may pose a safety or security risk to the United States. This information allows the USCG to facilitate effectively and efficiently the entry and departure of vessels into and from the United States and assist the USCG with assigning priorities while conducting maritime safety and security missions in accordance with international and domestic regulations." United States Coast Guard, "Privacy Impact Assessment Update for the Vessel Requirements for the Notice of Arrival and Departure (NOAD) and Automatic Identification System (AIS) Rulemaking," DHS/USCG/PIA-006(b), Department of Homeland Security, April 28, 2015.

7. For Maersk's official press release on the attack, see: https://investor.maersk.com/news-releases/news-release-details/cyber-attack-update.
8. Andy Greenberg, "The Untold Story of NotPetya, the Most Devastating Cyberattack in History," *Wired*, August 22, 2018, https://www.wired.com/story/notpetya-cyberattack-ukraine-russia-code-crashed-the-world/.
9. Ibid.
10. Ibid.
11. Doug Macdougall, *Endless Novelties of Extraordinary Interest: The Voyage of H.M.S. Challenger and the Birth of Modern Oceanography* (New Haven: Yale University Press, 2019), 68–73.
12. Calculations by the author, based on Andrea Murphy et al., "Global 2000 - The World's Largest Public Companies 2020," Forbes, May 13, 2020, https://www.forbes.com/global2000/, and the categorizations of Sean Starrs, "American Economic Power Hasn't Declined—It Globalized! Summoning the Data and Taking Globalization Seriously," *International Studies Quarterly* 57, no. 4 (December 2013): 817–30. Starrs separates banks and insurance companies from Forbes's larger category of financial services, meaning that this category consists largely of investment services and consumer financial services.

3: Charting Today's World

1. Roger Crowley, *Conquerors: How Portugal Forged the First Global Empire* (New York: Random House, 2015), 43–44.
2. Alfred Thayer Mahan, *The Interest of America in Sea Power, Present and Future* (Boston: Little, Brown, 1897), 124.
3. In a major recent study, the historian Andrew Lambert argues that only a small number of states in history have actually generated their power by the seas, as opposed to projecting power onto the seas; and married that to a maritime culture and republican values. Only this small number of states—of which Venice and Britain are his key exemplars—deserve the term "seapower"; he removes the hyphen to accentuate the point. See Andrew Lambert, *Seapower States: Maritime Culture, Continental Empires, and the Conflict That Made the Modern World* (New Haven: Yale University Press, 2018). Other scholars place less emphasis on culture and governance structure, and look more to the interplay between state management, naval power, and naval projection.
4. Jonathan Clements, *A Brief History of the Vikings: The Last Pagans or the First Modern Europeans?* (New York: Carroll & Graf, 2005), chs. 2, 7. Also Simon Winchester, *Atlantic: Great Sea Battles, Heroic Discoveries, Titanic Storms, and a Vast Ocean of a Million Stories* (New York: Harper Perennial, 2010).
5. Edward A. Alpers, *The Indian Ocean in World History* (New York: Oxford University Press, 2013), 28.
6. William J. Bernstein, *A Splendid Exchange: How Trade Shaped the World* (New York: Atlantic Monthly Press, 2008), 94–95.
7. The archaeological evidence now suggests at least some limited commerce between the Malay and Islamic coasts of the Indian Ocean for as much as seven

centuries before the arrival of the Portuguese. See inter alia Alpers, *The Indian Ocean in World History*.

8. Mark Cartwright, "Trade in Medieval Europe," in *Ancient History Encyclopedia*, January 8, 2019, https://www.ancient.eu/article/1301/trade-in-medieval-europe/.
9. Jack Turner, *Spice: The History of a Temptation* (New York: Knopf, 2004), xii.
10. Crowley, *Conquerors*, 12.
11. James Stavridis, *Sea Power: The History and Geopolitics of the World's Oceans* (New York: Penguin Press, 2017), 55–56.
12. For more on the connection between naval and global power, see George Modelski and William R. Thompson, *Seapower in Global Politics, 1494–1993* (Houndmills, UK: Macmillan Press, 1988).
13. Quoted in Alpers, *The Indian Ocean in World History*, 5.
14. Crowley, *Conquerors*, 51–52.
15. Alpers, *The Indian Ocean in World History*, 63.
16. For an overview of the competing theories on their size, see Christopher Wake, "The Myth of Zheng He's Great Treasure Ships," *International Journal of Maritime History* 16, no. 1 (June 1, 2004): 59–76, https://doi.org/10.1177/084387140401600105.
17. Louise Levathes, *When China Ruled the Seas: The Treasure Fleet of the Dragon Throne, 1405–1433* (New York: Oxford University Press, 1996).
18. In *Empires of the Weak: The Real Story of European Expansion and the Creation of the New World Order* (Princeton, NJ: Princeton University Press, 2019), J. C. Sharman highlights that the major Asian empires of the fifteenth century—the Chinese, the Ottomans, the Mamluks—were at least as sophisticated as their puny European counterparts. Certainly the ships sailed by Zheng He's Treasure Fleet were significantly more advanced than anything sailed by the Europeans at the same time. But the Asian empires, on the whole, chose not to develop their capacity for seafaring and focused their empire building inland in their own territories and their land neighbors. Europe was able to dominate them from the oceans in part because they did not contest them on land. Only in the early nineteenth century did this begin to change.
19. Bernstein, *A Splendid Exchange*, 101.
20. Edward L. Dreyer, *Zheng He: China and the Oceans in the Early Ming Dynasty, 1405–1433*, Library of World Biography (New York: Pearson Longman, 2010), 192.
21. See, for instance, Paul Musgrave and Daniel Nexon, "Zheng He's Voyages and the Symbolism Behind Xi Jinping's Belt and Road Initiative," *The Diplomat*, December 22, 2017, https://thediplomat.com/2017/12/zheng-hes-voyages-and-the-symbolism-behind-xi-jinpings-belt-and-road-initiative/.
22. Bruce Swanson, *Eighth Voyage of the Dragon: A History of China's Quest for Seapower* (Annapolis, MD: Naval Institute Press, 1982), 43.
23. Crowley, *Conquerors*, 52.
24. Bernstein, *A Splendid Exchange*, ch. 7.
25. Arthur Herman, *To Rule the Waves: How the British Navy Shaped the Modern World* (New York: Harper Perennial, 2004), xvii–xviii.
26. Dag Avango, Per Högselius, and David Nilsson, "Swedish Explorers, In-Situ Knowledge, and Resource-Based Business in the Age of Empire," *Scandinavian Journal of History* 43, no. 3 (May 27, 2018): 324–47, https://doi.org/10.1080/03468755.2017.1380923.

27. For an overview of the scramble for Africa, see Thomas Pakenham, *The Scramble for Africa: White Man's Conquest of the Dark Continent from 1876 to 1912* (New York: Random House, 1991); On Belgium's colonial brutality, see Adam Hochschild, *King Leopold's Ghost: A Story of Greed, Terror, and Heroism in Colonial Africa* (Boston: Houghton Mifflin, 1998).
28. Lincoln P. Paine, *The Sea and Civilization: A Maritime History of the World* (New York: Knopf, 2013), 377.
29. Sven Beckert, *Empire of Cotton: A Global History* (New York: Knopf, 2014), ch. 6.
30. Eric Hobsbawm, *The Age of Empire: 1875–1914* (New York: Vintage, 1989), ch. 2.
31. Erika Monahan, *The Merchants of Siberia: Trade in Early Modern Eurasia* (Ithaca, NY: Cornell University Press, 2016), 1.
32. The Dutch established the Dutch East India Company (also known as the United East India Company, or in Dutch, the *Vereenigde Oostindische Compagnie*, VOC) in 1602.
33. Om Prakash, *European Commercial Enterprise in Pre-Colonial India* (New York: Oxford University Press, 1998), ch. 3.
34. Bernstein, *A Splendid Exchange*, 215.
35. William Dalrymple, *The Anarchy: The Relentless Rise of the East India Company* (London: Bloomsbury, 2019).
36. William Dalyrmple, *White Mughals: Love and Betrayal in Eighteenth-Century India* (New York: Penguin Books, 2004).
37. Sharman, *Empires of the Weak.*
38. Adam Tooze, a celebrated historian of the interwar period and the author of *The Deluge*, spoke to this theme during a public debate with Robert Kagan, "World Order Without America?," Brookings Institution, November 13, 2018.
39. Niall Ferguson, *Empire: The Rise and Demise of the British World Order and the Lessons for Global Power* (New York: Basic Books, 2004), 83.
40. A fine history of first the Ottoman and then the Turkish, British, and French rivalry that reshaped the Middle East into its modern form is to be found in Jason Goodwin's *Lords of the Horizon: A History of the Ottoman Empire* (New York: Henry Holt, 1998).
41. Weimin Zhong, "The Roles of Tea and Opium in Early Economic Globalization: A Perspective on China's Crisis in the 19th Century," *Frontiers of History in China* 5, no. 1 (2010): 86–105, https://doi.org/10.1007/s11462-010-0004-0.
42. Bernstein, *A Splendid Exchange*, 294.
43. The essential account of this trade and the dynamics of British, American, and European contestation with the Qing emperor during this period is Stephen Platt's *Imperial Twilight: The Opium War and the End of China's Last Golden Age* (New York: Alfred A. Knopf, 2018).
44. Platt, *Imperial Twilight*, ch. 13; Jonathan Fenby, *Modern China: The Fall and Rise of a Great Power, 1850 to the Present* (New York: Ecco, 2008), 9.
45. Peter Auber, *China: An Outline of Its Government, Laws, and Policy, and of the British and Foreign Embassies to, and Intercourse with, That Empire* (London: Parbury, Allen, 1834), 200.
46. Bruce A. Elleman, *Modern Chinese Warfare, 1795–1989* (London: Routledge, 2001), 18–20.
47. Swanson, *Eighth Voyage of the Dragon*, 72.

48. Peter C. Perdue, "The First Opium War: The Anglo-Chinese War of 1839–1842," MIT Visualizing Cultures, 2011, https://visualizingcultures.mit.edu/opium_wars_01/ow1_essay03.html.
49. Quoted in Platt, *Imperial Twilight*, 344.
50. Perdue, "The First Opium War."
51. Song-Chuan Chen, *Merchants of War and Peace: British Knowledge of China in the Making of the Opium War* (Hong Kong University Press, 2017), 114.
52. Platt, *Imperial Twilight*, xxii–xxiii.
53. For explorations of the naval dimensions of the Anglo-French rivalry across the eighteenth and nineteenth centuries, see, for instance, Charles M. Andrews, "Anglo-French Commercial Rivalry, 1700–1750: The Western Phase, I," *The American Historical Review* 20, no. 3 (1915): 539–56, https://doi.org/10.2307/1835856; C. I. Hamilton, *Anglo-French Naval Rivalry, 1840–1870* (New York: Oxford University Press, 1993); Matthew S. Seligmann, "Britain's Great Security Mirage: The Royal Navy and the Franco-Russian Naval Threat, 1898–1906," *Journal of Strategic Studies* 35, no. 6 (December 1, 2012): 861–86, https://doi.org/10.1080/01402390.2012.699439.
54. For a broader overview of French imperialism, see Raymond F. Betts, *Tricouleur: The French Overseas Empire* (London: Gordon & Cremonesi, 1978).
55. Zachary Karabell, *Parting the Desert: The Creation of the Suez Canal* (New York: Alfred A. Knopf, 2003), 5.
56. Noël Mostert, *Supership* (New York: Knopf, 1974), 83.
57. Max E. Fletcher, "The Suez Canal and World Shipping, 1869–1914," *The Journal of Economic History* 18, no. 4 (1958): 556–73.
58. Donald Malcolm Reid, "The Urabi Revolution and the British Conquest, 1879–1882," in *The Cambridge History of Egypt*, ed. M. W. Daly (Cambridge, UK: Cambridge University Press, December 10, 1998), https://doi.org/10.1017/CHOL9780521472111.010; Efraim Karsh and Inari Karsh, *Empires of the Sand: The Struggle for Mastery in the Middle East, 1789–1923* (Cambridge, MA: Harvard University Press, 1999), chap. 4.
59. Paine, *The Sea and Civilization*, 525. Paine quotes the ever-pithy *The Economist* (in 1869), noting that the canal was "cut by French energy and Egyptian money for British advantage."
60. Jean Allain, *International Law in the Middle East: Closer to Power Than Justice* (London: Routledge, 2017), ch. 2.
61. Fletcher, "The Suez Canal and World Shipping, 1869–1914," and Richard C. Whiting, "The Suez Canal and the British Economy, 1918–1960," in *Imperialism and Nationalism in the Middle East: The Anglo-Egyptian Experience, 1882–1982*, ed. Keith M. Wilson (London: Mansell, 1983).
62. The best single account of this is Paul Kennedy's *The Rise and Fall of British Naval Mastery*; Kennedy takes the core structure of Mahan's arguments and applies and tests them against developments in the Royal Navy and in other aspects of British power. It is an essential read for anyone seeking to understand the unique role that naval power played in the British empire, or to apply Mahanian concepts to the United States, or to China. Andrew Lambert's *Seapower States*, a more recent work, takes issue with some parts of Kennedy's thesis and with the ubiquitous use of the concept of sea power, arguing that only a small handful of states—Athens, Carthage, Venice, briefly the Dutch, and Britain—count as true sea powers: powers for whom

naval culture was married to an inclusive republican politics and a national identity tied to the sea. In a review of Lambert's book, Francis Fukuyama acknowledges part of Lambert's argument, conceding that there is a "clear relationship between access to oceans and modernization, both economic and political." However, he argues that Lambert goes too far in claiming a strong tie between naval power and the creation of modern, liberal political institutions. See Francis Fukuyama, H-Diplo Review Essay 259, July 22, 2020, https://networks.h-net.org/node/28443/discussions/6259944/h-diplo-review-essay-259-fukuyama-lambert-seapower-states.

63. For a general explanation of this phenomenon, see John H. Maurer, "Arms Control and the Anglo-German Naval Race before World War I: Lessons for Today?," *Political Science Quarterly* 112, no. 2 (1997), 287–93.
64. Paul Ham, *1914: The Year the World Ended* (London: Doubleday, 2014); Max Hastings, *Catastrophe 1914: Europe Goes to War* (New York: Vintage, 2014); Christopher M. Clark, *The Sleepwalkers: How Europe Went to War in 1914* (London: Allen Lane, 2012).
65. Sibyl Crowe, *Our Ablest Public Servant: Sir Eyre Crowe, 1864–1925* (Braunton, UK: Merlin Books, 1993), ch. 7.
66. See, for instance, Zhengyu Wu, "The Crowe Memorandum, the Rebalance to Asia, and Sino-US Relations," *Journal of Strategic Studies* 39, no. 3 (April 15, 2016): 389–416, https://doi.org/10.1080/01402390.2016.1140648.
67. Eyre Crowe, "Memorandum on the Present State of British Relations with France and Germany" (January 1, 1907), Wikisource, http://en.wikisource.org/wiki/Memorandum_on_the_Present_State_of_British_Relations_with_France_and_Germany.
68. Quoted in James Joll and Gordon Martel, *The Origins of the First World War*, 3rd ed. (Harlow, UK: Pearson Longman, 2007), 148.
69. Robert K. Massie, *Dreadnought: Britain, Germany, and the Coming of the Great War* (New York: Random House, 1991), 180.
70. Patrick J. Kelly, *Tirpitz and the Imperial German Navy* (Bloomington: Indiana University Press, 2011), ch. 10; Massie, *Dreadnought*, ch. 9.
71. Massie, *Dreadnought*, ch. 26.
72. For a more in-depth discussion, see Lawrence Sondhaus, *German Submarine Warfare in World War I: The Onset of Total War at Sea* (Lanham, MD: Rowman & Littlefield, 2017); R. H. Gibson and Maurice Prendergast, *The German Submarine War, 1914–1918* (Annapolis, MD: Naval Institute Press, 2003).
73. Kennedy, *The Rise and Fall of British Naval Mastery* (New York: Scribner, 1976), 267–68.
74. Adam Tooze, *The Deluge: The Great War, America and the Remaking of the Global Order, 1916–1931* (New York: Penguin, 2014), introduction.
75. Marshall Smelser, *The Congress Founds the Navy, 1787–1798* (Notre Dame, IN: University of Notre Dame Press, 1959), 7–8; Stephen Howarth, *To Shining Sea: A History of the United States Navy, 1775–1998* (Norman: University of Oklahoma Press, 1999), 55–57.
76. Quoted in Howarth, *To Shining Sea*, 5.
77. Michael Green, *By More Than Providence: Grand Strategy and American Power in the Asia Pacific Since 1783* (New York: Columbia University Press, 2017), 23.
78. Howarth, *To Shining Sea*, ch. 5.

79. For an excellent history of this conflict, see Brian Kilmeade and Don Yaeger, *Thomas Jefferson and the Tripoli Pirates: The Forgotten War That Changed American History* (New York: Sentinel, 2015).
80. Howarth, *To Shining Sea*, 127.
81. Green, *By More Than Providence*, ch. 1.
82. Peter Booth Wiley, *Yankees in the Land of Gods: Commodore Perry and the Opening of Japan* (New York: Viking, 1990), 399–400.
83. Robert Erwin Johnson, *Far China Station: The U.S. Navy in Asian Waters, 1800–1898* (New York: Naval Institute Press, 2013), 10.
84. Ibid., 15.
85. Howarth, *To Shining Sea*, 216.
86. For a more detailed exploration of the naval role in the Spanish-American War, see Jim Leeke, *Manila and Santiago: The New Steel Navy in the Spanish-American War* (Annapolis, MD: Naval Institute Press, 2013); Vernon L. Williams, "Naval Service in the Age of Empire," in *Crucible of Empire: The Spanish-American War and Its Aftermath*, ed. James C. Bradford (Annapolis, MD: Naval Institute Press, 1993), 183–204.
87. Nathan Miller, *The U.S. Navy: A History* (Annapolis, MD: Naval Institute Press, 1997), 144, 155.
88. Ibid., 164–65.
89. "United States Maritime Expansion Across the Pacific During the 19th Century," Milestones in the History of U.S. Foreign Relations, Office of the Historian, https://history.state.gov/milestones/1830-1860/pacific-expansion, accessed April 30, 2020.
90. Miller, *The U.S. Navy: A History*, 154.
91. United States Department of State, International Organization and Conference Series 164 (Washington, DC: U.S. Government Printing Office, 1984), 97–98.
92. Miller, *The U.S. Navy: A History*, 166.
93. For more on Roosevelt, Mahan, and how the two thought about sea power, see: Peter Karsten, "The Nature of 'Influence': Roosevelt, Mahan and the Concept of Sea Power," *American Quarterly* 23, no. 4 (1971): 589, https://doi.org/10.2307/2711707.
94. Miller, *The U.S. Navy: A History*, 170; for a more detailed exploration of the Great White Fleet, see Kenneth Wimmel, *Theodore Roosevelt and the Great White Fleet: American Seapower Comes of Age* (Washington, DC: Brassey's, 1998).
95. Howarth, *To Shining Sea*, 324.
96. Ibid., 339–42.
97. Tooze, *The Deluge.*
98. "Lend-Lease and Military Aid to the Allies in the Early Years of World War II," Milestones in the History of U.S. Foreign Relations, Office of the Historian, https://history.state.gov/milestones/1937-1945/lend-lease, accessed April 30, 2020.
99. On the importance of anti-submarine warfare in World War I, see Andrew J. Krepinevich, "Calvary to Computer: The Pattern of Military Revolutions," *The National Interest*, no. 37 (September 1994): 30–42; and on its role in World War II, see Max Boot, *War Made New: Technology, Warfare, and the Course of History, 1500 to Today* (New York: Gotham Books, 2006).
100. Howarth, *To Shining Sea*, bk. 2, pt. 5.

101. David Burbach et al., "Weighing the US Navy," *Defense Analysis* 17, no. 3 (2001): 261.
102. The authoritative book on how the US built world order after World War II is G. John Ikenberry, *After Victory: Institutions, Strategic Restraint, and the Rebuilding of Order After Major Wars* (Princeton, NJ: Princeton University Press, 2001).
103. "The Chargé in the United Kingdom [Gallman] to the Secretary of State," June 16, 1947, *Foreign Relations of the United States, 1947*, vol. 3, pp. 254–55, quoted in Ikenberry, *After Victory*, 168.
104. Howarth, *To Shining Sea*, 476.
105. For a broad overview of the post–World War II US-Saudi relationship, see Bruce Riedel, *Kings and Presidents: Saudi Arabia and the United States Since FDR* (Washington, DC: Brookings Institution Press, 2017).
106. For more information on the February 14, 1945, meeting, see "President Roosevelt and King Abdulaziz—the Meeting at Great Bitter Lake: A Conversation with Rachel Bronson," Saudi-U.S. Relations Information Service, March 17, 2005, available at www.susris.com/2005/03/17/president-roosevelt-and-king-abdulaziz-the-meeting-at-great-bitter-lake-a-conversation-with-rachel-bronson/; "Memorandum of Conversations Between the King of Saudi Arabia (Abdul Aziz al Saud) and President Roosevelt, February 14, 1945, Aboard the U.S.S. 'Quincy,'" *Foreign Relations of the United States*, U.S. Department of State, 1945, pp. 2–3, 7–9, available at digicoll.library.wisc.edu/cgi-bin/FRUS/FRUS-idx?type=header&id=FRUS.FRUS1945v08&isize=M; William A. Eddy, *F.D.R. Meets Ibn Saud*, Washington, DC: America-Mideast Educational & Training Services, 1954, available at www.social-sciences-and-humanities.com/pdf/FDR_Meets_Ibn_Saud.pdf; Thomas W. Lippman, "The Day FDR Met Saudi Arabia's Ibn Saud," *The Link* (Americans for Middle East Understanding) 38, no. 2 (April–May 2005). Also see Riedel, *Kings and Presidents*.
107. Douglas Little, "Pipeline Politics: America, TAPLINE, and the Arabs," *Business History Review* 64, no. 2 (1990): 255–85, https://doi.org/10.2307/3115583.
108. Riedel, *Kings and Presidents*, 10–11.
109. Roger J. Stern, "United States Cost of Military Force Projection in the Persian Gulf," *Energy Policy* 38, no. 6 (June 2010), www.sciencedirect.com/science/article/pii/S0301421510000194.
110. Riedel, *Kings and Presidents*, 11.
111. See, for instance, Ronald Hyam, *Britain's Declining Empire: The Road to Decolonisation, 1918–1968* (Cambridge, UK: Cambridge University Press, 2007).
112. See Barry Turner, *Suez 1956: The Inside Story of the First Oil War* (London: Hodder & Stoughton, 2012).
113. Eric Hammel, "How the Suez Crisis Was a Win for Israel (And a Major Defeat for Britain and France)," *The National Interest*, October 13, 2018, https://nationalinterest.org/blog/buzz/how-suez-crisis-was-win-israel-and-major-defeat-britain-and-france-33316.
114. See, for instance, Keith Kyle, *Suez: Britain's End of Empire in the Middle East* (London: I. B. Tauris, 2011); Derek Varble, *The Suez Crisis 1956* (London: Bloomsbury, 2003).
115. Michael Scott Doran, *Ike's Gamble: America's Rise to Dominance in the Middle East* (New York: Free Press, 2016), 197.

116. Ibid., ch. 11; Kyle, *Suez*; Eugene L. Rogan, *The Arabs: A History* (New York: Basic Books, 2009); Turner, *Suez 1956.*
117. For a detailed account of the UN's role in the Suez Crisis, see Matthew Walker, "The Lost Art of Interdependency: United Nations Leadership in the Suez Crisis of 1956 and Its Ramifications in World Affairs," University of Nebraska, Lincoln, 2010, https://digitalcommons.unl.edu/cgi/viewcontent.cgi?article=1033&context=historydiss.
118. Conor McLaughlin, "The Suez Crisis: Security Implications for the Transatlantic Relationship and the Shift in Global Power," Student Scholarship & Creative Works by Year (Carlisle, PA: Dickinson College, 2016), https://scholar.dickinson.edu/cgi/viewcontent.cgi?article=1048&context=student_work.
119. Paine, *The Sea and Civilization*, 597.
120. James D. Hamilton, "Historical Oil Shocks," Working Paper Series, National Bureau of Economic Research, February 2011, pp. 10–12, https://doi.org/10.3386/w16790.

4: Western Tide Rising

1. G. C. Peden, "Suez and Britain's Decline as a World Power," *The Historical Journal* 55, no. 4 (December 2012): 1073–96, https://doi.org/10.1017/S0018246X12000246.
2. See Michael North, *The Baltic: A History*, trans. Kenneth Kronenberg (Cambridge, MA: Harvard University Press, 2015), ch. 7.
3. C. S. Christensen, "The History of the Russian Orthodox Church in Denmark (1741–2016) Seen in a Danish-Russian Historical Perspective," *Studia Humanitatis*, no. 2 (2017): 470–89; Vitaliy Zherdyev, "The Russian Orthodox Church in Copenhagen: A View from the Architect's Homeland," *Konsthistorisk Tidskrift/Journal of Art History* 87, no. 4 (October 2, 2018): 234–50, https://doi.org/10.1080/00233609.2018.1518342.
4. Paul Bairoch, "Europe's Gross National Product: 1800–1975," *Journal of European Economic History* 5, no. 2 (Fall 1976): 281.
5. Artur Attman, "The Russian Market in World Trade, 1500–1860," *Scandinavian Economic History Review* 29, no. 3 (September 1981): 184, https://doi.org/10.1080/03585522.1981.10407958.
6. North, *The Baltic: A History*, 301.
7. "Review of Maritime Transport 2018" (New York: United Nations Conference on Trade and Development, 2019), 32.
8. "The Connected City," National Museum of American History, February 28, 2017, https://americanhistory.si.edu/america-on-the-move/connected-city.
9. Author interview, Henning Morgen, Copenhagen, January 17, 2020. For more, see Chris Jephson and Henning Morgen, *Creating Global Opportunities: Maersk Line in Containerization, 1973–2013* (Cambridge, UK: Cambridge University Press, 2014).
10. Jephson and Morgen, *Creating Global Opportunities*.
11. Brian Cudahy, "The Containership Revolution: Malcolm McLean's 1956 Innovation Goes Global," *TR News*, October 2006, http://onlinepubs.trb.org/onlinepubs/trnews/trnews246.pdf.

12. Marc Levinson, *The Box: How the Shipping Container Made the World Smaller and the World Economy Bigger* (Princeton, NJ: Princeton University Press, 2016), ch. 2.
13. Ibid., 20.
14. Bernstein, *A Splendid Exchange*, 361.
15. Levinson, *The Box*, 38.
16. Hans van Ham and Joan Rijsenbrij, *Development of Containerization: Success Through Vision, Drive and Technology* (Amsterdam: IOS Press, 2012), 8.
17. Patrick Chung, "From Korea to Vietnam: Local Labor, Multinational Capital, and the Evolution of US Military Logistics, 1950–97," *Radical History Review* 2019, no. 133 (January 1, 2019): 38–39, https://doi.org/10.1215/01636545-7160053.
18. Levinson, *The Box*, ch. 3.
19. Marc Levinson, "The Now-Ubiquitous Shipping Container Was an Idea Before Its Time," *Smithsonian Magazine*, June 16, 2017, https://www.smithsonianmag.com/innovation/shipping-container-idea-before-time-180963730/.
20. Levinson, *The Box*, chs. 5–6.
21. Ibid., 94.
22. Ibid., 170.
23. Ibid., ch. 7.
24. "About the Industry: Containers," World Shipping Council, 2020, http://www.worldshipping.org/about-the-industry/containers.
25. Levinson, *The Box*, 277.
26. Bremer Ausschuss für Wirtschaftsforschung, *Container Facilities and Traffic in 71 Ports of the World* (Bremen, 1971).
27. "Choked Off: The Six Day War's Impact on Maritime Trade," Winton, June 6, 2017, https://www.winton.com/longer-view/the-six-day-wars-impact-on-trade.
28. James D. Hamilton, "Historical Oil Shocks," Working Paper Series (National Bureau of Economic Research, February 2011), 14, https://doi.org/10.3386/w16790.
29. Matthew Heins, "The Shipping Container and the Globalization of American Infrastructure" (PhD, Ann Arbor, University of Michigan, 2013), 19.
30. Jephson and Morgen, *Creating Global Opportunities*; Levinson, *The Box*.
31. "World Trade Report 2013: Factors Shaping the Future of Global Trade" (Geneva: World Trade Organization, 2013), 11.
32. Sudripto Khasnabis, "Choosing a Hull Form for Ships: A Naval Architect's Perspective," Marine Insight, August 27, 2019, https://www.marineinsight.com/naval-architecture/choosing-a-hull-form-for-ships-a-naval-architects-perspective/.
33. On the engineering challenges of U- and V-shaped hulls, see Larrie D. Ferreiro, *Bridging the Seas: The Rise of Naval Architecture in the Industrial Age, 1800–2000* (Cambridge, MA: MIT Press, 2019), ch. 4.
34. Mike W. Peng, *Global Business* (Boston: Cengage Learning, 2016), 470.
35. Phil Thomas, "Suez Spawns Supertankers," *Evening Independent*, July 15, 1968.
36. Levinson, *The Box*, 307.
37. "World Trade Report 2013," 52.
38. Global Financial Data, "United States Real GDP in 2012 Dollars."
39. Levinson, *The Box*, 281.
40. "World Trade Report 2013," 64.
41. Nguyen Dinh, "A Strategic Study of the Top 20 Liners During Period 1980–2001" (Master's, Malmo, Sweden, World Maritime University, 2002), 27.

42. Global Financial Data, "United States Quarterly Exports of Goods and Services."
43. Ham and Rijsenbrij, *Development of Containerization*, 65.
44. Jephson and Morgen, *Creating Global Opportunities*, 94.
45. Ibid., 176.
46. "Merchandise: Total Trade and Share, Annual," UNCTAD Stat, 2020, https://unctadstat.unctad.org/wds/TableViewer/tableView.aspx?ReportId=101.
47. Levinson, *The Box*, 16.
48. "Merchandise: Total Trade and Share, Annual."

5: Taipans of Globalization

1. Quoted in Mark Rivett-Carnac, "Hong Kong's Port Comes to Terms with Declining Trade," *Time*, July 3, 2016, https://time.com/4390790/hong-kong-port-harbor-shipping-trade/.
2. Ibid.
3. Richard Hu and Weijie Chen, *Global Shanghai Remade: The Rise of Pudong New Area* (London: Routledge, 2019), ch. 1.
4. Linsun Cheng, "Globalization and Shanghai Model: A Retrospective and Prospective Analysis," *Journal of International and Global Studies* 4, no. 1 (November 1, 2012): 60–62.
5. As recounted by his son, C. H. Tung, in an interview with the author, Hong Kong, office of the former chief executive of the SAR, 28 Kennedy Road, November 1, 2019.
6. Excerpts from C.Y. Tung diaries, C.Y. Tung Maritime Museum, Shanghai Jiao Tong University. A Chinese version is published as *Dong Haoyun ri ji, 1948–1982* [The Diary of Dong Haoyun, 1948–1982] (Hong Kong: Chinese University of Hong Kong Press, 2004).
7. C.Y. Tung diaries.
8. "Founding Father," *South China Morning Post*, January 17, 2003, https://www.scmp.com/article/403750/founding-father.
9. Elizabeth J. Perry, *Shanghai on Strike: The Politics of Chinese Labor* (Stanford, CA: Stanford University Press, 1993), ch. 5.
10. For the definitive English-language account of the battle, see Peter Harmsen, *Shanghai 1937: Stalingrad on the Yangtze* (Havertown, PA: Casemate, 2015).
11. Daniel Brook, *A History of Future Cities* (New York: W. W. Norton & Company, 2013), 244.
12. In his controversial book *1421: The Year China Discovered America* (New York: Harper Perennial, 2002), Gavin Menzies asserts that Zheng He actually visited the Americas on his famous voyages. The evidence for this is contested. In any case, no Chinese national had owned and operated a ship that sailed from Chinese shores to Europe or the United States in the intervening six hundred years.
13. Hugh Farmer, "SS Tien Loong—1947 a Chinese First," Industrial History of Hong Kong Group, May 24, 2020, https://industrialhistoryhk.org/tien-loong-chinese/.
14. C. Y. Tung, *Chinese Shipping Industry and Chinese Maritime Trust Ltd.* (Hong Kong, 1953), 60.

15. "Milestones in the Life of C. Y. Tung," Chinese University Press, November 18, 2004, http://www.cuhk.edu.hk/ipro/pressrelease/milestones.pdf.
16. Levinson, *The Box*, 281.
17. Ibid., 294–95.
18. "China Bank Linked to OOCL Bailout," JOC, March 9, 1997, https://www.joc.com/china-bank-linked-oocl-bailout_19970309.html.
19. Nguyen Dinh, "A Strategic Study of the Top 20 Liners During Period 1980–2001" (Master's, Malmo, Sweden, World Maritime University, 2002), 27.
20. Lau Chi-pang, "Getting to World Class: The Container Terminals," Marine Department of Hong Kong, https://www.mardep.gov.hk/theme/port_hk/en/p1ch7_1.html, accessed June 4, 2020.
21. Elena Holodny, "The Rise, Fall, and Comeback of the Chinese Economy over the Past 800 Years," *Business Insider*, January 8, 2017, https://www.businessinsider.com/history-of-chinese-economy-1200-2017-2017-1.
22. Richard M. Nixon, "Asia After Viet Nam," *Foreign Affairs*, October 1967, https://www.foreignaffairs.com/articles/asia/1967-10-01/asia-after-viet-nam.
23. "Memorandum from President Nixon to His Assistant for National Security Affairs (Kissinger)," *Foreign Relations of the United States*, 1969–1976, *vol. XVII, China, 1969–1972*, eds. Daniel J. Lawler and Erin R. Mahan (Washington, DC: Government Printing Office, 2010), doc. 3, Office of the Historian, https://history.state.gov/historicaldocuments/frus1969-76v17/d3.
24. Henry Kissinger, "National Security Decision Memorandum 17," June 26, 1969, Federation of American Scientists, https://fas.org/irp/offdocs/nsdm-nixon/nsdm-17.pdf.
25. Henry Kissinger, *White House Years* (Boston: Little, Brown, 1979), 190–91.
26. Jussi Hanhimäki, *The Flawed Architect: Henry Kissinger and American Foreign Policy* (New York: Oxford University Press, 2004), 119.
27. Chris Tudda, *A Cold War Turning Point: Nixon and China, 1969–1972* (Baton Rouge: Louisiana State University Press, 2012), ch. 5.
28. Ibid., ch. 10.
29. For a macro-level account of the rapprochement between the United States and China, see Dong Wang, *The United States and China: A History from the Eighteenth Century to the Present* (Lanham, MD: Rowman & Littlefield, 2013), ch. 9.
30. Maureen Dowd, "2 U.S. Officials Went to Beijing Secretly in July," *New York Times*, December 19, 1989, https://www.nytimes.com/1989/12/19/world/2-us-officials-went-to-beijing-secretly-in-july.html.
31. In current USD. World Bank national accounts data, "GDP (current US$)," accessed November 16, 2019.
32. In 1975, China's GDP per capita was $178.34 in current USD; the US's was $7,801.45. World Bank national accounts data, "GDP per capita (current US$)," accessed November 16, 2019.
33. For a more detailed exploration, see Harold Karan Jacobson and Michel Oksenberg, *China's Participation in the IMF, the World Bank, and GATT: Toward a Global Economic Order* (Ann Arbor: University of Michigan Press, 1990).
34. Jeffrey J. Schott, "The Soviet Union and the GATT," *Washington Post*, September 1, 1986, https://www.washingtonpost.com/archive/opinions/1986/09/01/the-soviet-union-and-the-gatt/ca6362b6-5cbf-4824-871e-20672e130ae7/.

35. "OOCL Names Its First 8,000-TEU Containership," FreightWaves, April 30, 2003, https://www.freightwaves.com/news/oocl-names-its-first-8000-teu-containership.

6: The Great Closing

1. Michael J. Enright, *Developing China: The Remarkable Impact of Foreign Direct Investment* (London: Routledge, 2016), 125.
2. Daniel Brook, "Head of the Dragon: The Rise of New Shanghai," *Places Journal*, February 18, 2013, https://doi.org/10.22269/130218.
3. Seth Faison, "Shanghai Journal; China Stands Tall in the World, and Here's Proof," *New York Times*, July 26, 1995, https://www.nytimes.com/1995/07/26/world/shanghai-journal-china-stands-tall-in-the-world-and-here-s-proof.html.
4. John Berra and Wei Ju, eds., *World Film Locations: Shanghai* (Bristol, UK: Intellect Books, 2014), 76.
5. Chengxi Yang, "30 Years of Pudong: A Story of China's Economic Rise," CGTN, April 21, 2020, https://news.cgtn.com/news/2020-04-21/30-years-of-Pudong-A-story-of-China-s-economic-rise--PS2yrWuXTO/index.html.
6. Howard W. French, "In World Skyscraper Race, It Isn't Lonely at the Top," *New York Times*, May 8, 2007, https://www.nytimes.com/2007/05/08/world/asia/08shanghai.html.
7. Amy Cortese, "Fashioning Skylines, Not a Personality Cult," *New York Times*, April 20, 2008, https://www.nytimes.com/2008/04/20/realestate/commercial/20sqft.html.
8. Tanya Powley, John Burn-Murdoch, and Cleve Jones, "World's Fastest Lifts Race to the Top of the Tallest Buildings," *Financial Times*, November 6, 2014, https://ig.ft.com/worlds-fastest-lifts/.
9. Choco Tang, "Five of Asia's Tallest Typhoon-Resistant Skyscrapers," *South China Morning Post*, August 22, 2017, https://www.scmp.com/magazines/style/news-trends/article/2107839/five-asias-tallest-typhoon-resistant-skyscrapers.
10. Ned Kelly, "The Epic Wonder of Shanghai's Yangshan Deep-Water Port," *That's*, August 8, 2019, https://www.thatsmags.com/suzhou/post/13788/throwback-thursday-yangshan-deep-water-port.
11. Bob Davis, "When the World Opened the Gates of China," *Wall Street Journal*, July 27, 2018, https://www.wsj.com/articles/when-the-world-opened-the-gates-of-china-1532701482.
12. World Bank national accounts data, "GDP (current US$)," accessed June 4, 2020.
13. Zhu Yu et al., "Population Geography in China Since the 1980s: Forging the Links Between Population Studies and Human Geography," *Journal of Geographical Sciences* 26, no. 8 (2016): 1,134.
14. Anthony Lambert, "Trans-Siberian Railway: Everything You Need to Know About Tackling the World's Greatest Train Journey," *The Telegraph*, February 4, 2016, https://www.telegraph.co.uk/travel/rail-journeys/Trans-Siberian-Great-Train-Journeys/.
15. Lance E. Hoovestal, *Globalization Contained: The Economic and Strategic Consequences of the Container* (London: Palgrave Macmillan, 2013), ch. 3.
16. Toh Ting Wei, "China Opens World's Longest Sea Bridge: Other Impressive

Bridges," *Straits Times*, October 24, 2018, https://www.straitstimes.com/world/longest-bridges-over-water-in-the-world.

17. Ci Song, "A Critical Analysis of the Donghai Bridge, Shanghai, China," Bridge Engineering 2 Conference, Bath, UK, 2008, https://people.bath.ac.uk/jjo20/conference2/2008/SONG%20PAPER%2021.pdf.
18. Any honest reading of the industrial development of Britain or other major Western economies will reveal episodes of forced displacement, coerced labor, appalling labor conditions, and industrial blight that echo the conditions that apply to modern industrializing China.
19. Dong-Wook Song and Ki-Tae Yeo, "A Competitive Analysis of Chinese Container Ports Using the Analytic Hierarchy Process," in *Port Management*, ed. Hercules Haralambides (London: Palgrave Macmillan, 2015), 341.
20. "Shanghai Surpasses Singapore as World's Busiest Port," Bloomberg, January 8, 2011, https://www.bloomberg.com/news/articles/2011-01-08/shanghai-surpasses-singapore-as-world-s-busiest-port-as-trade-volumes-jump.
21. "World's Largest Automated Container Terminal Opens in Shanghai," *Straits Times*, December 11, 2017, https://www.straitstimes.com/asia/east-asia/worlds-largest-automated-container-terminal-opens-in-shanghai.
22. Rosalina Tan, "Foreign Direct Investment Flows to and from China," PASCN Discussion Papers (Manila: Philippine APEC Study Center Network, 1999), 25.
23. Hongying Wang, "The Asian Financial Crisis and Financial Reforms in China," *The Pacific Review* 12, no. 4 (January 1, 1999): 538.
24. Nargiza Salidjanova, "Going Out: An Overview of China's Outward Foreign Direct Investment" (Washington, DC: U.S.-China Economic & Security Review Commission, March 30, 2011), https://www.uscc.gov/sites/default/files/Research/GoingOut.pdf; David Dollar, "Understanding China's Belt and Road Infrastructure Projects in Africa" (Washington, DC: Brookings Institution, September 2019), https://www.brookings.edu/wp-content/uploads/2019/09/FP_20190930_china_bri_dollar.pdf.
25. "Foreign Direct Investment, Net Outflows (BoP, current US$)—China," distributed by the World Bank, 2019, https://data.worldbank.org/indicator/BM.KLT.DINV.CD.WD?locations=CN.
26. "World Trade Report 2010: Trade in Natural Resources" (Geneva: World Trade Organization, 2013), 54.
27. Daniel Yergin, *The Quest: Energy, Security, and the Remaking of the Modern World* (New York: Penguin, 2011), 193. Also see Ruchir Sharma, "The Next Global Crash: Why You Should Fear the Commodities Bubble," *The Atlantic*, April 16, 2012, https://www.theatlantic.com/business/archive/2012/04/the-next-global-crash-why-you-should-fear-the-commodities-bubble/255901/.
28. Paul Collier, *The Plundered Planet* (New York: Oxford University Press, 2010), xiii.
29. Ruchir Sharma, *Breakout Nations: In Pursuit of the Next Economic Miracles* (London: Penguin Books, 2012), ch. 1.
30. The World Bank, *World DataBank*, available at databank.worldbank.org/data/home.aspx.
31. Bruce D. Jones and David Steven, *The Risk Pivot: Great Powers, International Security, and the Energy Revolution* (Washington, DC: Brookings Institution

Press, 2014); Ruchir Sharma, *The Rise and Fall of Nations: Forces of Change in the Post-Crisis World* (New York: W. W. Norton & Company, 2016).

32. "Review of Maritime Transport, 2001" (New York: United Nations Conference on Trade and Development, 2001), 67, https://unctad.org/en/Docs/rmt2001_en.pdf.
33. "Ranking of Container Ports of the World," Marine Department of Hong Kong, May 20, 2020, https://www.mardep.gov.hk/en/publication/pdf/portstat_2_y_b5.pdf.
34. James Kynge et al., "How China Rules the Waves," *Financial Times*, January 12, 2017, https://ig.ft.com/sites/china-ports.
35. "Ranking of Container Ports of the World."
36. "United States Trade Summary 2000," World Integrated Trade Solution, https://wits.worldbank.org/CountryProfile/en/Country/USA/Year/2000/Summarytext; "Foreign Trade," United States Census Bureau, https://www.census.gov/foreign-trade/statistics/highlights/top/index.html.
37. On Shanghai's burgeoning cultural significance, see Cheng Li, https://www.brookings.edu/essay/shanghais-dynamic-art-scene/; as well as Cheng Li, *Middle Class Shanghai: Reshaping U.S.-China Engagement* (Washington, DC: Brookings Press, 2021).

7: Global Supply Ships

1. In current USD. Giovanni Federico and Antonio Tena Junguito, "Federico-Tena World Trade Historical Database : World Trade," e-cienciaDatos, V2, Consorcio Madroño, 2018, https://doi.org/10.21950/JKZFDP.
2. "Shipping and World Trade," International Chamber of Shipping, 2017, https://www.ics-shipping.org/shipping-facts/shipping-and-world-trade.
3. "Maersk Line—from One Route to a Global Network," Maersk, February 21, 2019, https://www.maersk.com/news/articles/2019/02/21/maersk-line-from-one-route-to-a-global-network.
4. "A. P. Møller–Mærsk A/S Q2 2019 Report" (Copenhagen: Maersk, June 2019), 34, https://investor.maersk.com/static-files/5b3b9863-5220-4645-8021-1cecb7bad26f.
5. Marcus Hand, "The World's Largest Ships," Seatrade Maritime, November 3, 2017, https://www.seatrade-maritime.com/asia/world-s-largest-ships.
6. "The Evolution of the PCTC Cascade," Maritime Executive, September 25, 2014, https://www.maritime-executive.com/article/The-Evolution-of-the-PCTC-Cascade-2014-09-25.
7. Hans van Ham and Joan Rijsenbrij, *Development of Containerization: Success Through Vision, Drive and Technology* (Amsterdam: IOS Press, 2012), 288.
8. Ibid.
9. John Konrad, "Mærsk McKinney-Møller—Meet The World's Largest Ship! [Multimedia Gallery]," gCaptain, May 14, 2013, https://gcaptain.com/worlds-largest-ship-photos-maersk-moller/.
10. "Madrid Maersk Snatches Record from MOL Triumph," Maritime Executive, April 3, 2017, http://www.maritime-executive.com/article/madrid-maersk-snatches-record-from-mol-triumph.

11. "Fact File: Aircraft Carriers," United States Navy, July 15, 2019, https://www.navy.mil/navydata/fact_display.asp?cid=4200&tid=200&ct=4.
12. "Top 10 World's Largest Container Ships in 2019," Marine Insight, February 25, 2019, https://www.marineinsight.com/know-more/top-10-worlds-largest-container-ships-in-2019/.
13. "South China Sea, Mediterranean and North Sea Are Shipping Accidents Hotspots," World Wildlife Foundation, June 7, 2013, http://wwf.panda.org/wwf_news/press_releases/?208839/South-China-Sea-Mediterranean-and-North-Sea-are-shipping-accidents-hotspots.
14. Craig B. Smith, *Extreme Waves* (Newport Beach, CA: Dockside Sailing Press, 2010), 207.
15. Chris Dixon, *Ghost Wave: The Discovery of Cortes Bank and the Biggest Wave on Earth* (San Francisco: Chronicle, 2011), 86.
16. For an accessible account of the evolution of ship architecture and its focus on stability, see Larrie D. Ferreiro, *Bridging the Seas: The Rise of Naval Architecture in the Industrial Age, 1800–2000.*
17. On the dynamics of ultra-large ships rolling, see Mostert, *Supership*, 114.
18. The industry has been struggling with fires on container ships recently. Costas Paris, "Spate of Fires Has Shipping Industry Looking at How Dangerous Goods Are Handled," *Wall Street Journal*, November 24, 2019, https://www.wsj.com/articles/spate-of-fires-has-shipping-industry-looking-at-how-dangerous-goods-are-handled-11574600400.
19. Mark Twain, *Following the Equator* (Hartford, CT: American Publishing Company, 1897), 616–17.
20. "Frequently Asked Questions," All About AIS, 2012, http://www.allaboutais.com/index.php/en/faqs; "Tracking Apps That Reveal Location of British Warships Spark Security Fears," *The Independent*, February 5, 2018, http://www.independent.co.uk/news/uk/home-news/royal-navy-tracking-app-warship-nato-russia-china-military-security-a8191896.html.
21. Costas Paris and Mike Sudal, "With Container Ships Getting Bigger, Maersk Focuses on Getting Faster," *Wall Street Journal*, December 20, 2018, https://www.wsj.com/articles/with-container-ships-getting-bigger-maersk-focuses-on-getting-faster-11545301800.
22. See David Ricardo, *On the Principles of Political Economy and Taxation* (London: John Murray, 1817), ch. 6.
23. Eric Eng, "Asia's Reefer Trade: An Ocean Carrier's Perspective," Asia Fruit Congress, Hong Kong, September 7, 2011, https://globalmaritimehub.com/wp-content/uploads/attach_506.pdf.
24. Daniel Stone, "Why Are Bananas So Cheap?," *National Geographic*, August 10, 2016, https://www.nationalgeographic.com/culture/food/the-plate/2016/08/bananas-are-so-cool/.
25. Daniel Stone, "The Miracle of the Modern Banana," *National Geographic*, August 8, 2016, https://www.nationalgeographic.com/culture/food/the-plate/2016/08/the-miracle-of-bananas/.
26. Rose George, *Deep Sea & Foreign Going* (London: Portobello Books, 2014), 3.
27. Levinson, *The Box*, 359.
28. Ibid., 355–59.

29. "How Much Trade Transits the South China Sea?," *ChinaPower Project: Center for Strategic and International Studies* (blog), August 2, 2017, http://chinapower.csis.org/much-trade-transits-south-china-sea/.
30. Sam Costello, "Where Is the iPhone Made? (Hint: Not Just China)," Lifewire, March 31, 2020, https://www.lifewire.com/where-is-the-iphone-made-1999503.
31. "Let's Talk About Quality," Nutella, 2020, https://www.nutella.com/int/en/lets-talk-about-quality#7-ingredients.
32. "Mapping Global Value Chains" (Paris: Organization for Economic Co-operation and Development, December 3, 2012), 17; http://www.oecd.org/dac/aft/MappingGlobalValueChains_web_usb.pdf.
33. Alice Kahn, "Filling Every Gap," *New York Times*, August 23, 1992, https://www.nytimes.com/1992/08/23/style/filling-every-gap.html.
34. Marc Gunther, "Protecting a Tangled Workforce That Stretches Across the World," *The Guardian*, April 28, 2015, https://www.theguardian.com/sustainable-business/2015/apr/28/gap-kindley-lawlor-human-rights-workers-jobs-garment-industry.
35. "Facts and Figures," Port of Los Angeles, https://www.portoflosangeles.org/business/statistics/facts-and-figures, accessed June 27, 2020.
36. "What Could You Fit Inside a 20ft Shipping Container?," Universal Container Shipping LTD, August 1, 2018, https://www.universal-containers.com/what-can-you-fit-inside-a-20ft-shipping-container/.
37. Levinson, *The Box*, 3.
38. Daron Acemoglu et al., "Import Competition and the Great US Employment Sag of the 2000s," *Journal of Labor Economics* 34, no. S1 (January 2016): S141.
39. Justin R. Pierce and Peter K. Schott, "The Surprisingly Swift Decline of US Manufacturing Employment," *American Economic Review* 106, no. 7 (July 1, 2016): 1632–62; Craig Martin, "The Shipping Container," *The Atlantic*, December 2, 2013, https://www.theatlantic.com/technology/archive/2013/12/the-shipping-container/281888/.
40. "How Global Trade Runs on U.S. Dollars," *Wall Street Journal*, January 22, 2020, https://www.youtube.com/watch?v=jsDwMGH5E8U.
41. "Trade (% of GDP)—United States" (2019), distributed by the World Bank, https://data.worldbank.org/indicator/NE.TRD.GNFS.ZS?locations=US.
42. Jeffrey Shane, "Toward More Golden Anniversaries: Securing Transportation's Place in the National Policy Agenda," *TR News*, September–October 2006, http://onlinepubs.trb.org/onlinepubs/trnews/trnews246.pdf.
43. Mark Perry, "We Hear About US Jobs Outsourced Overseas ('Stolen') but What About the 7.1M Insourced Jobs We 'Steal' from Abroad?," American Enterprise Institute—AEI, November 9, 2018, https://www.aei.org/carpe-diem/we-hear-about-us-jobs-outsourced-overseas-stolen-but-what-about-the-7-1m-insourced-jobs-we-steal-from-abroad-2/.
44. Stephen Young, "What Has Happened to the Middle Class?," p. 142, Caux Round Table, http://www.cauxroundtable.org/wp-content/uploads/2018/10/middle-class-Oct-2015.pptx.
45. See, e.g., Simon Johnson and James Kwak, *13 Bankers: The Wall Street Takeover and the Next Financial Meltdown* (New York: Vintage, 2011).
46. Uri Friedman, "Why Trump Is Thriving in an Age of Distrust," *The Atlantic*,

January 20, 2017, https://www.theatlantic.com/international/archive/2017/01/trump-edelman-trust-crisis/513350/.

47. Philip Bump, "At Last: A Map of Trump's Acreage Victory That's to the Proper Scale," *Washington Post*, May 13, 2017, https://www.washingtonpost.com/news/politics/wp/2017/05/13/at-last-an-electoral-map-thats-to-the-proper-scale/.
48. James Manyika et al., "Urban America: US Cities in the Global Economy" (McKinsey Global Insitute, April 2012), https://www.mckinsey.com/~/media/McKinsey/Featured%20Insights/Urbanization/US%20cities%20in%20the%20global%20economy/MGI_Urban_America_Full_Report.ashx.
49. G. John Ikenberry, *After Victory: Institutions, Strategic Restraint, and the Rebuilding of Order After Major Wars* (Princeton, NJ: Princeton University Press, 2001), 167.
50. See Ikenberry, *After Victory*, ch. 5, for an account of the postwar settlement, and Charles P. Kindleberger, "Dominance and Leadership in the International Economy: Exploitation, Public Goods, and Free Rides," *International Studies Quarterly* 25, no. 2 (1981): 242–54, https://doi.org/10.2307/2600355, for a political science explanation of "hegemonic stability theory," which attempts to explain why nations like the United States will stabilize the international system despite the costs.
51. Edward Luce, "The Changing of the Global Economic Guard," *The Atlantic*, April 29, 2017, https://www.theatlantic.com/international/archive/2017/04/china-economy-populism/523989/.
52. "An Illustrious Hong Kong Container Firm Sells to China," *The Economist*, July 15, 2017, https://www.economist.com/business/2017/07/15/an-illustrious-hong-kong-container-firm-sells-to-china. Jennifer Lo, "Trade, Not Politics: Orient Overseas Defends Cosco Takeover," Nikkei Asia, August 7, 2017, https://asia.nikkei.com/Business/Trade-not-politics-Orient-Overseas-defends-Cosco-takeover.
53. See Wang Jisi, "China's Search for Stability with America," *Foreign Affairs*, January 28, 2009, https://www.foreignaffairs.com/articles/asia/2005-09-01/chinas-search-stability-america.

Part III: The Flag Follows the Trade

1. See inter alia Øystein Tunsjø, *The Return of Bipolarity in World Politics: China, the United States, and Geostructural Realism* (New York: Columbia University Press, 2018); Avery Goldstein, "US–China Rivalry in the Twenty-First Century: Déjà Vu and Cold War II," *China International Strategy Review* 2, no. 1 (June 2020): 48–62, https://doi.org/10.1007/s42533-020-00036-w.
2. Michael Green, *By More Than Providence: Grand Strategy and American Power in the Asia-Pacific Since 1783* (New York: Columbia University Press, 2017), 20.

8: Pirates of the Twenty-First Century

1. Steven Johnson, *The Enemy of All Mankind: A True Story of Piracy, Power and History's First Global Manhunt* (New York: Riverhead, 2020), 21.

2. For broad histories of Singapore's role in world commerce, see Jim Baker, *Crossroads: A Popular History of Malaysia & Singapore*, 2nd ed. (Singapore: Marshall Cavendish Editions, 2008), and John Curtis Perry, *Singapore: Unlikely Power* (New York: Oxford University Press, 2017).
3. "World Economic Outlook Database 2019," International Monetary Fund, February 2019, https://www.imf.org/external/pubs/ft/weo/2019/02/weodata/index.aspx.
4. Edward A. Alpers, *The Indian Ocean in World History* (New York: Oxford University Press, 2013), 45–46.
5. Jack Turner, *Spice: The History of a Temptation* (New York: Vintage, 2005), ch. 1.
6. Ashley Jackson, *Buildings of Empire* (New York: Oxford University Press, 2013), 7.
7. Alpers, *The Indian Ocean in World History,* 102. For a broader narrative of this story, see Johnson, *The Enemy of All Mankind.*
8. "Malaysia, Indonesia, Singapore Agree to Boost Security in Malacca Strait," *New York Times*, August 2, 2005, https://www.nytimes.com/2005/08/02/world/asia/malaysia-indonesia-singapore-agree-to-boost-security-in-malacca.html.
9. Simon Montlake, "Hard Times for Pirates in Busy World Waterway," *Christian Science Monitor*, October 30, 2006, https://www.csmonitor.com/2006/1030/p01s04-woap.html; Lejla Villar and Mason Hamilton, "The Strait of Malacca, a Key Oil Trade Chokepoint, Links the Indian and Pacific Oceans," Energy Information Administration, August 11, 2017, https://www.eia.gov/todayinenergy/detail.php?id=32452.
10. Anna Bowden, "The Economic Cost of Maritime Piracy," One Earth Future Working Paper, December 2010.
11. Catherine Zara Raymond, "Piracy and Armed Robbery in the Malacca Strait: A Problem Solved?," *Naval War College Review* 62, no. 3 (Summer 2009), 38–39.
12. In *The Pirates of Somalia*, Jay Bahadur cites British naval officers noting that the pirates do track ships by accessing AIS and GPS data on commercially available websites. But that's a far cry from integrating hundreds of millions of pieces of data, using AI-enhanced processing, to track and predict the movement of global shipping.
13. See "Fact Sheet on Information Fusion Centre (IFC) and Launch of IFC Real-Time Information-Sharing System (IRIS)," Ministry of Defense of Singapore, May 14, 2019, https://www.mindef.gov.sg/web/portal/mindef/news-and-events/latest-releases/article-detail/2019/May/14may19_fs for more information on the IFC.
14. By the mid-1800s Zanzibar was one of the largest suppliers of cloves in the world and remains the third-largest producer today. Alpers, *The Indian Ocean in World History*, 107.
15. J. E. Peterson, "America and Oman: The Context for Nearly Two Centuries of Relations," Symposium on the Voyage of Sultana to New York in 1840, Muscat: Public Authority for Radio & TV, 2014, http://www.jepeterson.net/sitebuildercontent/sitebuilderfiles/Peterson_-_America_and_Oman_2014.pdf.
16. For a more comprehensive history of the Omani Empire in the Indian Ocean, see Jeremy Jones and Nicholas Ridout, *A History of Modern Oman* (Cambridge, UK: Cambridge University Press, 2015), ch. 2.
17. Neil Ford, "The Race to Become East Africa's Biggest Port," BBC News, June 7, 2016, https://www.bbc.com/news/world-africa-36458946.

18. Fumbuka Ng'wanakilala, "Tanzania Arrests 7 Pirates After Attack on Oil Vessel," Reuters, October 4, 2011, https://www.reuters.com/article/tanzania-pirates-id USL5E7L43LO20111004.
19. For an account of this episode, and more importantly for a detailed and insightful examination of the history, politics, and economics of this phenomenon, see Bahadur, *The Pirates of Somalia*, 77–79 especially.
20. Ed Pilkington, "Somali Teen Faces First US Piracy Charges in over a Century," *The Guardian*, April 22, 2009, https://www.theguardian.com/world/2009/apr/21 /somali-pirate-trial-new-york. Muse was found guilty and sentenced to thirty -three years in US federal prison. A later appeal of his conviction was rejected by a judge. See http://graphics8.nytimes.com/packages/pdf/nyregion/22pirate _Complaint.pdf.
21. "IMO Assembly Calls for Action on Piracy off Somalia," Press Briefing, International Maritime Organization, November 24, 2005.
22. "Transnational Organized Crime Threat Assessment 2010" (Vienna: United Nations Office on Drugs and Crime, 2010), 209, https://www.unodc.org /documents/data-and-analysis/Studies/TOCTA_draft_2603_lores.pdf.
23. "Pirates Hijack UN Food Ship off Somalia," UN News, February 26, 2007, https:// news.un.org/en/story/2007/02/210172-pirates-hijack-un-food-ship-somalia.
24. UNSC Res 1816 (2008).
25. Tullio Treves, "Historical Development of the Law of the Sea," in *The Oxford Handbook of the Law of the Sea*, Oxford Public International Law (Oxford, UK: Oxford University Press, 2015), ch. 1.
26. The Charter of the United Nations, signed in San Francisco in 1945, is the operating system of the law of relations between states: the Charter makes it legal for states to use force only in one circumstance: self-defense. For every other circumstance, the Security Council is the only international body that has the legal power to authorize the use of force. That gives the body a unique role in international law and politics. Tullio Treves, "Piracy and the International Law of the Sea," in *Modern Piracy*, ed. Douglas Guilfoyle (Cheltenham, UK: Edward Elgar, 2013), 126, https://www-elgaronline-com.ezp-prod1.hul.harvard .edu/view/edcoll/9781849804844/9781849804844.xml; Bahadur, *The Pirates of Somalia*, ch. 10.
27. The full list of participants has fluctuated; for details, see: "About Combined Maritime Forces (CMF)," Combined Maritime Forces (CMF), August 18, 2010, https://combinedmaritimeforces.com/about/. At the time of drafting, participating states included: Australia, Bahrain, Belgium, Canada, Denmark, France, Germany, Greece, Italy, Japan, Jordan, the Republic of Korea, Kuwait, Malaysia, the Netherlands, New Zealand, Pakistan, Portugal, Saudi Arabia, Seychelles, Singapore, Spain, Thailand, Turkey, the United Arab Emirates, the United Kingdom, and the United States.
28. Details are available from EUNAVFOR: "European Union Naval Force Operation Atalanta," EUNAVFOR, https://eunavfor.eu/, accessed May 15, 2020.
29. "Ukraine Joins NATO's Counter-Piracy Operation Ocean Shield," NATO, September 24, 2013, http://www.nato.int/cps/en/natohq/news_103521.htm.
30. It's surprisingly hard to get up-to-date details of these operations; but good accounts of them can be found in NATO reports—for example: "Counter-Piracy

Operations (Archived)," NATO, December 19, 2016, http://www.nato.int/cps/en/natohq/topics_48815.htm.—and in studies of individual navies' participation. On China's involvement see: Alison A. Kaufman, "China's Participation in Anti-Piracy Operations off the Horn of Africa: Drivers and Implications," Conference Report (Arlington, VA: CNA, July 2009).

31. On the applicability of the law of the sea, see Bahadur, *The Pirates of Somalia*, ch. 10.
32. "The Economist Explains: What Is Happening to Africa's Pirates?," *The Economist*, January 16, 2018, https://www.economist.com/the-economist-explains/2018/01/16/what-is-happening-to-africas-pirates; Sandra L. Hodgkinson, "Current Trends in Global Piracy: Can Somalia's Successes Help Combat Piracy in the Gulf of Guinea and Elsewhere?," *Case Western Reserve Journal of International Law* 46, no. 1 (2013): 145–60.
33. See Kaufman, "China's Participation in Anti-Piracy Operations," 9–11; David Lai, "Chinese Military Going Global," *China Security* 5, no. 1 (Winter 2009): 3–10; and Richard Weitz, "Operation Somalia: China's First Expeditionary Force," *China Security* 5, no. 1 (Winter 2009): 27–44.

9: The Near Seas

1. CMSI proceedings. Xi's speech to the Chinese Politburo, July 30, 2013.
2. There were two brief exceptions: the period from 1368 to 1420, when China was ruled from Nanjing, and the years from 1928 to 1949, during the period of civil war and Japanese occupation, when various claimants to power established headquarters outside Beijing.
3. Nicholas D. Kristof, "Beijing Journal: Whatever the High Walls Hide, It Isn't Opulence," *New York Times*, January 25, 1991, https://www.nytimes.com/1991/01/25/world/beijing-journal-whatever-the-high-walls-hide-it-isn-t-opulence.html.
4. James R. Holmes and Toshi Yoshihara, *Chinese Naval Strategy in the 21st Century*, 1st ed. (London: Routledge, 2007), 53.
5. M. Taylor Fravel, *Active Defense: China's Military Strategy since 1949*, Princeton Studies in International History and Politics (Princeton, New Jersey: Princeton University Press, 2019), 162.
6. Liu went on to serve as the vice chairman of the Central Military Commission, which oversees the military. He also served on the Politburo Standing Committee. In 1987 he said: "Without an aircraft carrier, I will die with my eyelids open: the Chinese Navy needs to build an aircraft carrier." See Edward Wong, "Liu Huaqing Dies at 94; Oversaw Modernization of China's Navy," *New York Times*, January 16, 2011, https://www.nytimes.com/2011/01/18/world/asia/18liu.html.
7. Holmes and Yoshihara, *Chinese Naval Strategy in the 21st Century*, 29.
8. Alfred Thayer Mahan, *The Influence of Sea Power Upon History, 1660–1783* (New York: Little, Brown, 1918), 521.
9. Ibid.
10. Alfred Thayer Mahan, "The Persian Gulf and International Relations," *National Review* 40 (1902): 18–19.

11. For a rich account of the influence of Mahan on American strategy during this period, see in particular: Michael J. Green, *By More Than Providence: Grand Strategy and American Power in the Asia Pacific Since 1783* (New York: Columbia University Press, 2017).
12. H. J. Mackinder, "The Geographical Pivot of History," *The Geographical Journal* 23, no. 4 (1904): 421–44.
13. Holmes and Yoshihara, *Chinese Naval Strategy in the 21st Century*.
14. Mark Metcalf, "The Legacy of Admiral Liu Huaqing," Conference Paper, US Naval War College, presented May 6–7, 2019.
15. Wikileaks, "Public Library of US Diplomacy—MFA Maintains Claims to South China Sea: Urges U.S. Companies Not to 'Get Entangled,'" March 13, 2008, available at www.wikileaks.org/plusd/cables/08BEIJING924_a.html.
16. "South China Sea's Vague 9-Dash Line Underpins China's Claim," AP NEWS, March 23, 2016, https://apnews.com/b5d824f945434c39ba66c33378d51222.
17. Christopher Woody, "Scarborough Shoal Is Red Line amid US-China Tension in South China Sea," *Business Insider*, October 3, 2018, https://www.businessinsider.com/scarborough-shoal-is-red-line-amid-us-china-tension-in-south-china-sea-2018-10.
18. For an overview of China's territorial claims in the South China Sea, see "South China Sea Territorial Disputes (Continued)," Peace Palace Library, http://www.peacepalacelibrary.nl/south-china-sea-territorial-disputes-continued/, accessed September 5, 2020.
19. Clive Schofield, "Dangerous Ground: A Geopolitical Overview of the South China Sea," in *Security and International Politics in the South China Sea*, ed. Sam Bateman and Ralf Emmers (London: Routledge, 2008), 7–25.
20. "VIETNAM-CHINA: Tours, Bird-Watching Trigger New Row over Spratlys," Inter Press Service, April 5, 2004, http://www.ipsnews.net/2004/04/vietnam-china-tours-bird-watching-trigger-new-row-over-spratlys/.
21. Schofield, "Dangerous Ground," 11.
22. Kimberley Marten Zisk, "Japan's United Nations Peacekeeping Dilemma," *Asia-Pacific Review* 8, no. 1 (May 1, 2001): 21–39.
23. Yasuhiro Izumikawa, "Explaining Japanese Antimilitarism: Normative and Realist Constraints on Japan's Security Policy," *International Security* 35, no. 2 (Fall 2010): 123–60.
24. Bertil Lintner, "Japan Could Carry the Day in a US-China Conflict," *Asia Times*, May 13, 2020, https://asiatimes.com/2020/05/japan-could-carry-the-day-in-a-us-china-conflict/. For more on Japan's naval posture and strategy, see Takuya Shimodaira, "The Japan Maritime Self-Defense Force in the Age of Multilateral Cooperation: Nontraditional Security," *Naval War College Review* 67, no. 2 (Spring 2014): 1–17.
25. Kyle Mizokami, "Sorry, China: Why the Japanese Navy Is the Best in Asia," *The National Interest*, October 16, 2016, https://nationalinterest.org/blog/the-buzz/sorry-china-why-the-japanese-navy-the-best-asia-18056.
26. "Japan Coast Guard: Justice and Humanity" (Tokyo: Japan Coast Guard, 2018), 3.
27. David Axe, "Meet the Helicopter-Cruiser: The Half Aircraft Carrier," *The National Interest*, The Center for the National Interest, February 23, 2019, https://nationalinterest.org/blog/buzz/meet-helicopter-cruiser-half-aircraft-carrier-45482.

28. Shinichi Fujiwara, "Japan Avoids Flak by Refusing to Call Flattop 'Aircraft Carrier,'" *Asahi Shimbun*, December 6, 2018, http://web.archive.org/web/20200203181218; http://www.asahi.com/ajw/articles/AJ201812060055.html.
29. Ankit Panda, "Obama: Senkakus Covered Under US-Japan Security Treaty," The Diplomat, April 24, 2014, https://thediplomat.com/2014/04/obama-senkakus-covered-under-us-japan-security-treaty/.
30. Thom Shanker, "U.S. Sends Two B-52 Bombers into Air Zone Claimed by China," *New York Times*, November 26, 2013, https://www.nytimes.com/2013/11/27/world/asia/us-flies-b-52s-into-chinas-expanded-air-defense-zone.html.
31. "About USFJ," US Forces, Japan, https://www.usfj.mil/About-USFJ/, accessed September 10, 2020.
32. Lyle J. Morris et al., *Gaining Competitive Advantage in the Gray Zone: Response Options for Coercive Aggression Below the Threshold of Major War* (Santa Monica, CA: RAND Corporation, 2019), https://www.rand.org/pubs/research_reports/RR2942.html.
33. Justin McCurry, "Japan-China Row Escalates over Fishing Boat Collision," *The Guardian*, September 9, 2010, https://www.theguardian.com/world/2010/sep/09/japan-china-fishing-boat-collision.
34. Hiroko Tabuchi, "Japan Scrambles Jets in Islands Dispute with China," *New York Times*, December 13, 2012, https://www.nytimes.com/2012/12/14/world/asia/japan-scrambles-jets-in-island-dispute-with-china.html.
35. Tara Copp, "Japan Surges New Weapons, Military Roles to Meet China's Rise," *Military Times*, January 15, 2019, https://www.militarytimes.com/news/2019/01/15/japan-surges-new-weapons-military-roles-to-meet-chinas-rise/.
36. Denny Roy, *Taiwan: A Political History* (Ithaca, NY: Cornell University Press, 2003), 9–10.
37. Qiang Zhai, "Taiwan Strait Crises (1954–55, 1958)," in *Encyclopedia of the Cold War*, ed. Ruud van Dijk (New York: Routledge, 2008); Richard C. Bush, *At Cross Purposes: U.S.-Taiwan Relations Since 1942* (Armonk, NY: M. E. Sharpe, 2004), 97–98.
38. Margaret MacMillan, *Nixon and Mao: The Week That Changed the World* (New York: Random House, 2007), ch. 19; Bush, *At Cross Purposes*, 125–36.
39. Bush, *At Cross Purposes*, 150–60.
40. Keoni Everington, "Taiwan Navy Ranked '10th Most Powerful in World' by Viral Video," *Taiwan News*, January 24, 2017, https://www.taiwannews.com.tw/en/news/3080978.
41. Jyh-peng Wang and Chih-lung Tan, "Taiwan's Submarine Saga," The Diplomat, May 11, 2015, https://thediplomat.com/2015/05/taiwans-submarine-saga/.
42. Drew Thompson, "Hope on the Horizon: Taiwan's Radical New Defense Concept," War on the Rocks, October 2, 2018, https://warontherocks.com/2018/10/hope-on-the-horizon-taiwans-radical-new-defense-concept/.
43. Nicole Jao, "'Mask Diplomacy' a Boost for Taiwan," *Foreign Policy*, April 13, 2020, https://foreignpolicy.com/2020/04/13/taiwan-coronavirus-pandemic-mask-soft-power-diplomacy/.
44. Eleanor Freund, "Freedom of Navigation in the South China Sea: A Practical Guide," Belfer Center for Science and International Affairs, June 2017, https://www.belfercenter.org/publication/freedom-navigation-south-china-sea-practical-guide.

45. Kris Osborn, "America Is Using Its Navy to Deter China Around Taiwan and the Spratly Islands," The National Interest, June 8, 2020, https://nationalinterest.org/blog/buzz/america-using-its-navy-deter-china-around-taiwan-and-spratly-islands-161771.
46. Jane Perlez, "Tribunal Rejects Beijing's Claims in South China Sea," *New York Times*, July 12, 2016, https://www.nytimes.com/2016/07/13/world/asia/south-china-sea-hague-ruling-philippines.html.
47. Eleanor Ross, "How and Why China Is Building Its New Territory in the South China Sea," *Newsweek*, March 29, 2017, https://www.newsweek.com/china-south-china-sea-islands-build-military-territory-expand-575161.
48. Jeffrey Becker, "China's Military Modernization: The Legacy of Admiral Wu Shengli," China Brief, August 18, 2015, https://jamestown.org/program/chinas-military-modernization-the-legacy-of-admiral-wu-shengli/.

10: America's Lake

1. Michael Green, *By More Than Providence: Grand Strategy and American Power in the Asia Pacific Since 1783*, 32.
2. Formed in 2004 by a merger of Naval Base Bremerton and Naval Base Bangor.
3. Evan Thomas, *John Paul Jones: Sailor, Hero, Father of the American Navy*, reprint edition (New York: Simon & Schuster, 2004), ch. 3 onward.
4. Only a handful of naval ships in the world can exceed 67 kph, and none of them are destroyers. A class of ships known as "interceptors" can approach those speeds, but these are mainly used by Special Forces for covert insertion and by coast guards for littoral defense and counter-smuggling patrols.
5. The DF-21D, a medium-range ballistic missile, became in 2012 the world's first anti-ship ballistic missile built to attack ships at sea. It can reach speeds of up to Mach 10. David Webb, "Dong Feng-21D (CSS-5)," Missile Defense Advocacy Alliance, January 2017, https://missiledefenseadvocacy.org/missile-threat-and-proliferation/missile-proliferation/china/dong-feng-21d-df-21d/.
6. Most recently, the US Navy has successfully tested ship-based interception of an ICBM—an even more difficult challenge.
7. "Dong Feng-26," Missile Defense Advocacy Alliance, June 4, 2018, https://missiledefenseadvocacy.org/missile-threat-and-proliferation/todays-missile-threat/china/df-26/.
8. Jordan Wilson, "China's Expanding Ability to Conduct Conventional Missile Strikes on Guam" (Washington, DC: U.S.-China Economic & Security Review Commission, May 10, 2016), 3, https://www.uscc.gov/sites/default/files/Research/Staff%20Report_China's%20Expanding%20Ability%20to%20Conduct%20Conventional%20Missile%20Strikes%20on%20Guam.pdf.
9. Green, *By More Than Providence*, 529.
10. Andrew F. Krepinevich, "Why AirSea Battle?," Center for Strategic and Budgetary Assessments, February 19, 2010, https://csbaonline.org/research/publications/why-airsea-battle; Bill Sweetman and Richard Fisher, "AirSea Battle Concept Is Focused on China," Aviation Week, April 8, 2011, http://www.aviationweek.com/aw/generic/story_generic.jsp?channel=awst&id=news/awst/2011/04/04

/AW_04_04_2011_p62-299099.xml; Richard Halloran, "AirSea Battle," *Air Force Magazine*, August 2010, http://www.airforce-magazine.com/MagazineArchive/Documents/2010/August%202010/0810battle.pdf.

11. For an overview, see Peter Grier, "The First Offset," *Air Force Magazine*, June 2016.
12. Green, *By More Than Providence*, 531.
13. Author confidential interview, Washington, DC, April 2020.
14. Author confidential interview, Indo-Pacific Command HQ, February 2020.
15. Halloran, "AirSea Battle."
16. Stephen Biddle and Ivan Oelrich, "Future Warfare in the Western Pacific: Chinese Antiaccess/Area Denial, U.S. AirSea Battle, and Command of the Commons in East Asia," *International Security* 41, no. 1 (July 2016): 7–48.
17. Green, *By More Than Providence*, 10–11.

11: To Conquer the Seas

1. Information Office of the State Council of the People's Republic of China, "China's Military Strategy," Xinhua, May 26, 2015.
2. On China's port investments in Djibouti, see Peter A. Dutton, Isaac B. Kardon, and Conor M. Kennedy, "Djibouti: China's First Overseas Strategic Strongpoint," *China Maritime Report* no. 6, April 2020, China Maritime Studies Institute, US Naval War College.
3. See Jude Blanchette and Jonathan Hillman, "Hidden Harbors: China's State-Backed Shipping Industry," CSIS Briefs: July 8, 2020.
4. Rush Doshi, "The New Imperative: Protecting Overseas Interests," Draft conference paper, US Naval War College, presented May 6–7, 2019.
5. Conor M. Kennedy, "Strategic Strong Points and Chinese Naval Strategy", *China Brief* vol. 19, no. 6. Also see Andrew S. Erickson, "Power vs. Distance: China's Global Maritime Interests and Investments in the Far Sea," in Ashley J. Tellis, Alison Szalwinshi, and Michael Wills, eds., *Strategic Asia 2019: China's Expanding Strategic Ambitions*. Seattle: The National Bureau of Asian Research, 2019.
6. Isaac B. Kardon, "Building a World-Class Military: Missions, Modernization, and Bases," Testimony, on a "World-Class" Military: Assessing China's Global Military Ambitions, US China Economic and Security Review Commission, June 20, 2019, https://www.uscc.gov/sites/default/files/Kardon_USCC%20Testimony_FINAL.pdf.
7. For more, see Peter Dutton, Isaac Kardon, and Conor Kennedy, "China Maritime Report No. 6: Djibouti: China's First Overseas Strategic Strongpoint," CMSI China Maritime Reports, April 1, 2020, https://digital-commons.usnwc.edu/cmsi-maritime-reports/6; Conor Kennedy, "Strategic Strong Points and Chinese Naval Strategy," *China Brief* 19, no. 6 (March 22, 2019), Jamestown Foundation, https://jamestown.org/program/strategic-strong-points-and-chinese-naval-strategy/.
8. As quoted in Kennedy, "Strategic Strong Points and Chinese Naval Strategy."
9. Andrew Scobell and Nathan Beauchamp-Mustafaga, "The Flag Lags but Follows: The PLA and China's Great Leap Outward," in *Chairman Xi Remakes the PLA: Assessing Chinese Military Reforms*, eds. Phillip C. Saunders et al. (Washington, DC: NDU Press, 2019), 171–202.

10. U.S. Defense Intelligence Agency, "China Military Power: Modernizing a Force to Fight and Win," 51.
11. Zachary Keck, "India Has Reason to Fear China's Submarines in the Indian Ocean," National Interest, September 21, 2019, https://nationalinterest.org/blog/buzz/india-has-reason-fear-chinas-submarines-indian-ocean-82301.
12. U.S. Defense Intelligence Agency, "China Military Power: Modernizing a Force to Fight and Win," 51.
13. "Trade (% of GDP)," World Bank Data Bank, World Bank.
14. "How Much Trade Transits the South China Sea?," *ChinaPower Project* (blog), August 2, 2017, https://chinapower.csis.org/much-trade-transits-south-china-sea/.
15. Terrence Kelly et al., *Employing Land-Based Anti-Ship Missiles in the Western Pacific* (Arlington, VA: RAND Corporation, 2013), https://www.rand.org/pubs/technical_reports/TR1321.html.
16. Jan van Tol et al., "AirSea Battle: A Point-of-Departure Operational Concept" (Arlington, VA: Center for Strategic and Budgetary Assessments, 2010), https://csbaonline.org/research/publications/airsea-battle-concept/publication/1.
17. Sean Mirski, "Stranglehold: The Context, Conduct and Consequences of an American Naval Blockade of China," *Journal of Strategic Studies* 36, no. 3 (June 1, 2013): 397.
18. Ibid.
19. Gabriel Collins, "A Maritime Oil Blockade Against China—Tactically Tempting but Strategically Flawed," *Naval War College Review* 71, no. 2 (Spring 2018): 51. See also Henry Farrell and Abraham Newman, "The Folly of Decoupling from China," *Foreign Affairs*, June 3, 2020.
20. Craig L. Symonds, *World War II at Sea: A Global History* (New York: Oxford University Press, 2018), 153, 172, 192–93.
21. J. D. Simkins, "'We'll See How Frightened America Is'—Chinese Admiral Says Sinking US Carriers Key to Dominating South China Sea," *Navy Times*, January 7, 2019, sec. Your Navy, https://www.navytimes.com/news/your-navy/2019/01/04/well-see-how-frightened-america-is-chinese-admiral-says-sinking-us-carriers-key-to-dominating-south-china-sea/.
22. Evan Braden Montgomery, "Reconsidering a Naval Blockade of China: A Response to Mirski," *Journal of Strategic Studies* 36, no. 4 (August 1, 2013): 621.
23. Ashley Townshend, Brendan Thomas-Noone, and Matilda Steward, "Averting Crisis: American Strategy, Military Spending and Collective Defence in the Indo-Pacific" (Sydney, Australia: The United States Studies Centre at the University of Sydney, August 2019), 28, https://www.ussc.edu.au/analysis/averting-crisis-american-strategy-military-spending-and-collective-defence-in-the-indo-pacific.
24. Brad Lendon, "Keeping Up with China: US Navy Orders $22 Billion Worth of Submarines," CNN, December 3, 2019, https://www.cnn.com/2019/12/03/politics/us-navy-submarines-contract-intl-hnk/index.html.
25. Minnie Chan, "A Submarine Arms Race Is Heating Up in the Indo-Pacific amid a 'Great Threat' from China," *Business Insider*, February 17, 2019, https://www.businessinsider.com/threat-from-china-driving-submarine-arms-race-in-indo-pacific-2019-2. It's a sentiment echoed by the commander of the Carderock research facility, who wrote in 2015 that "the demand for undersea capability

continues to grow rapidly as adversary anti-access/area denial (A2/AD) systems that can challenge the ability of our maritime air and surface forces to operate freely continue to proliferate. Next-generation nuclear submarines are being fielded by our potential competitors, and extremely quiet diesel submarines continue to proliferate globally, increasing the burden on our ASW forces and capabilities." See https://www.public.navy.mil/subfor/underseawarfaremagazine/issues/PDF/USW_Fall_2015.pdf.

26. Zhenhau Lu, "US and China's Underwater Rivalry Fuels Calls for Submarine Code of Conduct to Cut Risk of Accidents," *South China Morning Post*, March 21, 2019, https://www.scmp.com/news/china/military/article/3002736/us-and-chinas-underwater-rivalry-fuels-calls-submarine-code.
27. Ibid.
28. Tyler Headley, "Submarines in the South China Sea Conflict," The Diplomat, August 10, 2018, https://thediplomat.com/2018/08/submarines-in-the-south-china-sea-conflict/.
29. Lu, "US and China's Underwater Rivalry Fuels Calls for Submarine Code of Conduct to Cut Risk of Accidents."
30. Lendon, "Keeping Up with China."
31. US Defense Intelligence Agency, "China Military Power: Modernizing a Force to Fight and Win" (Washington, DC, 2019), 72.
32. Lendon, "Keeping Up with China."
33. H. I. Sutton, "China's Submarines May Be Catching Up with U.S. Navy," *Forbes*, November 24, 2019, https://www.forbes.com/sites/hisutton/2019/11/24/latest-chinese-submarines-catching-up-with-us-navy/.
34. For a recent discussion, see Sanjaya Swain, K. Trinath, and Tatavarti, "Non-Acoustic Detection of Moving Submerged Bodies in Oceans," *International Journal of Innovative Research and Development* 1, no. 10 (December 2012).
35. Author interview, Washington, DC, April 2020.
36. For an analysis of Russia's naval and political tactics in the Black Sea since its annexation of Crimea, see Yuri Lapaiev, "Russia's Black Sea Dominance Strategy—A Blend of Military and Civilian Assets," *Eurasia Daily Monitor* 16, no. 163 (November 19, 2019), https://jamestown.org/program/russias-black-sea-dominance-strategy-a-blend-of-military-and-civilian-assets/.
37. Thomas B. Modly, "How a Modernized Navy Will Compete with China and Russia," Brookings Institution, February 28, 2020, https://www.brookings.edu/events/how-a-modernized-navy-will-compete-with-china-and-russia/.
38. Garret Hinck, "Evaluating the Russian Threat to Undersea Cables," *Lawfare* (blog), March 5, 2018, https://www.lawfareblog.com/evaluating-russian-threat-undersea-cables.
39. David E. Sanger and Eric Schmitt, "Russian Ships Near Data Cables Are Too Close for U.S. Comfort," *New York Times*, October 25, 2015, https://www.nytimes.com/2015/10/26/world/europe/russian-presence-near-undersea-cables-concerns-us.html.
40. For his deeper study on the evolution of British naval power, see Paul Kennedy, *The Rise and Fall of British Naval Mastery* (New York: Humanity Books, 1976), ch. 12.
41. Rebecca Strating, "Should Australia Be Involved in the South China Sea?,"

La Trobe Asia Brief, no. 2 (July 2019), https://www.latrobe.edu.au/news/announcements/2019/should-australia-be-involved-in-the-south-china-sea.

42. Holmes and Yoshihara, *Chinese Naval Strategy in the 21st Century*, 32; Sheila A. Smith, *Japan Rearmed: The Politics of Military Power* (Cambridge, MA: Harvard University Press, 2019).
43. "Statistics on Scrambles Through Fiscal Year 2018" (Tokyo: Japanese Ministry of Defense—Joint Staff, April 12, 2019), https://www.mod.go.jp/js/Press/press2019/press_pdf/p20190412_06.pdf.
44. For a good summary of how China's military engages with Japan in the East China see Edmund Burke et al., *China's Military Activities in the East China Sea: Implications for Japan's Air Self-Defense Force* (Alexandria, VA: RAND, 2018).
45. Confidential author interviews, US Department of Defense, February 2020.
46. One of India's leading scholar-diplomats, Shyam Saran, described India as a "premature power": Shyam Saran, "Shyam Saran: Premature Power," *Business Standard India*, March 17, 2010, https://www.business-standard.com/article/opinion/shyam-saran-premature-power-110031700019_1.html.
47. Daniel Kliman et al., "Imbalance of Power," Center for a New American Security, https://www.cnas.org/publications/reports/imbalance-of-power, accessed May 15, 2020.
48. "Indian Navy Aiming at 200-Ship Fleet by 2027," *Economic Times*, July 14, 2018, https://economictimes.indiatimes.com/news/defence/indian-navy-aiming-at-200-ship-fleet-by-2027/articleshow/48072917.cms.
49. Manu Pubby, "Indian Navy Cutting down on Procurement Due to Budget Cuts," *Economic Times*, January 16, 2020, https://economictimes.indiatimes.com/news/defence/indian-navy-trims-acquisition-list-due-to-budget-cuts/articleshow/73281243.cms).
50. Jonathan Soble, "Japan Summons Chinese Envoy After Naval Ship Nears Disputed Islands," *New York Times*, June 9, 2016, https://www.nytimes.com/2016/06/10/world/asia/japan-china-navy-protest.html.
51. "Chinese Nuclear Attack Submarine That Raised Flag in International Waters May Have Been Testing Japan's Patrol Capabilities," *South China Morning Post*, January 15, 2018, https://www.scmp.com/news/asia/east-asia/article/2128284/chinese-nuclear-attack-submarine-spotted-near-disputed-diaoyu.
52. "Northern Fights: America and Britain Play Cold-War Games with Russia in the Arctic," *The Economist*, May 10, 2020, https://www.economist.com/europe/2020/05/10/america-and-britain-play-cold-war-games-with-russia-in-the-arctic.
53. David H. Berger, "Commandant's Planning Guidance," US Marine Corps, July 16, 2019, https://www.hqmc.marines.mil/Portals/142/Docs/%2038th%20Commandant%27s%20Planning%20Guidance_2019.pdf?ver=2019-07-16-200152-700.
54. Mike Gallagher, "To Deter China, the Naval Services Must Integrate," War on the Rocks, February 4, 2020, https://warontherocks.com/2020/02/to-deter-china-the-naval-services-must-integrate/.

NOTES

12: The Salt of the Oceans

1. Richard Rhodes, *Energy: A Human History* (New York: Simon & Schuster, 2018), 259.
2. Daniel Yergin, *The Quest: Energy, Security, and the Remaking of the Modern World* (New York: Penguin Books, 2011).
3. "The Energy Industry in Houston," Greater Houston Partnership, https://www.houston.org/why-houston/industries/energy, accessed March 23, 2021.
4. Jordan Blum, "Houston Leads the Way as Texas Ships 80 Percent of Nation's Crude Exports," *Houston Chronicle*, March 18, 2019, https://www.chron.com/busines/energy/article/Houston-leads-as-Texas-ships-out-80-of-nation-s-13696641.php.
5. Matt Egan, "Oil Boom: Texas Achieves Major Export Landmark," CNN Money, August 23, 2018, https://money.cnn.com/2018/08/23/investing/oil-exports-texas-houston/index.html.
6. For a detailed account of the political machinations, in New Orleans and in Washington, DC, required to open up the Gulf to energy exploration, see in particular Tyler Priest, "Extraction Not Creation: The History of Offshore Petroleum in the Gulf of Mexico," *Enterprise & Society* 8, no. 2 (2007): 227–67.
7. In a later interview, Gordon Lill, who directed Project Mohole, was frank about using the Russian competition as a rationale for the project: Gordon Lill, interview by David van Keuren, March 20, 1995, Santa Barbara, CA, transcript, http://scilib.ucsd.edu/sio/oral/Lill.pdf.
8. Clyde W. Burleson, *Deep Challenge!: The True Epic Story of Our Quest for Energy Beneath the Sea* (Houston: Gulf Publishing, 1999).
9. "Project No Hole?" *Newsweek*, June 10, 1963.
10. For more on the mismanagement of the project, see D. S. Greenberg, "Mohole: The Project That Went Awry (III)," *Science* 143, no. 3604 (January 24, 1964): 334–37.
11. "About the Deep Sea Drilling Project," Deep Sea Drilling Project Reports and Publications, http://deepseadrilling.org/about.htm, accessed April 17, 2021.
12. "Project Azorian: The Story of the *Hughes Glomar Explorer*," *Studies in Intelligence*, Fall 1985, https://nsarchive2.gwu.edu/nukevault/ebb305/doc01.pdf.
13. Norman Polmar and Michael White, "Top Secret: Project Azorian," *Invention and Technology*, Winter 2011, https://www.inventionandtech.com/content/top-secret-project-azorian.
14. Scott L. Montgomery and Dwight "Clint" Moore, "Subsalt Play, Gulf of Mexico: A Review," *AAPG Bulletin*, 81, no. 6 (June 1997): 871–896
15. See Dev George, "Seismic Exploration," https://www.offshore-mag.com/regional-reports/article/16760640/seismic-exploration-taking-another-look-at-bright-spots. For more on the development of advanced exploration and drilling techniques, see inter alia Clyde W. Burleson, *Deep Challenge!: Our Quest for Energy Beneath the Sea* (Ukraine: Elsevier Science, 1998).
16. Burleson, *Deep Challenge!*, 47.
17. Priest, "Extraction Not Creation," 235. Priest documents that "a unique geology created opportunities for a wide range of companies and oil hunters and for an even greater number of subsidiary businesses. The Gulf's gradually sloping,

deltaic plain permitted experimentation with building free-standing structures in the open water. The sedimentary layers of the Gulf's ocean bed are relatively soft, making them easier to drill than hard-rock layers in other regions, onshore or offshore. The water is shallow for many miles, and the conditions are mild, except for hurricanes." Priest also documents the extensive corruption and pork barrel politics that went into opening up the coastal waters of Louisiana for drilling.

18. "The Offshore Petroleum Industry in the Gulf of Mexico: A Continuum of Activities" (Washington, DC: Bureau of Ocean Energy Management, US Department of the Interior, 2008), 2, https://www.boem.gov/sites/default/files/boem-education/BOEM-Education-Images-and-Resources/TheOffshorePetroleumIndustryOrganizationalScheme.pdf.
19. B. A. Wells and K. L. Wells, "Secret History of Drill Ship Glomar Explorer," American Oil & Gas Historical Society, February 8, 2020, https://aoghs.org/oil-almanac/secret-offshore-history-of-the-glomar-explorer/.
20. "Gulf of Mexico Fact Sheet," US Energy Information Administration, https://www.eia.gov/special/gulf_of_mexico/, accessed April 18, 2021.
21. Presentation by David Victor, "National Oil Companies and the World Oil Market," University of California at San Diego, November 15, 2011.
22. Some of the story of the Tengiz blowout can be found in "Kazakhstan: Kashagan—Mad, Bad, and Dangerous," *Petroleum Economist*, August 2002.
23. Although Brazil's first democratic constitution, in 1988, actually prohibited contracting with international firms, it protected a preexisting exception for Petrobras; and then a constitutional amendment in 1995 removed restrictions on foreign capital and established competitive markets in sectors previously governed by a monopoly. Petrobras retained monopoly ownership of the minerals found from drilling, but was able fully to partner with foreign companies in the process of discovery and extraction.
24. Yergin, *The Quest*, 247.
25. "Lula Oil Field Development," NS Energy, https://www.nsenergybusiness.com/projects/lula-oil-field-development/, accessed April 18, 2021.
26. Yergin, *The Quest*, 215.
27. "Contested Areas of South China Sea Likely Have Few Conventional Oil and Gas Resources," US Energy Information Administration, April 3, 2013, https://www.eia.gov/todayinenergy/detail.Php?id=10651.
28. Ibid.
29. Tim Daiss, "South China Sea Energy Politics Heat Up," OilPrice.com, March 2, 2019, https://oilprice.com/Geopolitics/Asia/South-China-Sea-Energy-Politics-Heat-Up.html.
30. "Update: China Risks Flare-Up Over Malaysian, Vietnamese Gas Resources," Asia Maritime Transparency Initiative (blog), December 13, 2019, https://amti.csis.org/china-risks-flare-up-over-malaysian-vietnamese-gas-resources/.
31. Ralph Jennings, "Beijing Preps 10-Story Oil Drilling Platform for South China Sea Despite Wary Vietnam," *Voice of America*, September 30, 2019, https://www.voanews.com/east-asia-pacific/beijing-preps-10-story-oil-drilling-platform-south-china-sea-despite-wary-vietnam.
32. "East China Sea," US Energy Information Administration, September 17, 2014, https://www.eia.gov/international/analysis/regions-of-interest/East_China_Sea.

33. "Update: Beijing Keeps Busy in East China Sea Oil and Gas Fields," Asia Maritime Transparency Initiative (blog), August 23, 2018, https://amti.csis.org/busy-summer-beijings-rigs/.
34. "Circum-Arctic Resource Appraisal: Estimates of Undiscovered Oil and Gas North of the Arctic Circle" (Menlo Park, CA: US Geological Survey, 2008), 4, https://pubs.usgs.gov/fs/2008/3049/fs2008-3049.pdf.
35. C. J. Chivers, "Russians Plant Flag on the Arctic Seabed," *New York Times*, August 3, 2007, https://www.nytimes.com/2007/08/03/world/europe/03arctic.html.
36. Louie Palu, "A Thawing Arctic Is Heating up a New Cold War," *National Geographic*, August 19, 2019, https://www.nationalgeographic.com/adventure/2019/08/how-climate-change-is-setting-the-stage-for-the-new-arctic-cold-war-feature/.
37. The Russian national accused in the case, Valery Mitko, was at the time the president of the Arctic Academy of Sciences in St. Petersburg. Mitko's lawyer Ivan Pavlov denied the charges leveled against him. See https://team29.org/story/arkticheskaya-doktrina-professora-mitko/.
38. "Natural Gas Explained: Liquefied Natural Gas," US Energy Information Administration, June 4, 2019, https://www.eia.gov/energyexplained/natural-gas/liquefied-natural-gas.php.
39. "BP Statistical Review of World Energy" (BP, 2019), 38, https://www.bp.com/content/dam/bp/business-sites/en/global/corporate/pdfs/energy-economics/statistical-review/bp-stats-review-2019-full-report.pdf.
40. "China Overtakes Japan as World's Top Natural Gas Importer," Reuters, November 12, 2018, https://www.reuters.com/article/china-japan-lng-idUSL4N1XN3LO.
41. "BP Statistical Review of World Energy."
42. "World Trade Report 2013," 53; Andrew G. Spyrou, *From T-2 to Supertanker: Development of the Oil Tanker, 1940–2000*, Revised (Bloomington, IN: iUniverse, 2011).
43. Mostert, *Supership*, 15.
44. "Offshore Energy Outlook," 15.
45. "Assessment of Undiscovered Oil and Gas Resources of the Nation's Outer Continental Shelf, 2016a," (Washington, DC: Bureau of Ocean Energy Management, US Department of the Interior, 2016), https://www.boem.gov/sites/default/files/documents/oil-gas-energy/resource-evaluation/resource-assessment/2016a.pdf.
46. "BP Statistical Review of World Energy," 38.
47. A concern well documented in Daniel Yergin, *The New Map: Energy, Climate, and the Clash of Nations* (New York: Penguin Press, 2020).
48. "Annual Energy Outlook 2011" (Washington, DC: US Energy Information Administration, April 2011), https://www.eia.gov/outlooks/aeo/pdf/0383(2011).pdf.
49. "World Energy Outlook 2019" (Paris: International Energy Agency, 2019), 166.
50. Ibid., 167.
51. Ibid.
52. Ibid., 130.
53. "International Energy Outlook 2019" (Washington, DC: U.S. Energy Information Administration, September 24, 2019), 42.
54. International Energy Agency, 165.

NOTES

13: Oceanography and Power

1. Anthony Brandt, *The Man Who Ate His Boots: The Tragic History of the Search for the Northwest Passage* (New York: Anchor, 2011); Doug Macdougall, *Endless Novelties of Extraordinary Interest: The Voyage of H.M.S.* Challenger *and the Birth of Modern Oceanography*, illustrated ed. (New Haven, CT: Yale University Press, 2019).
2. William Ragan Stanton, *The Great United States Exploring Expedition of 1838–1843* (Berkeley: University of California Press, 1975).
3. Nathaniel Philbrick, *Sea of Glory: America's Voyage of Discovery: The U.S. Exploring Expedition, 1838–1842* (New York: Viking, 2003); Simon Winchester, *Atlantic: Great Sea Battles, Heroic Discoveries, Titanic Storms, and a Vast Ocean of a Million Stories* (New York: Harper, 2010).
4. Sidney Hart, "Titian Ramsay Peale and the Great U.S. South Seas Exploring Expedition," Smithsonian Libraries, https://www.sil.si.edu/DigitalCollections/usexex/learn/Hart.htm.
5. Neil Smith, *American Empire: Roosevelt's Geographer and the Prelude to Globalization* (Berkeley: University of California Press, 2013).
6. See Harvey Sapolsky, *Science and the Navy: The History of the Office of Naval Research* (Princeton, NJ: Princeton University Press, 1990).
7. David K. van Keuren, "An Interview with Dr. Gordon Lill," March 20, 1995, Naval Research Laboratory, Scripps Institution of Oceanography History, p. 8, available at http://scilib.ucsd.edu/sio/oral/Lill.pdf.
8. Walter Munk, "The Sound of Climate Change," *Tellus A* 63, no. 2 (March 2011).
9. For example, see David M. Hart and David G. Victor, "Scientific Elites and the Making of US Policy for Climate Change Research, 1957–74," *Social Studies of Science* 23, no. 4 (November 1993).
10. Zoom interviews, May and June 2020, Washington, DC, and La Jolla, CA.
11. Roger Revelle and Hans E. Suess, "Carbon Dioxide Exchange Between Atmosphere and Ocean and the Question of an Increase of Atmospheric CO_2 During the Past Decades," *Tellus* 9, no. 1 (February 1957): 18–27.
12. Ibid., 18.
13. Ibid., 19.
14. Ibid., 18.
15. "Restoring the Quality of Our Environment: Report of the Environmental Pollution Panel, President's Science Advisory Committee," The White House, November 1965, 126, http://www.climatefiles.com/climate-change-evidence/presidents-report-atmospher-carbon-dioxide/.
16. Margaret Thatcher, Speech at 2nd World Climate Conference, Geneva, Switzerland, November 6, 1990, https://www.margaretthatcher.org/document/108237.
17. Hearing before the Committee on Energy and Natural Resources, United States Senate, 100th Congress, First Session on the Greenhouse Effect and Global Climate Change, part 2, June 23, 1988, available at https://babel.hathitrust.org/cgi/pt?id=uc1.b5127807&view=1up&seq=1. Hansen's testimony begins on page 39.
18. Growth between 2010 and 2012. Zhu Liu, "China's Carbon Emissions Report

2015" (Cambridge, MA: Harvard Kennedy School, Belfer Center for Science and International Affairs, Energy Technology Innovation Policy, May 2015), 2.
19. Author interview, David Victor, via Zoom, November 2020.
20. Andrew C. Revkin, "Google Earth Fills Its Watery Gaps," *New York Times*, February 2, 2009, https://www.nytimes.com/2009/02/03/science/earth/03oceans.html.
21. Sylvia Earle, "Introduction," in Rachel Carson, *The Sea Around Us*, revised ed. (Oxford, UK: Oxford University Press, 2018).
22. Rachel Carson, *The Sea Around Us* (Oxford, UK: Oxford University Press, 1950/1979), 17.
23. Ibid., 19.
24. Kathy A. Svitil, "The 50 Most Important Women in Science," *Discover*, November 1, 2002, http://discovermagazine.com/2002/nov/feat50/.
25. For more information, see "Argo Center," National Oceanic and Atmospheric Administration, Atlantic Oceanographic and Meteorological Laboratory, Physical Oceanography Division (PhOD), available at https://www.aoml.noaa.gov/phod/argo/, accessed August 13, 2020.
26. This was the key finding of the IPCC's 2019 "Special Report on the Oceans," 9.
27. David Alexander, "'Great Green Fleet' Using Biofuels Deployed by U.S. Navy," Reuters, January 21, 2016, https://www.reuters.com/article/us-usa-defense-greenfleet-idUSKCN0UY2U4; Meghann Myers, "Great Green Fleet Readies to Sail in January," *Navy Times*, August 7, 2017, https://www.navytimes.com/news/your-navy/2015/12/14/great-green-fleet-readies-to-sail-in-january/.
28. Bryan Bender, "Chief of US Pacific Forces Calls Climate Biggest Worry," *Boston Globe*, March 9, 2013.
29. "Effects of a Changing Climate to the Department of Defense" (Washington, DC: Office of the Under Secretary of Defense for Aquisition and Sustainment, January 2019).

14: Hot Waters Rising

1. Thant Myint-U, *Where China Meets India: Burma and the New Crossroads of Asia* (New York: Farrar, Straus and Giroux, 2011).
2. Brian Fagan, *The Attacking Ocean: The Past, Present, and Future of Rising Sea Levels* (New York: Bloomsbury Press, 2013), 116–17.
3. "Linking Snow Cover and the Monsoon," *Earth Observatory*, NASA, February 21, 2006, https://earthobservatory.nasa.gov/features/Monsoon/monsoon4.php, accessed August 13, 2020.
4. Science Mission Directorate National Aeronautics and Space Administration, "Climate Variability," NASA, March 2, 2020, https://science.nasa.gov/earth-science/oceanography/ocean-earth-system/climate-variability.
5. For example, see Kim Cobb et al., "Highly Variable El Niño–Southern Oscillation Throughout the Holocene," *Science* 339, no. 6115 (January 4, 2013); Wenju Cai et al., "Increasing Frequency of Extreme El Nino Events Due to Greenhouse Warming," *Nature Climate Change* 4 (2014): 111–16.
6. S. Soloman et al., eds., *Climate Change 2007: The Physical Science Basis:*

Contribution of Working Group I to the Fourth Assessment Report of the IPCC (New York: Cambridge University Press, 2007), 16.

7. For detailed modeling of this, see Marshall Burke and Kyle Emerick, "Adaptation to Climate Change: Evidence from US Agriculture," *American Economic Journal: Economic Policy* 8, no. 3 (August 2016): 106–40.
8. IPCC, "Special Report on the Ocean and Cryosphere in a Changing Climate" (Geneva: IPCC, November 2019), 10, https://www.ipcc.ch/srocc/.
9. J.-P. Gattuso et al., "Contrasting Futures for Ocean and Society from Different Anthropogenic CO2 Emissions Scenarios," *Science* 349, no. 6243 (July 3, 2015).
10. IPCC, "IPCC Special Report on the Ocean and Cryosphere in a Changing Climate," 9.
11. Wallace S. Broecker, "Glaciers That Speak in Tongues and Other Tales of Global Warming," *Natural History* 110, no. 8 (2001).
12. IPCC, "IPCC Special Report on the Ocean and Cryosphere in a Changing Climate," 10.
13. Kasha Patel, "Antarctica Melts Under Its Hottest Days on Record," Earth Observatory, NASA, February 21, 2020, https://earthobservatory.nasa.gov/images/146322/antarctica-melts-under-its-hottest-days-on-record, accessed August 13, 2020.
14. Neil Mostert, *Supership* (New York: Knopf, 1974), 211.
15. IPCC, "IPCC Special Report on the Ocean and Cryosphere in a Changing Climate," 205.
16. Arctic Monitoring and Assessment Programme, "Arctic Climate Issues 2011: Changes in Arctic Snow, Water, Ice, and Permafrost" (Oslo, Norway, 2012), available at https://www.amap.no/documents/download/2267/inline.
17. "Facts," Global Climate Change—Vital Signs of the Planet, NASA, August 4, 2020, https://climate.nasa.gov/vital-signs/arctic-sea-ice/, accessed August 13, 2020.
18. World Ocean Review, *World Ocean Review 6: The Arctic and Antarctic—Extreme, Climatically Crucial and in Crisis* (Hamburg, Germany: Maribus, 2019), 173.
19. IPCC, "IPCC Special Report on the Ocean and Cryosphere in a Changing Climate," 352.
20. Ibid., 22.
21. Ibid., 12.
22. Ibid., 513.
23. IPCC, "IPCC Special Report on the Ocean and Cryosphere in a Changing Climate," 5.
24. Ibid., 10.
25. O. Hoegh-Guldberg et al., "The Human Imperative of Stabilizing Global Climate Change at 1.5°C," *Science* 365, no. 6459 (September 20, 2019).
26. Juli Trtanji and Lesley Jantarasami et al., "Climate Impacts on Water-Related Illness," in Allison Crimmins et al., *The Impacts of Climate Change on Human Health in the United States: A Scientific Assessment* (Washington, DC: U.S. Global Change Research Program, 2016).
27. Charles B. Beard and Rebecca J. Eisen et al., "Vector-Borne Diseases," in Allison Crimmins et al., *The Impacts of Climate Change on Human Health in the United States.*
28. IPCC, "IPCC Special Report on the Ocean and Cryosphere in a Changing Climate," 13.

29. Ibid., 17.
30. "Climate Change Indicators in the United States, 2016" (Washington, DC: U.S. Environmental Protection Agency, 2016), 35.
31. Ibid., 36–37.
32. Ibid., 36.
33. Ibid.
34. IPCC, "IPCC Special Report on the Ocean and Cryosphere in a Changing Climate," 20.

Conclusion

1. "Germany is taking on more responsibility for the Arctic," German Federal Foreign Office, August 21, 2019, https://www.auswaertiges-amt.de/en/aussenpolitik/themen/internatrecht/einzelfragen/arctic-guidelines/2240000.
2. A good account of this framing can be found in Geoffrey Gresh, "The New Great Game at Sea," War on the Rocks, December 8, 2020, https://warontherocks.com/2020/12/the-new-great-game-at-sea/.
3. Manu Pubby, "India and UK in Final Stages of Signing Defence Logistics Pact, Will Extend Reach," *Economic Times*, October 9, 2020, https://economictimes.indiatimes.com/news/defence/seventh-logistics-pact-to-extend-naval-reach-from-japan-to-bahrain/articleshow/78562338.cms.
4. "China Reacts Cautiously to Indian Navy's New Air Base in Andaman and Nicobar Islands," *Economic Times*, January 25, 2019, https://economictimes.indiatimes.com/news/defence/china-reacts-cautiously-to-indian-navys-new-air-base-in-andaman-and-nicobar-islands/articleshow/67691969.cms?from=mdr.
5. Bruce Jones and Samir Saran, "An 'India Exception' and India-U.S. Partnership on Climate Change," *Planet Policy* (blog), January 12, 2015, https://www.brookings.edu/blog/planetpolicy/2015/01/12/an-india-exception-and-india-u-s-partnership-on-climate-change/.
6. Zhitao Xu et al., "Impacts of Covid-19 on Global Supply Chains: Facts and Perspectives," in *IEEE Engineering Management Review* 48, no. 3, 153–66.
7. For a similar argument, see James Goldgeier and Lindsey Ford, "Retooling America's Alliances to Manage the China Challenge," Brookings Blueprint Series, January 25, 2021, https://www.brookings.edu/research/retooling-americas-alliances-to-manage-the-china-challenge/.

Bibliography

Abulafia, David. *The Boundless Sea: A Human History of the Oceans*. New York: Oxford University Press, 2019.

Acemoglu, Daron, David Autor, David Dorn, Gordon H. Hanson, and Brendan Price. "Import Competition and the Great US Employment Sag of the 2000s." *Journal of Labor Economics* 34, no. S1 (January 2016): S141–98.

"ADP 3-0: Operations." Washington, DC: U.S. Army, October 2017. https://fas.org/irp/doddir/army/adp3-0.pdf.

Allain, Jean. *International Law in the Middle East: Closer to Power Than Justice*. London: Routledge, 2017.

Alpers, Edward A. *The Indian Ocean in World History*. New Oxford World History. New York: Oxford University Press, 2013.

Andrade, Tonio, and Xing Hang, eds. *Sea Rovers, Silver, and Samurai: Maritime East Asia in Global History, 1550–1700*. Honolulu: University of Hawai'i Press, 2019.

Andrews, Charles M. "Anglo-French Commercial Rivalry, 1700–1750: The Western Phase, I." *The American Historical Review* 20, no. 3 (1915): 539–56.

"Annual Energy Outlook 2011." Washington, DC: US Energy Information Administration, April 2011. https://www.eia.gov/outlooks/aeo/pdf/0383(2011).pdf.

"A.P. Møller - Mærsk A/S Q2 2019 Report." Copenhagen: Maersk, June 2019. https://investor.maersk.com/static-files/5b3b9863-5220-4645-8021-1cecb7bad26f.

"Assessment of Undiscovered Oil and Gas Resources of the Nation's Outer Continental Shelf, 2016a." Washington, DC: Bureau of Ocean Energy Management, US Department of the Interior, 2016. https://www.boem.gov/sites/default/files/documents/oil-gas-energy/resource-evaluation/resource-assessment/2016a.pdf.

Attman, Artur. "The Russian Market in World Trade, 1500–1860." *Scandinavian Economic History Review* 29, no. 3 (September 1981): 177–202.

Auber, Peter. *China: An Outline of Its Government, Laws, and Policy, and of the British and Foreign Embassies to, and Intercourse with, That Empire*. London: Parbury, Allen, 1834.

Avango, Dag, Per Högselius, and David Nilsson. "Swedish Explorers, In-Situ Knowledge, and Resource-Based Business in the Age of Empire." *Scandinavian Journal of History* 43, no. 3 (May 27, 2018): 324–47.

Bahadur, Jay. *The Pirates of Somalia: Inside Their Hidden World*. New York: Pantheon Books, 2011.

Bain, Kenneth Ray. *The March to Zion: United States Policy and the Founding of Israel*. College Station: Texas A&M University Press, 1980.

Bairoch, Paul. "Europe's Gross National Product: 1800–1975." *Journal of European Economic History* 5, no. 2 (Fall 1976): 273–340.

BIBLIOGRAPHY

Baker, Jim. *Crossroads: A Popular History of Malaysia & Singapore*. 2nd ed. Singapore: Marshall Cavendish Editions, 2008.

Ballantyne, Iain. *The Deadly Deep: The Definitive History of Submarine Warfare*. New York: Pegasus Books, 2018.

Bateman, Sam, and Ralf Emmers. "Dangerous Ground: A Geopolitical Overview of the South China Sea." In *Security and International Politics in the South China Sea*, 7–25. London: Routledge, 2008.

Beckert, Sven. *Empire of Cotton: A Global History*. First edition. New York: Alfred A. Knopf, 2014.

Beer, Andrew, and Terry L. Clower. *Globalization, Planning and Local Economic Development*. Routledge, 2019.

Berger, David H. "Commandant's Planning Guidance." US Marine Corps, July 16, 2019. https://www.hqmc.marines.mil/Portals/142/Docs/%2038th%20Commandant%27s%20Planning%20Guidance_2019.pdf?ver=2019-07-16-200152-700.

Bernstein, William J. *A Splendid Exchange: How Trade Shaped the World*. New York: Atlantic Monthly Press, 2008.

Berra, John, and Wei Ju, eds. *World Film Locations: Shanghai*. Bristol, United Kingdom: Intellect Books, 2014.

Betts, Raymond F. *Tricouleur: The French Overseas Empire*. London: Gordon & Cremonesi, 1978.

Biddle, Stephen, and Ivan Oelrich. "Future Warfare in the Western Pacific: Chinese Antiaccess/Area Denial, U.S. AirSea Battle, and Command of the Commons in East Asia." *International Security* 41, no. 1 (July 2016): 7–48.

Bitzinger, Richard, and Michael Raska. "The AirSea Battle Debate and the Future of Conflict in East Asia." Singapore: S. Rajaratnam School of International Studies, 2013. https://www.rsis.edu.sg/rsis-publication/idss/221-the-airsea-battle-debate-and-t/.

Blanchette, Jude, Jonathan E. Hillman, Maesea McCalpin, and Mingda Qiu. "Hidden Harbors: China's State-Backed Shipping Industry." Washington, DC: Center for Strategic and International Studies, July 2020.

Boot, Max. *War Made New: Technology, Warfare, and the Course of History, 1500 to Today*. New York: Gotham Books, 2006.

Bowden, Anna, Kaija Hurlburt, Eamon Aloyo, Charles Marts, and Andrew Lee. "The Economic Cost of Maritime Piracy." One Earth Future Working Paper. Broomfield, CO: Oceans Beyond Piracy, December 2010. https://oceansbeyondpiracy.org/sites/default/files/attachments/The%20Economic%20Cost%20of%20Piracy%20Full%20Report.pdf.

Bowring, Philip. *Empire of the Winds: The Global Role of Asia's Great Archipelago*. New York: I.B. Tauris, 2019.

"BP Statistical Review of World Energy." BP, 2019. https://www.bp.com/content/dam/bp/business-sites/en/global/corporate/pdfs/energy-economics/statistical-review/bp-stats-review-2019-full-report.pdf.

Brandt, Anthony. *The Man Who Ate His Boots: The Tragic History of the Search for the Northwest Passage*. New York: Alfred A. Knopf, 2010.

Broecker, Wally. *The Great Ocean Conveyor: Discovering the Trigger for Abrupt Climate Change*. Princeton: Princeton University Press, 2010.

BIBLIOGRAPHY

Brook, Daniel. *A History of Future Cities*. New York: W. W. Norton, 2013.

———. "Head of the Dragon: The Rise of New Shanghai." *Places Journal*, February 18, 2013.

Burbach, David T., Marc Devore, Harvey M. Sapolsky, and Stephen Van Evera. "Weighing the US Navy." *Defense Analysis* 17, no. 3 (December 1, 2001): 259–65.

Burke, Edmund J., Timothy R. Heath, Jeffrey W. Hornung, Logan Ma, Lyle J. Morris, and Michael S. Chase. "China's Military Activities in the East China Sea: Implications for Japan's Air Self-Defense Force." Santa Monica, CA: RAND Corporation, December 3, 2018. https://www.rand.org/pubs/research_reports/RR2574.html.

Burleson, Clyde W. *Deep Challenge! The True Epic Story of Our Quest for Energy Beneath the Sea*. Houston, TX: Gulf Professional Publishing, 1998.

Bush, Richard C. *At Cross Purposes: U.S.-Taiwan Relations since 1942*. Armonk, NY: M.E. Sharpe, 2004.

Cai, Wenju, Simon Borlace, Matthieu Lengaigne, Peter van Rensch, Mat Collins, Gabriel Vecchi, Axel Timmermann et al. "Increasing Frequency of Extreme El Niño Events Due to Greenhouse Warming." *Nature Climate Change* 4, no. 2 (February 2014): 111–16.

Carson, Rachel. *The Sea around Us*. New York: Oxford University Press, 1979.

Cartwright, Mark. "Trade in Medieval Europe." In *World History Encyclopedia*, January 8, 2019. https://www.ancient.eu/article/1301/trade-in-medieval-europe/.

Charlwood, David. *Suez Crisis 1956: End of Empire and the Reshaping of the Middle East*. Barnsley, UK: Pen & Sword Military, 2019.

Chaudhuri, K.N. *Trade and Civilization in the Indian Ocean: An Economic History from the Rise of Islam to 1750*. New York: Cambridge University Press, 1985.

Chen, Song-Chuan. *Merchants of War and Peace: British Knowledge of China in the Making of the Opium War*. Hong Kong: Hong Kong University Press, 2017.

Cheng, Linsun. "Globalization and Shanghai Model: A Retrospective and Prospective Analysis." *Journal of International and Global Studies* 4, no. 1 (November 1, 2012): 59–81.

"China Military Power: Modernizing a Force to Fight and Win." Washington, DC: Defense Intelligence Agency, 2019. https://www.dia.mil/Portals/27/Documents/News/Military%20Power%20Publications/China_Military_Power_FINAL_5MB_20190103.pdf.

Christensen, C.S. "The History of the Russian Orthodox Church in Denmark (1741–2016) Seen in a Danish-Russian Historical Perspective." *Studia Humanitatis*, no. 2 (2017): 470–89.

Chung, Patrick. "From Korea to Vietnam: Local Labor, Multinational Capital, and the Evolution of US Military Logistics, 1950–97." *Radical History Review* 2019, no. 133 (January 1, 2019): 31–55. https://doi.org/10.1215/01636545-7160053.

"Circum-Arctic Resource Appraisal: Estimates of Undiscovered Oil and Gas North of the Arctic Circle." USGS Fact Sheet. Menlo Park, CA: US Geological Survey, 2008.

Clark, Christopher M. *The Sleepwalkers: How Europe Went to War in 1914*. London: Allen Lane, 2012.

Clements, Jonathan. *A Brief History of the Vikings: The Last Pagans or the First Modern Europeans?* New York: Carroll & Graf Publishers, 2005.

BIBLIOGRAPHY

Climate Change 2007: The Physical Science Basis: Contribution of Working Group I to the Fourth Assessment Report of the Intergovernmental Panel on Climate Change. Cambridge: Cambridge University Press, 2007.

"Climate Change Indicators in the United States, 2016." Washington, DC: U.S. Environmental Protection Agency, 2016. https://www.epa.gov/sites/production/files/2016-08/documents/climate_indicators_2016.pdf.

Cobb, Kim M., Niko Westphal, Hussein R. Sayani, Jordan T. Watson, Emanuele Di Lorenzo, H. Cheng, R. L. Edwards, and Christopher D. Charles. "Highly Variable El Niño–Southern Oscillation Throughout the Holocene." *Science* 339, no. 6115 (January 4, 2013): 67–70.

Coll, Steve. *Private Empire: ExxonMobil and American Power.* New York: Penguin Books, 2012.

Collier, Paul. *The Plundered Planet: Why We Must—and How We Can—Manage Nature for Global Prosperity.* Oxford: Oxford University Press, 2010.

Conn, Stetson, Rose C. Engelman, and Byron Fairchild. *Guarding the United States and Its Outposts.* United States Army in World War II. Washington, DC: U.S. Government Printing Office, 1964. https://history.army.mil/books/wwii/Guard-US/.

Crimmins, Allison, J. Balbus, J. L. Gamble, and C. B. Beard, eds. *The Impacts of Climate Change on Human Health in the United States: A Scientific Assessment.* Washington, DC: United States Global Change Research Program, 2016. https://health2016.globalchange.gov/.

Crowe, Sibyl. *Our Ablest Public Servant: Sir Eyre Crowe, 1864–1925.* Braunton, UK: Merlin Books, 1993.

Crowley, Roger. *Conquerors: How Portugal Forged the First Global Empire.* New York: Random House, 2015.

Dalrymple, William. *The Anarchy: The Relentless Rise of the East India Company.* London: Bloomsbury, 2019.

———. *White Mughals: Love and Betrayal in Eighteenth-Century India.* New York: Penguin Press, 2004.

Davis, Lance E., and Stanley L. Engerman. *Naval Blockades in Peace and War: An Economic History Since 1750.* Cambridge: Cambridge University Press, 2006.

Denison, Edward, and Guang Yu Ren. *Building Shanghai: The Story of China's Gateway.* Hoboken, NJ: John Wiley & Sons, 2013.

Dicks, Lynn, Rosamunde Almond, Anna McIvor, and Arctic Monitoring and Assessment Programme. *Arctic Climate Issues 2011: Changes in Arctic Snow, Water, Ice and Permafrost.* Oslo: Arctic Monitoring and Assessment Programme, 2012. http://www.deslibris.ca/ID/239935.

Dixon, Chris. *Ghost Wave: The Discovery of Cortes Bank and the Biggest Wave on Earth.* San Francisco: Chronicle Books, 2011.

Dolin, Eric Jay. *When America First Met China: An Exotic History of Tea, Drugs, and Money in the Age of Sail.* 1st ed. New York: Liveright PubCorp, 2012.

Dollar, David. "Understanding China's Belt and Road Infrastructure Projects in Africa." Washington, DC: Brookings Institution, September 2019. https://www.brookings.edu/wp-content/uploads/2019/09/FP_20190930_china_bri_dollar.pdf.

Donner, Michel, and Cornelis Kruk. "Supply Chain Security Guide." Washington, DC: World Bank, January 2009.

BIBLIOGRAPHY

Doran, Michael Scott. *Ike's Gamble: America's Rise to Dominance in the Middle East.* New York: Free Press, 2016.

Dreyer, Edward L. *Zheng He: China and the Oceans in the Early Ming Dynasty, 1405–1433.* The Library of World Biography. New York: Pearson Longman, 2010.

Dunn, Ross E. *The Adventures of Ibn Battuta: A Muslim Traveler of the Fourteenth Century.* Berkeley: University of California Press, 2012.

Dutton, Peter A., Isaac B. Kardon, and Conor M. Kennedy. "China Maritime Report No. 6: Djibouti: China's First Overseas Strategic Strongpoint." CMSI China Maritime Reports. Newport, RI: US Naval War College, April 1, 2020. https://digital-commons.usnwc.edu/cgi/viewcontent.cgi?article=1005&context=cmsi-maritime-reports.

Earle, Sylvia. "Introduction." In *The Sea Around Us*, by Rachel Carson, revised. Oxford: Oxford University Press, 2018.

Elleman, Bruce A. *Modern Chinese Warfare, 1795–1989.* Warfare and History. London: Routledge, 2001.

Enright, Michael J. *Developing China: The Remarkable Impact of Foreign Direct Investment.* London: Routledge, 2016.

Erickson, Andrew S. "Power vs. Distance: China's Global Maritime Interests and Investments in the Far Sea." In Ashley J. Tellis, Alison Szalwinshi, and Michael Wills, eds., *Strategic Asia 2019: China's Expanding Strategic Ambitions.* Seattle: The National Bureau of Asian Research, 2019.

Erickson, Andrew S., ed. *Chinese Naval Shipbuilding: An Ambitious and Uncertain Course.* Annapolis, MD: Naval Institute Press, 2017.

Erickson, Andrew S., Lyle J. Goldstein, and Carnes Lord, eds. *China Goes to Sea: Maritime Transformation in Comparative Historical Perspective.* Annapolis, MD: Naval Institute Press, 2009.

Evans, David C., and Mark R. Peattie. *Kaigun: Strategy, Tactics, and Technology in the Imperial Japanese Navy, 1887–1941.* Annapolis, MD: Naval Institute Press, 2012.

Fagan, Brian M. *Fishing: How the Sea Fed Civilization.* New Haven: Yale University Press, 2017.

———. *The Attacking Ocean: The Past, Present, and Future of Rising Sea Levels.* New York, NY: Bloomsbury Press, 2013.

———. *Floods, Famines and Emperors: El Nino and the Fate of Civilizations.* New York: Basic Books, 2009.

Fenby, Jonathan. *Modern China: The Fall and Rise of a Great Power, 1850 to the Present.* New York: Ecco, 2008.

Ferguson, Niall. *Empire: The Rise and Demise of the British World Order and the Lessons for Global Power.* New York: Basic Books, 2004.

Ferreiro, Larrie D. *Bridging the Seas: The Rise of Naval Architecture in the Industrial Age, 1800–2000.* Transformations: Studies in the History of Science and Technology. Cambridge, MA: The MIT Press, 2019.

Fletcher, Max E. "The Suez Canal and World Shipping, 1869–1914." *The Journal of Economic History* 18, no. 4 (1958): 556–73.

Fravel, M. Taylor. *Active Defense: China's Military Strategy since 1949.* Princeton Studies in International History and Politics. Princeton: Princeton University Press, 2019.

Fukuyama, Francis. "Review of Seapower States: Maritime Culture, Continental Empires and the Conflict That Made the Modern World." *H-Diplo*, July 22, 2020. https://issforum.org/essays/PDF/E259.pdf.

Gattuso, J.-P., A. Magnan, R. Billé, W. W. L. Cheung, E. L. Howes, F. Joos, D. Allemand et al. "Contrasting Futures for Ocean and Society from Different Anthropogenic CO_2 Emissions Scenarios." *Science* 349, no. 6243 (July 3, 2015): aac4722.

George, Rose. *Deep Sea & Foreign Going*. London: Portobello Books Ltd, 2014.

Ghafar, Adel Abdel, and Anna Jacobs. "Beijing Calling: Assessing China's Growing Footprint in North Africa." Washington, DC: Brookings Institution, September 18, 2019. https://www.brookings.edu/research/beijing-calling-assessing-chinas-growing-footprint-in-north-africa/.

Gibson, R. H., and Maurice Prendergast. *The German Submarine War, 1914–1918*. Annapolis, MD: Naval Institute Press, 2003.

Gilmour, David. *Curzon: Imperial Statesman*. 1st American ed. New York: Farrar, Straus and Giroux, 2003.

Godfroy, Jeanne, and Liam Collins. "Iraq, 2003–2011: Succeeding to Fail." *Small Wars & Insurgencies* 30, no. 1 (January 2, 2019): 140–75.

Goldstein, Avery. "US–China Rivalry in the Twenty-First Century: Déjà vu and Cold War II." *China International Strategy Review* 2, no. 1 (June 2020): 48–62.

Goodall, Jamie L.H. *Pirates of the Chesapeake Bay: From the Colonial Era to the Oyster Wars*. Charleston, SC: The History Press, 2020.

Goodwin, Jason. *Lords of the Horizons: A History of the Ottoman Empire*. New York: Henry Holt, 1999.

Green, Michael. *By More Than Providence: Grand Strategy and American Power in the Asia-Pacific Since 1783*. New York: Columbia University Press, 2017.

Greenberg, D. S. "Mohole: The Project That Went Awry." *Science* 143, no. 3602 (1964): 115–19.

Haddick, Robert. *Fire on the Water: China, America, and the Future of the Pacific*. Annapolis, MD: Naval Institute Press, 2014.

Ham, Hans van, and Joan Rijsenbrij. *Development of Containerization: Success Through Vision, Drive and Technology*. Clifton, VA: IOS Press, 2012.

Ham, Paul. *1914: The Year the World Ended*. London: Doubleday, 2014.

Hamilton, C. I. *Anglo-French Naval Rivalry, 1840–1870*. New York: Clarendon Press, 1993.

Hamilton, James D. "Historical Oil Shocks." Working Paper Series. National Bureau of Economic Research, February 2011.

Hanhimäki, Jussi. *The Flawed Architect: Henry Kissinger and American Foreign Policy*. Oxford: Oxford University Press, 2004.

Harmsen, Peter. *Shanghai 1937: Stalingrad on the Yangtze*. Havertown, PA: Casemate Publishers, 2015.

Hart, David M., and David G. Victor. "Scientific Elites and the Making of US Policy for Climate Change Research, 1957–74." *Social Studies of Science* 23, no. 4 (November 1, 1993): 643–80.

Hastings, Max. *Catastrophe 1914: Europe Goes to War*. Reprint edition. New York: Vintage, 2014.

Hayton, Bill. *The South China Sea: The Struggle for Power in Asia*. New Haven: Yale University Press, 2014.

Heins, Matthew. "The Shipping Container and the Globalization of American Infrastructure." PhD thesis, University of Michigan, 2013.

Herman, Arthur. *To Rule the Waves: How the British Navy Shaped the Modern World.* New York: Harper Perennial, 2004.

Hobsbawm, E. J. *The Age of Empire, 1875–1914.* New York: Vintage, 1989.

Hochschild, Adam. *King Leopold's Ghost: A Story of Greed, Terror, and Heroism in Colonial Africa.* Boston: Houghton Mifflin, 1998.

Hodgkinson, Sandra L. "Current Trends in Global Piracy: Can Somalia's Successes Help Combat Piracy in the Gulf of Guinea and Elsewhere?" *Case Western Reserve Journal of International Law* 46, no. 1 (2013): 145–60.

Hodgson, Godfrey. *Lloyd's of London: The Risky Business, Colorful History, and Turbulent Future of the World's Most Famous Insurance Group.* New York: Penguin, 1984.

Hoegh-Guldberg, O., D. Jacob, M. Taylor, T. Guillén Bolaños, M. Bindi, S. Brown, I. A. Camilloni et al. "The Human Imperative of Stabilizing Global Climate Change at 1.5°C." *Science* 365, no. 6459 (September 20, 2019).

Holmes, James R., and Toshi Yoshihara. *Chinese Naval Strategy in the 21st Century: The Turn to Mahan.* New York: Routledge, 2008.

Hoovestal, Lance E. *Globalization Contained: The Economic and Strategic Consequences of the Container.* London: Palgrave Macmillan, 2013.

Howarth, Stephen. *To Shining Sea: A History of the United States Navy, 1775–1998.* Norman, OK: University of Oklahoma Press, 1999.

Hu, Richard, and Weijie Chen. *Global Shanghai Remade: The Rise of Pudong New Area.* London: Routledge, 2019.

Husain, Amir. *The Sentient Machine: The Coming Age of Artificial Intelligence.* New York: Scribner, 2017.

Hyam, Ronald. *Britain's Declining Empire: The Road to Decolonisation, 1918–1968.* Cambridge: Cambridge University Press, 2007.

Ikenberry, G. John. *After Victory: Institutions, Strategic Restraint, and the Rebuilding of Order after Major Wars.* Princeton: Princeton University Press, 2001.

"International Energy Outlook 2019." Washington, DC: U.S. Energy Information Administration, September 2019. https://www.eia.gov/outlooks/ieo/pdf/ieo2019.pdf.

IPCC. "Special Report on the Ocean and Cryosphere in a Changing Climate." Geneva: IPCC, November 2019. https://www.ipcc.ch/srocc/.

Izumikawa, Yasuhiro. "Explaining Japanese Antimilitarism: Normative and Realist Constraints on Japan's Security Policy." *International Security* 35, no. 2 (Fall 2010): 123–60.

Jackson, Ashley. *Buildings of Empire.* Oxford: Oxford University Press, 2013.

Jacobson, Harold Karan, and Michel Oksenberg. *China's Participation in the IMF, the World Bank, and GATT: Toward a Global Economic Order.* Ann Arbor: University of Michigan Press, 1990.

"Japan Coast Guard: Justice and Humanity." Tokyo: Japan Coast Guard, 2018.

Jephson, Chris, and Henning Morgen. *Creating Global Opportunities: Maersk Line in Containerisation 1973–2013.* Cambridge: Cambridge University Press, 2014.

Johnson, Robert Erwin. *Far China Station: The U.S. Navy in Asian Waters, 1800–98.* New York: Naval Institute Press, 2013.

Johnson, Simon, and James Kwak. *13 Bankers: The Wall Street Takeover and the Next Financial Meltdown*. Reprint edition. New York: Vintage, 2011.

Johnson, Steven. *Enemy of All Mankind: A True Story of Piracy, Power, and History's First Global Manhunt*. New York: Riverhead Books, 2020.

Joll, James, and Gordon Martel. *The Origins of the First World War*. 3rd ed. Origins of Modern Wars. Harlow, England: Pearson Longman, 2007.

Jones, Bruce D., and David Steven. *The Risk Pivot: Great Powers, International Security, and the Energy Revolution*. Washington, DC: Brookings Institution Press, 2014.

Jones, Jeremy, and Nicholas Ridout. *A History of Modern Oman*. Cambridge: Cambridge University Press, 2015.

Karabell, Zachary. *Parting the Desert: The Creation of the Suez Canal*. New York: Alfred A. Knopf, 2003.

Karsh, Efraim, and Inari Karsh. *Empires of the Sand: The Struggle for Mastery in the Middle East, 1789–1923*. Cambridge, MA: Harvard University Press, 1999.

Karsten, Peter. "The Nature of 'Influence': Roosevelt, Mahan and the Concept of Sea Power." *American Quarterly* 23, no. 4 (1971): 585–600.

Kaplan, Robert D. *Monsoon: The Indian Ocean and the Future of American Power*. New York: Random House, 2011.

———. *Asia's Cauldron: The South China Sea and the End of a Stable Pacific*. New York: Random House, 2015.

Kaufman, Alison. "China's Participation in Anti-Piracy Operations off the Horn of Africa: Drivers and Implications." Arlington, VA: Center for Naval Analyses, July 2009. https://apps.dtic.mil/dtic/tr/fulltext/u2/a503697.pdf.

Kelly, Patrick J. *Tirpitz and the Imperial German Navy*. Bloomington, IN: Indiana University Press, 2011.

Kennedy, Conor. "Strategic Strong Points and Chinese Naval Strategy," *China Brief* 19, no 6. (March 22, 2019).

Kennedy, Paul M. *The Rise and Fall of British Naval Mastery*. New York: Scribner, 1976.

Kilmeade, Brian, and Don Yaeger. *Thomas Jefferson and the Tripoli Pirates: The Forgotten War That Changed American History*. New York: Sentinel, 2015.

Kindleberger, Charles P. "Dominance and Leadership in the International Economy: Exploitation, Public Goods, and Free Rides." *International Studies Quarterly* 25, no. 2 (1981): 242–54.

Kissinger, Henry. *White House Years*. Boston: Little, Brown, 1979.

Kuo, Raymond. *Contests of Initiative: Countering China's Gray Zone Strategy in the East and South China Seas*. Washington, DC: Westphalia Press, 2020.

Kyle, Keith. *Suez: Britain's End of Empire in the Middle East*. London: I. B. Tauris, 2011.

Lai, David. "Chinese Military Going Global." *China Security* 5, no. 1 (Winter 2009): 3–10.

Lambert, Andrew. *Seapower States: Maritime Culture, Continental Empires and the Conflict That Made the Modern World*. New Haven, CT: YUP New Haven and London, 2018.

Leeke, Jim. *Manila and Santiago: The New Steel Navy in the Spanish-American War*. Annapolis, MD: Naval Institute Press, 2013.

Lehman, John. *Oceans Ventured: Winning the Cold War at Sea*. New York: W. W. Norton, 2018.

Levathes, Louise. *When China Ruled the Seas: The Treasure Fleet of the Dragon Throne, 1405–1433*. New York: Oxford University Press, 1996.

Levinson, Marc. *The Box: How the Shipping Container Made the World Smaller and the World Economy Bigger*. Princeton: Princeton University Press, 2016.

Little, Douglas. "Pipeline Politics: America, TAPLINE, and the Arabs." *Business History Review* 64, no. 2 (1990): 255–85.

Longworth, Richard C. *Caught in the Middle: America's Heartland in the Age of Globalism*. New York: Bloomsbury, 2008.

Low, Charles Rathbone. *The History of the Indian Navy (1613–1863)*. Cambridge: Cambridge University Press, 2012.

Macartney, George. *An Embassy to China: Being the Journal Kept by Lord Macartney during His Embassy to the Emperor Ch'ien-Lung, 1793–1794*. Hamden, CT: Archon Books, 1963.

Macdougall, J. D. *Endless Novelties of Extraordinary Interest: The Voyage of H.M.S. Challenger and the Birth of Modern Oceanography*. New Haven: Yale University Press, 2019.

Mackinder, H. J. "The Geographical Pivot of History." *The Geographical Journal* 23, no. 4 (1904): 421–44.

MacMillan, Margaret. *Nixon and Mao: The Week That Changed the World*. New York: Random House, 2007.

Mahan, Alfred Thayer. *The Influence of Sea Power Upon History, 1660–1783*. Boston: Little, Brown and Company, 1918.

———. *The Interest of America in Sea Power, Present and Future*. Boston: Little, Brown and Company, 1897.

———. "The Persian Gulf and International Relations." *National Review* 40 (1902): 27.

Manyika, James, Jaana Remes, Richard Dobbs, Javier Orellana, and Fabian Schaer. "Urban America: US Cities in the Global Economy." McKinsey Global Insitute, April 2012. https://www.mckinsey.com/~/media/McKinsey/Featured%20Insights/Urbanization/US%20cities%20in%20the%20global%20economy/MGI_Urban_America_Full_Report.ashx.

"Mapping Global Value Chains." Paris: Organisation for Economic Co-operation and Development, December 3, 2012.

Massie, Robert K. *Dreadnought: Britain, Germany, and the Coming of the Great War*. New York: Random House, 1991.

Maurer, John H. "Arms Control and the Anglo-German Naval Race before World War I: Lessons for Today?" *Political Science Quarterly* 112, no. 2 (1997): 285–306.

McLaughlin, Conor. "The Suez Crisis: Security Implications for the Transatlantic Relationship and the Shift in Global Power." Student Scholarship & Creative Works by Year. Carlisle, PA: Dickinson College, 2016. https://scholar.dickinson.edu/cgi/viewcontent.cgi?article=1048&context=student_work.

Menzies, Gavin. *1421: The Year China Discovered America*. New York: William Morrow, 2003.

Metcalf, Thomas R. *Imperial Connections: India in the Indian Ocean Arena, 1860–1920*. Berkeley, CA: University of California Press, 2007.

Miller, Edward S. *War Plan Orange: The U.S. Strategy to Defeat Japan, 1897–1945*. Annapolis, MD: Naval Institute Press, 1991.

Miller, Nathan. *The U.S. Navy: A History*. Annapolis, MD: Naval Institute Press, 1997.

Mirski, Sean. "Stranglehold: The Context, Conduct and Consequences of an American

Naval Blockade of China." *Journal of Strategic Studies* 36, no. 3 (June 1, 2013): 385–421.

Modelski, George, and William R. Thompson. *Seapower in Global Politics, 1494–1993.* Houndmills, England: Macmillan Press, 1988.

Mohan, C. Raja. *Samudra Manthan: Sino-Indian Rivalry in the Indo-Pacific*. Washington, DC: Carnegie Endowment for International Peace, 2012.

Monahan, Erika. *The Merchants of Siberia: Trade in Early Modern Eurasia*. Ithaca, NY: Cornell University Press, 2016.

Montgomery, Evan Braden. "Reconsidering a Naval Blockade of China: A Response to Mirski." *Journal of Strategic Studies* 36, no. 4 (August 1, 2013): 615–23.

Morris, Lyle J., Michael J. Mazarr, Jeffrey W. Hornung, Stephanie Pezard, Anika Binnendijk, and Marta Kepe. "Gaining Competitive Advantage in the Gray Zone: Response Options for Coercive Aggression Below the Threshold of Major War." Santa Monica, CA: RAND Corporation, June 27, 2019. https://www.rand.org/pubs/research_reports/RR2942.html.

Mostert, Noël. *Supership*. New York: Knopf, 1974.

———. *The Line Upon a Wind: The Great War at Sea, 1793–1815*. New York: W. W. Norton, 2007.

Muller, David G. *China as a Maritime Power*. Westview Special Studies on East Asia. Boulder, CO: Westview Press, 1983.

Munk, Walter. "The Sound of Climate Change." *Tellus A: Dynamic Meteorology and Oceanography* 63, no. 2 (January 2011): 190–97. https://doi.org/10.1111/j.1600-0870.2010.00494.x.

Myles, Douglas. *The Great Waves: Tsunami*. New York: McGraw-Hill, 1985.

Newman, Peter C. *Company of Adventurers: How the Hudson's Bay Empire Determined the Destiny of a Continent*. Toronto: Penguin Canada, 2005.

Nguyen Dinh. "A Strategic Study of the Top 20 Liners During Period 1980–2001." Master's dissertation, World Maritime University, 2002.

Nield, Robert. *China's Foreign Places: The Foreign Presence in China in the Treaty Port Era, 1840–1943*. Hong Kong: Hong Kong University Press, 2015.

North, Michael. *The Baltic: A History*. Translated by Kenneth Kronenberg. Cambridge, MA: Harvard University Press, 2015.

O'Hanlon, Michael E. *The Senkaku Paradox: Risking Great Power War Over Small Stakes*. Washington, DC: Brookings Institution Press, 2019.

Pagden, Anthony. *Peoples and Empires: A Short History of European Migration, Exploration, and Conquest, from Greece to the Present*. Modern Library Chronicles. New York: Modern Library, 2001.

Paine, Lincoln P. *The Sea and Civilization: A Maritime History of the World*. New York: Knopf, 2013.

Pakenham, Thomas. *The Scramble for Africa: White Man's Conquest of the Dark Continent from 1876 to 1912*. New York: Random House, 1991.

Palivos, Theodore, Ping Wang, and Chong Yip. "The Colonization of Hong Kong: Establishing the Pearl of Britain-China Trade." *IDEAS Working Paper Series from RePEc*, 2011. http://search.proquest.com/docview/1699219509/?pq-origsite=primo.

Payne, Craig M. *Principles of Naval Weapon Systems*. Annapolis, MD: Naval Institute Press, 2006.

Peden, G. C. "Suez and Britain's Decline as a World Power." *The Historical Journal* 55, no. 4 (December 2012): 1073–96. https://doi.org/10.1017/S0018246X12000246.

Peng, Mike W. *Global Business*. Boston: Cengage Learning, 2016.

Perry, Elizabeth J. *Shanghai on Strike: The Politics of Chinese Labor. Fulcrum.Org*. Stanford, CA: Stanford University Press, 1993.

Perry, John Curtis. *Singapore: Unlikely Power*. Oxford: Oxford University Press, 2017.

Peterson, J. E. "America and Oman: The Context for Nearly Two Centuries of Relations." Muscat: Public Authority for Radio & TV, 2014. http://www.jepeterson.net/sitebuildercontent/sitebuilderfiles/Peterson_-_America_and_Oman_2014.pdf.

Philbrick, Nathaniel. *Sea of Glory: America's Voyage of Discovery: The U.S. Exploring Expedition, 1838–1842*. New York: Viking, 2003.

Pierce, Justin R., and Peter K. Schott. "The Surprisingly Swift Decline of US Manufacturing Employment." *American Economic Review* 106, no. 7 (July 1, 2016): 1632–62. https://doi.org/10.1257/aer.20131578.

Platt, Stephen R. *Imperial Twilight: The Opium War and the End of China's Last Golden Age*. First edition. New York: Alfred A. Knopf, 2018.

Pletcher, Kenneth. "Opium Wars." In *Britannica Academic*. Encyclopaedia Britannica, June 20, 2018.

Pomeranz, Kenneth, and Steven Topik. *The World that Trade Created: Society, Culture, and the World Economy, 1400 to the Present*. Fourth edition. New York: Routledge, 2018.

Potter, E. B., ed. *Sea Power: A Naval History*. Second edition. Annapolis, MD: Naval Institute Press, 1981.

Prakash, Om. *European Commercial Enterprise in Pre-Colonial India*. Oxford: Oxford University Press, 1998.

Priest, Tyler. "Extraction Not Creation: The History of Offshore Petroleum in the Gulf of Mexico." *Enterprise & Society* 8, no. 2 (2007): 227–67.

Raymond, Catherine Zara. "Piracy and Armed Robbery in the Malacca Strait: A Problem Solved?" *Naval War College Review* 62, no. 3 (Summer 2009): 31–42.

Reid, Donald Malcolm. "The 'Urabi Revolution and the British Conquest, 1879–1882." In *The Cambridge History of Egypt*, edited by M. W. Daly, 217–38. Cambridge, UK: Cambridge University Press, December 10, 1998. https://doi.org/10.1017/CHOL9780521472111.010.

"Restoring the Quality of Our Environment: Report of the Environmental Pollution Panel, President's Science Advisory Committee." Washington, DC: The White House, November 2, 1965. http://www.climatefiles.com/climate-change-evidence/presidents-report-atmospher-carbon-dioxide/.

Revelle, Roger, and Hans E. Suess. "Carbon Dioxide Exchange Between Atmosphere and Ocean and the Question of an Increase of Atmospheric CO2 during the Past Decades." *Tellus* 9, no. 1 (January 1, 1957): 18–27. https://doi.org/10.3402/tellusa.v9i1.9075.

"Review of Maritime Transport, 2001." New York: United Nations Conference on Trade and Development, 2001. https://unctad.org/en/Docs/rmt2001_en.pdf.

"Review of Maritime Transport, 2018." New York: United Nations Conference on Trade and Development, 2019. https://unctad.org/webflyer/review-maritime-transport-2018.

Rhodes, Richard. *Energy: A Human History*. New York: Simon & Schuster, 2018.

Ricardo, David. *On the Principles of Political Economy and Taxation*. London: John Murray, 1817.

Riedel, Bruce. *Kings and Presidents: Saudi Arabia and the United States Since FDR*. Washington, DC: Brookings Institution Press, 2017. http://muse.jhu.edu/book/56367/.

Rogan, Eugene L. *The Arabs: A History*. New York: Basic Books, 2009.

Ross, Robert S. "Balance of Power Politics and the Rise of China: Accommodation and Balancing in East Asia." *Security Studies* 15, no. 3 (September 2006): 355–95. https://doi.org/10.1080/09636410601028206.

Roy, Denny. *Taiwan: A Political History*. Ithaca, NY: Cornell University Press, 2003. https://catalog.hathitrust.org/Record/004307407.

Salidjanova, Nargiza. "Going Out: An Overview of China's Outward Foreign Direct Investment." Washington, DC: U.S.-China Economic & Security Review Commission, March 30, 2011. https://www.uscc.gov/sites/default/files/Research/GoingOut.pdf.

Sapolsky, Harvey M. *Science and the Navy: The History of the Office of Naval Research*. Princeton: Princeton University Press, 2014.

Schofield, Clive. "Dangerous Ground: A Geopolitical Overview of the South China Sea." In *Security and International Politics in the South China Sea: Towards a Cooperative Management Regime*, edited by W. S. G. Bateman and Ralf Emmers, 7–25. London: Routledge, 2009.

Scobell, Andrew, and Nathan Beauchamp-Mustafaga. "The Flag Lags But Follows: The PLA and China's Great Leap Outward." In *Chairman Xi Remakes the PLA: Assessing Chinese Military Reforms*, edited by Phillip C. Saunders, Arthur S. Ding, Andrew Scobell, Andrew N. D. Yang, and Joel Wuthnow. Washington, DC: National Defense University Press, 2019.

Seligmann, Matthew S. "Britain's Great Security Mirage: The Royal Navy and the Franco-Russian Naval Threat, 1898–1906." *Journal of Strategic Studies* 35, no. 6 (December 1, 2012): 861–86.

Shackleton, Sir Ernest. *South: The Story of Shackleton's Last Expedition, 1914–1917*. New York: Dover Publications, 2019.

Sharma, Ruchir. *Breakout Nations: In Pursuit of the Next Economic Miracles*. 1st ed. New York: W. W. Norton, 2012.

———. *The Rise and Fall of Nations: Forces of Change in the Post-Crisis World*. New York: W. W. Norton, 2016.

Sharman, Christopher H. "China Moves Out: Stepping Stones Toward a New Maritime Strategy." China Strategic Perspectives. Washington, DC: Institute for National Strategic Studies, April 2015.

Sharman, J. C. *Empires of the Weak: The Real Story of European Expansion and the Creation of the New World Order*. Princeton: Princeton University Press, 2019.

Sherlock, Stephen. "Hong Kong and the Transfer to China: Issues and Prospects." Current Issues Briefs. Sydney: Parliament of Australia, June 23, 1997. https://www.aph.gov.au/sitecore/content/Home/About_Parliament/Parliamentary_Departments/Parliamentary_Library/Publications_Archive/CIB/CIB9697/97cib33.

Shimodaira, Takuya. "The Japan Maritime Self-Defense Force in the Age of Multilateral Cooperation: Nontraditional Security." *Naval War College Review* 67, no. 2 (Spring 2014): 1–17.

Shlapak, David A., David T. Orletsky, Toy I. Reid, Murray Scot Tanner, and Barry Wilson. *A Question of Balance: Political Context and Military Aspects of the China-Taiwan Dispute*. Santa Monica, CA: RAND Corporation, 2009. https://www.rand.org/pubs/monographs/MG888.html.

Smelser, Marshall. *The Congress Founds the Navy, 1787–1798*. South Bend, IN: University of Notre Dame Press, 1959.

Smith, Craig B. *Extreme Waves*. Newport Beach, CA: Dockside Sailing Press, 2010.

Smith, Crosbie. *Coal, Steam and Ships: Engineering, Enterprise and Empire on the Nineteenth-Century Seas*. Cambridge: Cambridge University Press, 2018.

Smith, Neil. *American Empire: Roosevelt's Geographer and the Prelude to Globalization*. California Studies in Critical Human Geography 9. Berkeley, CA: University of California Press, 2003.

Smith, Sheila A. *Japan Rearmed: The Politics of Military Power*. Cambridge, MA: Harvard University Press, 2019.

Smith, Simon, ed. *Reassessing Suez 1956: New Perspectives on the Crisis and Its Aftermath*. New York: Routledge, 2016.

Sondhaus, Lawrence. *German Submarine Warfare in World War I: The Onset of Total War at Sea*. Lanham, MD: Rowman & Littlefield, 2017.

Song, Ci. "A Critical Analysis of the Donghai Bridge, Shanghai, China." Bath, United Kingdom, 2008. https://people.bath.ac.uk/jjo20/conference2/2008/SONG%20PAPER%2021.pdf.

Song, Dong-Wook, and Ki-Tae Yeo. "A Competitive Analysis of Chinese Container Ports Using the Analytic Hierarchy Process." In *Port Management*, edited by Hercules Haralambides, 339–59. London: Palgrave Macmillan, 2015.

Spyrou, Andrew G. *From T-2 to Supertanker: Development of the Oil Tanker, 1940–2000*. Revised. Bloomington, IN: iUniverse, 2011.

Stanton, William Ragan. *The Great United States Exploring Expedition of 1838–1842*. Berkeley, CA: University of California Press, 1975.

Starrs, Sean. "American Economic Power Hasn't Declined—It Globalized! Summoning the Data and Taking Globalization Seriously." *International Studies Quarterly* 57, no. 4 (December 2013): 817–30.

Stavridis, James. *Sea Power: The History and Geopolitics of the World's Oceans*. New York: Penguin Press, 2017.

Stefanick, Tom. *Strategic Antisubmarine Warfare and Naval Strategy*. Lexington, MA: Lexington Books, 1987.

Stern, Roger J. "United States Cost of Military Force Projection in the Persian Gulf, 1976–2007." *Energy Policy* 38, no. 6 (June 2010): 2816–25.

Swain, Sanjaya Kumar, K. Trinath, and Tatavarti. "Non-Acoustic Detection of Moving Submerged Bodies in Ocean." *International Journal of Innovative Research and Development* 1, no. 10 (December 2012): 361–72.

Swanson, Bruce. *Eighth Voyage of the Dragon: A History of China's Quest for Seapower*. Annapolis, MD.: Naval Institute Press, 1982.

Symonds, Craig L. *World War II at Sea: A Global History*. New York: Oxford University Press, 2018.

Tan, Rosalina. "Foreign Direct Investment Flows to and from China." PASCN Discussion Papers. Manila: Philippine APEC Study Center Network, 1999.

Thant Myint-U. *Where China Meets India: Burma and the New Crossroads of Asia*. New York: Farrar, Straus and Giroux, 2011.

"The Offshore Petroleum Industry in the Gulf of Mexico: A Continuum of Activities." Washington, DC: Bureau of Ocean Energy Management, US Department of the Interior, 2008. https://www.boem.gov/sites/default/files/boem-education/BOEM-Education-Images-and-Resources/TheOffshorePetroleumIndustryOrganizationalScheme.pdf.

Thomas, Evan. *John Paul Jones: Sailor, Hero, Father of the American Navy*. New York: Simon & Schuster, 2003.

Till, Geoffrey. *Seapower: A Guide for the Twenty-First Century*. Fourth edition. New York: Routledge, 2018.

Till, Geoffrey, Emrys Chew, and Joshua Ho, eds. *Globalization and Defense in the Asia-Pacific: Arms Across America*. New York: Routledge, 2009.

Tol, Jan van, Mark Gunzinger, Andrew Krepinevich, and Jim Thomas. "AirSea Battle: A Point-of-Departure Operational Concept." Washington, DC: Center for Strategic and Budgetary Assessments, 2010. https://csbaonline.org/research/publications/airsea-battle-concept/publication/1.

Toll, Ian W. *Six Frigates: The Epic History of the Founding of the U.S. Navy*. New York: W. W. Norton, 2006.

———. *Pacific Crucible: War at Sea in the Pacific, 1941–1942*. (Volume 1 of the Pacific War Trilogy.) New York: W. W. Norton, 2012.

Tolley, Kemp. *Yangtze Patrol: The U.S. Navy in China*. Annapolis, MD: Naval Institute Press, 1971.

Tooze, Adam. *The Deluge: The Great War, America and the Remaking of the Global Order, 1916–1931*. New York: Penguin Press, 2014.

"Transnational Organized Crime Threat Assessment 2010." Vienna: United Nations Office on Drugs and Crime, 2010. https://www.unodc.org/documents/data-and-analysis/Studies/TOCTA_draft_2603_lores.pdf.

Trethewey, Laura. *The Imperiled Ocean: Human Stories from a Changing Sea*. New York: Pegasus Books, 2019.

Treves, Tullio. "Historical Development of the Law of the Sea." In *The Oxford Handbook of the Law of the Sea*. Oxford Public International Law. Oxford: Oxford University Press, 2015.

———. "Piracy and the International Law of the Sea." In *Modern Piracy*, edited by Douglas Guilfoyle. Cheltenham, England: Edward Elgar, 2013.

Tudda, Chris. *A Cold War Turning Point: Nixon and China, 1969–1972*. Baton Rouge: Louisiana State University Press, 2012.

Tung, C. Y. *Dong Haoyun ri ji, 1948–1982*. Xianggang: Zhong wen da xue chu ban she, 2004.

Tunsjø, Øystein. *The Return of Bipolarity in World Politics: China, the United States, and Geostructural Realism*. New York: Columbia University Press, 2018.

Turner, Barry. *Suez 1956: The Inside Story of the First Oil War*. London: Hodder & Stoughton, 2012.

Turner, Jack. *Spice: The History of a Temptation*. New York: Knopf, 2004.

Twain, Mark. *Following the Equator*. Hartford, CT: American Publishing Company, 1897.

United States Coast Guard. "Privacy Impact Assessment (PIA) Update for the Vessel Requirements for the Notice of Arrival and Departure (NOAD) and Automatic Identification System (AIS) Rulemaking." Washington, DC: Department of Homeland Security, April 28, 2015. https://www.dhs.gov/publication/dhs-uscg-pia-006b-vessel-requirements-noad-and-ais-rulemaking.

United States Department of State. International Organization and Conference Series 164. Washington, DC: U.S. Government Printing Office, 1984.

Urbina, Ian. *The Outlaw Ocean: Crime and Survival in the Last Untamed Frontier*. London: The Bodley Head, 2019.

Varble, Derek. *The Suez Crisis 1956*. London: Bloomsbury, 2003.

Wake, Christopher. "The Myth of Zheng He's Great Treasure Ships." *International Journal of Maritime History* 16, no. 1 (June 1, 2004): 59–76.

Walker, Matthew. "The Lost Art of Interdependency: United Nations Leadership in the Suez Crisis of 1956 and Its Ramifications in World Affairs." Lincoln, NE: University of Nebraska, 2010. https://digitalcommons.unl.edu/cgi/viewcontent.cgi?article=1033&context=historydiss.

Wallenfeldt, Jeff. "Strait of Malacca." In *Encyclopaedia Britannica*, June 20, 2019. https://www.britannica.com/place/Strait-of-Malacca.

Wang, Dong. *The United States and China: A History from the Eighteenth Century to the Present*. Lanham, MD: Rowman & Littlefield, 2013.

Wang, Hongying. "The Asian Financial Crisis and Financial Reforms in China." *The Pacific Review* 12, no. 4 (January 1, 1999): 537–56.

Weitz, Richard. "Operation Somalia: China's First Expeditionary Force." *China Security* 5, no. 1 (Winter 2009): 27–44.

Whipple, A.B.C. *To the Shores of Tripoli: The Birth of the U.S. Navy and Marines*. Annapolis, MD: Naval Institute Press, 1991.

Whiting, Richard C. "The Suez Canal and the British Economy, 1918–1960." In *Imperialism and Nationalism in the Middle East: The Anglo-Egyptian Experience, 1882–1982*, edited by Keith M. Wilson. London: Mansell, 1983.

Wiley, Peter Booth. *Yankees in the Land of Gods: Commodore Perry and the Opening of Japan*. New York: Viking, 1990.

Williams, Vernon L. "Naval Service in the Age of Empire." In *Crucible of Empire: The Spanish-American War and Its Aftermath*, edited by James C. Bradford, 183–204. Annapolis, MD: Naval Institute Press, 1993.

Wilson, Jordan. "China's Expanding Ability to Conduct Conventional Missile Strikes on Guam." Washington, DC: U.S.-China Economic & Security Review Commission, May 10, 2016. https://www.uscc.gov/sites/default/files/Research/Staff%20Report_China's%20Expanding%20Ability%20to%20Conduct%20Conventional%20Missile%20Strikes%20on%20Guam.pdf.

Wimmel, Kenneth. *Theodore Roosevelt and the Great White Fleet: American Seapower Comes of Age*. Washington, DC: Brassey's, 1998.

Winchester, Simon. *Atlantic: Great Sea Battles, Heroic Discoveries, Titanic Storms, and a Vast Ocean of a Million Stories*. New York: Harper, 2010.

"World Energy Outlook 2019." Paris: International Energy Agency, 2019. https://www.iea.org/reports/world-energy-outlook-2019.

World Ocean Review. "World Ocean Review 6: The Arctic and Antarctic - Extreme, Climatically Crucial and in Crisis." Hamburg, Germany: maribus, 2019.

"World Trade Report 2010: Trade in Natural Resources." Geneva: World Trade Organization, 2013.

"World Trade Report 2013: Factors Shaping the Future of Global Trade." Geneva: World Trade Organization, 2013.

Wu, Zhengyu. "The Crowe Memorandum, the Rebalance to Asia, and Sino-US Relations." *Journal of Strategic Studies* 39, no. 3 (April 15, 2016): 389–416.

Xu, Zhitao, Adel Elomri, Laoucine Kerbache, and Abdelfatteh El Omri. "Impacts of COVID-19 on Global Supply Chains: Facts and Perspectives." *IEEE Engineering Management Review* 48, no. 3 (September 2020): 153–66.

Yergin, Daniel. *The New Map: Energy, Climate, and the Clash of Nations*. New York: Penguin Press, 2020.

———. *The Quest: Energy, Security, and the Remaking of the Modern World*. New York: Penguin Press, 2011.

Yoshihara, Toshi, and James R. Holmes. "Japanese Maritime Thought: If Not Mahan, Who?" *Naval War College Review* 59, no. 3 (Summer 2006). https://digital-commons.usnwc.edu/cgi/viewcontent.cgi?article=1930&context=nwc-review.

———. *Red Star over the Pacific: China's Rise and the Challenge to U.S. Military Strategy*. Annapolis, MD: Naval Institute Press, 2018.

Zhai, Qiang. "Taiwan Strait Crises (1954–55, 1958)." In *Encyclopedia of the Cold War*, edited by Ruud van Dijk, 2:879–81. New York: Routledge, 2008.

Zherdyev, Vitaliy. "The Russian Orthodox Church in Copenhagen: A View from the Architect's Homeland." *Konsthistorisk Tidskrift/Journal of Art History* 87, no. 4 (October 2, 2018): 234–50.

Zhong, Weimin. "The Roles of Tea and Opium in Early Economic Globalization: A Perspective on China's Crisis in the 19th Century." *Frontiers of History in China* 5, no. 1 (2010): 86–105.

Zhu Liu. "China's Carbon Emissions Report 2015." Cambridge, MA: Belfer Center for Science and International Affairs, May 2015. https://scholar.harvard.edu/files/zhu/files/carbon-emissions-report-2015-final.pdf.

Zhu, Yu, Ding Jinhong, Wang Guixin, Shen Jianfa, Lin Liyue, and Ke Wenqian. "Population Geography in China since the 1980s: Forging the Links between Population Studies and Human Geography." *Journal of Geographical Sciences* 26, no. 8 (2016): 1133–58.

Zisk, Kimberley Marten. "Japan's United Nations Peacekeeping Dilemma." *Asia-Pacific Review* 8, no. 1 (May 1, 2001): 21–39.

Index

INDEX

INDEX

INDEX

INDEX

INDEX

INDEX

INDEX

INDEX

INDEX

INDEX

INDEX

INDEX

INDEX

INDEX

About the Author

BRUCE D. JONES directs the Project on International Order and Strategy of the Foreign Policy program at the Brookings Institution, where for four years he was also vice president. He has lived and worked in Asia, Africa, and Europe, including serving with UN operations in Kosovo and the Middle East. He has documented the changing dynamics of world power in several previous books about international affairs. He has been a senior adviser to the World Bank and has lectured or been a nonresident fellow at Princeton, Stanford, Yale, and New York University.